THE CAMBRIDGE COMPANION TO SHAKESPEAREAN TRAGEDY

Second edition

This revised and updated *Companion* acquaints the student reader with the forms, contexts, critical and theatrical lives of the ten plays considered to be Shakespeare's tragedies. Thirteen essays, written by leading scholars in Britain and North America, address the ways in which Shakespearean tragedy originated, developed and diversified, as well as how it has fared on stage, as text and in criticism. Topics covered include the literary precursors of Shakespeare's tragedies, cultural backgrounds, subgenres and receptions of the plays. The book examines the four major tragedies and, in addition, *Titus Andronicus*, *Romeo and Juliet*, *Julius Caesar*, *Antony and Cleopatra*, *Coriolanus* and *Timon of Athens*. Essays from the first edition have been fully revised to reflect the most up-to-date scholarship; the bibliography has been extensively updated; and four new chapters have been added, discussing Shakespearean form, Shakespeare and philosophy, Shakespeare's tragedies in performance, and Shakespeare and religion.

CLAIRE McEACHERN is Professor of English at the University of California, Los Angeles. She is the author of *The Poetics of English Nationhood, 1590–1612* (1996), co-editor (with Debora Shuger) of *Religion and Culture in the English Renaissance* (1997), and editor of the Arden 3 *Much Ado About Nothing*, as well as several other Shakespeare plays for various series.

A complete list of books in the series is at the back of the book.

THE CAMBRIDGE COMPANION TO SHAKESPEAREAN TRAGEDY

Second Edition

EDITED BY

CLAIRE McEACHERN

CAMBRIDGE
UNIVERSITY PRESS

CAMBRIDGE
UNIVERSITY PRESS

University Printing House, Cambridge CB2 8BS, United Kingdom

Published in the United States of America by Cambridge University Press, New York

Cambridge University Press is part of the University of Cambridge.

It furthers the University's mission by disseminating knowledge in the pursuit of education, learning and research at the highest international levels of excellence.

www.cambridge.org
Information on this title: www.cambridge.org/9781107643321

© Cambridge University Press 2013

First published 2002
Second edition 2013

Printed in the United Kingdom by Clays, St Ives plc

A catalogue record for this publication is available from the British Library

Library of Congress Cataloguing in Publication data
The Cambridge companion to Shakespearean tragedy / edited by Claire McEachern. – Second edition.
pages cm
Includes bibliographical references and index.
ISBN 978-1-107-01977-5 (Hardback) – ISBN 978-1-107-64332-1 (Paperback)
1. Shakespeare, William, 1564–1616 – Tragedies – Handbooks, manuals, etc.
2. Tragedy – Handbooks, manuals, etc.   I. McEachern, Claire, 1963–
PR2983.C28   2013
822.3'3–dc23
2013004142

ISBN 978-1-107-01977-5 Hardback
ISBN 978-1-107-64332-1 Paperback

Contents

Illustrations

Contributors

CATHERINE BATES, University of Warwick

CATHERINE BELSEY, University of Cardiff

DAVID BEVINGTON, University of Chicago

COLIN BURROW, University of Oxford

MICHAEL HATTAWAY, New York University in London

COPPÉLIA KAHN, Brown University

PAUL A. KOTTMAN, The New School for Social Research

RUSS MCDONALD, Goldsmiths, University of London

CLAIRE MCEACHERN, University of California, Los Angeles

LUCY MUNRO, Keele University

GAIL KERN PASTER, Director Emerita, Folger Shakespeare Library, Washington, DC

MICHAEL WARREN, University of California, Santa Cruz

ROBERT N. WATSON, University of California, Los Angeles

Preface to the second edition

The Cambridge Companion to Shakespearean Tragedy seeks to acquaint the undergraduate reader with the forms, context, kinds and critical and theatrical lives of the ten plays we consider Shakespeare's tragedies: *Titus Andronicus, Romeo and Juliet, Hamlet, Othello, King Lear, Macbeth, Julius Caesar, Antony and Cleopatra, Coriolanus* and *Timon of Athens*. The following thirteen chapters address the ways in which Shakespearean tragedy originated, developed and diversified, as well as how it has fared on stage, the page and in critical history.

Although the first edition of this volume has remained in print throughout the decade since it first appeared, the amount of Shakespeare criticism extant in the world has done nothing to abate its current volume and pace, just as Shakespeare's tragedies and works inspired by them continue to occupy a vital place in today's performance repertoire. Shakespeare's work remains as insistent a presence in our culture as ever, even as many of the historical or cultural frames of reference necessary to an informed understanding of his work ever recede from today's undergraduate audience. A revised edition of this text seemed not inopportune, and I was happy to respond to the request of the Press to ask the authors of the chapters to revisit their work with an eye to accounting to recent developments in the field. I was guided in this process by the reports commissioned by Cambridge University Press, which also urged the inclusion of four new chapters. I hope the result reflects an adequate response to their thoughtful suggestions, and also that the present list of contributors reflects the worldwide distribution achieved by the first edition.

The book is structured in four parts. The initial group of chapters takes up the forms and definitions of the genre which Shakespeare inherits and develops. Colin Burrow introduces the models of tragedy that may have influenced Shakespeare's composition and the ways these have influenced critical apprehension of the tragedies; Russ McDonald reviews the rhetorical resources which fuel Shakespeare's tragic voice; David Bevington undertakes a holistic account of Shakespeare's repeated revisitations of the form throughout his career (often in plays not considered tragedies), and Michael Warren provides an account of the curious nature of the material texts on which critical castles are built.

The second section treats the Tudor–Stuart political and social identities which inform these plays. My own chapter considers the religious cultures of Shakespeare's moment, and Michael Hattaway the political. Catherine Belsey introduces us to the early modern family, and Gail Paster to the mysterious realm of the early modern body. The next three chapters, on 'themes', address traditional subgenres of Shakespearean tragedy – the plays of revenge and ambition, love, and classical history – albeit from new perspectives. R. N. Watson re-evaluates the contemporary historical and philosophical understandings of the revenge form; Catherine Bates explores the paradoxes of love and loss that tragedy forces, and Coppélia Kahn describes the ways in which early modern understandings of classical civilization inform the texture of the five Greco-Roman plays. The final two pieces treat the ways in which reading and playing have shaped our experience of these plays. Paul A. Kottman introduces the reader to the important role of Shakespeare in philosophical thought and the ways in which philosophical thinkers have served to shape our notion of Shakespeare. Lucy Munro provides an account of performance traditions, with special attention to the role of texts, spectacle and the actor's body; her chapter concludes with consideration of two hallmark features of Shakespearean tragedy, the soliloquy and the representation of violence.

While this book will profit from being read sequentially, each chapter is designed to be a self-contained study of its object. The authors have avoided a chapter-per-play approach, and thus the reader will encounter different plays in different lights and from different perspectives (*Titus Andronicus*, for instance, receives consideration in terms of the family, revenge tragedy and classical models). At the same time, care has been taken to provide sustained coverage of each tragedy somewhere in the volume (the index reveals these concentrations). This prismatic design, in which a given play appears from multiple vantage points, is intended to avoid the restriction of the identity of any one play to any particular critical category or meaning, and urge the reader to the juxtapositions of an organic and cross-referenced critical appreciation.

Chronology

Dates given for plays are of first performance unless otherwise specified; most of these dates are approximate and those cited in individual chapters of the *Companion* may differ. For a fuller record of plays in the period, see the *Cambridge Companion to Renaissance Drama*, ed. Braunmuller and Hattaway.

1564	Shakespeare born in Stratford-upon-Avon
1566	Red Lion playhouse opens
1576	The Theatre opens
1577	Curtain playhouse opens; Blackfriars Theatre opens
1581	*Seneca His Tenne Tragedies* (trans. Newton) published
1582	Shakespeare marries Anne Hathaway; the licence is issued on November 27 and the first child (Susanna) is born six months later
1585	Shakespeare's twin son and daughter, Hamnet and Judith, born
c. 1586	Shakespeare leaves Stratford; nothing is known for certain of his life between this date and 1592, by which time he is in London
1587	Rose playhouse opens. Kyd, *The Spanish Tragedy*; Marlowe, *Tamburlaine 1* and *2*
1590	Anon., *King Leir*
c. 1591	Shakespeare, *Titus Andronicus*
c. 1592	Marlowe, *Doctor Faustus, Edward II*
1593	Marlowe, *The Massacre at Paris*
c. 1594	Around this time Shakespeare becomes a sharer in the Chamberlain's Men. Swan Theatre built
c. 1595	Shakespeare, *Romeo and Juliet*
c. 1599	Globe Theatre opens; Shakespeare's principal clown, Will Kempe, leaves the company; his successor is Robert Armin. Shakespeare, *Julius Caesar*
1600	Fortune Theatre built. Shakespeare, *Hamlet*

Abbreviations

Shakespeare's works

Cor. Coriolanus
Ham. Hamlet
H5 King Henry the Fifth
JC Julius Caesar
Lear King Lear
Luc. The Rape of Lucrece
Mac. Macbeth
Oth. Othello
R3 King Richard the Third
Rom. Romeo and Juliet
Tim. Timon of Athens
Tit. Titus Andronicus

General

F   Folio
Q1   First Quarto
Q2   Second Quarto
s.d.   stage direction

CHAPTER I

What is a Shakespearean tragedy?

Colin Burrow

Aristotle (384–322 BC) defined tragedy as 'a *mimēsis* of a high, complete action ... in speech pleasurably enhanced ... in dramatic, not narrative form, effecting through pity and fear the *catharsis* of such emotions'.[1] Aristotle was explicating and evaluating tragedies written in fifth-century Athens by Aeschylus, Sophocles and Euripides, all of whom were dead before he was born, and whose work he was attempting to assimilate into his own systematic philosophy. That philosophy encompassed rhetoric and ethics as well as biological theory. Aristotle's range of intellectual interests both enriches and confuses his definition of tragedy. Scholars have fretted in particular over what Aristotle meant by 'catharsis'. Did he believe that tragedy 'purges' excessive emotions in the way that medicines could purge excessive humours from the body? Did he think of tragedy as providing a kind of emotional education, which might help an audience learn how to experience the right kinds of emotion on appropriate occasions?[2] Which of those aims Aristotle wished to foreground is anybody's guess. Whether any of his concerns were actually on the minds of the fifth-century tragedians about whom Aristotle principally writes is extremely doubtful.

There are two clear lessons here. Definitions of tragedy necessarily come after the fact, and are usually embedded in larger philosophical systems. As a result they tend to be messier and less widely applicable than they sound. Nonetheless, theoretical writing about tragedy has had a massive influence on the ways in which Shakespearean tragedy is read, understood and even performed. *Shakespearean Tragedy* (1904) by A. C. Bradley (1851–1935), perhaps now more often criticized than read, is the most influential single book on this subject. Bradley's view of Shakespearean tragedy was deeply influenced by Aristotle, on whose *Metaphysics* Bradley wrote an essay early in his career, but his adaptation of Aristotle's theory to suit Shakespeare is often awkward. Bradley argues that a 'fatal imperfection or error'[3] in the character of the hero is the driver of Shakespearean tragedy. This is an Edwardian simplification of Aristotle's *Poetics*, which argues that the high-born and virtuous characters who are the principal subject of tragedy should, in a perfect example of the genre such as *Oedipus Rex*, suffer as a result of 'some *hamartia*' (*Poetics*, ch. 13, 1453a). By *hamartia* Aristotle probably meant not an ethical weakness or a flaw in character but a particular kind of 'acting in ignorance', when a protagonist unwittingly does something which under its proper description he would know to be wrong. This happens when Oedipus inadvertently kills his father at a crossroads.[4] In the Christian era *hamartia* was often rendered simply as 'sin', and became associated with both the general weakness of fallen beings and the specific vices of particular agents. Bradley is heir to that transformation of terms and of ethical values, and his heirs in turn produced from his work the cod-moralizing belief that Shakespearean tragic heroes display a 'tragic flaw' (Bradley himself never uses this phrase) which is punished in the course of the play. That is a recipe for drama which could only appeal to those who want simply to see the bad bleed, and who have a clear idea of what 'bad' is. It is not the recipe by which Shakespearean tragedy was created, and does not even correspond very closely to what Bradley himself said about Shakespearean tragedy.

Bradley was not just a student of Aristotle. He worked with the idealist philosopher T. H. Green at Oxford, and spent a period in Germany. His brother, the philosopher F. H. Bradley (1846–1924), was one of the leading English followers of the German Romantic philosopher G. W. F. Hegel (1770–1831). Bradley himself was the most influential English popularizer of Hegel's theory of tragedy. For Hegel tragedy was the highest form of literary art, which dramatized and then resolved conflicts in the ethical sphere. So in Sophocles's *Antigone* (which is Hegel's exemplary tragedy) loyalty to the family prompts the heroine to bury her brothers, while King Creon's allegiance to the state leads him to have the bodies of rebels exposed to the air. In the tragic climax there is for Hegel a resolution of those distinct ethical perspectives, in which each is reabsorbed into a higher totality. Tragedy could therefore act as an engine of development in ethical thinking, which for Hegel, as for his follower Marx, evolves through a dialectic between two interconnected but opposing elements. Hegel regarded Shakespearean tragedy as a product of a late and 'subjective' stage of ethical thought, in which conflicts and their resolution were internal to its heroes rather than objectively embodied in different agents. The result is heroes like Hamlet who vacillate.[5] Bradley's focus on heroes who are 'torn by an inward struggle' marks him as a popularizer of Hegel as well as of Aristotle.[6]

It would be naïve to suppose that to understand the 'real' character of Shakespearean tragedy we should try simply to forget this critical tradition.

The idea that there is something called 'Shakespearean tragedy' which has its own rationale and which offers unique insights into the world and into the conflicts that shape and misshape the lives of human beings is the reason this book is called *The Cambridge Companion to Shakespearean Tragedy*. However, it is tempting to try, by way of a thought-experiment, to set aside the theoretical arguments which developed after Shakespeare's death, and initially ask not 'what *is* a Shakespearean tragedy?' but a rather different, historical question: 'what *was* a Shakespearean tragedy so far as Shakespeare and his contemporaries were concerned?' As we shall see, this question is not easy to answer, but asking it can alert us to many elements within Shakespeare's tragedies which did not matter much to Bradley but which probably did matter to Shakespeare and his audiences.

What might one of Shakespeare's contemporaries have thought while watching *Hamlet*, and what could it tell us? Perhaps not much. The responses of seventeenth-century theatregoers to Shakespeare's plays were probably not much more interesting than the average remark overheard in the foyer during the interval of a theatrical performance today. We do have a few records of such thoughts, and they are not on the whole inspiring. When the diarist Samuel Pepys (1633–1703) saw a production of *Hamlet* in 1663 the main thing that struck him was not the prince's psychological irresolution, but the fact that his wife's maid was onstage in a non-speaking role. He loyally noted that 'she becomes the stage very well'. Pepys certainly believed Shakespearean tragedy mattered: he devoted an afternoon a year later to learning '"To bee or not to bee" without book',[7] but when he saw *Othello* in 1660 he just described it as 'well done' and remarked that 'a very pretty lady that sot by me cried to see Desdimona smothered'.[8] Had the lady in question not been pretty it's unlikely that Pepys would have noticed her tragic reaction. In the 1640s Abraham Wright (1611–90) was similarly cavalier, describing *Hamlet* as 'but an indifferent play, the lines but meane: and in nothing like *Othello*', though he did enjoy the gravedigger scene.[9] Simon Forman, however, left a more revealing record of a performance of *Macbeth* on 20 April 1610:

> The next night, beinge at supper with his noble men whom he had to bid to a feaste to the which also Banco should have com, he began to speake of Noble Banco, and to wish that he wer ther. And as he thus did, standing up to drincke a Carouse to him, the ghoste of Banco came and sate down in his cheier behind him. And he turninge About to sit down Again sawe the goste of Banco, which fronted him so, that he fell into a great passion of fear and fury, Utteringe many wordes about his murder, by which, when they hard that Banco was Murdred they Suspected Makbet. Then MackDove fled to

England to the kinges sonn, And soe they Raised an Army, And cam into Scotland, and at Dunston Anyse overthrue Mackbet. In the meantyme whille Macdovee was in England, Makbet slewe Mackdoves wife & children, and after in the battelle Mackdove slewe Makbet. Observe Also how Mackbetes quen did Rise in the night in her slepe, & walke and talked and confessed all, & the docter noted her wordes.[10]

Forman mainly records what we call plot rather than describing the emotions of the characters onstage or their effect on the audience. Nonetheless, he clearly brought notions of suspicion and guilt to his experience of tragedy: he thought about what the doctor infers from Lady Macbeth's madness and what the diners at the banquet scene think of Macbeth – about which there is very little evidence in the surviving text of the play. This could well indicate that educated members of Elizabethan and Jacobean audiences responded to plays in general and to tragedies in particular by thinking about how and what characters onstage knew. The processes of inference and conjecture that operated in Elizabethan courts of law, in which jurors would make conjectures about the conduct and motives of individuals, does seem to have influenced the ways plays were written and perhaps also how they were experienced.[11] That *is* a kind of psychological response to tragedy, although it differs profoundly from Bradley's conception of 'psychology' because it concentrates more on cognitive than emotional questions. Forman asks himself not 'what is Macbeth feeling now?' but 'who knows what about whom on the stage?'. That question may have been one which Shakespeare wanted his audience to ask, since it has suggestive parallels with Hamlet's attempt to use the play called *The Mousetrap* to probe Claudius's guilt: 'guilty creatures sitting at a play / ... have proclaimed their malefactions' (2.2.542–5). Shakespearean tragedies after Bradley were often treated as dramas of emotion; for Elizabethans they may have been at least in part dramas of knowledge.

Northumberland in *2 Henry IV* describes a messenger entering to bring the news that Hotspur his son is dead: 'Yea, this man's brow, like to a title-leaf, / Foretells the nature of a tragic volume' (1.1.60–1). Can we learn anything further about what Shakespearean tragedy was by looking at the way tragedies were presented to their early readers? The picture here is again complex. Of the thirty-five plays listed in the contents page of the 1623 First Folio edition of Shakespeare's dramatic works eleven fall under the section headed 'Tragedies'. Curiously enough only three of these are actually called 'tragedies' in the printed list (*The Tragedy of Coriolanus*, *The Tragedy of Macbeth* and *The Tragedy of Hamlet*), while others are presented as just plain *Romeo and Juliet* or *Cymbeline King of Britain*. Several of the plays given these bald titles in the preliminaries, including *Titus Andronicus* and *King Lear*, are described as 'tragedies' on the running-titles at the top of each page of the play itself. Even here there seems to be little rhyme or reason to the titles: *Timon of Athens* is grouped with the tragedies, but remains just *Timon of Athens* even on the running-titles, except at the very start of the play when it's called *The Life of Tymon of Athens*. The folio is a far from perfect guide to anything that went on in Shakespeare's head, since it was published seven years after his death. It includes among the tragedies one play, which it variously calls *Cymbeline King of Britain* and *The Tragedie of Cymbeline*, which tends now to be described as a 'romance' or a 'tragicomedy'. *Troilus and Cressida* (to which it is notoriously hard to assign a genre) sits anomalously at the end of the Histories and before the start of the Tragedies section of the folio, as though it doesn't quite belong with either group. This was probably a result of disputes over the copyright for the play rather than a sign that a scrupulous printer worried about its genre, but there are good reasons to believe that even the publishers who were attempting to produce a volume called *Mr William Shakespeares Comedies Histories & Tragedies* did not feel secure about the generic boundaries between tragedies and other plays. In the smaller and cheaper quarto format editions in which a number of Shakespeare's plays were published during his lifetime several plays classed as 'histories' in the First Folio were first called 'tragedies', notably *The Tragedie of King Richard the Second* (printed in 1597) and *The Tragedy of King Richard the third* (also printed in 1597). Meanwhile two plays that Bradley included among the 'big four' tragedies have in their quarto texts titles that make them sound as much like 'histories' (a word which can in this period mean little more than 'story' or 'narrative') as tragedies: *The Tragicall Historie of Hamlet Prince of Denmark* (1603) is at least 'tragicall', but the *True Chronicle History of the Life and Death of King Lear and his three Daughters* (1608) sounds like a history play.

So a play's title leaf might foretell the nature of the tragic volume. Or it might not. The evidence of title pages suggests that the category 'tragedy' was very elastic in this period. That is of course borne out by the extraordinary fluency with which Shakespeare modulates between chronicle history, tragedy and moments of comedy throughout his oeuvre. Shakespeare himself used the words 'tragedy' and 'tragic' in different ways at different times. In the history plays those words are generally used to heighten moments of fear, as when Northumberland anticipates the worst from the frowning messenger. By the very end of the sixteenth century, however, Shakespeare was tending to restrict the word 'tragical' to contexts in which characters are rather stiltedly attempting to raise their language beyond its normal social register, or which are actually comic. In *A Midsummer Night's Dream* (c. 1596) the rude mechanicals' play of Pyramus and Thisbe is described as 'very tragical mirth' (5.1.57). By the later 1590s 'tragical' seems to have dropped from Shakespeare's vocabulary entirely, with the telling exception of its use by the arch-pedant Polonius in *Hamlet* (c. 1600) when he describes the players who come to Elsinore as 'The best actors in the world, either for tragedy, comedy, history, pastoral, pastoral-comical, historical-pastoral, tragical-historical, tragical-comical-historical-pastoral, scene individable or poem unlimited' (2.2.363–6). Polonius once played Julius Caesar, and his vocabulary here marks him as being at least a decade out of date in both his tastes and his critical language. Printers continued to use the word 'tragical' on title pages well into the seventeenth century, but for Shakespeare himself that word seems to have evoked the literary landscape of the 1560s and 1570s – in which the source for *Romeo and Juliet* was called *The Tragical History of Romeus and Juliet*. For him 'tragical' came to connote unrelenting woe, and a slightly outmoded literary manner.

These aren't just lexical curiosities. The slippage between plays called 'histories' and plays called 'tragedies' indicates the extent to which readers, printers and Shakespeare himself identified tragedy with the fall of historical figures (particularly kings and Caesars) who were crushed by the grinding rotations of fortune's wheel. Geoffrey Chaucer (c. 1340–1400) gathered together 'tragedies' of this kind (as well as several which don't quite fit that model) in the 'Monk's Tale', and seems to have been the first English writer call this kind of story a 'tragedy'. 'The Fall of Princes' by Chaucer's follower John Lydgate (c. 1370–1449/50?) developed Chaucerian 'tragedy' into a form which could sharply address Lydgate's own Lancastrian political context.[12] The appetite for tragedies about the fall of princes, modelled loosely on Lydgate and on Boccaccio, remained unquenched through the sixteenth century. In *A Mirror For Magistrates*, which grew in regular editions from 1559 through to the next century, the ghosts of historical characters end their tales with warnings along the lines of 'Who reckles rules, right soone may hap to rue'.[13] This vernacular model of tragedy established both a general moral framework for Elizabethan tragedy and a crude boundary to the social origins of people whose lives could be described as a 'tragedy'. A play called *The Tragedy of Bottom the Weaver* would be intrinsically comical, since a weaver is so clearly, even in his name, close to the bottom of the social ladder. Falling requires a measure of social elevation. Being part of a historical record implies a degree of prominence too.

But the most important single fact to bear in mind when thinking about any aspect of Shakespeare, or indeed about his contemporary dramatists, is that he worked in a relatively new and rapidly changing medium under a high degree of commercial pressure. If he did not do something new in each play then his audience would take their pennies down the road to the Swan or the Rose or one of the other rival playhouses. In this environment the 'fall of princes' was one of several tragic conventions which were not passively followed but continually transformed. Shakespeare did indeed write plays about the fall of kings and (Julius) Caesars, but the way he did so was usually slightly offbeat. *Richard II* (printed 1597) concentrates with operatic intensity on the fall of a king and the rhetorical arias with which he washes away his own balm. Most of the central characters of later tragedies tend to be just slightly out of place, or not quite as socially elevated as they want to think of themselves, or are even men on the make. Macbeth is not a king but a would-be king, whose desire to get on is accelerated by the prophecies of the witches. Hamlet is a prince who has lost the prospect of succession. Othello is a mercenary warrior whose own conception of his status is qualified by both his and the Venetians' sense that his blackness makes him not quite belong. Even Coriolanus is an aristocratic anachronism in a period of Rome's history in which power is shifting towards the plebeians, while Antony is left behind by the realpolitik of the rising emperor Octavian. When Shakespeare returned to a 'fall of princes' narrative in *King Lear* (*c.* 1603–6) he again did something odd with it: Lear wilfully divides his kingdom right at the start of the play as though he is determined to spin Fortune's wheel right off its axle by his own efforts, while the Gloucester sub-plot relates the rise and fall of another socially marginal and aspiring character, Edmund. This preoccupation with upward social mobility suggests how profoundly the plays of Shakespeare's contemporary Christopher Marlowe (1564–93) influenced his way of writing tragedies. Marlowe – who died just as Shakespeare's career as a dramatist was taking off – tended to dramatize efforts by people on the edges of society – shepherds like Tamburlaine, Jews like Barabas, or scholars like Dr Faustus – to dominate the world and the stage. The foregrounding of such figures in Elizabethan tragedy also has some connection with the relatively low social origins of most playwrights in the period: Shakespeare, like Marlowe, could barely claim to belong to the middling sort of men by birth, but by writing for the popular stage he came to be wealthy and relatively well known. The tragedy of *Macbeth* is certainly not, as the more reductive kinds of Marxist criticism would have it, a fable about the rise and self-destruction of the bourgeoisie,[14] but it is not surprising that a provincial glover's son should have felt that stories about the falls of princes might not speak directly to an audience that consisted partly of London apprentices and artisans. Characters who, like the semi-tragic socially aspirational steward Malvolio in *Twelfth Night*, were not born great but who wanted to believe that they could achieve greatness were much closer to the aspirations of his audience.

The literary criticism of the period suggests some further answers to the question 'what was a Shakespearean tragedy?', although again the answers it provides are neither clear nor simple. For Sir Philip Sidney (1554–86), the most influential writer on poetics in Shakespeare's lifetime, tragedy could shake the bodies of tyrants and assist the government of the state: the 'high and excellent tragedy . . . openeth the greatest wounds, and showeth forth the ulcers that are covered with tissue; that maketh kings fear to be tyrants, and tyrants manifest their tyrannical humours; that with stirring the affects of admiration and commiseration teacheth the uncertainty of this world, and upon how weak foundations gilden roofs are builded'.[15] Sidney ends his sentence with a nod to the conventional view that tragedy represents the mutability of fortune and the fragility of high office, but he begins it with a real bite: tragedy is a genre that 'maketh kings fear to be tyrants' – in the present tense. That aim was a strong component in the *Mirror for Magistrates*, which began life under its Protestant editors in the reign of the Catholic Queen Mary as not just a series of plangent wailings by dead kings and councillors, but as such a biting critique of government that it was initially suppressed, and was not published until the reign of the Protestant Elizabeth.[16] Shakespeare's historical dramas (which include the plays set in ancient Britain, *King Lear*, *Macbeth* and *Cymbeline*), repeatedly establish nervy intersections between present events and past tyrannies, as Chapter 6 explores in detail. Whether or not Shakespeare's *Richard II* was staged shortly before the ill-judged rebellion of the Earl of Essex against the Queen in 1601, and whether or not the Queen was referring to Shakespeare's play when she famously declared 'I am Richard II, know ye not that?', the scene in which Shakespeare dramatized the deposition of the king was deemed too hot to print until the fourth quarto edition, which appeared five years after the death of Elizabeth.[17] Shakespeare, like Sidney, certainly regarded tragedy as a form which could probe the wounds of the state.[18]

Sidney's view of tragedy was restated in slightly muffled form by George Puttenham (1529–91) in his *Art of English Poesy* (1589). Puttenham locates the historical origins of tragedy in the (supposed) period in which tyrants had become things of the past. Again, the function of tragedy is both morally and politically reforming:

> But after that some men among the more became mighty and famous in the world, sovereignty and dominion having learned them all manner of lusts

and licentiousness of life, by which occasions also their high estates and felicities fell many times into most low and lamentable fortunes, whereas before in their great prosperities they were both feared and reverenced in the highest degree, after their deaths, when the posterity stood no more in dread of them, their infamous life and tyrannies were laid open to all the world, their wickedness reproached, their follies and extreme insolencies derided, and their miserable ends painted out in plays and pageants, to show the mutability of fortune, and the just punishment of God in revenge of a vicious and evil life.[19]

Puttenham's *Art*, however, did not simply present tragedy as form of political retrospect, which looks back to the tyrannical past to find lessons for the present. It was itself retrospective: although printed in 1589 it was probably written during the 1570s and 1580s. Sidney's *Apology* also appeared in print almost a decade after its author had died. The slight antiquity of both these works was offset by their social cachet, since both Sidney and Puttenham wrote, or said they wrote, for courtly poets and readers, and Puttenham in particular regarded poetry as one of the arts of self-presentation by which an aspirant courtier could win advancement.[20] The styles and manners of socially elite groups generally trickle down through time to less elevated members of a society. That trickle-down effect certainly shaped the poetic tastes of the sixteenth century, since courtly fashions in verse tended to hit the press, the market and a popular readership around a decade after their first dissemination. But we should not expect this process of cultural diffusion to have occurred in quite the same way in drama as it did in poetry. Sidney and Puttenham chiefly valued plays written for small elite groups at the Inns of Court or other small, closed venues. Neither of them had a clue about how to appeal to the popular audience who paid to see Shakespeare's plays. As a result we might expect Shakespeare to have read the theorists, to have thought about them (respectfully), but not necessarily to have been guided by them in his practice.

One particular element in Sidney's *Apology* might have influenced Shakespeare much more than it actually did. In the latter part of the *Apology* Sidney accuses contemporary dramatists of 'mingling kings and clowns' onstage, and of being 'faulty both in place and time', by which he means that they failed to obey what came to be called the unities of time and place.[21] Sidney probably got his understanding of Aristotle's 'unities' not from the *Poetics* itself (of which a Latin translation appeared in 1498 and a Greek text in 1508, but which was not translated into English until the eighteenth century) but from Italian commentaries. Nevertheless he used 'Aristotelian' principles as a stick with which to bash the popular stage. Ben

Jonson ventriloquized this aspect of Sidney's criticism in the prologue to the Folio edition of *Every Man in his Humour* (1616), in which he scolded the writers of contemporary history plays, including Shakespeare, who 'with three rusty swords, / And help of some few foot-and-half foot words, / Fight over York and Lancaster's long jars / And in the tiring-house bring wounds to scars' (9–12). That was the moment when the prescriptive Aristotelian voice of Sidney spoke to Shakespeare as though from the grave.

But by the time it did so, probably around 1616, Shakespeare himself may have been in his grave too, although it is not known exactly when Jonson composed his prologue.[22] If Shakespeare did live to hear Jonson's Sidneian attack on him there is no sign that it influenced the way he wrote tragedies, in which references to the passage of time are usually markers of mood and atmosphere rather than signs of the playwright's Aristotelian aspirations to unity. When the notoriously anachronistic clock chimes repeatedly in the background of *Julius Caesar* it serves as a reminder that this is the moment at which the conspirators must act, and that time is slipping away. *Macbeth* also contains bells, knockings and clocks, but time in that play is so elastic that it's almost impossible to track its literal passage: the witches offer Macbeth kingship at an unspecified period 'hereafter', but he labours to make their 'hereafter' happen now, or tomorrow. After the murder of Duncan time stretches on, spreading from the bank and shoal of the present through tomorrow and tomorrow and tomorrow to the very crack of doom. Theatrical time and place stretch and bend too: the scene shifts to England in Act 4 while Macduff and Malcolm slow down the pace of the play by their dialogue about kingship and tyranny. This kind of time-stretching, in which the anxious pause before an action can seem like an age, and the period after it extend to eternity, would have been incomprehensible, and perhaps deplorable, to Sidney. It was also very different from the treatment of time in Shakespeare's comedies, in which, despite Orlando's claim that 'there is no clock in the forest' (*As You Like It*, 3.3.254–5), time tends to be more 'classically' regulated than it is in the tragedies. The action of the early *Comedy of Errors* (1594) is restricted to a single place and day, while Shakespeare's last single-authored play *The Tempest* (1610–11) is punctuated with near clockwork regularity by allusions to the hour, which remind the audience that the play's action occupies not the Aristotelian twenty-four hours but a magically compressed three.

Shakespeare's comedies tended to be more 'regular' (in the neo-classical sense) in their treatment of time and place than most of his tragedies for one simple and highly significant reason. So far as most sixteenth-century English readers were concerned there was a far more developed and accessible body of theoretical writing about comedy than there was about tragedy. The standard Renaissance editions of the classical comedians Plautus (*c.* 254–184 BC) and Terence (*c.* 190–158 BC) included elaborate introductions which discussed the ideal structure of a comic plot and the principles underlying that structure.[23] The prologues to Terence's plays also include critical reflections on his own practices. Classical tragedy could offer no equivalent to any of this. If Shakespeare read (as he probably did) some Greek tragedies in Latin translation he would not have found in them any systematic discussion of the structure or function of tragedy.[24] The surviving Roman tragedies by Lucius Annaeus Seneca (*c.* 4 BC – AD 65) are also silent about what a 'tragedy' might be or how it should be structured. In the nineteenth century – and indeed in the fourth century BC – tragedy was the genre on which most theories of drama were centred, and was regarded as the most intellectually rigorous kind of theatre. For the sixteenth century that role was filled by comedy. It was from comic theory and practice that playwrights could develop their ideas about form, about plot construction, and indeed about how to represent theatrical characters in action.

This had profound consequences for Shakespeare in general and for Shakespearean tragedy in particular. The presence of comic scenes in Shakespeare's tragedies was traditionally an embarrassment to critics, although Samuel Johnson memorably defended his 'interchange of seriousness and merriment, by which the mind is softened at one time, exhilarated at another'. These comic episodes – the porter in *Macbeth*, the clown who wishes Cleopatra 'all joy of the worm' before her death – could just be a sign, as Johnson believed, that comedy was 'congenial to [Shakespeare's] nature'.[25] They also show the banal fact that throughout most of Shakespeare's career the Fool was the most recognizable and at least the second most famous actor in his company. Writing plays which would give Will Kempe or Robert Armin an evening off would be a bit like putting on a Rolling Stones concert without Keith Richards. Writing a tragedy in which the Fool suddenly and without explanation disappears, as happens in *King Lear*, on the other hand, was the strongest means of showing an audience that catastrophe had finally arrived, and that all normal theatrical expectations were blown apart.

But the relationship between Shakespearean tragedy and comedy goes much further than this. Classical comedy provided much of Shakespeare's thinking about psychology and human action. In the plays of Plautus characters often form beliefs about what is happening around them. Very often they do so on the basis of hints, clues and tokens rather than of clear evidence. Sometimes these hints and clues are illusions, and at other times they are deliberately misleading performances (in a theatrical sense) put on by other characters in order to trick or beguile their onstage audience. Sometimes when characters discover the falsity of these illusory beliefs Plautus's comedies move into potentially tragic terrain, in which people wonder who they are, or whether the world actually is as they believe it to be. So in Plautus's *Amphitryon*, which is the only classical play to describe itself as a 'tragicomedia', Jove and Mercury disguise themselves as a warrior and his slave in order to seduce the warrior's wife. The real slave meets his divine impersonator, who turns him away from his own house. He thinks he's gone mad. Elsewhere in Plautus characters are frequently persuaded that what they thought was one person is in fact another person, and feel the world melt around them as a result. In Plautus's *Braggart Soldier* a slave who apparently witnesses his master's mistress kissing another man says 'I didn't see her and yet I did see her' ('non vidi eam, etsi vidi', 407).[26]

These moments, and the deeper interest in the nature of belief and theatrical illusion from which they arise, had an incalculable influence on Shakespearean comedy and tragicomedy. When Troilus sees a woman kissing Diomed who seems to be the Cressida who has just sworn to love him for ever he cries out 'This is and is not Cressid' (5.2.145), in a direct echo of Plautus's comic slave which occurs at the moment when the generically uncategorizable *Troilus and Cressida* comes closest to tragedy. A world in which actions and beliefs are founded on inference rather than evidence provides a perfect ground for error; and perceptual error – particularly when it concerns love and acts of sexual infidelity which by their nature cannot be directly witnessed – can become a ground for tragedy.

Othello is in this respect not so much a tragedy as a classical comedy gone wrong.[27] The play starts in a conventionally comic landscape, in which an enraged father blunders about at night while his daughter elopes, and young men-about-town cook up schemes for self-advancement. Throughout the play characters insist that they, like characters in Plautus, ground their actions and beliefs on probability rather than certain knowledge. Brabantio declares that ''Tis probable and palpable to thinking' (1.2.76) that Othello has used magic to make Desdemona love him, and so assumes it to be true although it is false. Even the Duke of Venice supposes 'it is possible enough to judgement' (1.3.9) that the Turks are attacking Cyprus rather than knowing it for a fact. Othello himself – and in a sense this is his tragedy – has a predisposition to short-circuit the process of coming to a well-founded belief: 'I'll see before I doubt; when I doubt, prove; / And on the proof, there is no more but this: / Away at once with love or jealousy' (3.3.192–4). He does not quite say 'when I'm doubtful I'll look for more evidence and assess the case accordingly'. Doubt seems to become in the

course of his sentence almost a foundation of proof: 'when I doubt, prove'.
Othello is constructed as a thought-experiment which is also a generic
experiment. It asks what would happen if you put a powerful and eloquent
warrior who simply cannot bear to experience doubt into a social landscape
drawn from classical comedy, in which human mental realities are founded
on beliefs rather than on certain knowledge.

The ultimate outcome of that experiment is not just Othello's lethal
jealousy, but the unleashing of intense physical and rhetorical violence that
makes the hero sound not like a character from Plautus, but like an import
from one of the tragedies of Seneca:

> Like to the Pontic Sea,
> Whose icy current and compulsive course
> Ne'er feels retiring ebb but keeps due on
> To the Propontic and the Hellespont,
> Even so my bloody thoughts with violent pace
> Shall ne'er look back, ne'er ebb to humble love,
> Till that a capable and wide revenge
> Swallow them up. (3.3.454–61)

Most of the ten tragedies ascribed to Seneca in the sixteenth century were
about ancient mythical heroes, although one (and this is significant given
the connections between Shakespearean tragedies and history plays), the
Octavia, was a tragedy about recent Roman history. Seneca wrote for and
often about periods of tyranny. He served as tutor to the Emperor Nero,
and eventually was ordered to commit suicide by his former pupil. His plays
can present acts of spectacular violence, but underlying them is often an
ideal of emotional 'autarchy' or self-government, which might enable subjects of tyranny to experience some measure of control over the universe
which they inhabit.[28] The combination of crafted rhetoric and physical
violence in Seneca's plays has been given a rough time by the critical
tradition, and their influence on Shakespearean tragedy has often been
seriously underestimated as a result.[29] Shakespeare, however, would have
been mad to neglect Seneca, whom he could have read comfortably in the
original Latin or in the collection of English translations which appeared in
1581. Playwrights in the generation just older than Shakespeare whom he
sought to emulate and supersede – Thomas Kyd (1558–94) and George Peele
(1556–96) in particular – had made their debts to Senecan tragedies of blood
instantly obvious. The analogy which Othello develops between his
thoughts and the uncontrollable movements of the oceans is profoundly
but not directly Senecan, since very often in Seneca's plays the universe
reverberates to the passions of his heroes and heroines. Other moments in

the tragedies are explicitly indebted to particular passages of Seneca. King
Lear on the heath is Shakespeare's strongest Senecan voice:

> Let the great gods,
> That keep this dreadful pudder o'er our heads,
> Find out their enemies now. Tremble, thou wretch,
> That hast within thee undivulgèd crimes
> Unwhipped of justice. Hide thee, thou bloody hand,
> Thou perjured and thou simular of virtue
> That art incestuous. Caitiff, to pieces shake,
> That under covert and convenient seeming
> Has practised on man's life. Close pent up guilts,
> Rive your concealing continents and cry
> These dreadful summoners grace. I am a man
> More sinned against than sinning.   (3.2.47–58)

Lear echoes, amplifies and transfigures a speech from the *Hippolytus*, a Senecan
play to which Shakespeare repeatedly returned in the course of his career:

> Magne regnator deum,
> tam lentus audis scelera? tam lentus vides?
> et quando saeva fulmen emittes manu,
> si nunc serenum est? omnis impulsus ruat
> aether et atris nubibus condat diem,
> ac versa retro sidera obliquos agant
> retorta cursus. tuque, sidereum caput,
> radiate Titan, tu nefas stirpis tuae
> speculare? lucem merge et in tenebras fuge.
> cur dextra, divum rector atque hominum, vacat
> tua, nec trisulca mundus ardescit face?
> in me tona, me fige, me velox cremet
> transactus ignis: sum nocens, merui mori.   (673–86)

Great king of the gods, do you hear about crimes so slowly? Do you see them
so slowly? And when will you send the lightning bolt from your vengeful
hand, since now the heavens are clear? Let the whole sky collapse inwards and
hide the day in black clouds, let the stars turn backwards and swerving run
their course askew. And you, head of stars, radiant Titan, do you look down
at this crime by your offspring? Drown the light, and flee into darkness. Why
is your hand empty, ruler of gods and men, why do you not singe the world
with your three-pronged brand? Strike me with lightning, transfix me, let the
swift fire cremate me: I am guilty. I deserve to die.

The thunder of dissolution and retribution was, however, by no means
Shakespeare's only debt to Senecan tragedy. As early as 1589 the pamphleteer
Thomas Nashe was complaining that the Senecan style, with its heroes who

utter *sententiae* (one-line memorable aphorisms) like 'blood is a beggar', was old hat.[30] Shakespeare, always acutely sensitive to fashion, took this prompt, and never imitated Seneca without giving a twist of novelty to his imitations. Lear's speech turns Hippolytus's cry of guilt upside-down, insisting on his own innocence, and calling down destruction not on himself but on others. The storm and thunderbolts – which in *Hippolytus* are only wished for but are pointedly *not* happening – are realized onstage. *Hamlet* (which probably derives from an earlier lost play in the Senecan style that Nashe deplored) also has Senecan moments, but again these are deliberately transformed. At the start of Seneca's goriest play, *Thyestes* – at the climax of which, as at the climax of *Titus Andronicus*, a father is made to eat his own flesh and blood – Atreus berates himself for failing to act:

> Ignave, iners, enervis et (quod maximum
> probrum tyranno rebus in summis reor)
> inulte, post tot scelera, post fratris dolos
> fasque omne ruptum questibus vanis agis
> iratus Atreus? fremere iam totus tuis
> debebat armis orbis, et geminum mare
> utrimque classes agere; iam flammis agros
> lucere et urbes decuit, ac strictum undique
> micare ferrum.   (176–84)

Lazy, useless, gutless, and (what I think is the worst failing in a tyrant who is dealing with the most important matters of all) unrevenged! Angry Atreus, after your brother's trickery and the violation of all good principles, are you just whining on with vain complaints? Now the whole world should thunder with your weapons, and fleets should be setting sail from both shores of the twin sea; now the fields ought to be alight with flames and the cities too, and the drawn sword should flash on all sides.

Any member of Shakespeare's audience who had a smattering of Latin – and that meant all those who had been to grammar school – would hear these lines behind the soliloquy which Hamlet delivers after the players leave him:

> O what a rogue and peasant slave am I!
>
>   . . .
>
> Why, what an ass am I! This is most brave,
> That I, the son the dear murderèd,
> Prompted to my revenge by heaven and hell,
> Must like a whore unpack my heart with words,
> And fall a-cursing like a very drab,
> A scullion!
> Fie upon't, foh!   (2.2.502–41)

No one who knew Seneca's *Thyestes* would have missed the differences between those speeches either. Atreus goes on to make his brother feed on his own children. Hamlet by contrast persuades himself to 'act' in the theatrical rather than the practical sense, by staging his play designed to 'catch the conscience of the king'. Shakespeare heard in Seneca not just the sound of fury and cosmic destruction, but also a voice of contingency and possibility, in which characters don't just simply do violent deeds, but deliberate over what they might do and what should happen. Seneca's Atreus does not just describe his actual revenge but a hypothetical revenge introduced by the modal verbs 'should' and 'ought' ('Now the whole world *should* thunder with your weapons'). That tiny grammatical detail, which is something of a habit in Seneca's heroes, was of immense importance for Shakespeare. He teased his *Hamlet* out from those modal verbs, and made from them a play which is grounded on 'might' in the grammatical rather than in the physical sense. Hamlet is throughout the play captivated by verbs and grammatical moods which evoke possibility: 'Now *might* I do it pat' (3.3.73), he says when he catches Claudius at prayer; 'Now *could* I drink hot blood' he says just before he visits his mother (3.2.351). And when that fell sergeant Death carries him off, Hamlet again speaks the language of possibility rather than of actuality, with 'oh I *could* tell you – / But let it be' (5.2.316–17). Hamlet is a quizzical and almost a parodic response to the physically mighty heroes of Senecan tragedy; but his indecision – which Bradley, and before him Coleridge, and before him Hegel, put at the centre of his character – grows from the space between speaking and doing which is such a strong element in the language of Seneca's heroes.

That observation takes us close to the heart of Shakespearean tragedy. It would be only a slight exaggeration to say that *acting* is the central concern of the tragedies Shakespeare wrote in the period roughly from 1599 to 1606, and which Bradley regarded as the high-point of his 'tragic phase'. Picking up a sword and killing a king is an uncomplicated matter in the heat of battle, but deliberating beforehand, imagining a dagger, rehearsing the role, putting on the borrowed robes of Senecan rhetoric in order to persuade yourself to do it: these are the theatrical and mental spaces explored in *Hamlet* and *Macbeth* in particular. The point at which an agent is deciding to act, or is imagining the consequences of what he or she might do, provides a perfect occasion for soliloquies which represent the processes of deliberation. This pause before action, full of potential and of fear, was not a moment that Shakespeare simply discovered in the 'mature' tragedies, however. In *Titus Andronicus* (c. 1593–4) there is a long delay between the rape of Lavinia and Titus's revenge. In the interim between this action and

Titus's reaction Titus himself *acts* strangely, plays mad, dresses up as a cook. In *Julius Caesar* (1599) the pause before action is shorter, but for Brutus it becomes the occasion for what was called 'deliberative rhetoric', in which the pros and cons of a particular course of action are debated:

> Between the acting of a dreadful thing
> And the first motion, all the interim is
> Like a phantasma or a hideous dream. (2.1.63–5)

What Brutus describes as 'the interim' is the temporal space between the first 'motion', or impulse to action, and its performance. That period gives an agent time to imagine what he should do, and it may spawn dreams and nightmares about what might happen if he does it. Shakespeare, like most Elizabethan schoolboys, was trained to compose speeches in which a real or imagined person might produce arguments both for and against a particular course of action – a skill he deployed most famously in his theatrical career in Hamlet's deliberation whether 'To be or not to be'. Shakespeare also read manuals of ethics which described the complex interplay between acts of imagination and will and the workings of the bodily humours and passions (discussed in Chapter 8). This enabled him – in a very different way from Sophocles or Euripides – to write dramas which address questions about action, agency and responsibility.

Greek ethical thought was also part of the amalgam that made Shakespearean tragedy, even if Shakespeare, as seems likely, never read a word of Sophocles in Greek. Plutarch's 'Life of Coriolanus', which was the source for Shakespeare's *Coriolanus*, includes an extended discussion of how in Homer a mixture of human appetites and external promptings could prompt someone to act:

> But in wonderous and extraordinarie thinges, which are done by secret inspirations and motions, he [that is, Homer] doth not say that God taketh away from man his choyce and freedom of will, but that he doth move it: neither that he doth worke desire in us, but objecteth to our mindes certaine imaginations whereby we are lead to desire, and thereby doth not make this our action forced, but openeth the way to our will, and addeth thereto courage, and hope of successe.[31]

Shakespeare was also an inheritor of a complex set of arguments, which had run through sixteenth-century Protestant theology, about the role played by the human will in determining the ultimate destination of the soul in heaven or hell. As well as all of this, Shakespeare spent his days 'acting' in a rather more humdrum sense: he learned lines, some of which he had written himself and some of which were written for him, and so experienced almost every day the actor's sense of inevitability, in which he knew the words he was going to speak and the events which simply had to happen. He was therefore equipped to think about the grounds on which people act, was trained to represent through rhetoric the processes of deliberation which might precede action, and he was skilled at using his own voice and body in another form of 'acting', by performing in plays. That made 'acting' in Shakespearean tragedy a far richer concept than it was even to the Greek tragedians, since it fused together religious, rhetorical and ethical thought with professional practice. When Hamlet laments that he has the 'motive and the cue for passion' but not passion itself, he is speaking from this richly multiple view of what it is to act.

This leads to a point where discussion of what a Shakespearean tragedy *was* begins to suggest answers to the question of what a Shakespearean tragedy *is*. The temptation to provide a tidy formula for Shakespearean tragedy which resembles the quotation from Aristotle with which this chapter began should be resisted. Shakespearean tragedies have eclectic origins, and that is the principal reason for their aesthetic power. Shakespeare's own conception of what might be achieved by a play which its printers might want to call a 'tragedy' kept on changing. He experimented with late medieval traditions of tragedies about the falls of princes, and hybridized these with Tudor thought about historical process, and gave them political force in the light of contemporary beliefs that tragedies could influence the government of the state. Shakespeare also absorbed and refashioned Marlowe's tragedies of social aspiration and moral transgression, which gives a profoundly unclassical edginess and sense of displacement to his central characters. His tragedies absorbed a whole range of thinking about imagination and probability, which can be traced to origins in legal and rhetorical traditions, as well as to classical comedy. Many of them show an interest in the nature of the will and of human desires which is at once philosophically sophisticated and finally unresolvable to a single philosophical position. That fuses with his skill in fashioning speeches of deliberation to suit particular characters and occasions. Some Shakespearean tragedies explore how human aspirations and desires are imaginatively projected on to the world, and the multiple ways in which those desires do not quite manage to turn into actions in quite the way the agent wanted. Some present agents whose destruction seems to resonate with the surrounding world. Those features of the plays show Shakespeare's deep debt to the tragedies of Seneca.

But these plays – the products of rapid and deep thought, which have ever since their composition provided occasions for deep thought in their readers and audiences – are by no means purely cerebral. Shakespeare's audiences could, not far from the Globe, pay a penny or so to witness dogs being torn apart by bears chained to posts. They could also see public executions, which were often explicitly compared to tragedies – as when Chidiock Tichborne, about to be partially strangulated, disembowelled while still alive and then cut up into segments by the public hangman for his part in the Babington plot in 1586, declared 'Here you see a company of young men (and that Generosi too) playing a woefull Tragedy.'[32] Tichborne's theatrical metaphors ('company', 'Tragedy') were not simply conventional. Elizabethan tragedies can make the body scream in pain. When King Lear says 'I am bound / Upon a wheel of fire, that mine own tears / Do scald like molten lead' (4.6.43–5) Tichborne's theatrical metaphors are inverted: a player king lays claim in metaphor to the physical torment which was literally enacted close by on the scaffold of execution. Running right through Shakespearean tragedy, from the mutilation of Lavinia in *Titus Andronicus* to the blinding of Gloucester in *King Lear*, and from the sacrificial slaughter of Julius Caesar, so thoughtfully planned and yet so carnal to witness, to the butchery of Coriolanus, there is a perplexing conjunction between raw physicality and refined questions about motive and agency. This diversity of purpose and origin, in which physical violence meets metaphysical speculation, is not simply an accidental element of Shakespearean tragedy. Diversity of purpose makes it thrilling, and also makes it defy simple definition. Watching *Hamlet* is not a matter of working out what the Prince is thinking or feeling, as it was for Bradley. Nor is it a matter of experiencing pity and terror in an elevated form, as a neo-Aristotelian critic might wish. Nor is it simply (as the most radical attempt to break free of character-based readings of the play proposes)[33] a play that broods on the material fact of losing one's inheritance. The play is a quizzical act of conjunction and comprehension. An audience watches a player and a playwright pull together a whole range of divergent interests and intellectual preoccupations in order to make a kind of tragic drama that seemed new. The play requires its audience, like Simon Forman when he watched *Macbeth*, to make inferences about who has done what and who knows what, and it presses that process of making inferences to the outer limit of uncertainty. Sometimes the play and the Prince seem to sprawl off to meditate on death and the destruction of the body in ways that seem beyond the immediate purpose; sometimes the terror of death slows the action to a crawl; sometimes the collectivity of laughter weaves itself in with the shared experience of mortality, as when the gravediggers banter about time and death and bodily decay.

This diversity of purpose, origins and effects means that responses to the play are likely to be as various and numerous as its audiences. A guilty king watching it might give himself away by displaying what Sidney called the 'ulcers that are covered with tissue' of his usurped state, as Claudius does when he calls for 'light' in the middle of the performance of *The Mousetrap*. A stoic like Horatio might see in it a simple moral, a tale of 'accidental judgements, casual slaughters' (5.2.361). A pedant like Polonius might see in it a mixture of generic conventions. A self-improving man about town like Samuel Pepys might think that learning to recite 'To be or not to be' was a very ribbon in the cap of youth. Hamlet himself might hear in it the untold tale which he 'would tell' if death did not carry him off. Any mortal might witness in the play a primal panic in the face of death, which is given an additional impulse by the cloudy imperative to revenge, to die and to go you know not where. But then again an apprentice butcher in the audience might think the climactic sword-fight was really the best bit, and might laugh if his friend were spattered by sheep's blood when Claudius is finally stabbed. These plays are very nearly overburdened by the multiplicity of their purposes and origins, and that is what makes them permanently great – not as works of art consciously grounded in determinable principles, but as hyper-principled, hyper-ambitious and endlessly overdetermined fictions.

Notes

1. D. A. Russell and Michael Winterbottom, *Ancient Literary Criticism: The Principal Texts in New Translations* (Oxford University Press, 1972), p. 97.
2. See Stephen Halliwell, *Aristotle's Poetics* (London: Duckworth, 1986), pp. 184–201 and Martha C. Nussbaum, *The Fragility of Goodness: Luck and Ethics in Greek Tragedy and Philosophy* (Cambridge University Press, 1986), pp. 378–91.
3. A. C. Bradley, *Shakespearean Tragedy: Lectures on Hamlet, Othello, King Lear, Macbeth* (London: Macmillan, 1957), p. 22.
4. Halliwell, *Aristotle's Poetics*, pp. 215–22.
5. Georg Wilhelm Friedrich Hegel, *Aesthetics: Lectures on Fine Art*, ed. and trans. T. M. Knox, 2 vols. (Oxford University Press, 1975), vol. ii, pp. 1192–237.
6. Bradley, *Shakespearean Tragedy*, p. 18.
7. Samuel Pepys, *The Shorter Pepys*, ed. Robert Latham (London: Bell and Hyman, 1985), pp. 281, 442.
8. *Ibid.*, p. 86.
9. Arthur C. Kirsch, 'A Caroline Commentary on the Drama', *Modern Philology* 66 (1969): 256–61; 257–8.
10. Bodleian Ashmole MS 208, fol. 207, transcribed in E. K. Chambers, *William Shakespeare: A Study of Facts and Problems*, 2 vols. (Oxford University Press, 1930), vol. iii, pp. 337–8. Forman's notes were discovered by the forger John Payne Collier, and doubt has sometimes been cast on their authenticity.

11. Lorna Hutson, *The Invention of Suspicion: Law and Mimesis in Shakespeare and Renaissance Drama* (Oxford University Press, 2007).

12. See Nigel Mortimer, *John Lydgate's Fall of Princes: Narrative Tragedy in its Literary and Political Contexts* (Oxford University Press, 2005), especially pp. 153–218.

13. William Baldwin, *The Mirror for Magistrates*, ed. Lily B. Campbell (Cambridge University Press, 1938), p. 345.

14. Terry Eagleton, *William Shakespeare* (Oxford University Press, 1986), p. 6: 'Like Macbeth, the bourgeoisie will become entangled in its own excess, giving birth to its own gravedigger (the working class).'

15. Gavin Alexander, ed., *Sidney's The Defence of Poesy and Selected Renaissance Literary Criticism* (London: Penguin, 2004), pp. 27–8.

16. See Scott Lucas, *A Mirror for Magistrates and the Politics of the English Reformation* (Amherst: University of Massachusetts Press, 2009).

17. For the arguments, see Blair Worden, 'Which Play Was Performed at the Globe Theatre on 7 February 1601?', *London Review of Books* (12 July 2003): 22–4 and Jason Scott-Warren, 'Was Elizabeth Richard II: The Authenticity of Lambarde's "Conversation"', *Review of English Studies* (2012), http://res.oxfordjournals.org/content/early/2012/07/14/res.hgs062.full.pdf.

18. See Rebecca W. Bushnell, *Tragedies of Tyrants: Political Thought and Theater in the English Renaissance* (Ithaca, NY: Cornell University Press, 1990).

19. Alexander, *Renaissance Literary Criticism*, p. 85.

20. See Daniel Javitch, *Poetry and Courtliness in Renaissance England* (Princeton University Press, 1978).

21. Alexander, *Renaissance Literary Criticism*, pp. 45–6.

22. See David Bevington, Martin Butler and Ian Donaldson, eds., *The Cambridge Edition of the Works of Ben Jonson*, 7 vols. (Cambridge University Press, 2012), vol. IV, p. 624.

23. Joel B. Altman, *The Tudor Play of Mind: Rhetorical Inquiry and the Development of Elizabethan Drama* (Berkeley and London: University of California Press, 1978), pp. 107–47.

24. Emrys Jones, *The Origins of Shakespeare* (Oxford University Press, 1977), pp. 85–118.

25. Samuel Johnson, *Works*, ed. Walter Jackson Bate, 23 vols. (New Haven, CT: Yale University Press, 1958–2010), vol. VII, pp. 68–9.

26. See further Robert S. Miola, *Shakespeare and Classical Comedy: the Influence of Plautus and Terence* (Oxford University Press, 1994) and Alison Sharrock, *Reading Roman Comedy: Poetics and Playfulness in Plautus and Terence* (Cambridge University Press, 2009).

27. See Joel B. Altman, *The Improbability of Othello: Rhetorical Anthropology and Shakespearean Selfhood* (Chicago and London: University of Chicago Press, 2010) and Hutson, *Invention of Suspicion*.

28. See Gordon Braden, *Renaissance Tragedy and the Senecan Tradition: Anger's Privilege* (New Haven, CT and London: Yale University Press, 1985), Robert

S. Miola, *Shakespeare and Classical Tragedy: The Influence of Seneca* (Oxford University Press, 1992).

29. For parallels see John William Cunliffe, *The Influence of Seneca on Elizabethan Tragedy: An Essay* (London: Macmillan, 1893); for a claim that these do not derive directly from Seneca see G. K. Hunter, *Dramatic Identities and Cultural Tradition: Studies in Shakespeare and his Contemporaries* (Liverpool University Press, 1978), pp. 159–73. For the pro-Senecan backlash, see Emrys Jones, *The Origins of Shakespeare* (Oxford University Press, 1977), pp. 267–72.

30. Thomas Nashe, *Works*, ed. Ronald B. McKerrow and F. P. Wilson, 4 vols. (Oxford University Press, 1958), vol. III, pp. 315–16.

31. *Plutarch's Lives of the Noble Grecians and Romans*, trans. Thomas North, ed. George Wyndham, 6 vols. (London: D. Nutt, 1895), vol. II, p. 181.

32. Richard S. M. Hirsch, 'The Works of Chidiock Tichborne', *English Literary Renaissance* 16 (1986): 303–18; 313.

33. See Margreta de Grazia, *'Hamlet' without Hamlet* (Cambridge University Press, 2007).

Further reading

Altman, J. B., *The Improbability of Othello: Rhetorical Anthropology and Shakespearean Selfhood* (Chicago and London: University of Chicago Press, 2010).

Braden, Gordon, *Renaissance Tragedy and the Senecan Tradition: Anger's Privilege* (New Haven, CT and London: Yale University Press, 1985).

Bradley, A. C., *Shakespearean Tragedy: Lectures on Hamlet, Othello, King Lear, Macbeth* (London: Macmillan, 1957).

Bushnell, Rebecca W., *Tragedies of Tyrants: Political Thought and Theater in the English Renaissance* (Ithaca, NY: Cornell University Press, 1990).

de Grazia, Margreta, *'Hamlet' without Hamlet* (Cambridge University Press, 2007).

Hutson, Lorna, *The Invention of Suspicion: Law and Mimesis in Shakespeare and Renaissance Drama* (Oxford University Press, 2007).

Jones, Emrys, *The Origins of Shakespeare* (Oxford University Press, 1977).
  Scenic Form in Shakespeare (Oxford: Clarendon Press, 1971).

Kerrigan, J., *Revenge Tragedy: Aeschylus to Armageddon* (Oxford: Clarendon Press, 1996).

Miola, Robert, S., *Shakespeare and Classical Tragedy: The Influence of Seneca* (Oxford: Clarendon Press, 1992).

Smith, Emma, *Shakespeare's Tragedies* (Oxford: Blackwell, 2004).

CHAPTER 2

The language of tragedy

Russ McDonald

In the middle of *The Second Part of King Henry the Fourth*, during the long nocturnal tavern scene, Shakespeare abruptly alters the elegiac mood by introducing a new character – Pistol. Significantly, his entrance is announced in advance: as soon as his name is mentioned Doll Tearsheet denounces him as 'a swaggering rascal' and 'the foul-mouthed'st rogue in England'. Her complaint instantly identifies his essential attribute, for like so many secondary characters in the second tetralogy, Pistol speaks a distinctive language.

> PISTOL What, shall we have incision? Shall we imbrue?
> [*Snatches up his sword.*]
> Then Death rock me asleep, abridge my doleful days!
> Why then, let grievous ghastly gaping wounds
> Untwind the sisters three; come, Atropos, I say!
> HOSTESS Here's goodly stuff toward! (2.4. 157–61)

'Stuff' indeed. Attempting to pass himself off as a valiant warrior, the coward has filched the rhetoric of a hero, and we need look no further for the source of his grandiloquent speech than the Elizabethan playhouse. Pistol wants to sound like a Marlovian hero – in one of his first utterances he misquotes Marlowe's *Tamburlaine* – and thus assembles his speeches with the verbal materials of the tragedian. Since parody or caricature exaggerates and thus identifies the fundamental properties of a style, Pistol's extravagant, pretentious, colourful speech provides an appropriate introduction to the language of Shakespearean tragedy.

Before considering the authentic idiom that Pistol counterfeits, it will be helpful to glance briefly at the growth of tragedy as a theatrical phenomenon in the last decades of the sixteenth century. Thanks partly to the emergence of a few brilliant playwrights, particularly Thomas Kyd and Christopher Marlowe, the English theatre made enormous presentational, social, commercial, and poetic advances at the end of Elizabeth's reign. By 1603 the

tragic actor, whether he spoke Shakespeare's verse or Ben Jonson's or
someone else's, sounded radically different from his counterpart of thirty
years earlier. To a considerable extent the spoken words sounded different
because, as the sixteenth century gave way to the seventeenth, the world
being spoken of was changing, becoming ever more alien, confusing, and
disturbing. The language of English tragedy at this crucial moment was
shaped by a wide range of cultural phenomena: the rise of literacy, the
emerging artistic dignity of the English language, the emerging existential
dignity of the human being, corresponding scepticism about such an
evaluation, the accelerating reassessment of monarchical, ecclesiastical,
and divine authority, and the concomitant upheaval in the political, religious, social, and philosophical spheres. Although I shall touch on such
trends and movements, they are treated more thoroughly elsewhere in this
volume.[1] My aim is to elucidate Shakespeare's response to such developments as it manifests itself in the speech of his principal tragic characters.

Hamlet, Othello, and their theatrical kin are among the most charismatic
speakers in all of world drama, and this essay is an attempt to identify and
analyse the sources of their unexcelled authority. In one sense such a
taxonomic effort is inherently vain, in that Shakespeare's tragic language
works just as the rest of Shakespeare's language works: the dynamic effect of
patterned words upon the listener's mind is much the same whether the
speaker is Petruchio or Portia or King Lear. And yet the visionary propensities of the tragic heroes, the extremes of tragic action, and the historical–
cultural sovereignty of the tragic mode help to generate a distinctive poetic
intensity. Lofty diction, repetition of words and syntactical patterns, classical allusions, rhetorical questions, sophisticated metrical schemes and
effects, poetic and thematic recapitulation, overstatement – all these characteristics mocked in Pistol's outbursts constitute the 'stuff' of Shakespearean
tragic speech. After the two initial efforts in the early and mid-1590s, *Titus
Andronicus* and *Romeo and Juliet*, the playwright committed himself in
mid-career to the darkly sceptical mode of tragedy. That turn coincides
with his attainment of poetic maturity, with his having mastered and
developed the technical practices and formal innovations inherited from his
theatrical predecessors: blank verse as a medium for poetic drama, for
example, was less than fifty years old when Shakespeare wrote *Hamlet*. This
technical proficiency afforded him the means of articulating with unparalleled
force the terms of the tragic paradox – that the sources of human greatness
and the sources of human failure are identical. And the artistic manifestation
of that paradox is that the limits of language are set forth in language of almost
illimitable power.

Antecedents and commentary

Two distinct traditions shaped the way English writers thought about tragedy in the middle of the sixteenth century. The first is the native strain deriving from the medieval stories and poems typified in John Lydgate's *The Fall of Princes* (1431). The public thrilled to this collection of tales, which their authors regularly describe as 'tragedies' but which resemble classical tragedy much less than they do the Christian tradition of *contemptus mundi*. In the English popular mind, devoted as it was to 'this proliferating body of mortuary verse,'[2] the term 'tragedy' meant simply a spectacular fall from high place. In the dramatic tradition, 'tragedy' usually meant Roman tragedy, specifically and almost exclusively the plays of Seneca. The Elizabethans automatically identified Senecan drama with blood, vengeance, violent death, and supernatural intervention. For present purposes, the more significant Senecan characteristic is the prominence of sublime expression. In the *Apology for Poetry* (pub. 1595), Sir Philip Sidney famously praises Sackville and Norton's *Gorboduc*, the first important English stage tragedy, because 'it is full of stately speeches and well-sounding phrases, climbing to the height of Seneca's style'.[3] It is worth pausing here to heed Sidney's figurative language, particularly 'stately' and 'climbing'. From the sixteenth century to the twenty-first, metaphors of altitude are inescapable in discussions of tragic language. 'Stately', meaning 'majestic' or 'regal', invokes height in relation to social class. The decorum of tragic language, of Seneca's style in particular, is aristocratic, refined, associated with and limited to the small world of the court. And Sidney's use of such descriptive terms is utterly conventional and consistent with the attitudes of the period.

Thomas Newton introduces his 1581 edition of *Seneca His Tenne Tragedies* by defending the Roman's works against charges of immorality. At just about that time opponents of the stage were busy attacking the London theatres as showcases of depravity, condemning plays and players for providing instruction in vice. Seeking to refute such criticism by asserting the morality of drama, Newton ascribes great moral efficacy to Seneca's style, and his commendation provides a typical example of early modern rhetoric about dramatic rhetoric:

> For it may not at any hand be thought and deemed the direct meaning of Seneca himself, whose whole writings (penned with a peerless sublimity and loftiness of style), are so far from countenancing vice, that I doubt whether there be any among all the catalogue of heathen writers, that with more gravity of Philosophical sentences, more weightiness of sappy [vigorous, juicy] words, or greater authority of sound matter beateth down sin, loose

life, dissolute dealing, and unbridled sensuality; or that more sensibly, pithily, and bitingly layeth down the guerdon [reward, consequences] of filthy lust, cloaked dissimulation, and odious treachery, which is the drift whereunto he leveleth the whole issue [i.e. the resolution] of each of his tragedies.[4]

The sentiments and the language of Sidney and Sidney's contemporaries – not to mention Polonius, who approvingly mentions Seneca's 'heavy' style – are clearly and forcefully expressed here. Newton establishes the morality of the dramatic enterprise in the series of adverbs that describes the excoriation of vice, 'sensibly, pithily, and bitingly', but even more relevant is his figurative analysis of the style: 'peerless sublimity', 'loftiness of style', 'weightiness', 'sappy words'.

The nobility of tragic language is intimately connected with the aristocratic pedigree of tragedy as an artistic form. Renaissance literary critics were no less hierarchical than political writers or religious apologists, and tragedy stood near the very top of the order of fictional or poetic forms, second only to the epic. Virtually everyone in the period who writes about tragedy invokes its exalted status: Sidney ('the high and excellent tragedy'), Roger Ascham ('the goodliest Argument of all'), William Webbe ('bringing in the persons of Gods and Goddesses, Kynges and Queenes, and great states'), George Puttenham ('besides those poets comic there were other who served also the stage, but meddled not with so base matters'), Kyd's Hieronimo ('Fie! comedies are fit for common wits; . . . Give me a stately written tragedy').[5] The tragic playwright addresses, and addresses self-consciously, fundamental problems of human experience – the inevitability of death, the desire for transcendence, the vanity of terrestrial aspiration, the consequences of pride, heroic self-assertion, the effects of evil in the world. Such heavy matters require heightened, uncommon language.

The burgeoning of Elizabethan tragedy owed much to the invention of a poetic language suitable for it – unrhymed iambic pentameter, or blank verse. Until poets and playwrights began to experiment with blank verse and made it the standard for Renaissance tragedy, those writers who sought to tell tragic stories were hampered by the available poetic forms, as we hear in John Studley's translation of a passage from Act 3 of Seneca's *Agamemnon* (1566). Miserable humans are happy to be summoned

> By death, a pleasaunt port, for aye in rest them selves to shroude,
> Where dreadfull tumultes never dwell nor stormes of fortune proude:
> Nor yet the burning firy flakes of Jove the same doth doubt,
> When wrongfully with thwacking thumpes he raps his thunder out:
> Heere Lady Peace th'inhabitours doth never put in flight,

> Nor yet the victors threatning wrath approching nygh to sight,
> No whyrling western wynde doth urge the ramping seas to praunce,
> No dusty cloude that raysed is by savage Mimilaunce,
> On horseback riding rancke by rancke, no fearce and cruell host,
> No people slaughtred, with their townes cleane topsie turvey tost.[6]

The point of citing such a passage is not to gain a cheap laugh at Studley's expense or to belittle him for not being Marlowe or Shakespeare. Writers like Studley were admired in their day, and their translations are notable because they attest to the poetic taste of the age just prior to Shakespeare's and to the kind of verse considered appropriate for the highest form of drama.

In Studley's case the poetic crudeness (which to our ears approaches burlesque) is attributable in part to the modest talents of the translator, but such apparent ineptitude owes much to the comparatively undeveloped state of English poetry. Studley's translation is hampered by his chosen prosodic form: the fourteen-syllable or septenary line almost inevitably tends to split in two, producing a clumsy and puerile-sounding monotony, and this long line also gives the ham-handed alliterator more space and material – more syllables – with which to embarrass himself. Further, the unremitting jingle of the rhymes enhances the impression of naïveté. As poets and dramatists were happily beginning to discover, the unrhymed ten-syllable line, neither so long as to split nor so short as to sound juvenile, provides a more congenial medium than fourteeners for extended flights of English verse.[7]

Thomas Sackville and Thomas Norton seem to have been the first to write blank verse for the theatre in *Gorboduc, or Ferrex and Porrex*, their tragedy about English politics, specifically the problem of royal succession, composed at the beginning of Elizabeth's reign and published in 1562. Although their poetry is significantly less complex and polished than that to be heard fifty years later, it is serviceable and relatively easy on the ear:

> O my beloved son! O my sweet child!
> My dear Ferrex, my joy, my life's delight!
> Is my beloved son, is my sweet child,
> My dear Ferrex, my joy, my life's delight,
> Murdered with cruel death? O hateful wretch!
> O heinous traitor both to heaven and earth!
> Thou, Porrex, thou this damned deed hath wrought;
> Thou, Porrex, thou shalt dearly bye [pay for] the same.
> Traitor to kin and kind, to sire and me,
> To thine own flesh, and traitor to thyself,
> The gods on thee in hell shall wreak their wrath.   (4.1.23–33)[8]

Representing English blank verse in an early manifestation, this passage offers the ear possibilities that later poets would enthusiastically develop.

The lack of rhyme in poetic drama would probably have puzzled the first audiences of *Gorboduc*. Tragedy demanded verse, not the quotidian prose of comedy, and verse usually supplied some form of end rhyme. Sackville and Norton create their poetic effects not with rhymed line-endings but with noticeable repetitions and other rhetorical turns, tropes that assert themselves without rudely clamouring for attention. The tendency of the pre-Shakespearean poets to stop at the end of a line is audible, but it is striking that these writers are unusually alert to the possibilities of rhythmic variation in the line. The frequent pauses within the pentameter line are remarkable because they are rare in such early blank verse. Here they serve to accent the repetitions achieved with appositives and doubled nouns: 'my joy, my life's delight' or 'to kin and kind, to sire and me'. In other words, the ordering effect of the decasyllabic rhythm is supplemented with and supported by other shaping patterns. It is just these variations that will, in the hands of the later poetic innovators, break the monotony of dramatic dialogue organized into endlessly repeated ten-syllable units. Until the arrival of Shakespeare, the most gifted and significant of those theatre poets was Christopher Marlowe.

Marlowe showed his theatrical contemporaries how to characterize the tragic hero by means of language, creating a dignified verse style appropriate to his subjects. *Tamburlaine*, his first great success, opens with a prologue consciously asserting theatrical originality and poetic superiority. The audience will be rescued 'From jigging veins of rhyming mother wits' and invited instead to 'hear the Scythian Tamburlaine / Threatening the world with high astounding terms' (Prologue, 1, 4–5).[9] Explicitly advertising novelty, the playwright rejects sing-song rhyme in favour of the more neutral and more modern medium of blank verse. In a series of tragedies written for the celebrated tragedian Edward Alleyn at Henslowe's Rose playhouse, Marlowe was the first English poet to introduce great flexibility into the rigid verse line of the 1570s and '80s.[10] Building upon the example of Sackville and Norton and exploiting the latent variety in their lines, he experimented boldly with the rhythmic possibilities of iambic pentameter, inserting pauses at various points in the line and exaggerating the aural effect of such stops. Above all, he consciously played with the inherent tension between the poetic frame and the semantic energy of the sentence: the intellectual hunger of a Doctor Faustus and the gleeful vengeance of a Barabas, the Jew of Malta, for example, tend to push the sentences so hard as to threaten the regularity of the pentameter. Marlowe's other major contribution was to demonstrate the appeal of majestic diction. The *Tamburlaine* Prologue means what it says in promising 'high astounding terms'. Everywhere the audacious young playwright indulges his fondness for the exotic proper noun, either of place – *Persepolis, Trebizon, Bithynia, Campania, Elysium* – or of person – *Bajazeth, divine Zenocrate, Usumcasane, Ithamore*. Rather than dispense entirely with the rhetorical patterns and artificial verbal structures that stiffen the verse of his predecessors, he summons them for particular theatrical effects without allowing them to tyrannize over the structure of his verse.

These and other Marlovian innovations are significant in moving dramatic speech to a new level of sophistication and possibility. The poet complicates the use of dialogue, for example, enhancing verisimilitude by allowing characters to speak *to* each other rather than *past* each other. But perhaps most important is that Marlowe figures words explicitly as weapons. This equation has become axiomatic, and yet it is impossible to consider the subject without restating it, and plainly: in Marlowe, language is power. Tamburlaine, for example, talks his way into geopolitical supremacy, control of words symbolizing other forms of domination – political, sexual, emotional, financial – and usually his characters know it. The extraordinary self-consciousness about language that we observe in Marlowe's speakers is a clue to his vital role in changing the English theatre. Even before Marlowe's death in 1593 Shakespeare the novice was beginning to exploit some of these same ways of thinking about theatrical representation, and in just a few years Shakespeare had created some of his greatest successes with Marlowe's poetic and theatrical tools. It is idle to speculate on what Shakespeare's verse would have looked like had Marlowe never written a play, but it seems indisputable that the young Shakespeare was enthralled by the Marlovian poetry he heard declaimed from the stage of the Rose.

'The style which shows'

Familiarity with earlier Elizabethan plays (or sonnets, or prose fiction, or any other literary form, for that matter) makes it easier to overcome one of the greatest obstacles to appreciating Shakespeare's tragic language: its obvious and unapologetic artificiality. In this respect, as in many others, it is like everything else he wrote. Ordinary people in Elizabethan England did not sound like dramatic characters. Hamlet and Doctor Faustus and Volpone talk the way they do because their creators have selected and arranged the raw linguistic materials, have 'wrought' the words into art. And the extremes of tragic emotion and eloquence of the heroes' speech make the stylization especially conspicuous. One of Shakespeare's primary contributions to the development of English drama was his capacity for making dramatic speech sound 'natural'. He extends Marlowe's technique of having his persons engage with one another's speech, interacting directly and responding to or modifying the utterance of the conversational partner. His construction of their speeches also makes characters seem dynamic, as they change their minds in mid-speech or work through an idea rather than merely expound it.[11]

And yet for all this verisimilitude, Shakespeare's tragic speakers still employ many of the same rhetorical patterns audible in the language of John Lyly and Thomas Kyd and their Tudor predecessors. Such obviously arranged verbal structures are most easily discerned in his early plays, particularly the histories. In *3 Henry VI*, for example, the doomed King Henry imagines a meeting which decides his future, the participants being his Queen Margaret and the Earl of Warwick:

> Ay, but she's come to beg, Warwick to give:
> She on his left side, craving aid for Henry,
> He on his right, asking a wife for Edward;
> She weeps and says her Henry is depos'd,
> He smiles and says his Edward is installed.   (3.1.42–6)

Here the oppositions and complements are well suited to the subject of the passage, the complementary nature of royal politics, specifically the fall of one king with the rise of another. Characteristic syntactical forms include the similarly shaped lines, particularly with antithetical contents, the reiterative diction ('and says her ... / ... and says his'), and the obviously 'poetic' or 'arranged' sound of the passage. In the early comedies, too, the give-and-take of flirtation and courtship is often represented in symmetrically arranged phrases and words. Although the 'flowers of rhetoric' become less ostentatious as Shakespeare gains experience, he never abandons artifice altogether but depends upon subtler, less exposed forms of verbal patterning.

Renaissance playwrights wrote for audiences who relished 'the style which shows'.[12] Shakespeare in the tragedies depends upon conventional rhetorical forms and overt structures not because he can't escape them but because he likes them, and his taste reflects his culture's unashamed delight in craft. People in early modern England took pleasure in art that was obviously art: they expected to see evidence of labour, they relished the highly wrought object, they delighted in the ornamented sentence, the intricate phrase, the clever rhyme. Thus Ben Jonson's poem that prefaces the 1623 Folio praises

Shakespeare's 'well turned, and true-filèd lines'. Such an attitude also accounts for the sixteenth-century humanists' general preference for Virgil over Homer, since the *Aeneid* was thought to be more polished and artful than its more primitive Greek antecedents.[13] To look at Elizabethan tragedy under this lens is to recognize one of its principal appeals, that its noble characters and extreme actions gave opportunity for highly wrought, extravagant declamation. Sidney's praise of 'stately speeches and well sounding phrases, climbing to the height of Seneca's style' in *Gorboduc* reveals the expectations that audiences brought with them to the public theatres. It was for such ears and tastes that Shakespeare created the eloquent heroes of the tragedies.

The heroic register

The sound of any Shakespearean tragedy is dominated, of course, by the extraordinary voice of the tragic hero.[14] Each of the title characters speaks distinctively, such is Shakespeare's gift for individualizing them linguistically, but they do share some common rhetorical traits, and it will be worthwhile to identify and illustrate some basic features of the heroic style. This sort of enterprise must be approached with caution, however. First, each of the protagonists is so vividly particularized that lumping all together can seem to misrepresent their modes of expression. Second, in addition to differences from play to play, there are variations within each play: the hero is by no means the only speaker of exalted or impressive verse. Since the tragic mode implies an elevated verbal decorum, most members of the cast speak a relatively formal, dignified style of poetry. And given the extremity of the passions represented, as well as the rank of the characters, many supporting players speak an appropriately noble language – Claudius, Bolingbroke, Macduff, Octavius, Volumnia. Finally, any such taxonomy is bound to be unsatisfying. Knowing and naming components cannot account for the mysterious power of Hamlet's speech, or that of any of his tragic counterparts: poetry is much more than the sum of its parts.[15] Still, we can say that the keynote in tragedy is set by the tragic hero, and that keynote is hyperbole.

When Sidney asserts that tragedy should 'stir the affects [emotions] of admiration and commiseration', 'admiration' is synonymous with 'wonder', and the hero's poetic flights are among the poet's most effective tools for stimulating such a response.[16] They confer upon the protagonist what we would call charisma, a verbal authority that supplements and reinforces the natural attractions of the lead actor, be he Burbage or Branagh. In Shakespearean tragedy the sound and fury signify something: the heroic idiom is calculated to suggest the visionary propensities of the tragic hero. Heightened speech attests to idealism, aspiration, the desire for transcendence. The dimensions of this heroic vision are suggested in Brutus's refusal to swear an oath to assassinate Caesar:

> What need we any spur but our own cause
> To prick us to redress? What other bond
> Than secret Romans that have spoke the word
> And will not palter? And what other oath
> Than honesty to honesty engaged
> That this shall be or we will fall for it?
> Swear priests and cowards and men cautelous,
> Old feeble carrions, and such suffering souls
> That welcome wrongs: unto bad causes swear
> Such creatures as men doubt. But do not stain
> The even virtue of our enterprise,
> Nor th'insuppressive mettle of our spirits,
> To think that or our cause or our performance
> Did need an oath.   (*JC* 2.1.123–36)

This is the hero's early, idealistic mode. It is marked by command, by self-assertion, by rejection of the common or conventional. Poetry and vision convert murder into sacrifice, conspiracy into a sacred cause. Hamlet, Macbeth, Coriolanus, all speak in similar accents.

During the course of each tragic narrative the heroic voice changes radically in response to conflict and suffering. This linguistic alteration signifies the metamorphosis by which the hero is transformed into his opposite. It is clearly audible in Mark Antony's language after the battle of Actium:

>   All is lost!
> This foul Egyptian hath betrayèd me.
> My fleet hath yielded to the foe, and yonder
> They cast their caps up and carouse together
> Like friends long lost. Triple-turned whore! 'Tis thou
> Hast sold me to this novice, and my heart
> Makes only wars on thee. Bid them all fly;
> For when I am revenged upon my charm,
> I have done all. Bid them all fly. Begone!
>
>   [*Exit Scarus*]
>
> O sun, thy uprise shall I see no more.
> Fortune and Antony part here; even here
> Do we shake hands. All come to this? The hearts
> That spanieled me at heels, to whom I gave
> Their wishes, do discandy, melt their sweets

On blossoming Caesar; and this pine is barked
That overtopped them all. Betrayed I am.   (*Ant.* 4.12.9–24)

Experience and the tragic environment exert a pressure on the hero that
magnifies, intensifies, and violently changes the tones of speech. In Antony's
case the language is no longer magnanimous and self-assured, but vindictive,
cruel, and to some extent desperate. He reaches for the poetic conventions that
will furnish him with a language appropriate to adversity, e.g., apostrophe
('O sun'), personification ('Fortune and Antony'), images ('cast their caps up'),
grand metaphors ('this pine is barked'), imperatives ('Bid them . . . Bid them'),
rare diction ('spanieled', 'discandy'), extravagant alliteration ('Like friends long
lost. Triple-turned . . .'), rhetorical questions ('All come to this?'), syntactic
inversion ('Betrayed I am'), and other forms of patterning and intensification.

Othello offers an even clearer paradigm of this verbal mutation. The
Moor owes his success before the Senate to the same rhetorical powers
that won the heart of Desdemona and that he then proceeds to turn against
himself. The sonorous verbal music of the opening becomes, by the middle
of the third act, destructive, vengeful, and bombastic, and in the fourth act
glorious poetry yields to prosaic gabbling and filthy images hurled at his
innocent wife. Such audible variations not only support but help to create
the arc of each hero's experience. Hamlet's assault on Ophelia in the
Nunnery Scene (3.1), for example, or his vulgar treatment of his mother
in the Closet Scene (3.4) are as brutal as some of his other speeches are
sensitive and lyrical, one register depending upon the other for its impact.

Usually the tragic hero regains poetic authority and power just before the
end, before death. Othello in his final speech, 'Soft you; a word or two
before you go', has recovered some control of the rhythms and imagery that
were so initially winning. Even King Lear, perhaps the most reduced and
damaged of the tragic protagonists, attains a degree of eloquence and
authority in the speech to Cordelia about their living 'like birds in the
cage' (5.3.8–19). Then in his final moments he unleashes another kind of
affective power in the imprecations and wrenching pleas over her lifeless
body. In each play the hero's eloquence results from the poet's manipulation of patterns: the establishment and subsequent modification of these
expected forms signal or underscore the emotional, psychological, and
spiritual permutations that so thoroughly move the audience.

'Big and boisterous words'

Of the particular elements from which Shakespeare fashions his heroes'
extraordinary speech, one of the most potent is diction. As William Webbe

wrote in 1586, 'To the tragical writers belong properly the big and boisterous words.'[17] Shakespeare's heroes are bigger than life and, putting the matter crudely, they use bigger words than other characters, magnificent polysyllables that contribute substantially to their eloquence: Othello's 'Anthropophagi' and 'chrysolite'; Hamlet's 'the Everlasting', 'malefactions', and 'consummation / Devoutly to be wished'; Richard II's 'Discomfortable cousin' and 'glistering Phaeton'; Romeo's 'o'erperch' and 'unsubstantial Death is amorous'; Juliet's 'cockatrice'; Macbeth's 'multitudinous seas incarnadine', 'Tarquin's ravishing strides', and 'If th'assassination / Could trammel up the consequence'; Lear's 'cataracts and hurricanoes'; Coriolanus's 'acclamations hyperbolical'; Cleopatra's 'make / My country's high pyramides my gibbet'. Some of these, such as 'o'erperch', 'incarnadine', and 'assassination', seem to have been Shakespeare's invention, or in some cases his adaptation of an existing word. Many were as unusual and striking in his day as they are in ours. Just as his heroes are magnified by the presence of foils and opposites – Hamlet and both Horatio and Polonius, Macbeth and Banquo, Lear and Kent or the Fool – so the hero's speech stands out by virtue of its difference from the languages spoken around him. The poet has selected verbal elements that connote distinction and rarity: such splendid diction is to common speech as the hero is to common people.[18]

The dazzling word, like a precious gem, benefits from an appropriate setting, and much depends upon placement. Webbe goes on to say in his brief comments on 'big ... words' that 'Examples must be interplaced, according fitly to the time and place'.[19] As some of the phrases cited above will have indicated, Shakespeare often underwrites the equation of speech and stature by locating exceptional words against a relatively neutral background. Richard II's eloquent metaphor for his downfall is one such passage, in which the stunning phrase is embedded among monosyllables: 'Down, down I come, like glistering Phaeton' (3.3.178). So it is in Romeo's 'shake the yoke of inauspicious stars', the hard consonants of the first monosyllables preparing for the sibilant sweep of the last two words. Romeo's phrase also illustrates another typical form, an impressive adjective linked with a plain noun. Often the adjective is Latinate and the concluding noun Anglo-Saxon in origin, although sometimes the combination is reversed. In Romeo's final soliloquy alone we find 'inauspicious stars' accompanied by a multitude of such contrasting doublets: 'betossèd soul', 'triumphant grave', 'slaughtered youth', 'unsubstantial Death', 'everlasting rest', 'world-wearied flesh', 'righteous kiss', 'engrossing Death', 'true apothecary'. This characteristic verbal device creates a systole–diastole rhythm, another long–short pattern that mimics other forms of rhythmic contrast, most notably the iambic structures of which the lines are made.

But no one, not even an eloquent Shakespearean hero, speaks this way all the time. For all their command of a brilliant vocabulary, these characters may, especially at moments of extreme passion, express themselves with unwonted simplicity. A striking form of this tactic is the unlooked-for series of powerful monosyllables:

> OTHELLO Damn her, lewd minx! O, damn her! damn her!   (3.3.476)

> LEAR Why should a dog, a horse, a rat have life,
> And thou no breath at all?   (5.3.279–80)

> MACBETH ... a poor player
> That struts and frets his hour upon the stage
> And then is heard no more.   (5.5.23–5)

> RICHARD III Chop off his head!   (3.1.193)

> HAMLET To be, or not to be   (3.1.56).

These simple nouns and verbs are powerful, to be sure, but subtle poetic forces are at work to complicate their plainness. The apparently lone monosyllables are supported by an array of rhythmic devices, particularly duplication or reiteration. The verbs in Macbeth's image ('struts and frets') are acoustically matched; Othello's outburst depends upon a triply repeated verb and the unexpected spondee ('lewd minx'), a foot that breaks the iambic pattern with two syllables of identical weight; the repeated article in Lear's question separates and emphasizes the iambs; and the most famous of all Shakespearean phrases benefits from its opposed infinitives, duplicated with a difference.

Such phrases also register powerfully because their simplicity contrasts so markedly with the surrounding poetic grandeur. Othello's blunt curse, the first example, follows several rhythmically propulsive speeches, one of which develops the elaborate simile comparing his 'wide revenge' to the 'icy current and compulsive course' of the Pontic Sea. Macbeth's monosyllabic doublet 'struts and frets' occurs in the soliloquy that begins with the famously reiterated polysyllables, 'Tomorrow, and tomorrow, and tomorrow', and proceeds to 'the last syllable of recorded time'. An obverse but no less impressive instance occurs in the last act of *Othello*, in the opening lines of 'It is the cause, it is the cause, my soul': as one critic puts it, 'In Othello's priestlike speech before the sacrifice of Desdemona forty monosyllables fall like the waterdrops of Chinese torture before the crowning grandeur of "monumental alabaster"'.[20] This juxtaposition of the majestic and the simple exemplifies a larger principle, one that governs not only verbal registers but also such features as scenic arrangement, contrasting characters, and comparable plots. All these combinations inhabit the category of rhythm.

The most pervasive form of rhythm found in tragedy is the pulsating beat of the blank verse. In its basic pattern the poetry spoken by the tragic heroes is no different from that given to Titania or Bolingbroke or any verse speaker from any other kind of play. But by the time Shakespeare commits himself to the tragic mode, i.e., by mid-career, he has already developed a sophisticated, tractable approach to the pentameter line, and this flexible command of verse structure permits him to adapt and shape dramatic speech according to the demands of character and narrative. Considering the state of English blank verse in 1590, it is astonishing to observe how far he had pushed the boundaries of the form by 1600, his first decade of composition. He was able to rely on the audience's familiarity with the underlying beat, both the give and take of the iambs and the general length of the pentameter line, so that when he came to write *Hamlet* his profound understanding of the relation between sound and sense allowed him to modify the line for specific effects. The major tragedies exhibit an unparalleled intuition of how acoustic variation and irregularity make meaning.

The sound of Hamlet's speeches, to take one of the most audible examples, profits from Shakespeare's experiments with enjambment, with variously and multiply segmented lines, with reversed feet, and with other rhythmic subtleties.

> I am dead, Horatio. Wretched queen adieu.
> You that look pale, and tremble at this chance,
> That are but mutes or audience to this act,
> Had I but time, as this fell sergeant death
> Is strict in his arrest, oh I could tell you –
> But let it be. (5.2.312–17)

The tactics by which Shakespeare slackened and varied the relative uniformity characteristic of early English dramatic verse are clearly exhibited here. The first line begins by eliding two words ('I am') into one syllable, then quickly performs another elision as the 'i-o' of Horatio is reduced to one syllable. Including the stop at the end of the line, the speaker must pause four times: the medial period divides the line in two, and a comma sub-divides each half. The second line begins with a trochaic inversion ('Yóu thăt'); the fourth adds a spondee ('thís féll seŕgeănt') to promote a crucial metaphor; the fifth appends an additional syllable to the end; grammatical intrusions disrupt the rhythmic uniformity ('I could tell you'); and only one line allows the sweep of an unbroken pentameter.

Such hesitations and rhythmic instability focus the ear on Hamlet's dying words, of course, and many other passages reveal, in their distinctive rhythmic imprint, a similarly intimate relation to their narrative context. We might note Macbeth's metrical disarray when, after having killed Duncan, he justifies his killing the guards who have apparently killed the king:

> Who can be wise, amazed, temp'rate, and furious,
> Loyal and neutral, in a moment? No man.   (2.3.101–2)

or Coriolanus's emotional division over having to ask for the consulship:

>   [I] for your voices have
> Done many things, some less, some more. Your voices!
> Indeed, I would be consul.   (2.3.115–17)

or Cleopatra's

> Give me my robe. Put on my crown. I have
> Immortal longings in me.   (5.2.274–5)

Repeatedly local meanings are thus enhanced by the poet's manipulation of sound. The rhythmic baldness of Coriolanus's last five words establishes the opposition of talk and action, the contrast between the reiterated 'voices' of the previous lines and the 'Indeed' of the conclusion.

Particular significance, however, is much less important than the larger rhythms to which sound and sense contribute. The extraordinary metrical variety that Shakespeare achieves in the tragedies is only one component in a larger musical structure. This pervasive system is not much commented on, but it is vital in our experience not only of the tragic voice but also of its echoes produced throughout the play. Hamlet's short phrases and broken lines play off our memory of contrary rhythms we have been assimilating from the beginning of the play. 'But let it be. Horatio, I am dead, / Thou livest' (5.2.317–18) depends for its effect upon our having absorbed such expansive phrases as 'Whether 'tis nobler in the mind to suffer / The slings and arrows of outrageous fortune' (3.1.57–8). The tragedies offer what we might call dramatic polyphony, a simultaneous sounding of different voices, accents, patterns, and tempi. Lear's extravagant outbursts, from the early speech about 'the barbarous Scythian' (1.1.110) to 'Blow winds, and crack your cheeks! Rage, blow' (3.2.1), require the counterpoint of Cordelia's 'Nothing' (1.1.82, 84), the Fool's jingling reversals, and Edmond's verbal bravado. The alternation between verse and prose is another manifestation of this rhythmic pattern, as is the contrast in tempo between differently paced lines of blank verse within the same play, or between the same speaker's use of different styles and speeds.

Often a single speech exhibits a deliberate acceleration and accumulation of verbal power that seems uniquely Shakespearean. Mark Antony's famous soliloquy just after the assassination of Julius Caesar, beginning 'O, pardon me, thou bleeding piece of earth' (3.1.254), palpably increases in velocity as it moves towards its rhythmic climax. Other familiar examples would be Othello's 'Farewell the tranquil mind! Farewell content!' (3.3.348–57), Lady Macbeth's 'Come, you spirits / That tend on mortal thoughts' (1.5.40–54), or Coriolanus's 'You common cry of curs' (3.3.120–35). In these cases, and others like them, clauses and phrases of approximately the same length follow one another in succession, generating something like a perpetual motion machine that pushes the listener forward to the memorable conclusion. Also, a lightening of punctuation seems to intensify the reiterative pulse of the iambs. This sudden intensification in a crucial speech promotes increased tension and power in the play as a whole.

Such manipulation of tempo signals another rhythmic effect, here perceptible in Othello's repetition of 'Farewell' and in the harsh alliteration of Coriolanus's line. The reproduction of various sounds certainly creates poetic coherence, binding together words and phrases, but a more important function is that it increases the formality and thus the gravity or momentousness of a speech. By this point in his career Shakespeare knows the difference between stiffness and formality, and thus the rhetorical schemes and self-conscious patterns of the early plays have yielded to the extravagant but more spontaneous repetitions of the tragic figure in conflict. To look at the pressure points in most of the tragedies is to notice how frequently such acoustic duplication appears at such moments.

> CLEOPATRA   Where art thou, Death?
> Come hither, come! Come, come, and take a queen
> Worth many babes and beggars.
> CHARMIAN   O, temperance, lady! (*Ant.*5.2.45–7)

'Temperance' is exactly what the tragic figure disdains: extravagance makes the character exceptional, and this magnificent intemperance is heard in such effusions as the four instances of 'come' in the second line, or the alliterative 'queen [with its embedded 'w'] ... worth' and 'babes and beggars'. So significant and widespread is such pleonasm that many of the passages already cited depend upon it, from Richard II's 'Down, down I come, like glistering Phaeton' to Macbeth's 'Tomorrow, and tomorrow, and tomorrow'.

Figures and their function

To first-time readers or playgoers, the highly figurative texture of Shakespeare's plays is most immediately impressive and can make the verse appear unduly ornamented and disorienting. So it seemed to no less a critic than John Dryden:

> [His] whole style is so pestered with figurative expressions that it is as affected as it is obscure . . .'Tis not that I would exclude the use of metaphors from passions, . . . but to use 'em at every word, to say nothing without a metaphor, a simile, an image, or description, is I doubt to smell a little too strongly of the buskin.[21]

Dryden and the Augustans who followed him especially deplored Shakespeare's practice of mixing images and piling metaphor upon metaphor, probably because such fluent or mercurial treatment violated their taste for discrete categories of action and thought. But these objections, which motivated eighteenth-century editors' attempts to tidy up and regularize the Shakespearean text, serve ironically to prove the centrality of figurative language in it. Prose speakers in comedy and tragedy also use imagery constantly, Iago being one of the most notorious of such speakers, and so do we all, even in ordinary conversation. But in poetry, particularly the heroic style, the images and image clusters colour and thereby intensify the passionate verse.

The first effect of figurative language proceeds from the materiality of the image, the way that an image *as an image* stimulates the reader's imagination and enriches the texture of speech. This ornamental or affective value is suggested by the Elizabethan poetic theorist and cataloguer George Puttenham when he asserts that 'figure itself is a certain lively or good grace set upon words, speeches, and sentences, to some purpose and not in vain, giving them ornament or efficacy by many manner of alterations in shape, in sound, and also in sense'. The excellent poet will produce verse that 'is gallantly arrayed in all his colours which figure can set upon it'.[22] This is not to imply that even in this limited sense images perform no thematic work: on the contrary, they establish atmosphere, modify our perception of character, comment on the action, and otherwise contribute in a multitude of ways. But many images do not primarily serve to elucidate another thing; instead, they make a powerful impact on their own.

Images can forcefully affect the senses of the imaginative mind. Shakespeare often seeks a visceral effect, attempting to move the audience by means of word pictures and their associations. Pictorial or other sensory images account for some of the most memorable and characteristic passages in the tragedies:

Hamlet's disposal of the body of Polonius:

> I'll lug the guts into the neighbor room.   (3.4.213)

The Nurse's recollection of Juliet's weaning:

> For I had then laid wormwood to my dug,
> Sitting in the sun under the dove-house wall.   (1.3.27–8)

Cleopatra's angling for 'tawny finned fishes':

> My bended hook shall pierce
> Their slimy jaws.   (2.5.12–13)

Aufidius's greeting to Coriolanus:

> Let me twine
> Mine arms about that body, where against
> My grainèd ash an hundred times hath broke
> And scarred the moon with splinters.   (4.5.103–6)

Enobarbus's lengthy and detailed recital of Cleopatra's river journey:

> The barge she sat in, like a burnished throne
> Burned on the water. The poop was beaten gold;
> Purple the sails, and so perfumèd that
> The winds were lovesick with them. The oars were silver,
> Which to the tune of flutes kept stroke.   (2.2.201–5)

And yet as luscious as the sounds and pictures may be, even those images employed for their material effect are likely, as the barge speech indicates, to be exploited for their symbolic possibilities.

All language, linguistic theorists contend, is in some sense metaphoric: a word is a verbal sign, an image, that calls to mind – through a process of symbolic representation – the object or concept it names.[23] Therefore poets, attracted to the materiality of language as well as to its symbolic capacities, are naturally drawn to metaphor because it multiplies what the ordinary word can do. Metaphor was known to humanist rhetoricians as 'the figure of transport', since in the process of apprehension the perceiver's mind is moved, impelled from one image to another. Abundant figurative language is vital to the great arias because in those crucial moments of passion speakers seem transported beyond themselves and seem to carry the audience with them. Shakespeare's metaphoric practice is once again especially conspicuous in the early work. *Romeo and Juliet*, for instance, is saturated with figures, particularly metaphors that beget other metaphors. Readers can recall their own favourite metaphoric clusters from this lavishly figurative play: perhaps the religious discourse with which the lovers flirt on first meeting; the heavenly bodies, flowers, lights, colours, and other beauties of the balcony scene; Juliet's 'Gallop apace, ye fiery footed steeds', with its multiple, vivid comparisons ('thou wilt lie upon the wings of night / Whiter than new snow upon a raven's back'); the oxymoronic combination of images – e.g. 'fiend angelical' – that express Juliet's irreconcilable feelings about her husband just after the death of Tybalt (3.1.1). Metaphoric intensity is so prominent in *Romeo and Juliet* probably because the playwright was still discovering his gift for figuration and the story he chose to dramatize stimulated him to use it liberally.

A flair for metaphor is one trait that distinguishes the speech of the great tragic heroes and enriches the poetic texture of the middle and later tragedies. Metaphor and simile account for some of the most famous phrases and passages in the canon: 'the slings and arrows of outrageous fortune' with which Hamlet struggles (3.1.57–8); Othello's 'subdued eyes' that 'Drops tears as fast as the Arabian trees / Their medicinable gum' (5.2.346–7); Macbeth's 'I am in blood / Stepped in so far that should I wade no more, / Returning were as tedious as go o'er' (3.4.136–8). Such figuration contributes much to the monumental, irresistible sound of the hero's voice. But in the mature tragedies it does much more than that: metaphor is one of the primary means by which Shakespeare creates unity of effect and thus intensifies the affective power of these great plays. Unity is such a fundamental artistic principle, one that artists and critics worry over, because the strategies that promote unity help to concentrate meaning. In *King Lear*, the savage conditions of the playworld are given vivid reality for the audience because the playwright describes the characters and their actions as tigers, vultures, kites [birds of prey], 'pelican daughters' [spilling the blood of the parent], vultures, monsters, 'monsters of the deep', rats, serpents, asses, dragons, bears, hogs, foxes, she-foxes, lions, boars, fitchews [polecats], horses, multiple species of dogs, centaurs, fiends, and cannibals. Whatever his theme Shakespeare always represents the significance of that topic in a network of meaningful figures. *Coriolanus*, his late Roman tragedy, is a hard play, both in the sense of its difficulty and in its tough, unyielding tone: its hero is proud, unpleasant, and hard to like, keeping his distance both from others and from the audience. Thus it is apt that the language of the play strikes us as somewhat rigid. G. Wilson Knight, one of the twentieth-century critics most sensitive to poetic imagery, gives a persuasive account of this correspondence between image and theme:

> We are in a world of hard weapons, battle's clanging contacts ... the sickening crashes of war ... The imagery is often metallic – such as 'leaden pounds' (III.i.314), or 'manacles' (I.ix.57) or 'leaden spoons, irons of a doit' (I.v.5), or as when Coriolanus's harshness forces his mother to kneel 'with no softer cushion than the flint' (V.iii.53) ... Hostile cities are here ringed as with the iron walls of war, inimical, deadly to each other, self-contained. Thus our city imagery blends with war imagery, which is also 'hard' and metallic. And that itself is fused with the theme of Coriolanus's iron-hearted pride.[24]

Such a symbolic network enriches the play's interest in the problem of Coriolanus's masculinity, his effort to remain untouched by other beings, particularly the weak ones, more particularly women. An even more impressive and detailed symbolic structure informs *Macbeth*: blood. Blood not only gives rise to a complex network of related figures but also reveals the playwright's concern with such central issues as kinship and country. In every play the figurative patterns generate a symbolic world, an imaginary realm in which the means of comparison – in *Coriolanus*, the metallic images – take on an existence of their own and thus fortify the meaning of the tragic action.

Self-conscious speech

The contribution of these technical features to the voice of the tragic hero is less significant, finally, than one indispensable quality – verbal self-consciousness reflecting the poet's sensitivity to the uses of language. The modern world, given our technological advances and other cultural developments, seems dominated by visual images, and the supremacy of the eye may have dulled our acoustic sensitivities, at least compared to those of our early modern ancestors. With print in its adolescence, Shakespeare's England was largely an oral culture; consequently, the ability to do things with words was a coveted talent. The early modern feeling for words and verbal patterns is related to the increasing dignity of the English language, considered unsuitable for serious writing until well into the sixteenth century. As translators began to render the Bible into English, and as poets and scholars began to explore the expressive possibilities of their native tongue, educated English people began to take pride in their language. They fretted over it, relished it, sought to polish it, called attention to its felicities and opportunities for creativity and communication. This public consciousness meant that Shakespeare could have expected his audience to notice and take pleasure in linguistic virtuosity. And since tragedy occupied so exalted a position on the critical scale, the mode was especially hospitable to rhetorical ostentation.

Such verbal brilliance becomes a matter of alarm to Shakespeare around mid-career, just as he turns wholeheartedly to the creation of tragedy. In *Julius Caesar* (1599), young Antony's language is flamboyant and self-aware, particularly in the funeral oration, with its ironic digs at Brutus and the conspirators as 'honourable men'. Thus his eulogy contrasts pointedly with his adversary's prose defence of the assassination, for Brutus subordinates virtuosity to virtue, style to substance. However, Brutus's disdain of rhetoric also implies a kind of reverse virtuosity, a pride in undecorated statement. This juxtaposition of opposing forms embodies Shakespeare's growing doubts about pyrotechnical speech, suspicions he had begun to explore in the history plays, tentatively in *Richard III* and then more profoundly in the second tetralogy (1595–9).

All these anxieties come to fruition in the tragedies that immediately follow *Julius Caesar* – *Hamlet* and *Othello*. One of Hamlet's principal appeals is his sensitivity to language and his self-conscious manipulation of it:

> GERTRUDE Hamlet, thou hast thy father much offended.
> HAMLET Mother, you have my father much offended. (3.4.9–10)

Hamlet cannot resist showing off. His punning first line, 'a little more than kin, and less than kind' (1.2.65); his reply to Polonius's question about what he is reading, 'Words, words, words' (2.2.189); and his insolence to Claudius about the dead Polonius being 'At supper . . . Not where a eats, but where a is eaten' (4.3.17–19) – these are sophomoric applications of formidable linguistic prowess, a talent that Shakespeare both admires and deplores. Indeed, the prince's self-awareness about his words is a synecdoche for his larger existential difficulty, the potentially paralytic effects of self-consciousness. While Othello is not as verbally adroit, he too is knowing about his particular form of verbal showmanship. His apology to the Senate, 'Rude am I in my speech' (1.3.81), is a rhetorical tactic, the manoeuvre of a sure-handed storyteller who knows how to manipulate his audience and whose defence of his marriage is anything but unpolished: on the contrary, the tale of Othello's wooing is a brilliant performance, romantic, poetically powerful, convincing to the audiences on stage and in the theatre. Above all, the speaker is aware of his talent. The 'self-dramatizing' tendencies that T. S. Eliot and others have noticed in Othello – they intend the phrase pejoratively – hint at the hero's irresistible inclination to use such virtuosity against himself. According to the paradox that underlies most of Shakespeare's work in this mode, the tragic fact is that the hero who uses his talent to conquer others also employs it to undo himself.

Most of the tragic protagonists who follow Othello are not represented as rhetorical peacocks; in these later tragedies the self-consciousness is patently that of the playwright. King Lear and Macbeth, for example, are powerful speakers, but they are less obviously attentive to language as language than their earlier counterparts. Shakespeare, however, is no less interested in language as a human problem. To start with, other verbal dandies begin to appear, Iago being the model of villainous eloquence. In *King Lear*, Goneril and Regan evince a kind of glee in their flattery of their father, while Edmond in his soliloquy on primogeniture (1.2.1–15) takes delight in the pliability of the word, particularly in the quibbles on 'bastard' and in his mockery of that 'fine word, "legitimate"'.[25] Since Coriolanus is so absolute in his mistrust of language, the role of the self-conscious talker is taken by his mother, Volumnia, whose name indicates her passion for words. Having used her tongue incessantly, she concludes her loquacious plea that Rome be spared with an ironic look at her own prolixity: 'I am hushed until our city be afire, / And then I'll speak a little' (5.3.181–2). In *Antony and Cleopatra* Mark Antony reappears, older, more experienced, and manifestly less impetuous, but still conscious of his rhetorical gifts and his charismatic power. And Cleopatra, of course, is one of Shakespeare's most beguiling speakers. The arts of language are among Egypt's great attractions, along with music and other sensuous pleasures: much of her charm arises from her ear for language – 'he words me, girls' (5.2.190) – and her awareness of her verbal command.

The tragedy of language

Shakespeare's tragic conception of human experience must be seen, at least in part, as predicated on the failings of language itself. Throughout the Middle Ages and into the Renaissance, a bedrock of Christian doctrine was the linguistic catastrophe attendant on the Fall. Prelapsarian speech had been perfect and thus unmistakably clear, whereas in the fallen world language had become unreliable, potentially fraudulent, and dangerously ambiguous. The story of the Tower of Babel in Genesis 11 elaborated on the linguistic chaos to which fallen humanity was subject, and Reformation theologians regularly deplored their necessarily faulty medium of communication. At the same time, however, Shakespeare's culture had also inherited from the earlier Tudor humanists a faith in eloquence and in the power of language to educate, to civilize, and thus to help redeem the fallen race. In this respect Shakespeare's tragedies are faithful registers of a significant cultural division. They are among the most complex and subtle representations we have of this early modern ambivalence towards language. And that ambivalence extends beyond speech to the playwright's doubts about the theatre and his deeply divided estimation of the human species.

The tragedies everywhere imply an authorial obsession with the capacity of language to damage, deform, and mislead. Jean-Pierre Vernant, writing about language in Greek tragedy, proposes that

> The function of the words used on stage is not so much to establish communication between the various characters as to indicate the blockages and barriers between them and the impermeability of their minds, to locate the points of conflict. For each protagonist, locked into his own particular world, the vocabulary that is used remains for the most part opaque. For him it has one, and only one meaning. This one-sidedness comes into violent collision with another.[26]

The relevance of this formulation to the Shakespearean tragic speaker should be clear: conceived as a medium of communication, language in tragedy is a force of separation. Shakespeare's thinking about his verbal tools seems to darken appreciably as his career proceeds from Hamlet, who loves words, to Coriolanus, who loathes them. When Hamlet laments, in his second major soliloquy, that he 'Must like a whore unpack [his] heart with words', he identifies his own particular vulnerability, the propensity to substitute language for action and to exercise his gift for words to the point of self-indulgence and self-delusion. *Coriolanus*, written at the end of the tragic sequence, examines the opposite problem: the Roman soldier despises language so thoroughly that he cannot move into the parliamentary realm of politics ('Parliament' is from French *parler*, to talk). He confesses that, while he sought out warfare, he 'fled from words', and he objects to the recitation of his deeds, resents hearing his 'nothings monstered'. This last phrase captures his mistrust of language, specifically its inherent failure to represent the world accurately. The man of action cannot tolerate the slippage or lack of correspondence between sign and signified.

Between the extremes of *Hamlet* and *Coriolanus* stand the other tragic heroes, all inhabiting a world in which language is to some degree the enemy. Each play depicts a slightly different form of linguistic treachery, although certain pernicious modes of speech and many of the same woeful consequences recur again and again. *Othello* exhibits the power of words used maliciously, or, putting it another way, the danger of fiction in the hands of the wicked. A manipulator such as Iago can make words distort the truth, pierce the heart, and destroy the innocent. Similarly, Edmund invents and employs such lies in *King Lear*, a play that begins with two lessons in the art of fiction, Goneril's and Regan's extravagant and empty declarations of love for their father. Cordelia suffers because she rejects such empty signs, refuses to use 'that glib and oily art / To speak and purpose not' (1.1.219–20). Since the evil of flatterers, or 'mouth-friends', is the focus of the first half of *Timon of Athens*, it is not surprising that Timon should figure his suicide as a rejection of speech: 'Lips, let sour words go by and language end' (5.1.210).[27] Further instances might be adduced – Cassius's dishonest exploitation of Brutus's idealism; Hamlet's lashing out at Ophelia; Othello's insulting Desdemona in the brothel scene (4.2); or, in *Coriolanus*, the tribunes' inciting the people to taunt the hero into self-defeat. Each case represents the dangerous malleability of words, their utility as instruments of evil.

Language is not merely the apparatus of the wicked, however, but is itself treacherous and unreliable, even in the hands of the good or the well-meaning. Even when not maliciously intended, not employed as outright lies, words may be empty or misleading, as Shakespeare's complex portrait of Othello himself may prompt us to suspect. His romantic speech is colourful, even enthralling, but his self-dramatizing manner hints that his language may be hollow, an instrument of deception – especially self-deception – and that Iago may be partly right when he refers to the Moor's style as 'bombast'. As Puttenham puts it in *The Art of English Poesy*, 'generally the high style is disgraced and made foolish and ridiculous by all words affected, counterfeit, and puffed up, as it were a wind-ball carrying more countenance than matter...'[28]

Flatterers and liars can succeed because words are inherently limited in their capacity to represent the world. A measure of Lear's tragic pain is his discovery of the distance between sound and sense:

> They flattered me like a dog and told me I had the white hairs in my beard ere the black ones were there. To say 'ay' and 'no' to everything that I said 'ay,' and 'no' too was no good divinity. When the rain came to wet me once and the wind to make me chatter, when the thunder would not peace at my bidding, there I found 'em, there I smelt 'em out! Go to, they are not men o' their words. They told me I was everything; 'tis a lie, I am not ague-proof.   (4.5.95–107)

The mad king's ordeal on the heath, when he commands the elements to destroy the wicked world, teaches him not only the consequences of flattery but also the futility of language divorced from power. The world survives 'the pelting of this pitiless storm' (3.4.29); Lear's words have no effect. Even more bitterly tragic is the insufficiency of words to do good. Cordelia knows that feelings cannot be adequately expressed, that she cannot describe the bond of love between child and parent: 'I cannot heave my heart into my mouth' (1.1.86–7).

In *Macbeth* language is more sinister still, the tool of demonic forces and the means of error and deceit. There Shakespeare looks sceptically at the properties of language that permit its misuse, reacting with disgust and sympathy at the fatal vulnerability of even the greatest among us. The Porter's joke about the damned 'equivocator' arriving at hell's gate – he 'could not equivocate to heaven' (2.3.7–10) – is a darkly ironic expression of the multiple dangers that pervade the play: double talk, slithery language, wicked persuasion, lies. To overcome Macbeth's high-mindedness, Lady Macbeth resolves to 'chastise with the valour of [her] tongue' (1.5.25) everything that prevents him from killing the king. She bullies and ridicules him, using contemptuous terms to belittle his manliness: 'beast', '*infirm* of purpose', as timid as 'the poor cat i'th'adage'. Macbeth is finally destroyed and his bloody career halted by a pair of prophecies: that 'none of woman born / Shall harm Macbeth' (4.1.79–80), and that 'Macbeth shall never vanquish'd be until / Great Birnam wood to high Dunsinane hill / Shall come against him' (92–4). Both promises are deceptive, seeming to offer invulnerability and yet fulfilling themselves in unexpected ways. Macbeth learns too late his error in trusting 'th'equivocation of the fiend / That lies like truth', of believing the 'juggling fiends . . . / That palter with us in a double sense' (5.8.19–20). The wordplay that delightfully animates the comic realms of *Much Ado About Nothing* and *Twelfth Night* has turned lethal, and fatal ambiguity is everywhere: in the double meanings of words; in the riddling prophecies; in the duplicitous terms of Lady Macbeth's welcome to Duncan, that 'All our service / In every point twice done and then done double' (1.6.16–17) would be insufficient; in the witches' incantation, 'Double, double toil and trouble'.

Macbeth's 'Tomorrow, and tomorrow, and tomorrow' speech (5.4.18–27) urges a despairing assessment of all language: 'life' is nothing more than an empty verbal construct, 'a tale / Told by an idiot, full of sound and fury / Signifying nothing'. This dark passage, however, has proved to be among the most powerful and enduring of Shakespeare's words. The playwright was able to conceive of language in the darkest possible light, to identify the conditions of a tragic world with the verbal medium that constitutes it, and to imagine a character whose nihilism condemns even the means of expressing itself. But clearly he also appreciated the complementary position, recognizing that language had the capacity to fix such a dark point of view in a beautiful and lasting verbal artefact. Words are not entirely destructive but can be used creatively within the tragic narratives: in seeking to relieve his father and save the king Edgar modulates his speech, taking on the accents of disparate social classes; Emilia in *Othello* resolves to speak the truth despite the fatal consequences; Macbeth articulates the searing effect of evil on his soul; Volumnia persuades her stubborn son – at the cost of his life – to spare the city that has rejected him. Cleopatra constructs a 'monumental recreation of Antony' in the great speech to Dolabella (5.2.76–92), a word-picture that has been called 'the great generative act of the play'.[29] After the tragedies Shakespeare will devote himself to romance, and Cleopatra's creativity represents a step on the way to the affirmations of that mode.

Hamlet regrets unpacking his heart with words, but the forms in which he expresses his misery comprise some of the most meaningful verbal configurations ever created. This is one of the great paradoxes of Shakespearean tragedy, that language may convey its own failures and inadequacy in a form that is more than adequate, even triumphant. Thus Shakespeare's ambivalent conception of language, of his own artistic medium, corresponds exactly to the mixed view he takes towards his tragic protagonists: foolish and heroic, estimable and contemptible, undercut by the very quality that distinguishes them. This mixed assessment is congruent with the philosophical or religious contrarieties that had emerged from both medieval scholasticism and Tudor humanist thought and that characterized English literate culture at the beginning of the seventeenth century: the principle of the dignity of man, on the one hand; on the other, the belief in human depravity. All the tragedies invite the audience to entertain both positions, the infamy and the glory of the race, and the validity of each is encoded in Shakespeare's words.[30]

Having begun with Pistol, I conclude by recalling another of Shakespeare's tragic pretenders. In the first rehearsal scene of *A Midsummer Night's Dream* Bottom covets the part of a tyrant – 'I could play Ercles rarely' (1.2.24–5) – and proceeds to illustrate his gift for Herculean declamation. Bottom understands the prestige and the supreme power of the tragic idiom: even fools know that there is something special about the tragedies, something unavailable in the other modes. Shakespeare's command of language is one source of that distinction.

Notes

1. See the chapters by Burrow, McEachern, and Belsey, elsewhere in this volume.
2. Alfred Harbage, 'Introduction' to *Twentieth-Century Views of Shakespeare's Tragedies* (Englewood Cliffs, NJ: Prentice-Hall, 1964), p. 3.

3. *English Renaissance Literary Criticism*, ed. Brian Vickers (Oxford: Clarendon Press, 1999), p. 381.

4. 'To the Right Worshipful Sir Thomas Henneage, Knight', in Thomas Newton's *Seneca His Tenne Tragedies* (New York: Alfred A. Knopf, 1927; rpt University of Indiana Press, 1932), p. 5.

5. The first quotations are cited from Vickers, *English Renaissance Literary Criticism*, and from *Elizabethan Critical Essays*, ed. G. Gregory Smith (Oxford: Clarendon Press, 1904), 2 vols.: Sidney (Vickers, p. 363); Ascham (Vickers, p. 19); Webbe (Smith, vol. 1, p. 249). The passage from Puttenham is taken from *The Art of English Poesy*, ed. Frank Whigham and Wayne A. Rebhorn (Ithaca, NY: Cornell University Press, 2007), p. 115; this critical edition is indispensable for students of early modern rhetoric. The lines from *The Spanish Tragedy* are cited from Thomas Kyd, *'The First Part of Hieronimo' and 'The Spanish Tragedy'*, ed. Andrew S. Cairncross (Lincoln: University of Nebraska Press, 1967).

6. Quoted from Newton's *Seneca*, p. 123.

7. See, however, Lucy Munro's recent defence of this earlier verse: 'Although the fourteener line seems odd to early twenty-first century ears, its effect in performance can be unexpectedly powerful.' 'Tragic Forms', *The Cambridge Companion to Renaissance Tragedy*, ed. Emma Smith and Garrett A. Sullivan, Jr (Cambridge University Press, 2010), p. 94. Her discussion of style (pp. 92–6) constitutes one of the few recent attempts to connect tragic action and expression.

8. *Gorboduc, or Ferrex and Porrex* in *Drama of the English Renaissance: The Tudor Period*, ed. Russell A. Fraser and Norman Rabkin (New York: Macmillan, 1976).

9. *The Complete Works of Christopher Marlowe: Tamburlaine the Great Parts I and II*, ed. David Fuller (Oxford: Clarendon Press, 1998). I have modernized the spelling.

10. George T. Wright, *Shakespeare's Metrical Art* (Berkeley and Los Angeles: University of California Press, 1988), p. 98.

11. Raphael Lyne has profitably pursued this connection between language and thought, specifically the dramatist's poetic representation of the process of intellection in the words of the speaker. See his *Shakespeare, Rhetoric and Cognition* (Cambridge University Press, 2011), especially pp. 1–67.

12. Richard Lanham, *The Motives of Eloquence* (New Haven: Yale University Press, 1976), p. 1.

13. See Vickers, *English Renaissance Literary Criticism*, p. 623 n. 51.

14. 'Hero' is a problematic term. It seems to carry a positive valence – 'protagonist' is less evaluative – and it may appear to exclude those central figures who are women. But it is less cumbersome than the alternatives, and it is appropriate here because the hero's language is in the heroic register and sets the tone for the linguistic decorum of tragedy.

15. Lyne, in an analysis of conflicting critical responses to Macbeth's 'naked new-born babe' simile (1.7.2–15), speaks approvingly of its elusive quality: 'resistance

to explicability, even if it can be overcome, is still a property of the text'
(*Shakespeare, Rhetoric and Cognition*, p. 24). The wider applicability of this
statement is notable.

16. See J. V. Cunningham, *Tradition and Poetic Structure* (Denver, CO: Alan
Swallow, 1960), pp. 181ff.

17. William Webbe, *A Discourse of English Poetry*, in *Elizabethan Critical Essays*, ed.
Smith, vol. 1, p. 292.

18. A fascinating discussion of Othello's diction, especially Shakespeare's introduction of new, exotic words to characterize the Moor of Venice, is found in
Robert N. Watson, 'Shakespeare's New Words', *Shakespeare Survey* 65 (2012):
358–77.

19. Webbe, *A Discourse of English Poetry*, p. 292.

20. George Rylands, 'The Poet and the Player', *Shakespeare Survey* 7 (1954), 31.

21. Quoted in Kenneth Muir, 'Shakespeare's Imagery – Then and Now',
Shakespeare Survey 18 (1965), 46.

22. *The Art of English Poesy*, p. 243.

23. See Terence Hawkes, *Metaphor* (London: Methuen, 1972), *passim*.

24. *The Imperial Theme* (London: Methuen, 1965), pp. 155–6.

25. Paul Hammond writes astutely about the sensitivity of Edmond's ear, not only
in his quibbles on 'bastard' and 'legitimate' but also in his mocking of his
father's philosophical clichés: 'If Gloster has been listening to the Homilies,
Edmond has been reading Montaigne.' See *The Strangeness of Tragedy* (Oxford
University Press, 2009), p. 167.

26. 'Tensions and Ambiguities in Greek Tragedy', Jean-Pierre Vernant and
Pierre Vidal-Naquet, *Myth and Tragedy in Ancient Greece*, trans. Janet Lloyd
(New York: Zone Books, 1988), p. 42.

27. I have adopted 'sour words', an emendation often accepted by editors; NCS
prints the Folio's 'four words'.

28. *The Art of English Poesy*, p. 237.

29. Janet Adelman, *Suffocating Mothers: Fantasies of Maternal Origin in
Shakespeare's Plays, 'Hamlet' to 'The Tempest'* (New York and London:
Routledge, 1992), p. 187.

30. For an extensive treatment of this paradox, see Russ McDonald, *Shakespeare
and the Arts of Language* (Oxford University Press, 2001), especially the last
chapter, 'Words Effectual, Speech Unable', pp. 164–92.

CHAPTER 3

Tragedy in Shakespeare's career

David Bevington

In one sense, Shakespeare wrote tragedies throughout his career. To be sure, among the plays classified as tragedies in the great Folio edition of 1623, only *Titus Andronicus* (*c.* 1589–92) and *Romeo and Juliet* (1594–6) were written before 1599. Yet Shakespeare certainly pursued tragic themes and consequences in his early historical plays. The title page of *The First Part of the Contention betwixt the Two Famous Houses of York and Lancaster*, published in 1594 as a somewhat shortened version of what was to appear in the 1623 Folio as *The Second Part of Henry the Sixth*, announces among its subjects 'the death of the good Duke Humphrey', the 'banishment and death of the Duke of Suffolk', and 'the tragical end of the proud Cardinal of Winchester'. *The True Tragedy of Richard Duke of York, and the Death of Good King Henry the Sixth*, published in 1595 as a version of what was to appear in the 1623 Folio as *The Third Part of Henry the Sixth*, describes itself as a tragedy in that quarto title. So does *The Tragedy of Richard III*, registered and published in 1597 after having been written in about 1592–4. *The Life and Death of King John* (written in about 1594–6 and first published in the 1623 Folio) and *The Tragedy of Richard the Second* (registered and published in 1597) are similarly characterized as tragedies on their title pages, at least (in the case of *King John*) by the implications of tragedy in the King's 'death'.

To say that the early history plays explore tragic themes and consequences is not, however, to establish in Shakespeare's writing at this juncture a clear sense of tragedy as a genre. In all of these plays, as David Kastan has argued,[1] history is an ongoing and open-ended project that eclipses tragic form. Classical literary criticism, from Aristotle on down to the early modern period, afforded no precedent for 'the history play' as a dramatic structure; hence Francis Meres's categorization of all the plays of Shakespeare that he lists in 1598 as either comedies or tragedies.[2] *Richard III* in his taxonomy is a tragedy, while *Henry IV* is a comedy. These rough-hewn approximations make sense, but do not allow for the conception of 'the history play' as a genre in its own right. 'The history play' remains a different sort of classification, based primarily on subject matter in a way that comedy and tragedy are not; the English history play is a play about English history.

As such, the history play's commitment to tragedy remains radically ambiguous. *Richard III* is about the rise and fall of Richard, Duke of Gloucester, who became king; it is also about the accession to power of Henry Tudor, Queen Elizabeth's grandfather. The idea of 'tragedy' here seems indebted to the overarching scheme of the medieval English cycle plays, in which human failure and death are ultimately to be understood as a part of a larger cosmic plan aimed at eventual restoration of order and harmony. This is not to argue a theologically providential reading of Shakespeare's first tetralogy, or to see the account as allegorical. Yet these plays do interpret English history in such a way as to suggest that Richard's diabolical evil leads ultimately to his own downfall, having in the meantime inflicted on the English nation a scourging that it has richly earned through factionalism. The Earl of Richmond represents a deliverance and a new beginning under the Tudor monarchy. *The Tragedy of Richard II* similarly ends in the ascension of the Lancastrian king whose son will be Henry V. Tragedy is a prelude to historical change.

Shakespeare appears to owe his conception of tragedy in these early history plays not only to the English cycle plays (and to the larger cosmic idea of Christian history to which they are in turn indebted), but also to the tradition of the Fall of Princes. As enunciated in Chaucer's Prologue to 'The Monk's Tale',

> Tragedie is to seyn a certeyn storie,
> As olde bookes maken us memorie,
> Of hym that stood in greet prosperitee,
> And is yfallen out of heigh degree
> Into myserie, and endeth wrecchedly.[3]

Chaucer proceeds to illustrate this commonsense view of tragedy with illustrations of the fall of men and angels in divine and human history, from Lucifer and Adam to Samson, Hercules, Nebuchadnezzar, Nero, Antiochus, Alexander, Julius Caesar, Croesus, and still others. The idea of such a dolefully edifying catalogue is derived from Boccaccio's *De casibus virorum illustrium* and from the *Roman de la Rose* (5829–6901).[4] Boccaccio supplies the plan of the tale, with a similar catalogue of falls of great men; the *Roman* (indebted in turn to Boethius's *De consolatione philosophiae*)[5] supplies the motif of Fortune as the capricious goddess upon whose turning wheel no human can depend.

The list of fallen angels and men in Chaucer and Boccaccio contains some who are evil and villainous (Lucifer, Nero, Antiochus). As a result, the idea of tragedy bears little relation to Aristotle's definitions and classifications of tragedy in the *Poetics*, where the overthrow of a bad man is seen as distinctly less 'tragic' than the downfall of an essentially good man in whom can be identified a '*hamartia*' (variously translated as 'tragic flaw' and 'tragic error'). Instead, the prevailing view of tragedy in the Middle Ages becomes that of an edifying instance of the instability of fortune. Chaucer's essential definition is that the protagonist falls from high to low and ends wretchedly. The reader is invited to learn from such instances what it is to pin one's hopes on worldly advancement and one's own fatal pride.

This conception of tragedy continues strong into the late Middle Ages and early modern period, in John Lydgate's *The Fall of Princes* (1430–8), and in ever-expanding versions of *A Mirror for Magistrates*, begun (but prohibited from being published) in 1555 by William Baldwin and others, then published in 1559, 1563, 1574, 1578, and 1587, each time with additions. Tracing a direct line of descent back to Chaucer and Boccaccio, this compilation came to include exemplary 'Complaints' of Henry Duke of Buckingham (by Thomas Sackville) and Jane Shore, among others. New material contributed in the later editions by John Higgins and Thomas Blennerhasset took the story back to the legendary kings of early Britain, like Locrine, Lear, and King Arthur. The subject, increasingly, was English history and legendary history, in a form that was readily at hand to dramatists (Shakespeare most of all) eager to exploit a growing fascination with English national identity in the time of the Spanish Armada – 1588, just one year after the publication in 1587 of a major edition of *A Mirror*, as well as of the second edition of Holinshed's *Chronicles*.[6]

To be sure, *A Mirror for Magistrates* duplicated a good deal of the information Shakespeare could also have found in the chronicles of Holinshed and Hall, but it also firmly established a model of tragedy as applied to the history of England's royal families. This model offered a 'mirror' of the instability of fortune and the inevitable punishment of vice. Shakespeare's *Henry VI* plays and *Richard III*, insofar as they are tragedies, repeatedly illustrate this formula in the rise and fall of Henry VI, Richard Plantagenet, Duke Humphrey of Gloucester, the Dukes of Suffolk and Clarence, Edward IV, Hastings, Rivers, Grey, Buckingham, and many others. *Richard III* is, in these terms, the culmination and epitome of the model that Shakespeare inherited from a long tradition of the Fall of Princes. The model served him as a conceptual framework around which to dramatize civil conflict and provide a moral commentary which would have been familiar to his audiences.

As a basis for writing tragedy, on the other hand, its purposes were limited. It focused on political struggle to the virtual exclusion of the domestic and personal. The criteria of evaluation through which an audience might experience tragic emotion were largely those of judging success or failure in the performance of public duty. The audience is invited to deplore cynical manipulation of the political process as something to be punished by the workings of the plot, however engaging the manipulator (such as Richard III) might prove to be. Even a basically good-hearted man whose fall is due to what could be viewed as a tragic flaw, like Duke Humphrey of Gloucester in *Henry VI Part II*, appears more as a victim of conniving than as a tragic protagonist working out his own destiny; his story, however 'tragic' in the trite sense of *A Mirror for Magistrates*, is subsumed into a larger narrative of England's struggle for national identity. This narrative is ultimately comic in finding a positive and edifying outcome – 'comic' in the sense that Dante's *Divina commedia* is comic.

Concurrently with his early history plays, Shakespeare seems to have been thinking about a strikingly different conception of the tragic offered by Seneca's tragedies and Seneca's English imitators. Thomas Kyd's *The Spanish Tragedy*, first published in 1592 after having been written and acted as early as 1586 or 1587, was a major theatrical event in London during Shakespeare's first years in the city. Here was a model that was distinctly tragic in form, and wildly popular.[7] Just as he tried his hand at Plautine comedy in *The Comedy of Errors* during these same years, Shakespeare apprenticed himself to neo-classical Senecan tragedy in *Titus Andronicus* (*c.* 1589–92).

The parallels between *The Spanish Tragedy* and *Titus Andronicus* are so extensive, indeed, that we cannot be sure when Shakespeare is modelling his writing on Seneca and when on Kyd. Certainly Kyd was the closer at hand for Elizabethan audiences. The success of the genre of the revenge tragedy, in the early 1590s and on down for another generation, points to a formula that worked theatrically. As a pattern for tragedy, on the other hand, it has its limitations. The increasingly remorseless conduct of the protagonist as revenger comes at the expense of sympathetic identification. The emotional effect in the catastrophe is more ironic than personally tragic; Titus is the cunning avenger more than the fallen hero struggling to understand his destiny and his place in an uncertain cosmos. This is a problem to which Shakespeare will return in *Hamlet*, with stunning success. *Titus Andronicus*, for all its brilliance of effect and powerful theatrical moments, seems content to succeed in the way that Kyd had succeeded earlier.

Romeo and Juliet, the other play prior to 1599 that was published as a tragedy in the 1623 Folio, explores a strikingly different approach to tragedy. It is no revenge tragedy, even if a vendetta between two families is the ugly problem that the two lovers must face; vengeful street-fighting repeatedly sets in motion the fateful trajectory that the play must follow. Nor is the play a mirror for magistrates, clearly. To a remarkable extent, it is *sui generis* as a dramatic genre. Pragmatically, its conception of tragedy comes from its sources, which are non-dramatic: Arthur Brooke's long narrative poem in English called *The Tragical History of Romeus and Juliet* (1562), and, behind it, Matteo Bandello's *Novelle* of 1554, Pierre Boaistuau's French translation (1559), and, still further back, Luigi da Porto's *Novella* (*c.* 1530), Masuccio of Salerno's *Il Novellino* (1476), and so on back to the *Ephesiaca* of the fifth century AD. The much-admired story of two lovers destined to suffer the consequences of their families' animosity had grown in successive stages, adding new characters like Mercutio and the Nurse. As Brooke's title indicates, the word 'tragical' seemed an appropriate designator.

Shakespeare, then, inherited the 'tragic' dimensions of the story he chose to dramatize about fated young lovers. The idea of tragedy came with the sources, and it is not one for which either the Fall of Princes or revenge tragedy provided a formula. Nor does the pattern owe anything to classical and neo-classical theories of tragedy. The play's protagonists are young persons, unremarkable other than for the poetic intensity of their passion. Their families are not patrician; indeed, the plan to marry Juliet to Count Paris underscores a hope for social advancement that is appropriate to the Capulets' status as one of two 'households' in Verona. The families are well-to-do, able to employ a number of servants and put on impressive parties, but they are not from the ruling elite. The dual protagonists spend little time exploring the existential dimensions of the universe and their place in it, even if Romeo does exclaim at one point 'Then I defy you, stars!' (5.1.24).

Perhaps we can call *Romeo and Juliet* a 'love tragedy'. The need for such an improvised characterization bespeaks a sense of the anomalous. Sometimes the play is paired with *Antony and Cleopatra* as a later, more mature play about tragic protagonists,[8] but even at that the pairing seems a little desperate. *Antony and Cleopatra*, for all its fine comic scenes involving the queen of Egypt, is an unmistakably tragic action dramatizing great figures of the classical past in a way that classical theorists of drama would recognize, even if they might tear their hair out at the play's lack of chronological and geographical unity. Romeo and Juliet, contrastingly, are ordinary people.

Moreover, a major portion of the play is funny and delightful in the vein of the romantic comedies that Shakespeare was writing at about the same time, such as *A Midsummer Night's Dream* and *Much Ado about Nothing*. We are warned that disaster is looming, of course, by the Prologue and by the violence with which *Romeo and Juliet* begins, and yet the play's first two acts wonderfully evoke the ecstasy of falling in love, the playful adolescent camaraderie of the young men, and the domestic imbroglios of a large extended family. The bawdry is as colourful as anywhere in Shakespeare, chiefly in scenes involving the Nurse and Mercutio. Plainly, Shakespeare has no interest in adhering to the strictures of neo-Aristotelian theorists insisting that tragedy not be adulterated with comedy.

The play announces itself as about 'a pair of star-crossed lovers', prompting us to ask what it means to be 'star-crossed', and whether that phrase can be seen as a kind of synonym for tragedy. The answer, in this resolutely non-classical play, is as varied as the story itself. The hostility between the families must serve as a major cause of tragedy here, and yet we see that good-hearted persons on both sides of the quarrel are determined to stop the carnage. Mere accident plays an important part: if the Friar's letter had got to Romeo in time, or if the Friar himself had arrived at Juliet's tomb before Romeo killed himself, tragedy could have been averted. Misunderstanding is no less crucial: if Juliet's family had known of her secret marriage to Romeo, presumably they would not have insisted on her marrying Paris. The father's anger at Juliet's waywardness in refusing to take up so promising an offer of marriage (3.5) shows him to be choleric and dictatorial as patriarch of the family, and yet we see his intemperance with the ironic understanding that he really is trying to do what he thinks best. All these are factors that seem quite external to the young protagonists, and thus do not bear heavily on tragic choice in a way that we see in Aeschylus' *Oresteia*, for example.

At one moment in *Romeo and Juliet*, to be sure, tragic choice does become crucial. It is when Romeo determines that he must kill Tybalt in revenge for the death of Mercutio. We see him giving in to peer pressure and the contagious atmosphere of macho loyalties to one's friends, at the expense of the softer and more charitable ideas of turning the other cheek that he has begun to learn from his love of Juliet. We see Romeo struggling with this choice, and regretting that choice in the immediate aftermath of Tybalt's death, even if Romeo tries to blame it on something outside himself: 'O, I am fortune's fool!' (3.1.127). This is a fine moment, and suggests that Shakespeare is searching for a tragic pattern that will deeply explore the connection linking choice and fate and character. At the same time,

Shakespeare seems drawn to the story of *Romeo and Juliet* by other considerations, by a vision of young love as all the more exquisite for being misunderstood by an unfeeling world. In such a picture there is only limited room for an exploration of the inner self in relation to destiny. To talk about *hamartia* in *Romeo or Juliet* is, by and large, an exercise in futility. Such an approach imposes criteria on a play whose interests lie elsewhere, in the essentially beautiful pain of suffering for having fallen in love.

Shakespeare's disparate ventures into tragic expression in the years prior to 1599 suggest that he had not yet found the model or models he was looking for, or, more positively, that he was exploring tragic and near-tragic possibilities in the romantic comedies and English history plays for which he was rapidly becoming famous. In comedy, his inclination from the start was to threaten and complicate his comic world with tragic potential. *The Comedy of Errors* (c. 1589–94), despite its farcically Plautine plotting, is framed by the pending execution of old Egeon that is resolved only by the conclusion of the comic plot. This same formulation can be applied to *The Merchant of Venice* (c. 1596–7), in which Shylock's seemingly irresistible assault on the life of Antonio is foiled by the heroine of the love plot, and to *Much Ado About Nothing* (1598–9), where the terrible wrong done to Hero by Don John's slander and the assent of Claudio, Don Pedro, and even Hero's father to the undeserved accusation lead to her apparent death and to Benedick's resolution to challenge his best friend to a duel. Virtually all of the gentlemen are at the point of killing one another until the bumbling Dogberry and his Watch discover the truth, thus prompting the penance of those who have so erred in their faith. Even *A Midsummer Night's Dream* (c. 1595) darkens its comic vision with a perception that fairy magic can be malign. The banishment of the virtuous Duke Senior and his followers to the Forest of Arden in *As You Like It* (1598–1600) bespeaks a fallen world of ingratitude and treachery; Orlando's brother Oliver plans the death of his hated sibling by means of a rigged wrestling match. In his comedies generally, Shakespeare is continually fascinated by tragic possibility as a way of defining a human potential for failure that is redeemed solely by a comic and restorative move towards charity and forgiveness that is vested chiefly in Shakespeare's romantic heroines.[9]

The obsession of the so-called 'problem plays' in pursuing still further a problematic and even pessimistic view of human nature needs to be understood in the context of Shakespeare's full engagement with tragedy as a formal genre in the years beginning with 1599–1601. *Julius Caesar*, publicly acted at the new Globe Theatre in 1599, is set in the ancient classical world of Rome. Shakespeare had experimented with this setting in *Titus*

Andronicus, albeit in a fictional guise derived from his various sources for that play. Now, in 1599, he chose to dramatize one of the climactic and enduringly memorable scenes of Roman history. Both plays display a fascination with the spirit of Rome as material for tragical discourse. Roman history was, for Shakespeare and his contemporaries, the sole earlier civilization of which they had much knowledge. Through various legends about the founding of Great Britain by the grandson of Aeneas, Britain considered itself a scion of Rome and a direct inheritor of its culture. A story about the overthrow of a senatorial republican tradition by a strong single military leader was, moreover, a story that was bound to resonate in an England uncertain of its own political destiny at the end of Queen Elizabeth's reign, no matter how different the situation after Caesar's assassination might be from that of monarchist England.

What the story of Caesar's assassination offered Shakespeare was a chance to explore the tragic dimensions of that great account quite distanced from the moral and Christian imperatives of English history. *Julius Caesar* is a history play, but it is one that need not end in any providential sense of history as a confirmation of God's handiwork. Even in the English history plays, Shakespeare had done much to question such imperatives, but they were a given of his sources. In *Julius Caesar* he is free to delineate a radically different pattern of historical process. Indeed, as John Velz has shown,[10] that process in *Julius Caesar* is essentially one of undulation, in which one leader or one kind of governmental structure succeeds a predecessor and then yields to a successor without any clear sense of progress or even of plan. History is change; it is unstable; the outcome of a particular moment depends on the charisma or perhaps the luck of the individual leader.

The consequences of such an existential view of human history for tragedy are profound. Brutus, whom traditional neo-Aristotelian criticism inevitably singles out as the play's tragic protagonist,[11] is a man of noble and even worthy intentions whose seemingly best qualities help to undo him. Keenly aware of his descent from the first Brutus (Junius) who had liberated his city from Tarquinius Superbus, Brutus is selflessly devoted to public service but also proud. A devoted Stoic, he thinks himself invulnerable to flattery, but is for that very reason an easy target for the insinuations of those like Cassius who know how to appeal to Brutus's sense of his own integrity. A defender of republicanism, Brutus nonetheless assumes command of the revolutionary conspiracy he has been asked to join and proceeds to overrule his compatriots with a series of disastrous decisions: spare Mark Antony after the assassination, allow Antony to speak at Caesar's funeral, fight with Antony and young Octavius at Philippi in disregard of Cassius's judicious warnings of their military unpreparedness for the battle. Brutus's attempt to restore republicanism is undone by the very qualities that make him a great man: he sees the necessity of assassinating Caesar, but refuses to shed blood further than is necessary, and then grants Antony permission to speak at Caesar's funeral out of a sense of fair play and decency (along with his own proud sense that what he will have to say will silence any answer that Antony might give). Here is a tragedy at once personal and political. It illustrates the Fall of Princes, while at the same time it discovers tragic meaning in the protagonist himself. The ironies of history are best displayed in this leader of the cause of republicanism, who gives his life in a supreme effort, the result of which is to repress still further the liberties that Brutus held so dear.

Though Brutus is usually interpreted by neoclassical criticism as the play's tragic protagonist, other figures are also remarkable studies in tragic character. Julius Caesar is like Brutus in more ways than either of them recognize. Unshaken of purpose, holding steady when other men waver, Caesar is also deaf to counsel when he most needs it. Physically he is both the mightiest man of the world and a frail human being who cannot compete with Cassius in swimming the Tiber, and who must turn his head to one side when the senators address him because he is deaf in one ear. Like Brutus, he considers himself above flattery, and is for that reason prone to it; as Decius Brutus observes, 'when I tell him he hates flatterers,/ He says he does, being then most flattered' (2.1.208–9). Caesar is superstitious, even though he professes to scorn the interpretation of omens and signs. Like Brutus, Caesar is counselled by a wise and compassionate wife, who futilely urges him not to go to the Capitol on what they both know to be a fateful day. His character is his destiny. Shakespeare's astute strategy of pairing Brutus and Caesar in adjoining scenes (2.1 and 2.2), as these great men ignore their wives' urgings and march to their destinies, underscores the ironic and repetitive patterns of history through which this tragedy unfolds.[12] The great men of this play are victims of their own hubris, and experience a kind of blindness at the crucial moment of their destinies that is remarkably like that which the ancient Greeks called *até* or blind infatuation.

In *Hamlet*, written shortly after *Julius Caesar*, Shakespeare revisits the revenge-play motif of *Titus* in a way that transforms it into tragic greatness. A seemingly inherent problem in the formula of the revenge play, as we have seen, is that the protagonist, in his obsessive drive for necessary revenge, becomes dehumanized and unsympathetic to such a degree that the cathartic effect of tragedy is diverted into the kind of savage and wanton destruction we see in the end of *The Spanish Tragedy*, where the spirit of Revenge is not satisfied until nearly every person of the play lies dead onstage. *Hamlet* does not shy away from this problem. Hamlet himself is unquestionably hardened and even coarsened by his killing of Polonius (however mistaken in its object), his sending of Rosencrantz and Guildenstern to their deaths, his responsibility however indirect for the madness of Ophelia, and still more. The stage at the end of *Hamlet* is littered with corpses. Hamlet is the avenger, and as such he stands in a line of inheritance that is bloody.

To grasp the extent of this hold over the play exerted by the revenge tradition, we can look not only to the earlier revenge play that Shakespeare had written but also to his sources for *Hamlet*. The *Historia Danica* (1180–1208) of Saxo Grammaticus is unapologetically violent. Undeterred by any moral scruples, facing a cunning enemy in his uncle Feng, young Amlethus senses that he is being spied upon during his interview with his mother in her chamber. Finding the hidden courtier, Amlethus stabs the man to death, drags the body forth from the straw in which it has been concealed, cuts the body into morsels, boils them, and flings the bits 'through the mouth of an open sewer for the swine to eat'. Sent to England, as in Shakespeare's play, he arranges for the death of his escorts by substituting in their papers a forged document ordering their execution in his stead. Returning to Jutland a year later, after having married the king's daughter, Amlethus encourages the court to indulge in a wild drinking party, imprisons the drunken courtiers in a large tapestry stitched for him by his mother, and then sets fire to the palace.[13]

The later versions of the story to which Shakespeare was more directly indebted, including Belleforest's *Histoires Tragiques* (1576) and a lost anonymous play of *Hamlet* of the early 1590s, did little to ameliorate the carnage. What Thomas Lodge recollects from that theatrical experience is 'the vizard of the ghost which cried so miserably at the theatre, like an oyster wife, "Hamlet, revenge!"',[14] while Thomas Nashe speaks of the lost play as 'English Seneca read by candlelight'.[15] Later revenge plays as well, after Shakespeare's *Hamlet*, feature protagonists whose cunning overwhelms their (presumably) better natures; John Marston's *Antonio's Revenge* and *The Revenger's Tragedy* (perhaps by Thomas Middleton) are cases in point. Shakespeare's *Hamlet* is unique not only in being one of the finest tragedies ever written, but also in its attempts to exculpate and humanize the revenger. The play's greatness and the humanity that Shakespeare bestows on his protagonist are not unrelated.

Shakespeare's way of humanizing his revenger is to present a Hamlet who is thoughtful, introspective, witty, capable of enduring friendships, deeply moved by the need for human affection both in his family and in romantic attachments, and philosophically inquisitive. Ever since Coleridge, criticism of this play has been plagued by the notion that Hamlet's humanity renders him incapable of action,[16] despite the play's plentiful evidence to the contrary in his slaying of Polonius, his resolute behaviour at sea, and still other forthright actions. The observation seems more appropriate to Coleridge (and to Goethe and Hegel) than to Hamlet. In the context of our present argument about Shakespeare's developing sense of tragic form, a dramaturgical interpretation presents itself: the humanizing of Hamlet is the strategy needed to counter the dehumanizing thrust of the revenge tradition.

Viewed in this light, Hamlet is bound to question his own motives and the certainty of the information he has seemingly received about his father's apparent murder. His hesitancy and self-castigation are the appropriate responses in a student of philosophy who is also heir to the Danish throne. Shakespeare adroitly takes advantage of his play's location in Denmark (which is to say that he does not alter the location, as he certainly could have done) in order to present us with a world that stands between Scandinavia to the north (a land of pagan legends of revenge, prominently including that narrated by Saxo Grammaticus) and Europe to the south, bifurcated in our imagination between the Paris of pleasurable pursuit and the Wittenberg of scholarly learning and theology. Hamlet the man and *Hamlet* the play stand between these worlds. The pagan ethic of revenge, on the one hand, demands of Hamlet that he revenge the 'foul and most unnatural murder' of his father (1.5.26). The civilized world of Europe, on the other hand, brings with it Christian imperatives against suicide and murder. Hamlet is a Christian; he is also his father's son. Here, then, in Shakespeare's solution to the problem of sympathetic identification posed for him by the revenge-play tradition, Shakespeare found his most intensely satisfying pattern for the depiction of the tragic individual. Hamlet's internal conflict, in which civilized decency is posed with seemingly irreconcilable opposition against the need for brutally direct action, is the stuff of tragic greatness.

The danger in this pattern, on the other hand, is that the protagonist might turn out to be ineffectual, pitiable in his inability to act, unable to find a way out of his dilemma – the Hamlet of Coleridge's imagination. Shakespeare's dramaturgical solution to this is again integral to what makes this play so great as tragedy. Hamlet does find a solution, or, rather, one is found for him. Paradoxically, after he has flailed about in an attempt to carry out his father's commission and has managed in the process to kill the wrong man – a move that, as Hamlet sees, he will have to pay for – Hamlet submits himself to the will of Providence and is thereupon handed the solution he has devoutly sought for but has been unable to find on his own initiative. Without his connivance – a connivance that would inevitably smack of premeditation to commit murder – Hamlet finds himself in a fatal duel with Laertes that leads further to the death of his mother, the public exposure of Claudius's villainy, and thus the occasion for a violent act against Claudius that is essentially unpremeditated. The act seems fully justified to us as audience by the powerful emotions of the final scene. Hamlet comes to understand his fate and to see a pattern in the human suffering that has seemed to him earlier so pointlessly brutal. At the same time, the ending he did not devise for himself brings about his own death – a death he has longed for, yet without the suicidal self-infliction that his Christian teaching forbids. Even if Horatio offers a more sceptical reading of Hamlet's history, one in which 'carnal, bloody, and unnatural acts' have prevailed along with 'accidental judgment' and 'casual slaughters' (5.2.383–4), the play's ending notably strives towards philosophical comprehension of human suffering and evil. It is here that we find the catharsis so richly evident in *Oedipus Tyrannos*, and lacking in *Titus Andronicus*.

Once Shakespeare had succeeded so brilliantly with tragedy in *Hamlet*, the way may have seemed open for him to concentrate on what had eluded him earlier, or had seemed less pressing in terms of his own artistic agenda. Perhaps, as Richard Wheeler has argued, this turning point in his artistic career can best be understood as a grappling with new and deeply personal problems that Shakespeare had been unready to face in his younger years.[17] Having successfully manoeuvred the strategies of male maturation and courtship in his earlier plays, and having begun to explore darker themes in his Sonnets, particularly the agonies of betrayal and jealousy, Shakespeare was at a point where he could choose no longer to present female infidelity as primarily a phantasm of the diseased male imagination, but as something that could actually occur. The Dark Lady of the Sonnets is unfaithful in a way that Hero of *Much Ado* simply was not.

The 'problem plays', in this view, are of critical importance. Manifestly, in them Shakespeare is exploring the porousness of the generic boundaries between tragedy, history play, and comedy. A tragic outcome so threatens the major personages of *Measure for Measure* (1603–4) that the Duke, for all his secretive manipulations, is stymied in his attempt to save the life of Claudio until a prisoner providentially dies in the prison. The problematic nature of marriage in this play, and in *All's Well That Ends Well* (c. 1601–5), is inseparably linked to the human propensity (especially among males) for forced seduction, bribery, and attempted murder. Angelo's anguished discovery of his own diseased cravings produces soliloquies that are fully tragic in tone. The mutual recriminations of Claudio and his sister Isabella are as searing as anything Shakespeare wrote in his tragedies, and as fully revelatory of human failure. The Duke's meditation on the vanity of human wishes in his counselling of Claudio (3.1.5–41) to 'Be absolute for death' is no less tragic, even if its tragic import is qualified by the Duke's disguise and his announced intent to be a rescuer. *All's Well*, like *Much Ado*, invokes a mock death in its attempt to recuperate the undeserving hero through penance. *All's Well* shares with *Measure for Measure* the employment of an ethically dubious bed trick. *Troilus and Cressida* (*c.* 1601–2), the most problematic of these 'problem plays', defied the attempts of the Folio editors to find a tidy place for it in their generic categories: manifestly a history play about the Trojan war, it ends with the tragic death of Hector and with the failure of the love affair of its title figures, and yet spares the lives of most of its characters in a standoff that is more akin to satire than to tragedy; the hovering figures of Thersites and Pandarus strongly reinforce this satiric tone. Fittingly, *Troilus and Cressida* ended up in the Folio edition between the histories and the tragedies, unpaginated, ceaselessly enigmatic.

If, then, Shakespeare was ready to investigate human failure in a fully tragic dimension as never before, and with the very real successes of *Julius Caesar* and especially *Hamlet* as vital encouragement to proceed, we may well imagine a Shakespeare who now was ready to tackle the tragic dilemmas that his own advancing age must have compelled him to face: sexual jealousy in marriage (in *Othello*), the ingratitude felt by children towards their ageing parents (*King Lear*), the insane promptings of ambition (*Macbeth*), midlife crisis (*Antony and Cleopatra*), bitter resentment towards persons who fail to show proper gratitude and reciprocity for a lifetime of generosity (*Timon of Athens*), and, again, resentment towards a city that has not been properly grateful to its leading general and fledgeling political leader (*Coriolanus*).

This list of tragedies is remarkable in its own right as Shakespeare's greatest achievement. It is also remarkable for its variety of tragic experiences and tragic forms. *Othello* (*c.* 1603–4) is a play that might well illustrate Shakespeare's understanding of Aristotle's definitions of tragedy, if we had any reason to think that Shakespeare cared about Aristotle and the critical tradition that descended from him. Othello is a mighty figure in the heroic mould of classical tragedy, even if his being black marks him as a stranger. He is a good man in most ways: brave, capable of great leadership, strong in his affections, loyal, ordinarily calm under stress. His devotion to Desdemona is all-encompassing; indeed, it is the intensity of his love for her that prepares the extent of his fall into misery and self-hatred. If one looks for a *hamartia* or tragic flaw, Othello's characterization of himself as 'one that loved not wisely but too well' is readily at hand; he is one 'not easily jealous but, being wrought,/Perplexed in the extreme' (5.2.354–6).

The play's cathartic experience is deep, and depends on the protagonist's belated recognition of the wrong he has committed. The irrational fury that has seized Othello and has led to such a terrible crime is not unlike the *até* that afflicts Agamemnon in Aeschylus's *Oresteia*; it is an insanity from which the protagonist recovers too late, so that we are allowed to see the causal relationship between character and destiny. A larger scheme of justice ultimately prevails: Othello denounces his terrible act, clears Desdemona of any wrong, rediscovers his love for her even though she cannot be restored to him as his living wife, and (like Oedipus) punishes his own crime. The pattern of tragic recognition is not unlike that so admired by Aristotle and his followers; the tragic effect works on us in ways that Aristotle ably describes.

Macbeth (*c.* 1606–7) is another Shakespearean tragedy that is not unduly distorted by applying the framework of Aristotle's *Poetics*. Macbeth is an aristocratic figure of great personal bravery and public reputation. At the start of the play, he is the loyal soldier of his kind-hearted king. He is a man of poetic sensitivity and extraordinary insight into his own emotional drives. We are invited to sympathize with him, even in his torments of guilt, and to see things through his eyes. His *hamartia*, if we wish to call it that, is his intense ambition, combined with a dependence on the fatal urgings of his wife on the occasion of Duncan's visit to their castle. He knows his obsessive desire for the kingship is wrong, and yet his susceptibility to that desire makes him prone to the suggestions of his wife and the three Weird Sisters. The sisters know how to insinuate with him because they can read his heart and know that the longing to seize power by whatever means necessary has visited him long before they make known their enigmatic and seductive half-truths about his advancement from Glamis to Cawdor and thence to king.

Macbeth is thus an otherwise good man afflicted by a tragic flaw. Our understanding of the meaning of his tragedy lies in our perception of the necessary and just relationship between that craving and his ultimate fate. This pattern again sounds Aristotelian in its working out of discovery and recognition. As in *Othello*, order is restored through the punishment of the protagonist and the reaffirmation of political and social stability. At the same time, we must recognize that the terms of the tragic flaw in *Macbeth* are Christian and moral in a way that they are not in fifth-century Greek tragedy. Oedipus's *hamartia* has nothing to do with guilt or sin; his killing of his father and marrying his mother are polluted acts that he has committed however unintentionally, and he must pay for them, but he is not a sinner. Macbeth is a sinner, and he knows it: even before he kills Duncan, he confesses that Duncan's virtues will plead, 'like angels, trumpet-tongued, against/The deep damnation of his taking-off' (1.7.18–19). To see *Macbeth* as a kind of object lesson illustrating one of the Ten Commandments, 'Thou shalt not kill', would be to reduce the play to a platitude, perhaps, but this would not misrepresent the nature of Macbeth's *hamartia*. It is ambition, or Pride, the deadliest of the Seven Deadly Sins; it is the sin of Lucifer. The elucidation of meaning in Macbeth's tragedy thus depends on moral cause and effect in a way that Greek tragedy does not. The fact that Macbeth is a sympathetic character capable of a close marital relationship with his wife makes his fall into sin all the more terrifying, since it implies that, but for the grace of God, there go we as well. The cause and effect of sin and punishment in *Macbeth* thus reads as a kind of translation of Greek *hamartia* into terms that are more morally comprehensible to a Christian civilization.

The Aristotelian formula does not apply, on the other hand, to a play like *Romeo and Juliet*, where the protagonists are, by and large, innocent victims, even martyrs, to the unfeeling world that surrounds and engulfs them. Romeo is briefly caught up as agent of his own tragedy, but incidentally and as part of a larger pattern of guiltless suffering. Hamlet, too, despite the efforts of much criticism to shape him in the mould of *hamartia*, and despite his many failures of *caritas*, is better seen as one who must bear on his shoulders the 'slings and arrows of outrageous fortune' (3.1.59). He must die that the truth may be known and the debt of vengeance paid, not in relation to any crime of his own but that of his uncle. Denmark is 'an unweeded garden' (1.2.135) not through Hamlet's means, and yet he must die. Without in any way allegorizing this narrative, we can perceive that it bears a structural similarity to the story of Christ's suffering and death. That is to say, the meaning in tragedy resides not in a cause-and-effect discovery through which the protagonist comes to understand his own frightening inner self and to see a cosmic need for fall and punishment; rather, it is a tragedy of sacrifice. With it comes finally a cathartic sense of compensation and ultimate reward, if only the reward of knowing that one has tried to better a fallen world. As Capulet says at the end of *Romeo and Juliet*, the lovers are 'Poor sacrifices of our enmity' (5.3.305). The parents' rage has been such that, 'but their children's end, naught could remove' (Prologue, 11).

This distinctly non-Aristotelian tragic pattern, of a seemingly necessary sacrifice that atones for and partly ameliorates the wretched condition of humanity, can account for much that happens in *King Lear* (*c.* 1605–6). Lear himself, as protagonist, is one in whom one can easily find a *hamartia*; he is choleric, imperious, domineering, deaf to counsel, fatally wrong in his judgements of his daughters. His failures lead with exemplary directness to his fall from power. Yet we respond at once to his cry of pain that he is 'a man/More sinned against than sinning' (3.2.59–60). The inversions of madness and sanity, seeing and blindness, justice and tyranny that so overwhelm us in this play bring with them the perception that Lear does not deserve what happens to him. Accordingly, we must look for tragic meaning elsewhere than in a formula of crime and punishment. What is true of Lear is also true of Gloucester; however badly he misjudges his sons and persecutes Edgar, the blinding of this defenceless old man with the connivance of his illegitimate son Edmund, and the charitable sorrow with which Gloucester accepts blame for his own failures, create for him the role of sacrificial victim. The meeting of these two ruined old men at Dover (4.6) evokes our pity so compellingly that we nearly forget what they have done to bring this on themselves.

Even more so, those who win our unhesitating sympathy are sacrificial figures. However much Cordelia may have prompted Lear into banishing her, however much she may have wished to make clear to him that she had to have a life of her own, she does return from France to save him. She does the very thing she told him she wouldn't do: she puts her marriage and her very life at risk, because the things that her sisters are doing to her father are intolerable. There are times when one must stand up and be counted, at whatever cost to oneself, and Cordelia has the immense courage to do this.

So have Edgar, and Kent, and the Fool. They and Cordelia must make their choices to suffer for goodness in the face of an indifferent universe where the gods do not seem to care and indeed may not exist. Under these circumstances, what moral guidelines can be discovered to govern human action? Edmund embodies the principle that a naturalistic universe invites and even demands a naturalistic response; if there are no gods, if moral principles are mere contrivances of human culture, then why not proceed ruthlessly to obtain what one wants? Goneril and Regan, though less able than Edmund to verbalize philosophical and moral principles, act on the same basis of anarchic opportunism. Yet they are all struck down, by their own hands, and by the desiccating force of inward corruption that (in the apocalyptic vision of this play) necessarily attends on heartless self-sufficiency. Cordelia, Edgar, and Kent suffer, but they have made the choices by which they know they must live. Tragic meaning, in this devastating play, resides somewhere in this recognition that evil is its own worst reward and that the only way to be able to live with oneself as a human being is to embrace the role of sacrificial victim, suffering in order that an idea of goodness may not perish.

Antony and Cleopatra (1606–7) breaks away from the Aristotelian definition of tragedy in still another way. It is, first of all, a play that defies all classical and neo-classical strictures about the unities of time, place, and action, but that is of less importance than its conception of the main characters. By deploying dual protagonists, it wonderfully complicates the tragic formula. Traditional criticism has usually solved this problem by centring on Antony alone as the tragic protagonist; he is, after all, a male, and he is the subject of Plutarch's *Life of Antony*.[18] Not surprisingly, the traditional interpretation of him as tragic figure confirms Plutarch's view: Antony is a great general of personal courage, vitality, and charisma, but he is a man who throws away everything out of his infatuation for a trull. Cleopatra is an amazing woman, to be sure, but in Plutarch she represents fleshly temptation through which the great man is diverted from his appointed task. This is a perfect formula of *hamartia*; it sees moral and just cause and effect in Antony's downfall.

The trouble is, of course, that it fails to do justice to Shakespeare's amazing play. Shakespeare dramatizes the Plutarchan perspective, all right, but as an ideology against which to measure the daring of the lovers and of the poet who created them. All that can be said against the lovers is true: Antony deserts duty and hates himself for it, he is untrue to Octavia in despite of his oaths to her, and he is unmanned by Cleopatra, who, for her part, is presented as cunning, seductive, and deceiving.[19] Yet out of this story of human failure Shakespeare dares to imagine a spirit of greatness, a sharing of experiences between a man and a woman that transcends boundaries of gender, and a defiance of normal worldly expectations that entirely alters the nature of the tragic experience. This is no simple moral lesson in which we see *hamartia* leading to its necessary consequences. Instead, we are invited to admire a Cleopatra who is grandly capable of a noble resolution through which she will be able to call 'great Caesar ass/Unpolicied' (5.2.307–8). Antony and Cleopatra are not sacrifices like Romeo and Juliet, since they are far from innocent, but they do insist on being 'past the size of dreaming' (5.2.96). As such, they share with other tragic protagonists in Shakespeare a wish to challenge and surmount the dead weight of a world that imposes such a fearful cost on those who do not follow the world's ways.

Shakespeare's tragedies of disillusionment, *Timon of Athens* (*c.* 1605–8) and *Coriolanus* (*c.* 1608), suggest by their deep misanthropy a kind of sad and even bitter conclusion to Shakespeare's exploration of the genre of tragedy. What vision of tragedy is possible, we are invited to ask, after *King Lear*, *Macbeth*, and *Antony and Cleopatra*? Shakespeare writes as though the desolate conclusions found especially in *Lear* leave no further room for hope. Turning again in these plays to the ancient classical world where, as in *Julius Caesar*, he could step aside from Christian imperatives and ameliorating visions of human history, Shakespeare ponders human ingratitude with unsparing candour. Timon and Coriolanus are alike in their outspokenness, their disappointment in human behaviour, their mistrust of ordinary people. The protagonists are ultimately extreme and unattractive in their rejection of human consolation. Timon and Coriolanus are admirable in their relentless refusal to deceive themselves through illusion, but for them, and indeed for us, very little is left. Timon cuts off all human contact; Coriolanus not only leaves his family and his mother, but finds himself on the verge of attacking his own city of Rome, with his family among the intended victims. He is pulled back from matricide and wife-slaying not by an ennobling tragic vision but by the irony of a situation that paralyses him into helplessness: 'O Mother, Mother!/What have you done? Behold, the heavens do ope,/The gods look down, and this unnatural scene/They laugh at' (5.3.182–5). Shakespeare's final tragic vision is dispiriting indeed. He surveys the desolation found also in *Lear* but without the sacrificial and cathartic ending that offers some atonement. These tragedies of disillusionment offer scepticism as the only honest answer to humanity's tragic dilemma.

Without the romances to which Shakespeare turned in his last years as a writer, the vision would be bleak indeed. These plays are needed to repair and recuperate the tragic failures that this essay has been investigating. They do so by confronting tragic possibility, as the earlier romantic comedies had done. In fact they do so with a new intensity. *Pericles* (1606–8) deals with incest more relentlessly than the earlier plays, and allows the titular hero to suffer for the apparent abandonment of his wife at sea. *Cymbeline* (*c.* 1608–10) features the death and gross disfigurement of Cloten, along with the apparent death of Imogen, to the extent that the play was catalogued in the Folio as a tragedy. *The Tempest* (*c.* 1611) plays out its perfect comic structure on the island against a backdrop of political duplicity and attempted murder in mainland Italy, to which the unreconstructed Antonio and Sebastian will presumably return. Uniquely, *The Winter's Tale* (*c.* 1609–11) misleads its audience into an assurance that Queen Hermione is actually dead, since her spirit appears to Antigonus in requesting that he save the life of her daughter. The deception is needed to produce the splendid ambiguity surrounding Hermione's coming to life as a statue: is it an illusion staged for Leontes's spiritual edification, or a miracle of the dead restored to life? Certainly it is a *coup de théâtre*, one in which Shakespeare's supple exploration of the ambiguous boundaries between tragedy and comedy is perfectly encapsulated. To the end of his career, his interest is in mingled forms.

Notes

1. David Scott Kastan, *Shakespeare and the Shapes of Time* (Hanover, NH: University Press of New England, 1982).
2. Francis Meres, *Palladis Tamia* (London, 1598).
3. *The Riverside Chaucer*, ed. Larry D. Benson (Boston: Houghton Mifflin, 1987), 'The Monk's Prologue', 1973–7, 3163–7.
4. Giovanni Boccaccio, *De casibus virorum illustrium* (*Concerning the Falls of Illustrious Men*), mid-fourteenth century, and Guillaume de Lorris and Jean de Meung, *Le Roman de la Rose*, translated in part by Chaucer as The Romaunt of the Rose.
5. Anicius Manlius Severinus Boethius, *De consolatione philosophiae*, early sixth century.
6. See Claire McEachern, *The Poetics of English Nationhood, 1590–1612* (Cambridge University Press, 1996), and Richard Helgerson, *Forms of Nationhood: The Elizabethan Writing of England* (University of Chicago Press, 1992). The debate about nationhood also importantly involves Benedict Anderson, *Imagined Communities: Reflections on the Origin and Spread of Nationalism* (London: Verso, 1983).
7. Fredson Bowers, *Elizabethan Revenge Tragedy, 1587–1642* (Princeton University Press, 1940). On the question of whether George Peele was co-author with Shakespeare of *Titus Andronicus*, see 'Peele and *Titus Andronicus*', *George Peele*, ed. David Bevington, in the series on 'The University Wits', series editor, Robert A. Logan; Farnham and Burlington, VT: Ashgate, 2011. The article and its notes survey the various sides of the question of co-authorship.
8. See Franklin M. Dickey, *Not Wisely But Too Well: Shakespeare's Love Tragedies* (San Marino, CA: Huntington Library, 1957).
9. Robert Grams Hunter, *Shakespeare and the Comedy of Forgiveness* (New York: Columbia University Press, 1965). On the transitional years 1500–1601, see Harley Granville-Barker, 'From Henry V to Hamlet', *Proceedings of the British Academy* 11 (1925), 283–309.
10. John Velz, 'Undular Structure in *Julius Caesar*', *Modern Language Review* 66 (1971), 21–30.
11. See, for example, Ruth M. Levitsky, '"The Elements Were So Mix'd ..."', *PMLA* 88 (1973), 240–5, and Reuben A. Brower, *Hero and Saint: Shakespeare and the Graeco-Roman Heroic Tradition* (Oxford: Clarendon Press, 1971).

12. Norman Rabkin, 'The Polity', *Shakespeare and the Common Understanding* (New York: Free Press, 1967), pp. 105–21.

13. Saxo Grammaticus, *Historia Danica* (1180–1208), in Geoffrey Bullough, *Narrative and Dramatic Sources of Shakespeare*, 7 vols. (London: Routledge and Kegan Paul, 1966), vol. VII.

14. Thomas Lodge, *Wit's Misery, and the World's Madness* (London, 1596).

15. Thomas Nashe, *Epistle* prefixed to Robert Greene's *Menaphon* (London, 1589).

16. *Coleridge on Shakespeare: The Text of the Lectures of 1811–12*, ed. R. A. Foakes (Charlottesville: University Press of Virginia, 1971), and Ernest Jones, *Hamlet and Oedipus*, rev. edn (New York: 1949, 1954). For a powerful refutation of the Coleridgean line of interpretation, see Margreta de Grazia, *'Hamlet' without Hamlet* (Cambridge University Press, 2007). See also David Bevington, *Murder Most Foul: Hamlet through the Ages* (Oxford University Press, 2011).

17. Richard P. Wheeler, *Shakespeare's Development and the Problem Comedies: Turn and Counter-Turn* (Berkeley: University of California Press, 1981).

18. See Linda T. Fitz, 'Egyptian Queens and Male Reviewers: Sexist Attitudes in *Antony and Cleopatra* Criticism', *Shakespeare Quarterly* 28 (1977): 217–316.

19. See Janet Adelman, *The Common Liar: An Essay on 'Antony and Cleopatra'* (New Haven, CT: Yale University Press, 1973) and Linda Charnes, *Notorious Identity: Materializing the Subject in Shakespeare's Plays* (Cambridge, MA: Harvard University Press, 1993), pp. 103–47.

CHAPTER 4

Shakespearean tragedy printed and performed

Michael Warren

Throughout the twentieth century critical and popular opinion regarded Shakespeare's tragedies as his highest achievement; there is no sign that their pre-eminence will be modified in the twenty-first. In a largely secular world they have been invested with the status of secular scripture, often treated with reverence as spiritual masterpieces of transcendent literary art rather than as great plays written about four hundred years ago. The texts have sometimes appeared like sacred objects, especially in collected editions. Certainly the discussion of individual plays (sympathetic or hostile) has often been conducted as if the text of each were definitively established, canonically determined, and available for exegesis.

However, such is not the case. The notion of a single authentic text belongs to the tradition of reading plays rather than that of performing them in the playhouse, where performance admits variation. The texts of Shakespeare's tragedies, as of all of his plays, are unstable. The modern editions that we study are derived from documents of doubtful origin and imperfect execution about which there is less external evidence than we desire. Those early documents are constantly re-edited in the light of new knowledge, new theoretical concerns, and new hypotheses. The reading texts of the plays have changed and developed since their first publication; the texts of the plays have never been and cannot be truly fixed, although editions are frequently quite similar.

It will be advantageous to begin an introduction to the texts of Shakespeare's tragedies by reviewing briefly the facts about the plays' earliest publication.

Titus Andronicus is usually regarded as the earliest tragedy that he wrote. It was the first of the tragedies to be published and was, as far as we know, also the first of Shakespeare's plays to be published; even of that we cannot be truly certain, for all the details of Shakespeare's early career are not known. Only his poem *Venus and Adonis* had been published (1593) prior to the appearance of *Titus* in quarto in 1594; *Lucrece* appeared in 1594 also

about the same time as *Titus*. Both poems were printed in London by
Richard Field, a former resident of Stratford-upon-Avon, neither with the
author's name on the title page, but each with a dedicatory letter to the Earl
of Southampton signed by William Shakespeare. The title page of *Titus*
bore the following words: 'The Most Lamentable Romaine Tragedie of
Titus Andronicus: As it was Plaide by the Right Honourable the Earle of
Darbie, Earle of Pembrooke, and Earle of Sussex their Seruants'. A notable
inclusion is the names of the companies that played the play; a notable
omission, by modern standards, is any reference to the playwright. The
printer of that play was John Danter, who in 1597 also printed the next of
Shakespeare's tragedies to appear, *Romeo and Juliet*. Its title page reads: 'An
Excellent conceited Tragedie of Romeo and Iuliet. As it hath been often
(with great applause) plaid publiquely, by the right Honourable the L. of
Hunsdon his Seruants'. Again there is no identification of the playwright on
the title page. In 1599 appeared a second printing of the play, still anony-
mously, this time by Thomas Creede, with a title page that reads: 'The Most
Excellent and lamentable Tragedie, of Romeo and Iuliet. Newly corrected,
augmented, and amended: As it hath bene sundry times publiquely acted,
by the right Honourable the Lord Chamberlaine his Seruants'. The change
of name of the acting company is not particularly significant: its sponsor had
received a new appointment. However, the claim that the text is 'Newly
corrected, augmented, and amended' and the assertion that it is 'As it hath
bene sundry times publiquely acted' are important. The text that Creede
printed was markedly different from that published in 1597; variation
between the two texts is extensive, and Creede suggests that the earlier
printing was deficient in length and in accuracy. Such distinction between
texts presents challenges to the definition or even the description of a single
entity called *Romeo and Juliet*.

A similar situation obtains with *Hamlet*, the next tragedy to be printed.
In 1603 it appeared in quarto with a title page that reads: 'The Tragicall
Historie of Hamlet Prince of Denmarke By William Shake-speare. As it
hath beene diuerse times acted by his Highnesse seruants in the Cittie of
London: as also in the two Vniuersities of Cambridge and Oxford, and elsewhere'. Shakespeare's name appears on the title page (it had appeared first in
1598 on that of *Love's Labour's Lost*); King James I had become the company's sponsor. The book was printed by Valentine Simmes, working for
the publishers, Nicholas Ling and John Trundell. One of those publishers
of the first quarto (Q1), Nicholas Ling, employed James Roberts to print a
second quarto (Q2) late in 1604 (surviving copies are variously dated 1604 or
1605). Its title page reproduces the play's title and its author's name almost

exactly, but instead of the identification of the play's performance history it states: 'Newly imprinted and enlarged to almost as much againe as it was, according to the true and perfect Coppie'. The differences between the two quartos are even greater than those between the two quartos of *Romeo and Juliet*. Not the least significant is the discrepancy in length: the first quarto is 2,221 lines of type, and the second quarto is 3,803 lines of type. In 1608 a quarto of *King Lear* was published with a bold and elaborately informative title page that begins with the playwright's name: 'M. William Shakespeare: His True Chronicle Historie of the life and death of King Lear and his three Daughters. With the vnfortunate life of Edgar, sonne and heire to the Earle of Gloster, and his sullen and assumed humor of Tom of Bedlam: As it was played before the Kings Maiestie at Whitehall vpon S. Stephans night in Christmas Hollidayes. By his Maiesties seruants playing vsually at the Gloabe on the Bancke-side'.

These are the only tragedies of Shakespeare published before his death in 1616. Prior to his death *Titus* was reprinted in 1600 and 1611, *Romeo* in 1609, and *Hamlet* in 1611. A second quarto of *Lear* was published after his death: in 1619 Thomas Pavier reprinted the text of Q1 *Lear* with a title page that bears the false date 1608. In 1622, a year before the publication of the First Folio (F1), a fourth quarto of *Romeo* was published, and possibly a fourth, undated quarto of *Hamlet*. More importantly, however, a quarto of *Othello* appeared: 'The Tragœdy of Othello, The Moore of Venice. As it hath beene diuerse times acted at the Globe, and at the Black-Friers, by his Maiesties Seruants. Written by William Shakespeare'.

The other five tragedies – *Julius Caesar, Macbeth, Antony and Cleopatra, Timon of Athens*, and *Coriolanus* – did not see print until the publication of the First Folio in 1623: 'Mr. William Shakespeares Comedies, Histories, & Tragedies. Published according to the True Originall Copies'. Among the tragedies the Folio places *Troilus and Cressida* and *Cymbeline*, which are rarely considered as such, and which I shall not consider. The Folio provides the sole authoritative text for these five plays. In relation to the plays already published in quarto, the First Folio presents complications. In each case except *Romeo*, where the Folio text is close to that of Q2, there are significant and important variations between the Folio text and the earlier quarto record. The text of *Titus* contains a scene that is not in Q1 and its later reprints. If Q1 and Q2 *Hamlet* present radically different texts, the Folio *Hamlet* presents a third. The Folio *King Lear* contains material not in Q1 and does not contain some material that is in Q1. The Folio text of *Othello* contains sequences and language that are not in Q1, but it also lacks material that is in Q1. All these five texts are thus manifestly unstable at source; each play exists in more than one state or condition. Moreover, the fact of the variant states of these texts places in question the nature of those texts that exist in one state or condition only. What state of the play does each represent? What states of each play do we lack?

One cannot but be struck by two aspects of this review: first, the apparently arbitrary nature of the publication of the plays; second, the frequency of significant variation in texts of plays published more than once.

The former should not be a matter of surprise. Shakespeare was a working dramatist; performance was the primary medium for making his creations public. Moreover, he wrote within a culture in which plays, even tragedies, were not accepted as high art on a par with epic poetry or the works of the classical authors. The playhouses were centres of noble achievement but in a popular culture environment, and actors and playwrights did not command the dignity frequently claimed for and often ascribed to poets; it is not surprising that Jonson's bold act of publishing his collected plays, poems, and masques in 1616, the year of Shakespeare's death, under the title *Workes* drew mocking comment in his time. However, not only was there no high status attached to plays, but there was not a sufficiently demanding reading public for play texts to drive a publishing economy. Peter W. M. Blayney has pointed out that in the first decade of the seventeenth century on average fewer than six new plays were published each year, and that for the publisher there was little prospect of early profit from a first printing.[1] The hope of the publisher was that a play would be attractive to a reading public and would occasion a second printing, which would yield a substantial profit. Scholarship has frequently suggested that by withholding their plays from publication companies protected their performance rights, but it seems more likely that publishers were not enthusiastic about paying companies or playwrights for the right to publish their works. An absence of obvious profit to the publisher meant that the company would gain no great sum from the sale of its play (compared to the income from performance). Blayney suggests that the chief reason that companies wished to see their plays in print may have been publicity (pp. 396–9).

The second matter, the variation between printed texts, is a crucial issue for Shakespeare studies. What did the sixteenth- or seventeenth-century book buyer receive when he or she made a purchase? What do we read when we examine such texts? In the case of each quarto that I have recorded above, the title of the play is listed with some authenticating detail – one or all of the author's name, the name of the acting company that played the play, or the occasion of the play's performance. In the Folio's preliminaries John Heminge and Henry Condell protest the perfection of the texts that the Folio presents: in their letter 'To the great Variety of Readers' they state that the plays that have been previously published 'are now offer'd to your view cur'd, and perfect of their limbes', while those that appear for the first time are 'absolute in their numbers, as he [Shakespeare] conceived the[m]'. However impressive these statements may be, examination of the texts suggests that Heminge and Condell were engaged in hyperbolic praise of the book's contents and that the plays are manifestly not perfect. Apparent imperfections in the texts and variants from earlier published states, for instance, provoke scholars to try to discover more about the sources of what was printed, and specifically what may be known about the origins of the copy from which the compositors set the text. If Q1 *Lear*, the 'True Chronicle Historie of ... King Lear and his three Daughters', and F1 *Lear*, 'The Tragedie of King Lear', disagree in numerous ways, what is each? Where does each come from? In what sense is each or either *King Lear*? In what sense is there a single play called *King Lear*?

Textual scholars desire to understand what state or condition of a play its printing represents; by examining its features they attempt to establish the relation of the text to its authorial origins. In the absence of surviving examples of annotated printers' copy for a play, and with a limited number of extant playbooks or manuscript copies of plays to serve as guides, scholars work within a set of descriptive categories that are based on hypotheses about how plays were composed, what copies were made, and what materials were sent to printing houses. The conventional narrative distinguishes five basic forms of 'copy', the materials from which compositors set a play into type: (i) foul papers, authorial draft materials not in a finished state; (ii) fair copy, the finished state of the author's composition, which may have become or from which a scrivener may have produced (iii) the prompt-book, or 'the book of the play', the manuscript in the playhouse which bore the signature of approval of the Master of the Revels that authorized stage performance; (iv) transcripts prepared from any of these sources; (v) copies of an earlier printing of the play, possibly corrected by reference to 'the book of the play', or subjected to revision by the author or some other hand[s].

Each kind of copy is conventionally identified by particular features. For instance, the particular traits that identify a work as printed from foul papers include an observed level of confusion or absence of clarity in the language of a text that may be the consequence of the difficulty in the printing house of reading the working draft of the author as he writes, corrects, crosses out, rewrites, and introduces new material. A lack of specificity in stage directions (*Enter Gloster brought in by two or three*, in Q1 *Lear*) is interpreted as evidence of the vagueness of the composing author. Another indicator of foul papers is the presence of variant speech headings for a single role; in Q2 *Romeo* Lady Capulet is designated in the speech headings variously as *Wife*, *Old La*, *La*, *Mo*, and *M* (the last two indicating 'Mother'). Yet another is the presence of the actor's name in the text; in Act 4 Scene 5 of *Romeo* a Q2 stage direction reads *Enter Will Kemp*, presumably in the role of Peter coming to address the Musicians (Q1 *Romeo* reads *Enter Seruingman*). Significance is attached to the presence of unusual spellings that resemble the idiosyncratic forms that appear in the Hand D section of *The Book of Sir Thomas More*, which has been identified by many as in Shakespeare's hand. This system of discrimination assumes that, by contrast, the practical demands of the playhouse would not tolerate such imperfection and inconsistency in the book of the play. The presence of stage directions indicating more specific actions is seen as evidence of playhouse origins of some kind; for instance, in F *Lear*, *Stocks brought out*, and *Alarum within. Enter with Drumme and Colours, Lear, Cordelia, and Souldiers, ouer the Stage, and Exeunt*, and *Exeunt with a dead March*. Scribal copying is detected from the presence of non-theatrical elements such as act-and-scene divisions, and also from the distinctive features of the work of a known scrivener. For instance, the habit of grouping the names of all characters in a scene at the beginning of the scene and also some punctuation habits, particularly the heavy use of parentheses, betray the hand of Ralph Crane in a number of texts of the First Folio.

A small but important group of texts does not conform readily to these categorizations, however. While the second quartos of *Romeo* and *Hamlet* correspond well to the model of foul papers origins, the first quarto of each play does not. In each case the first quarto prints a text that is significantly shorter than the second, is relatively of much poorer quality, and contains notable differences in major features of plot and action. They – along with five other texts in the Shakespeare canon – have become known as Bad Quartos, an unfortunately prejudicial term that was invented in 1909 by A. W. Pollard, who believed that they were unauthorized publications of 'pirated' texts.[2] Their textual origins have usually been identified in 'memorial reconstruction', the efforts of one or more actors to reproduce a text of the play as they had performed it without the aid of any authoritative document. However, although they have been dismissed as non-authoritative because of their reported (i.e., second-hand) nature, their stage directions have nevertheless been seen as preserving possible information about stage practice, since, it is presumed, the actors were recalling the details of their performance. For instance, where the Q2 stage direction for Juliet's entrance to her wedding reads *Enter Iuliet*, the Q1 stage direction reads *Enter Iuliet somewhat fast, and embraceth Romeo*. Similarly, when Ophelia enters mad for the first time, Q2 *Hamlet* reads simply *Enter Ophelia*, but Q1 reads *Enter Ofelia, playing on a Lute, and her haire downe singing*.

In recent years both the criteria for identifying the printers' copy of plays and the category of Bad Quartos have come under attack. Paul Werstine has subjected the narratives of textual transmission to a sceptical criticism. He has argued that in the absence of any surviving example of 'foul papers' the ability of scholars to identify a text's origins in such material depends on commitment to a system of hypotheses rather than on extrapolations from observed data.[3] William B. Long has pointed out that thorough examination of surviving playbooks indicates that they reveal no signs of the kinds of regularization and conformity in the service of clarity and efficiency that are the criteria for discriminating text of playhouse origin.[4] Randall McLeod has demonstrated that even prompt-books of twentieth-century productions do not conform to conventional expectations of playbooks; he has noted that they often confuse the name of the role with that of the actor of the role.[5] With regard to Bad Quartos, Peter W. M. Blayney has refuted a foundational aspect of Pollard's theory (1909) that stressed that they were unauthorized or 'piratical' printings (pp. 383–4). The work of Laurie E. Maguire and Paul Werstine has eroded the certainty of identifying their origins in memorial reconstruction; Werstine has shown that the evidence on which Q1 *Romeo* and Q1 *Hamlet* have been identified as memorially reconstructed and the roles of the reconstructing actors discerned does not hold up under examination.[6] These texts remain troublesomely idiosyncratic. Nevertheless, in the absence of any more persuasive or useful hypotheses, many textual critics and editors continue to discriminate between texts by using the traditional categories.

The aim of the conventional hypotheses has been to identify the qualities of the printed work and from the data to recreate the 'play', usually in the form of the ideal authorial original. However, while the grounds for discriminating the individual printed texts have been challenged, the concept of the authorial original has been subjected to scrutiny also, and in such a way that the idea of the author as the site of interest for the textual scholar has been questioned. Two separate approaches produce this particular disruption. The first involves attention to the prevalence in sixteenth- and seventeenth-century playhouse culture of authorial collaboration. Gerald Eades Bentley asserts that collaborative composition was common among professional dramatists; he records his 'reasonable ... guess that as many as half of the plays by professional dramatists in the period incorporated the writing of more than one man' and that 'nearly two-thirds' of the plays mentioned in *Henslowe's Diary* are the result of collaboration.[7] While no scholar explicitly advances the idea of identifiable collaboration in the composition of the tragedies beyond the presence of George Peele in *Titus* and Thomas Middleton in *Macbeth* and probably *Timon*,[8] Shakespeare's texts are nevertheless perceived by many as far more permeable than those of the conventionally conceived solitary author. With the loss of authorial sanctity the play text becomes an entity separate from the author, whose original production is no longer the object of pursuit. The second influential approach emphasizes that the very nature of a play as a theatrical form frustrates the idea of the defined single entity that can be realized by any kind of historical or archaeological investigation. In this way of thinking a play is an unfixed object always subject to change in performance and to modification over time in the playhouse. Accordingly, any scholarly approach that seeks to reproduce some text of original purity is not true to the historical and generic nature of the play: the play is always in flux and impure. What survive are just print manifestations of moments in the history of the play.

In such a context of destabilization not only are the principles of the establishment of the authorial text subject to rethinking, but new modes of presentation of whatever text is established are also entertained. Editing Shakespearean tragedy has always been a process of imposing order on the unruly or creating provisional truth in an environment of uncertainty. Editions have always varied in textual detail one from another, but recently the variation in presentation has become greater than in the past as editors grapple with questions of what they are to represent and how best to represent it. Most conventional editions still aim to reproduce as a reading text something that can be described as the 'ideal of the authorial fair copy'[9] with a critical apparatus that records the choices made. The Riverside edition, for instance, is of this kind, even conservatively preserving some unusual spellings within its general modernization and marking significant editorial interventions with brackets. By contrast, the Oxford *Complete Works* has as its objective the recreation of the text as it existed in the playhouse as the foundation of performance. Since its editors believe that the revision of *King Lear* produced two distinct performance versions of the play, the Oxford is notable as the first collected edition to publish two separate reading texts of *King Lear* printed sequentially as *The History of King Lear* and *The Tragedy of King Lear*. The Oxford texts are printed without textual apparatus, although a full discussion of the textual situation is to be found in the separately published *Textual Companion*. The New Cambridge Shakespeare presents another approach, publishing both conventional critical editions of the plays and a complementary series of critical editions of 'The Early Quartos', including Q1 *Romeo*, Q1 *Hamlet*, Q1 *King Lear*, and Q1 *Othello*.[10] Some editions push beyond the conventional formats to draw attention to the textual history and the editor's practice. In the Arden 3 series of individual texts of plays some editors meet editorial challenges with arresting graphics. The edition of *Titus* prints the fly-scene (3.2) in a distinctive sanserif type that contrasts with the serif type used for the rest of the text, thus drawing attention to its F-only status. The edition of *Lear* presents only a single conflated text, but material that is exclusive to either Q1 or F is clearly identified by parenthetical superscripts of the appropriate letter.[11] It is not evident that any of these editions has abandoned the standard categories of the narrative of textual recension. However, in the New Folger Library Shakespeare series Barbara A. Mowat and Paul Werstine reject the standard narrative as insufficiently confirmed by evidence to be useful in identifying the source of the printer's copy for a text. Consequently they declare their ambition to present an edition of each play as a textual phenomenon, as manifested in one or more surviving printings and disengaged from the circumstances of its authorial origins.[12] They choose for their editions a format with markings designed to highlight their choices and introductions so that the constructedness of their work is always manifest. Such a reading text insists on its own provisionality; the editors seek to make the reader constantly aware of the unavoidable constitutive role of editorial activity that in most editions is only visible in the textual apparatus.

Other editions also seek to respond to the particularity of the material remains or to the perceived irreducibility of the phenomena to a single text. In their Shakespeare Originals series Graham Holderness, Bryan Loughrey, and Andrew Murphy present direct transcriptions of individual early printings, reducing editorial mediation to the minimum, and encouraging the reader's encounter with features of the 'unedited' text without engaging the costly process of photographic facsimile reproduction. In this context the problem presented by the two texts of *King Lear* has provoked instructive editorial design solutions. Michael Warren has produced parallel texts of Q and F in facsimile by cutting photographic images, thus retaining as far as possible the unedited features of the original print of both texts. René Weis has produced edited texts of both Q and F *Lear* and presented them in parallel format on facing pages. Stephen Orgel has edited each and presented them sequentially as in the manner of the Oxford *Complete Works* but with glossarial notes on the page. In *The Norton Shakespeare Based on the Oxford Edition* Stephen Greenblatt and his co-editors reprint the Q and F versions from the Oxford *Complete Works* on facing pages; a traditional Conflated Text succeeds them.[13]

Such variety is not a manifestation of prodigality or irresponsibility in scholarship. Rather it is an inventive response to current thinking about the nature of the historical remains, the purpose of editing, and the possibilities of the book format, albeit within the constraints of the economics of commercial publishing. An awareness of complexity and a scepticism about simple answers require that superficial representations of the phenomena be avoided, and the print medium be explored in imaginative ways.

Examples from four plays may illustrate the general issues that I have discussed above. Q1 *Lear* (1608) contains about 283 lines that are not present in F *Lear* (1623); F *Lear* contains about 100 lines that are not present in Q1 *Lear*; verbal variants between the two texts are numerous. There are two primary explanatory hypotheses for the variant states of the texts: first, that each is a degraded state of a lost complete original that contained all the mutually exclusive material; second, that each represents in some form a stage in the development or existence of the play. Texts that combine material from both printings, such as that in the Riverside edition, the Arden 3, or the Conflated Text in *The Norton Shakespeare*, represent the editorial consequences of the first mode of thinking. Dual text presentations, such as those of the Oxford *Complete Works* and that of Stephen Orgel, and parallel presentations, such as the editions by Warren and Weis and that in *The Norton Shakespeare*, reflect the second. The Folger edition represents an avoidance of choice in its resort to a concept of textuality. The New Cambridge Shakespeare series goes one step further by publishing separate editions entitled *The Tragedy of King Lear* (F) and *The First Quarto of King Lear* (Q).[14] To maintain the first position, which seeks to reconstruct the author's desired form of the play, one must assume that at any moment of disagreement between the texts one is correct and one incorrect, or alternatively that neither is correct. But that is not incontrovertibly the case with Q and F *King Lear*. If the two *Lear* texts are read with respect for their individual textual integrity it is possible to recognize that each has a characteristic dramaturgy and that each has the potential for the creation of a distinctive theatrical experience. Q1 is distinguished from F by the presence of the mock trial and Edgar's soliloquy in 3.6, the conversation of the two servants after the exit of Regan and Cornwall in 3.7, much of the conversation of Albany and Goneril in 4.2, the complete scene between Kent and the

Gentleman (normally numbered 4.3), and their further conversation at the end of 4.7. The presence or absence of these particular elements, which are only some of the most immediately conspicuous among many, affects aspects of stage action, characterization, and ultimately meaning in the literary or theatrical interpretation of each text. This will become evident from a discussion of two sequences in the last moments of each version of the play, occurring in both texts on the last printed page.

The death of Lear is portrayed in different ways in the two texts. All recent conflated editions of the play, assuming the inferior quality and greater corruption of the quarto text, reproduce in some form the Folio text of the event. Lear's last words are:

> And my poore Foole is hang'd: no, no, no life?
> Why should a Dog, a Horse, a Rat haue life,
> And thou no breath at all? Thou'lt come no more,
> Neuer, neuer, neuer, neuer, neuer.
> Pray you vndo this button. Thanke you Sir,
> Do you see this? Looke on her? Looke her lips,
> Looke there, looke there.   *He dies.*   (TLN 3277–83)[15]

In F and conflated editions the speech is succeeded by Edgar's 'He faints, my Lord, my Lord'. Kent then expresses his desire for release, 'Breake heart, I prythee breake'. But the quarto text presents a different sequence of events in relatively similar language. Lear's speech is shorter and in prose:

> And my poore foole is hangd, no, no life, why should a dog, a horse, a rat of life and thou no breath at all, O thou wilt come no more, neuer, neuer, neuer, pray you vndo this button, thanke you sir. O, o, o, o.   (L4r)

Here, after expressing his thanks, Lear does not draw the attention of others to Cordelia's lips, but instead utters a sigh or groan represented by 'O, o, o, o'. As in F, Edgar comments on the movement of Lear's fainting, but in Q Lear speaks again, uttering words that are ascribed in F to Kent: 'Breake hart, I prethe breake'. In this version Lear expresses his personal desire for his release and dies a willed death, not, as F may be interpreted as indicating, in some condition of happy illusion. These sequences present different scenarios for stage action; they permit different modes of interpretation of the characters' behaviour that are mutually exclusive; and they elicit possible different emotional and intellectual responses in readers and audiences to Lear's death.

The roles of Albany and Edgar are also affected by variation in a speech heading at the end of the play. In the familiar F reading that is customarily adopted by editors, Edgar speaks the last speech of the play:

The waight of this sad time we must obey,
Speake what we feele, not what we ought to say:
The oldest hath borne most, we that are yong,
Shall neuer see so much, nor liue so long.   (TLN 3298–301)

The quarto prints the same speech with only one minor variation in
punctuation, but it assigns the speech to *Duke*, that is Albany. The conclusions of the two texts are therefore different in a second respect; each
presents a different interpretive opportunity. In both texts Albany has just
invited Edgar and Kent to share Lear's kingdom: 'Friends of my soule, you
twaine,/Rule in this realme [Q: kingdome], and the gor'd state sustaine'
(TLN 3294–5); in both texts Kent declines the invitation. In F Edgar's
response to Albany's invitation to rule is oblique but presumably positive.
In Q, however, he is apparently unresponsive, and in the context of Albany's
final speech his silence suggests that he is not accepting the throne. The
quarto title page gives prominence to mentioning 'the vnfortunate life of
Edgar'; the conclusion of the Q text can be interpreted as related to that
statement. Although Edgar's life in the F text could be considered unfortu-
nate – he has undergone a severe test, lost his father, and fought his brother
to the death – it is not the epithet that seems appropriate to the man who
assumes the throne at the end of the play. The two endings are irreconcilable; scholars may argue that one or the other is corrupt, but that is a
judgement, not a necessary conclusion from the evidence. Each is justifiable
theatrically and intellectually. There are grounds for identifying more than
one text of a play called *King Lear*; *King Lear* is not a single stable entity.

   Othello also exists in two states, the quarto of 1622 and the Folio of 1623,
although the nature of the variance between the texts is different. The Folio
text is longer and fuller than the quarto text and so has been chosen usually
as the copy text for editions; there are numerous individual verbal variants
between the texts. One set of verbal variants is of particular interest, notably
oaths that are present in Q but not in F. For example, in Q the first line of the
play reads 'Tvsh, neuer tell me, I take it much vnkindly', but in F the initial
exclamation is missing; in the fourth line Iago says ''Sblood but you will not
hear me', whereas in F he says simply 'But you'l not heare me'. The presence
of such oaths in Q suggests that it derives from a manuscript that represents
a state of the play that dates from before 1606 when the Act to Restraine
Abuses of Players prohibited the uttering of oaths on the stage.[16] Their
absence from F indicates its later origin. However, Q is also notable for the
absence from it of several passages that are present in F, not least among
them Desdemona's Willow Song in 4.3, Emilia's justification of women's
sexual rights at the end of the same scene, and a number of other speeches of

Desdemona and Emilia in the fourth and fifth acts that appear to have serial interpretive connections. Nevill Coghill and E. A. J. Honigmann have both proposed that the interrelation of these passages suggests a systematic development and revision in the F text rather than corruption or cutting in Q, although Honigmann has recently withdrawn his support of this position.[17] Whatever the case, two distinct texts of the play exist. It is scholarly hypothesis that determines the constitution of one or two versions of *Othello* from this material, just as in the act of conflating to produce a single *Othello* it will be scholarly judgement that will select one or the other reading where there are verbal variants.

The textual condition of *Hamlet* is still more complicated because there are three texts, Q1 (1603), Q2 (1604/5), and F (1623). I shall ignore in this case the complex relation of Q2 and F, in which the familiar pattern of presence and absence in both texts and of local verbal variants is apparent, and focus instead on the relation of Q1, the 'Bad Quarto', to the term *Hamlet*. Because of the fullness and comparative goodness of the Q2 text, the edited text of *Hamlet* is usually based on Q2 with additions from F.[18] However, there exists, challengingly, Q1, a much shorter, verbally less felicitous text that is nevertheless ascribed to Shakespeare on the title page. As I have indicated earlier, the origin and status of 'Bad Quartos' are uncertain; nevertheless, whatever its origins, Q1 testifies to a version of the play different in kind from either Q2 or F. F may lack Hamlet's fourth-act soliloquy, 'How all occasions doe informe against me' (printed in Q2), and Q2 may lack the second-act conversations concerning Hamlet's perception of Denmark as a prison and the adult players' discomfiture at the hands of boys' companies, but Q1 contains a whole scene between Horatio and the Queen that has no equivalent in either Q2 or F, that is not manifestly non-Shakespearean, and that alters the interpretation of the Queen's role in the rest of the play: in it Horatio informs her of the King's conspiracy to have Hamlet killed in England. The scene cannot be easily dismissed except insofar as it is part of the derided Q1 and as it is irreconcilable with the rest of the Q2/F text; it is worth considering that the book purchaser of *Hamlet* in 1603 believed that it was part of *Hamlet*. Standard conflated editions of the play are created by ignoring the challenge to their constructed unity that Q1 presents; although editors may borrow stage directions from it as a text with its origins in performance, they do so only after assigning it a status inferior to the Q2 and F texts. The scene of the Queen and Horatio is rarely printed and seldom acknowledged (see figure 1).[19] It remains to assert that *Hamlet* is multiple, not a single fixed text.

By contrast with *Hamlet* there is only one text of *Macbeth*, so that no acts of comparison serve to complicate the identification of the work. However,

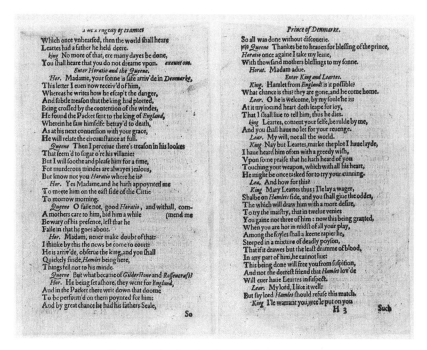

Figure 1. *Hamlet*, 1603 Quarto. Sigs. H2v–H3r.

the constitution of the work as Shakespearean is not simple. At two points in the Folio text the stage directions make reference to songs of which only a few words are supplied. In Act 3 Scene 5 F reads *Sing within. Come away, come away, &c.* In Act 4 Scene 1 a stage direction reads *Musicke and a Song. Blacke spirits &c.* Both appear to refer to songs by Thomas Middleton from his play *The Witch*. The date of composition of Middleton's play is unknown, though it is usually placed later than that of *Macbeth*. How these songs relate to the text of the play is not clear, since the references are very abbreviated.[20] However, it is noteworthy that the only source of information that establishes the foundation for a text of *Macbeth* manifestly contains non-Shakespearean elements. It is probable that there was a state of *Macbeth* that at some time did not contain the material derived from Middleton, but it is lost to us. Even though the text of *Macbeth* is single, the nature of what we know as *Macbeth* is not simple.

With the inclusion of the material from *The Witch*, the text of *Macbeth* appears to be associated with playhouse practice after initial composition; it may reflect what audiences saw at some time between 1606 and 1623. The record of performances of Shakespeare's tragedies before the closing of the theatres in 1642 is disappointingly slim. The title pages cited at the beginning of this essay provide information that may or may not be reliable about performances of *Titus, Romeo, Hamlet, Lear,* and *Othello,* or at least about the companies that performed them. There were three performances of *Titus* at the Rose playhouse and two at Newington Butts in 1594. A Swiss visitor to London, Thomas Platter, saw *Julius Caesar* at the Globe on 21 September 1599, and recorded that the actors performed a dance after the play; *Julius Caesar* was also played at court in the winter of 1612–13, at St James's Palace in 1637, and at the Cockpit in 1638. *Othello* was performed at court on 1 November 1604, at Oxford in September 1610 (Evans, *Riverside,* p. 1852), again at court in the winter of 1612–13, in 1629 at either the Globe or the Blackfriars, in 1635 at the Blackfriars, and in 1636 for the king and queen at Hampton Court. *Hamlet* was played twice on shipboard off Sierra Leone on 5 September 1607, and 31 March 1608, and at Hampton Court in 1637. A provincial company in Yorkshire performed *King Lear* in 1610 (Halio, *Tragedy,* p. 34). There are no surviving references to performances of *Antony and Cleopatra, Coriolanus,* or *Timon of Athens.* Few reports give insight into the nature of performances. A member of the audience for *Othello* in Oxford in 1610 described in a letter the moving quality of the actor playing Desdemona dead (Evans, *Riverside,* p. 1852), and the astrologer and alchemist Simon Forman recorded in his *Book of Plaies* his recollections of a performance of *Macbeth* at the Globe on 20 April 1611; he describes the Witches as 'women feiries or Nimphes'.[21] But what exactly was played on any occasion – the relation between the published text and the performance – is not known. If from the remark of the Chorus in the opening speech of *Romeo and Juliet* that he introduces 'the two houres trafficque of our Stage' (Q2) one is tempted to generalize the conventional length of presentation, then no audience can have seen all of Q2 or F *Hamlet,* both plays well in excess of 3,500 lines. Texts that editors have identified as of playhouse origins do not indicate how the play may have been played. Stephen Orgel suggests that the play performed was always shorter than the written text.[22] William B. Long (p. 116) has suggested that playbooks that do not provide adequate guides to playing by modern standards were nevertheless sufficient to the needs of the actors who knew how to use them, to play their contents. We have to conceive of a creative environment markedly different from our own.[23]

The desire of textual and historical scholarship is for certainty, but in contemplating the text of Shakespearean tragedies scholars work with a perplexing body of relatively fragmentary information, and generalizing narratives are frequently perilous; in regard to performance the information is extremely limited. The forms in which we conventionally read the plays may enable acts of interpretation, but it is imperative that we acknowledge the provisional and constructed nature of those forms.

Notes

1. Peter W. M. Blayney, 'The Publication of Playbooks', *A New History of Early English Drama*, ed. John D. Cox and David Scott Kastan (New York: Columbia University Press, 1997), p. 385.
2. Alfred W. Pollard, *Shakespeare Folios and Quartos: A Study in the Bibliography of Shakespeare's Plays, 1594–1685* (London: Methuen, 1909).
3. Paul Werstine, 'Narratives about Printed Shakespeare Texts: "Foul Papers" and "Bad" Quartos', *Shakespeare Quarterly* 41 (1990): 67–86; and 'Plays in Manuscript', *A New History of Early English Drama*, ed. Cox and Kastan, pp. 481–97.
4. William B. Long, '"A Bed/for Woodstock": a Warning for the Unwary', *Medieval and Renaissance Drama in England* 2 (1985): 91–118.
5. Randall McLeod, 'The Psychopathology of Everyday Art', *The Elizabethan Theatre IX*, ed. G. R. Hibbard (Port Credit, Ontario: P. D. Meany, 1986), pp. 100–68.
6. Laurie E. Maguire, *Shakespearean Suspect Texts* (Cambridge University Press, 1996); Paul Werstine, 'A Century of "Bad" Shakespeare Quartos', *Shakespeare Quarterly* 50 (1999): 310–33.
7. Gerald Eades Bentley, *The Profession of Dramatist in Shakespeare's Time* (Princeton University Press, 1971), p. 199; see also Jeffrey Masten, 'Playwrighting: Authorship and Collaboration', *A New History of Early English Drama*, ed. Cox and Kastan, pp. 357–82.
8. See Brian Vickers, *Shakespeare, Co-Author* (Oxford University Press, 2002).
9. Fredson Bowers describes the process of editing as the application of critical principles 'to the textual raw material of the authoritative preserved documents in order to approach as nearly as may be to the ideal of the authorial fair copy by whatever necessary process of recovery, independent emendation, or conflation of authorities', *Textual and Literary Criticism* (Cambridge University Press, 1966), p. 120.
10. *The Riverside Shakespeare*, general and textual editor G. Blakemore Evans with the assistance of J. J. M. Tobin (Boston: Houghton Mifflin, 1997); *The Complete Works*, gen. eds. Stanley Wells and Gary Taylor (Oxford: Clarendon Press, 1986), pp. 1025–98; Stanley Wells and Gary Taylor with John Jowett and William Montgomery, *William Shakespeare: A Textual Companion* (Oxford: Clarendon Press, 1987; rpt with corrections, New York: W. W. Norton, 1997); *The First Quarto of Romeo and Juliet*, ed. Lukas Erne (Cambridge University Press, 2007); *The First Quarto of Hamlet*, ed. Kathleen O. Irace (Cambridge University Press, 1998); *The First Quarto of King Lear*, ed.

Jay L. Halio (Cambridge University Press, 1994); *The First Quarto of Othello*, ed. Scott McMillin (Cambridge University Press, 2001).

11. *Titus Andronicus*, ed. Jonathan Bate (London: Routledge, 1995); *King Lear*, ed. R. A. Foakes (London: Thomas Nelson, 1997).

12. Barbara A. Mowat and Paul Werstine, 'An Introduction to This Text', *Hamlet* (New York: Washington Square Press, 1992), p. xlix.

13. *The Parallel 'King Lear' 1608–1623*, prepared by Michael Warren (Berkeley: University of California Press, 1989); *'King Lear': A Parallel Text Edition*, ed. René Weis (London: Longman, 1993); *'King Lear': The 1608 Quarto and 1623 Folio Texts*, ed. Stephen Orgel (New York: Penguin Putnam, 2000); *The Norton Shakespeare Based on the Oxford Edition*, ed. Stephen Greenblatt, Walter Cohen, Jean E. Howard and Katharine Eisaman Maus (New York: W. W. Norton, 1997), pp. 2307–553.

14. *King Lear*, ed. Barbara A. Mowat and Paul Werstine (New York: Washington Square Press, 1993); *The Tragedy of King Lear*, ed. Jay L. Halio (Cambridge University Press, 1992); *The First Quarto of King Lear*, ed. Jay L. Halio (Cambridge University Press, 1994).

15. TLN (Through Line Numbers) is the system developed by Charlton Hinman in *The Norton Facsimile: The First Folio of Shakespeare* (New York: W. W. Norton, 1968) to designate locations within individual Folio plays by line of type (spoken text or stage direction).

16. E. K. Chambers, *William Shakespeare: A Study of Facts and Problems*, 2 vols. (Oxford: Clarendon Press, 1930), I. 98–9.

17. Nevill Coghill, *Shakespeare's Professional Skills* (Cambridge University Press, 1964), pp. 164–202; E. A. J. Honigmann, 'Shakespeare's Revised Plays: *King Lear* and *Othello*', *The Library*, 6th ser., 4 (1982): 142–73; Honigmann expresses his doubts about the evidence for revision in *The Texts of 'Othello' and Shakespearian Revision* (London: Routledge, 1996), pp. 7–21.

18. The Oxford *Complete Works* prints a text based on F, printing the Q2-only material as 'Additional Passages'; in the Oxford Shakespeare *Hamlet*, ed. G. R. Hibbard (Oxford University Press, 1987), that material appears in Appendix A, 'Passages Peculiar to the Second Quarto'. Although based on the Oxford edition, *The Norton Shakespeare* reintroduces the passages into the body of the text but in italics.

19. The scene may also be located in *The Tragicall Historie of Hamlet Prince of Denmarke*, ed. Graham Holderness and Bryan Loughrey (Hemel Hempstead: Harvester Wheatsheaf, 1992); *The First Quarto of Hamlet*, ed. Kathleen O. Irace (Cambridge University Press, 1998); *The Three-Text Hamlet: Parallel Texts of the First and Second Quartos and First Folio*, ed. Paul Bertram and Bernice W. Kliman, second edition, revised and enlarged (New York: AMS Press, 2003); and the Arden 3 *Hamlet*, ed. Ann Thompson and Neil Taylor (London: Thomson, 2006), which is made up of two volumes, *Hamlet*, an edition of Q2, and *Hamlet: The Texts of 1603 and 1623*, editions of Q1 and F.

20. For a full discussion see A. R. Braunmuller, 'Thomas Middleton's Contribution to the Folio', in his edition of *Macbeth* (Cambridge University

Press, 1997), pp. 255–9; see also Inga-Stina Ewbank, 'Introduction' to *The Tragedy of Macbeth* in Thomas Middleton, *The Collected Works*, gen. eds. Gary Taylor and John Lavagnino (Oxford: Clarendon Press, 2006), pp. 1165–69.

21. All information about performances derives (unless otherwise stated) from Chambers, *William Shakespeare*, II. 303–53.

22. Stephen Orgel, 'The Authentic Shakespeare', *Representations* 21 (1988): 97.

23. See Simon Palfrey and Tiffany Stern, *Shakespeare In Parts* (Oxford University Press, 2007).

CHAPTER 5

Religion and Shakespearean tragedy

Claire McEachern

'Religion' and 'Shakespearean tragedy' are a nettlesome pair. Shakespeare's culture was both in ideology and in daily practices a Christian one, to a degree that can be difficult for us to imagine. Religion provided the languages of state and self, of family and nature, and described the relations between all of these domains. God's words in scripture told the story of how and why the world came to be and man's and woman's role within it, of good and evil, of why things happen and for what reason, of how we matter; it gave an account of human history and an anticipation of its future. Church bells organized the day into parts as the liturgical calendar did a given year. The first book most children learned to read (Shakespeare probably included) was the state-prescribed *Primer*, which packaged between its covers the ABCs, a Latin grammar, the catechism and a selection of prayers and psalms cued to the official state liturgy as specified in the *Book of Common Prayer*. In fact, we largely owe our notion of 'culture', i.e., a set of communal practices and understandings, to the sixteenth-century English church: the preface to the *Book of Common Prayer* asserted that 'where heretofore there hath been great diversity in saying and singing in churches within this realm, some following Salisbury use, some Hereford use, some the use of Bangor, some of York, and some of Lincoln, now from henceforth all the whole realm shall have but one use'.[1] From henceforth (or so the plan went), the entire realm would worship in one tongue, according to one script, at one time and in church. Attendance would be taken. It is not that every aspect of Tudor–Stuart culture was determined by religion, or that English persons in Shakespeare's day were on balance holier than we. The habit of imagining our ancestors as more credulous than urbane present-day persons is itself a legacy of Protestant Christianity, and rumours of the demise of religion in our post-modern world have been greatly exaggerated. Shakespeare's England did not resemble modern fundamentalist theocracies. But nor were the soul and other private domains entirely beyond official concern. It may well have been the case that a greater proportion of the population took the afterlife into regular consideration, and certain, given that church attendance was compulsory, that they were exhorted to.

Religion was thus a primary language through which Shakespeare's culture thought about itself, and religious vocabularies, images, stories and character types abound in Shakespeare's plays. At the same time, its very atmospheric quality can make the effects of religion difficult to pinpoint, in literature or in life. This difficulty notwithstanding, what early modern persons may well have understood far better than ourselves is what distances could exist between their theoretical and practical versions of community. What Shakespeare understood better than most is how fragile such visions of community and harmony could be. His tragedies explore what happens when social bonds fail us – when 'love cools, friendship falls off, brothers divide; in cities mutinies. In countries, discords, in palaces treason' (*King Lear*, 1.2.105–8).

This is not to say that the relations between Shakespeare's tragedies and religious discourse were straightforward ones. Precedents certainly exist, in the history of Western drama, of tragic drama working in tandem with supernatural systems of thought. Religious ritual possesses a theatrical dimension, and tales of human haplessness and the powerful emotions they solicit can be useful to metaphysical understandings. Wonder, awe, pity and terror (the latter pair Aristotle's terms for the tragic response) are common reactions to the contemplation of supernatural power and the reach of divinity relative to our own. Scholars of the earliest Western drama argue that plays served in the ancient world in some capacity to religious observances, such as the celebrations in fifth-century Athens consecrated to Dionysus. Hymns to that deity and his kin can be found, for instance, in the texts of Sophocles.

As we will see, the relationship of sixteenth-century English Christianity and the public professional theatre was considerably fraught, in no small part due to the contention that beset sixteenth-century English Christianity. But at a general conceptual level there is certainly some agreement between tragic norms and Christian ones. Genre is itself an important component of Christian thought. The founding story of Christianity begins with a – *the* – Fall, in which humans wittingly flout a law laid down by a generous Creator and incur the penalty (death). The grief of this lamentable episode is compounded by the doleful ways in which the consequences of their act resound throughout human history, impacting the entire species in a way that seems virtually genetic, and which include an inability to avoid repeating the initial error, let alone the power to repair it. The ensuingly and decidedly mixed quality of life on earth is a central tenet of Christian thought, which holds all earthly existence to be impoverished in comparison to the promised delights of salvation after death. As an expression of how forces larger than oneself and events occurring before birth impact one's choices and conspire to mock a sense of personal sovereignty, the concept of original sin is an elegant Judaeo-Christian version of sentiments also found, for instance, in Sophocles's *Oedipus Rex*. When preachers explained such suffering as divinely motivated – for instance, as a lesson meant punish or purify – it could serve as a reminder of why fear or at least deep respect should obtain in one's relation to God.

However, unlike classical understandings of divinity, which distribute various supernatural powers amongst a variety of gods, or even a Jewish one, which emphasizes the aspect of a single God as a lawgiver, Christian theology insists upon the dual nature of a single divinity. The Christian God is both just *and* benevolent – not just great but good. As in Judaism, the faithful are urged to fear and obey that deity as one might a stern parent, but they are also urged to love Him as a loving and gracious parent, one who understands how difficult such obedience can be, and has, mercifully, sought to mitigate the penalties of disobedience. This mercy operates chiefly through the compensatory promise of a heavenly afterlife made possible through God's sacrifice of His own child to earthly suffering in payment for sins not his own (a transaction which gives justice its due, but lends human beings divine assistance in order to satisfy the logic of sacrifice). The hope of this afterlife is meant to inspire an ethics of conduct guided, as in Judaism, by the Ten Commandments, but further shaped by the example and teachings of Christ, as recorded by his earliest disciples in the New Testament. The latter can be summarized under the heading of *caritas*: the love of others more than oneself, even if (as in Christ's instance) at the expense of oneself. Avoidance of self takes various forms: eschewing interpersonal rivalry and tribal allegiance in favour of less parochial bonds; forgiveness of injury; compassion for the sufferings of others; the denial of bodily appetites and attachments to worldly goods and goals. Tudor–Stuart propaganda considered charity 'the knot of all Christian society'.[2]

Not only awe but adoration are appropriate responses to a deity such as this. However, the Janus-faced notion of the deity as not only just but loving meant early modern Christianity approached instances of human misery very carefully indeed. Take, for example, the notion of original sin itself, the woeful and far-reaching consequences for the entire species of the actions of two (in John Milton's term) 'Grand Parents'. The notion of

disobedience punishable by death possesses a logical force, and tallies with
the notion of God as righteous. However, as an instance of judgement it can
also seem grossly disproportionate and even inaccurate, the paradigmatic
case of one bad apple unfairly spoiling the entire basket. (The adjective
'original', in fact, only works as a description of historical priority, as the
description of the first sin in which all subsequent sin originates; as for the
other sense, the burden of such a sin is that none of us are originals.)
Christian theology thus takes care to describe human misery as a result of
human error rather than divine wrath; indeed, it sources suffering's allevia-
tion to the generosity of divine grace, by which light even suffering serves
our ultimate good. Preachers of Shakespeare's day insisted on the miserable
and sinful quality of human existence, but always as contrasted with the
bountiful generosity of God and the future delights of heaven awaiting the
faithful.

'Christian tragedy' is thus in many respects an oxymoron. The *Commedia*
of the fourteenth-century Italian author Dante is termed so not because it is
funny but because the Christian understanding of existence is profoundly
providential, which is to say ordered by a beneficent God. Shakespeare's
comedies, notwithstanding their portraits of humans driven by base desires
and intent on earthly happiness, are perhaps the more theologically correct
precisely because of the reliance of comic harmonies on fortuitous coincidence. For in a universe governed by divine providence, all tragedy is
perforce local: temporary, temporal and, however sad for the individual in
question, sad only when – erroneously – considered in isolation from
eternal measures. (Most tragedies are, in fact, about isolation in its various
forms.) However, when viewed according to a cosmological perspective,
justice *will* be done – even if its accomplishment must await the Last
Judgement and the end of life on earth. Sooner or (more likely) later,
good is rewarded and evil punished. There is nothing tragic about the
long view.

Shakespeare's literary predecessors of the fourteenth and fifteenth centuries generally embrace this order of priorities. For instance, the medieval
storytelling tradition called *de casibus* tragedy, or 'the Fall of Princes', offered
stories of fortune's favourites inevitably brought low, usually due to their
confidence in the transient temporal blessings rather than eternal ones. Such
tales demonstrated the precariousness of earthly joys and urged the reader to
seek after the less instant but more permanent gratifications to be had by
following Christ's example. Similarly, the English 'cycle' plays – which, like
ancient Greek drama, were mounted under the aegis of official religious and
civic purposes – urge on a heavenly perspective upon human existence,

particularly in their formal architecture. Constructed of a series of individual plays based on key incidents of scripture organized chronologically, the narrative arc of the entire pageant encompasses a period stretching from the beginning to the end of human time, Creation to the Last Judgement (the Latin word for human time was 'saeculum', the root for our word 'secular'). Some plays address instances of terrible loss, most notably the Passion of Christ. But located as individual episodes always are within the larger 'cycle' of all human history, God's greater plan contextualizes them within a cosmic story whose ending is ultimately happy, and in which poetic justice is amply served; as such, there are no real tragedies, only optical illusions of tragedy that result from a myopic human emphasis on exclusively human measures of value. In Shakespeare's England, competing strains of Christianity differed in their understandings of what relationship existed between life on earth and life hereafter: whether, as some Catholics held, one's actions were a partial *cause* of arriving in heaven or hell, or rather, according to Calvinist Protestants, merely an *effect* of a destiny predetermined by God, sign and harbinger only. But all brands of Christianity were united in agreeing that, when considered in light of the entire story, life on earth is merely prologue, not the main event.

Shakespeare's tragedies, however, derive their power from the insistence that human life and loss command our attention in themselves. Divine perspectives do receive acknowledgement. Hamlet might, at the penultimate moment of his story, claim that divinity is in the details: 'there is special providence in the fall of a sparrow' (5.2.197–8). His friend Horatio hopes that 'flights of angels sing thee to thy rest' (5.2.343) – even though Hamlet himself imagines the afterlife as 'that undiscovered country, from whose bourn no traveler returns' (3.1.79–80). Macbeth, also nearing his conclusion, arrives at a world-weariness that belies his former ambition: 'Out, out, brief candle / Life's but a walking shadow, a poor player / That struts and frets his hour upon the stage / And then is heard no more' (5.4.23–6). As the metaphor suggests, the experience of watching a play can offer us a God's-eye view upon characters and their conflicts. This perspective can provide a certain protection, a certain ironic 'Lord, what fools these mortals be' distance upon human foibles (*A Midsummer Night's Dream*, 3.2.121). But the latter purchase is often a prerogative of comedy alone; for when watching a tragedy, our greater knowledge is often a source of intense and often painful involvement. That Emilia gave her husband the handkerchief; that Claudius did indeed murder his brother; that blind Gloucester is unwittingly led by the very son whose forgiveness he craves; that Juliet is not really dead: when we watch a tragedy, these facts matter intensely to us, as do the characters to whose fortunes they are pertinent. No matter how doctrinaire or frequent the passing mentions of a heavenly perspective on our lives might be in a Shakespearean tragedy, their power consists in commanding our concern for the here and now of human existence. The emotions they engender can beggar the powers of any consolation; we feel not just pity and terror at an object lesson in human impotence, but pity and charity, a compassionate bond with characters less condescending than it is loyal, an alliance as fellow humans ranged together against the forces greater than ourselves. If we manage, with their heroes, to renounce the world's 'uses', as 'weary, stale, flat and unprofitable' (*Hamlet* 1.2.133), it is not by dint of hoping for a better world, but because we have believed to the point of exhaustion in our own.

There are many different reasons for Shakespeare's striking departure from both Christian orthodoxy and native literary tradition. They include the dialogic nature of drama: in non-dramatic genres such as lyric poetry or a sermon, the charge of tragic tales can be managed by the narrative voice pointing a moral before and aft. Writers of plays, however, construct staged stories by bringing variety of perspectives into dialogue with each other, so that it often can be difficult to choose between them. Drama is not necessarily without the means to provide a celestial perspective (witness the design of the cycle plays), and in Shakespeare's tragedies the devices of an epilogue, or a chorus, or a character's speech can supply a moral gloss upon events. *King Lear*'s Edgar, for instance, describes his adulterous father's blinding with 'the Gods are just, and of our pleasant vices,/Make instruments to plague us' (5.3.172–3). But such homiletic statements risk sounding platitudinous, sanctimonious, or (at best) inadequate to the horrors they address; the overall experience of watching *King Lear* tends to lead one to suppose that the gods are otherwise occupied than with seeing justice, let alone mercy, done on earth. Certainly Edgar's words are peculiarly judgemental, and not necessarily delivered by an actor without irony. But even gentler words intended to soothe – Cordelia's heartbreaking balm 'No cause, no cause' (4.7.78) – are by their very nature and form less arresting than the spectacular calamities to which they respond. The frame is rarely as memorable as the picture it contains.

Another influence upon the focus of Shakespeare's tragedies on mortal rather than celestial measures of mattering lies in the sixteenth-century rediscovery of classical thought: the intellectual movement termed 'humanism'. This excavation and circulation of the literature of charismatic alien cultures, particularly one possessed of the enviable political success of imperial Rome, provided dramatists with rich new veins of story. The ancient world was not without its own metaphysical vision of daunting divinity, and one that also premised a bipartite afterlife (albeit with locations less strikingly opposite than Heaven or Hell: the Elysian fields, for exceptional heroes, and the more nebulous Hades for everyone else). Certain norms of classical ethical philosophy tallied with Christian ones: Stoicism, for instance, also viewed passion askance. However, the emphasis of the classical world-view on temporal values such as family honour and civic identity caught the attention of Renaissance thinkers, Shakespeare among them. A play such as *Titus Andronicus* demonstrates the catastrophic effect of fanatical allegiance to earthly bonds, and yet seemingly makes no apology for the satisfactions to be derived from defending them; hot or cold, revenge is a dish worth serving. Brutus's dark night, in *Julius Caesar*, concerns not his own soul but his country's: 'Shall Rome stand under one man's awe?' (2.1.52). Antony and Cleopatra may shake off political ambition as so much pettiness, but their heaven consists not in a renunciation but an embrace of erotic love: 'I am again for Cydnus,/To meet Mark Antony' (5.2.229–30). Shakespeare asks us to consider such characters not as benighted pagans who have their priorities mixed up, but people who find uniquely human concerns matters worth fighting and dying for.

The greatest contribution to an imaginative investment in human mattering may have come from the pressures brought to bear upon human–divine relations by the nature of Tudor–Stuart Christianity itself. Many longstanding questions of Christian theology were revisited in Shakespeare's England: why would a God both good and great permit suffering or evil?; what kind of relationship obtains between earthly experience and quality of afterlife?; what is the degree of God's involvement in our lives? In order to understand the relation of religion to Shakespeare's tragedies, we must take time to consider the momentous and contentious sixteenth-century transformation of Christianity known as the Reformation.

Any institution of 1,500 years' duration is subject to vicissitudes and variegation along the way (Byzantine vs. Western?; Ockamist vs. Thomist?; Benedictines vs. Franciscans?). The ninety-five theses nailed by the German cleric Martin Luther to a church door in Wittenberg in 1517 were by no means wholly unanticipated by earlier critics of the Roman Catholic church. The fifteenth century had witnessed movements advocating translation of Latin scripture into vernacular tongues, and satire of clerical greed and hypocrisy permeates Chaucer's *Canterbury Tales*. But the differences sowed by Luther did not remain, as it were, in-house. A variety of political, cultural and technological conditions made this the case, but it is also true that the comprehensiveness of Luther's critiques and his theological care taken to support them may well have made them harder to absorb or silence than earlier complaints.

Luther's objections touched on a host of practices and understandings (not least concerning 'the host' itself). Their initial target was the fiscal practice by which clerical officials were permitted to sell pardons or 'indulgences' for remittance from the eternal wages of sin in exchange for contributions of one's worldly goods to church coffers. This traffic in forgiveness relied on two assumptions, one cosmological and one theological. The former was the existence of Purgatory, an intermediate way-station or anteroom in the afterlife for those persons not good enough to go straight to Heaven but not bad enough for Hell. Its climate was thought to be similar to Hell's (Hamlet's father's ghost speaks of 'flaming fire' in which the 'foul crimes done in my days of nature/Are purged and burnt away' (1.5.4–6)). But time spent there was limited, and could be shortened by performing good deeds, or, for those with ready money, outsourcing them to the church through the purchase of indulgences, or masses or prayers, either paid for in advance of death or by one's family after it.

The theological premise that underwrote the sale of pardons was the notion that human actions ('works') could help to merit salvation. Luther shored up his critique of institutions by the theological masterstroke of claiming that salvation was, on the contrary, available only through divine gift, or grace, and experienced by faith alone ('*sola fida*'), unmediated by human guesses about divine purposes. Important corollaries of this understanding emphasized by later thinkers such as the French reformer Jean Calvin were that (1) salvation was thus not only in God's gift, but possibly determined before a given life was lived, perhaps even at the time of Creation itself; (2) faith is primarily an interior, affective experience, an encounter of a soul with God mediated solely by scripture; and (3) with the abolition of middle men went the abolition of middle ground and middle time, meaning the soul would arrive at its ultimate destination effectively immediately upon death. A given person might feel these changes as either a cause for relief or anxiety, but either way they made the question of salvation considerably more urgent than it had been in a Catholic dispensation, as well as perhaps more, or at least differently, suspenseful – instead of wondering whether death might unpleasantly catch you in arrears, it became a dénouement, a recognition scene where one would confirm one's true identity. English Protestants such as William Perkins, whose writings began to appear in the years Shakespeare's own career took flight, insisted that it was possible to obtain assurance of salvation during one's lifetime – were one diligent enough to examine the evidence of one's thoughts and feelings (and always humble enough to realize assurance was not absolute certainty). This was an intellectual and emotional labour signally different from the Catholic practice of striving to accumulate enough good deeds to offset one's sins. Detecting God's intentions towards oneself paradoxically meant that human thought and action were rendered experiences of enigma and scrutiny, whose meanings were to be parsed and weighed. The emphasis on self-examination can be felt in Shakespeare's tragedies by the weight given to the formal feature of soliloquy.

Luther's censure of human determinations of divine dispensations came to comprehend all manner of Roman Catholic religious practices: not only the sale of indulgences came under attack, but also the practices of pilgrimage and the celebration of shrines, the sale of talismanic relics meant to offer spiritual protection (e.g. the bones of martyr saints, or pieces of the true cross upon Christ was crucified), the use of religious art objects to inspire worship, the number of sacraments (those rituals marking special stages in a Christian's life) and even the understanding of the Eucharist, the central act of the Christian Mass. According to Roman Catholic theology, bread and wine were converted miraculously into the body and blood of Christ by the priest's Latin prayer; according to Protestants, the ceremony was a symbolic transaction, a re-enactment and commemoration of the Last Supper that signified the effects of grace. Protestants lumped all their opponents' practices together as means of duping a gullible soul into a superstitious reliance upon false forms of salvation and their predatory clerical purveyors – a hocus pocus song and dance of the seven veils performed by the Whore of Babylon meant to separate souls from their money, and worse, their true salvation.

'Idolatry' in particular, or the worship of an image of God rather than God Himself (reminiscent of the golden calf that had prompted God to issue his commandments), became a kind of blanket charge levied by Protestantism upon its opponents. The sights, sounds and smells of Roman Catholic ritual were described as appealing to the 'carnal imagination' via the ports of the senses, and preying upon the abject human desire for some tangible protection against the wages of sin. Protestants characterized their own practices, by contrast, as attending to the interior spiritual life, as a search for the feelings of grace and sinfulness guided by God's word, modelled after those of the earliest Christian church, now re-formed, cleansed of a millennium of accreted practices whose purpose had been to augment the power of the 'Bishop of Rome'. Scripture is of course itself replete with verbal imagery, whose function Reformers understood as

serving to translate abstract truths into the sensory terms more amenable to
fallen human understanding. Speech acts such as blessings, prayers and
oaths possess a magic of their own. The Protestant understanding of the
Eucharist as a historical re-enactment is in one respect even more theatrical
than the Catholic one – in effect, an Elizabethan history play *avant la lettre*.
Certainly such distinctions depend largely on nuance, entailing not so much
a revolution in what kinds of actions are performed upon an altar but a
change in how those actions are understood – one that may well be lost
upon an observer. But unlike visual aids like a statue or a relic, Protestants
considered the images in God's word less likely to deceive a reader or auditor
into taking them for the thing itself, and hence more likely to refer thought
heavenwards. Some scholars have argued that Shakespeare's metadramatic
emphasis on the nature of his representations as mere 'shadows' incorpo-
rates this Protestant aesthestic sensibility.[3]

Reformation controversy was thus to a great extent not only an image war
but a war about images: what they were and what they did. It was a war with
consequences for the public professional theatre in general and tragedy in
particular. Not the least of the consequences for the latter must have been
the spectacle of intense social and political conflict between and within
countries, communities and even families. Religion was the greatest source
of social tension in early modern England. In the two decades prior to
Shakespeare's birth, England experienced four changes of monarch and
three of religion; he was thus born into a country whose brand of
Christianity was of recent vintage and, for all anyone knew, tenuous
purchase, the cause of internal domestic tensions of a kind that led elsewhere in Europe to armed combat, and rendered England vulnerable to the
threats of Catholic superpowers on a regular basis.[4]

The most obvious ramifications of the Reformation for theatre in general
were simply legal ones that impacted the conditions and subjects of theatrical activity. Among the first acts of Elizabeth I in the year of her accession to
the throne (1558) was to outlaw the cycle plays, on the grounds that the
staged representations of scriptural events and the human impersonation of
holy personages, God most of all, constituted a violation of the scriptural
prohibition against 'graven images'. There was, however, no real pressure to
enforce the law until 1569/70 (and some performances survived into the
1600s), and much to the chagrin of the more strident preachers, Tudor–
Stuart governments made their peace with the emergent public professional
theatre. It could not have helped that the government was willing enough to
license public playing while prohibiting public debates of the meanings of
scripture. But those preachers had their revenge, and among the first acts of

the 'Puritan' government in the English Republic in the 1640s was to close the theatres – although, as David Kastan has argued, 'it is too simple to see this as the triumph of a precise puritanism over those who still enjoyed their cakes and ale'.[5]

During the near century between the opening and closing of the public theatre, censorship laws prohibited the playacting of what seems (to us) the most obvious religious content, such as doctrinal controversy, but also the less so: oaths, or religious ceremonies such as the marriage service or prayers. It would be decades after 1558 before preachers aimed the anti-idolatry rhetoric at theatre; this is partly because it would be a decade before there even was a professional theatre (the Red Lion opened in 1567), and longer still before it was successful enough to attract concerted animus. But preachers seized opportunities to describe plague or earthquakes as divine punishment for all things theatrical, and warned that actions on a stage would be re-enacted by a populace in their own lives.

Of course, there was plenty for a pious Christian not to like about the public theatre in and of itself: purveyor of tales of sex and violence; occasions for boys playing the parts of women; of commoners dressing up in the clothes of their betters and audiences mingling them; prostitutes soliciting audience members; apprentices shirking work to go to a play. Much of this may equally have also applied to the performance of the cycle plays, but the public theatres lacked even the ostensible virtue of educating the populace in scripture, precisely due to the religiously based prohibition against it (a case of God closing a door only to open a floodgate). Theatre's sardonic portraits of religious zeal and hypocrisy seem to indicate the contempt was mutual: Jonson's Zeal-of-the-Land-Busy and Shakespeare's Malvolio come to mind. We should be wary of extrapolating the opinions of all Reformers from the caricatures of an often sensational polemic. However, if you asked any contemporary what divines thought of plays, or players divines, the likeliest answer would be, not much.

Taking their cue from this antipathy, some modern scholars have in fact argued that the public theatre harnessed the thwarted energies of medieval cycle drama – the script may have changed, but the show went on – much as the cult of Elizabeth I as the Virgin Queen is thought to have repurposed devotional energies previously dedicated to the Virgin Mary.[6] In fact, Protestants and players (like Protestants and Catholics) may have had more in common than not, their antipathy sprung from the narcissism of small differences. Preachers consulted rhetorical handbooks in order to craft persuasive oratory, and plays were often penned by men university-trained as preachers but who chose to instead make their way in the word world of the theatre. Churches and theatres were the two kinds of architectural structures capable of containing large public assemblies, and both competed of a weekend for audiences, rivals for the imaginative energies of their audiences. While Tudor–Stuart plays, unlike sermons, lacked official imprimatur as a site for moral inquiry, both offered solace and terror, and stirring words to live and die by, with the difference that theatre possessed the additional resource (or special effects) of visual images, and the gratifications offered by even a generous two-hours' traffic on a stage were far more immediate than those that awaited in heaven (all advantages one might well begrudge were, one a preacher).[7] Thus religious animus against theatre may have had to do with the way the imaginative experience of playgoers resembled the habits of the faithful; antipathies ran high not because church and theatre offered alternative forms of imaginative engagement, but the same kind.

Certainly preachers and players shared conceptual fascinations. For instance, a central preoccupation of religious debate over what constituted a meretricious visual display was the relation between appearances and intentions, sincerity and insincerity, surface and substances. Debates over what kind of sights, sounds and gestures best shaped the soul drove doctrinal controversies from the 1570s onwards, as the contrast between the true church and the false one once drawn in terms of England vs. Rome became internal to the English church and ultimately the person (saved or damned?). They concerned issues such as how ornate clerical vestments should be (costume), whether congregants should kneel (gesture), where an altar rail should be located and whether there should be rood screens (the wooden barrier that separated clergy from lay persons in a medieval church – scenery). The greatest contest of all focused on script: whether or not the preacher should follow the state-sanctioned liturgy as laid out in the *Book of Common Prayer*, and read government-approved sermons from the *Book of Homilies*, or improvise as the spirit moved. The premise of the *Book of Common Prayer* is that the terms of common worship will shape souls amenable to communal harmony (or at least the appearance of it, good enough for government work). But it was this very premise that provoked widespread debate about the nature and purpose of religious behaviour. Proponents of the former position presumed the communal performance of unanimity and deference would work to shape pious thought and conduct; advocates of the latter considered such regulation-issue scripts yet another kind of screen behind which a sinner could hide, far less likely to penetrate to the soul than inspired preaching, for 'reading is not feeding, but it is as evil as playing upon a stage'.[8]

As the metaphor suggests, these are profoundly theatrical questions: what can a person infer from the speech and actions of another? How do we detect hypocrisy? What kinds of tokens of behaviour or feeling can we trust? How do you know – can you know? – whether someone loves you? How do you know yourself? What happens when we make mistakes about those significations, or when someone mistakes our own intentions? How do we build human community on such shifting sands of trust?

While confusion stemming from such mistakes can make for delightful comedy, they may matter even more fundamentally to tragedy. Othello's miseries, for instance, derive in large part from his reliance on Iago's self-professed power to interpret Venetian actions and intentions: 'I know our country disposition well: / In Venice they do let God see the pranks / they do not show their husbands' (3.3.201–3). This dependency could be attributed to Othello's cultural difference were it not that every other character in the play also believes Iago 'honest' – a fact in stark and distressing discrepancy with our own hard knowledge to the contrary. Othello demands evidence of Desdemona's infidelity: 'Villain, be sure thou prove my love a whore! / Be sure of it; give me the ocular proof' (3.3. 359–60), but the ease with which Iago is able to construe tokens such as the handkerchief, or his conversation with Cassio about Bianca, or the false report of Cassio's dream, so as to fuel Othello's suspicions, reveal the latter's faith in such signs to be grossly misplaced (the tragedy consists in the fact that you can never prove someone loves you, only that they don't).

In one light, Shakespeare seems to be offering a Reformation-style critique of the human dependence on tangible external evidence as opposed to interior conviction: even at his most confident, Othello's love is mediated: 'She loved me for the dangers I had pass'd, / And I loved her that she did pity them' (1.3.166–7). But as the play proceeds, we ourselves become desperately focused on the progress of the handkerchief; while we may well suspect that a despair as readily triggered as Othello's and an innocence as wilful as Desdemona's are beyond cure, the handkerchief nevertheless seems the sole means of proving Iago a liar, and this task alone still matters when all else is lost. The emotional and cognitive effect upon us of the latter half of the play comes from our being unsure how or when information about the hand-kerchief ought to be deployed, even as we are increasingly sure it must above all be carefully and precisely deployed. Hence Emilia's coming to 'acknown' what we know she knows becomes the focus of our desires, something we can hold on to and will not let drop. What she knows makes no difference to the play's outcome: it will not save Desdemona or reform Othello, and may well not serve to convict Iago once returned to Venice. It certainly won't solve the problem of evil. But it nonetheless matters intensely to us that she know it, and her final disclosure is the sole tangible proof of human (not divine) goodness and efficacy the play affords: 'I peace? / No I will speak as liberal as the north. / Let heaven and men and devils, let them all, / All, all cry shame against me, yet I'll speak' (5.2.218–22).

In some respects Othello, like many of Shakespeare's tragic heroes, can seem to undergo, in the difficulty of knowing the love of a woman, the difficulty of knowing whether God has chosen someone for salvation; the vicissitudes of humans attempting to believe they are loved or loveable mimic those that attended the inquiry into election. Shakespeare's tragic protagonists are generally men in the throes of a crisis of belief (to be or not to be? Does she or doesn't she? Is this a dagger or isn't it?). This susceptibility to crisis seems a rather gendered condition: men are the believers, women, for the most part, those believed in. But while most tragic protagonists express disappointments in the cosmos in terms of female infidelity, this is not a problem that afflicts erotic partners only; the precipitating calamities of *King Lear* are the inabilities of not just one but two fathers to acknowledge the love of their children. Tragic worlds are those where people are unable or unwilling to know each other, and perhaps even themselves. Iago confesses multiple times to his own motives, but each explanation revises its predecessor; when Othello asks what could possibly have motivated such malevolence – 'Will you, I pray, demand that demi-devil / Why he hath thus ensnared my soul and body?' – Iago's retort returns him to the proven deficiencies of his own knowledge capacities: 'What you know, you know' (5.2.301–3). Hamlet's Denmark is a world of spies and pretence, where Polonius urges his son 'This above all, to thine own self be true' after he has just told him to dissemble every aspect of his being (1.3.77). There are occasions during a play when we ourselves seem to have relatively more purchase on the events and characters: we know, unlike Hamlet, that (as Reformers foretold) while Claudius may go through the motions of penitence these have no effect upon his feelings: 'My words fly up, my thoughts remain below' (3.4.97). But usually what we know serves only to distress us, reminding us that even as advantageously placed as we are we must bow to the same epistemological difficulties that beset our characters, and know that what knowledge we have ourselves gleaned from 'the trappings and the suits of woe' may be just as partial or inaccurate as any belonging to a character within a play world (*Hamlet*, 1.2.86). Nor can it answer all the questions we have (e.g., *why* does Emilia give her mistress's handkerchief to a husband she knows to be 'wayward'?). Even the most confessional of Shakespeare's heroes raises more questions than he answers:

why is Hamlet so scrupulous in determining the ghost's credibility?; is he really mad or feigning it?; did he really love Ophelia (though if so, why be so cruel to her – unless it is to be kind)?; and why does his mother's marriage bother him so?

While much Reformation religious conflict focused on the questions of what symbolic practices best cultivated a godly soul, it was driven by deeply theological differences of opinion concerning the nature of salvation itself – *was it even possible to cultivate a godly soul?* Theories of salvation abounded. Was salvation something one could earn during one's lifetime, as Catholics thought? Or was it, as Calvin insisted, predestined by God, perhaps even before Creation of the world? If the latter, what role remained for the individual, besides waiting and hoping for the dénouement of death? Could one collaborate with the divine plan even just a little bit, or was one meant merely to stand by and watch one's own behaviour to see whether it indicated whether one might be saved or damned (and if so, how was one meant to judge the evidence of earthly fortunes: as a preview of coming events, or a contrast to it)? Could a person even *mean* to do anything, if actions were not a cause of salvation, but an effect of divine decree, in which case what was the point of humans having actions or intentions at all? If God had decided your fate, what difference did it make whether you sinned or not? Worst of all, what if you weren't saved, but doomed from before your birth to suffer the fires of hell, no matter how hard you tried to be good? And what kind of God damns the majority of his creation?[9]

These are discomfiting questions. Theologians struggled to find answers compatible with the notion of a loving God, but doing so could require a rather gymnastic turn of mind and inevitably required entertaining quite disturbing imaginative possibilities about the relation of God to evil; the government indeed recommended that such matters were best left to experts or avoided altogether: 'For curious and carnal persons, lacking the Spirit of Christ, to have continually before their eyes the sentence of God's predestination, is a most dangerous downfall, whereby the Devil may thrust them either into desperation, or into a recklessness of most unclean living, no less perilous than desperation.'[10] It is in posing such questions that Reformation religion could be said not merely to have influenced Shakespearean tragedy but to have virtually *caused* it.

Their thematic influence is everywhere. *Hamlet* poses the most obvious address: a prince of a philosophical bent is charged, by an apparition claiming to be the ghost of his father, with a brutal hands-on and soul-imperilling task highly unsuited to his talents. It is of neither his own devising nor inclination, but merely assigned to him by virtue of his birth, like original sin itself, 'so oft it chances in particular men/That for some vicious mole of nature in them / As in their birth, wherein they are not guilty, / Since nature can not choose his origin' (1.4.23–6). It is the kind of task whose execution will require of him both conviction and passion, but one that pits political against metaphysical concerns, family honour and masculine purpose against the prohibition against murder, which in this case is both regicide and a kind of parricide. Such conflicts vex purposeful-ness, at least for the thinking man. He must undertake this act of revenge in a dangerous political milieu where a person's very survival requires dissem-bling, where the actions and intentions of others are inscrutable, and where parents seek to control their children even from beyond the grave, where survival allows scant room for luxuries like love or even thought. Hamlet's ethical sensibility marks him out from his kind but also disables him for political action (neither Laertes nor Fortinbras scruples to avenge his father). We can find ourselves impatient with what seems like his inability to act, yet conscious that self-reflection upon the predicaments into which we are placed may be our only *raison d'être*, the only form of human mattering that remains to us.

Macbeth also poses the question of whether our desires are relevant to our destiny. Three witches greet a renowned warrior and leader of men with news of a fate that promises the fulfilment of his political ambition and talents. (It is a signature trait of Shakespeare's heroes that their God-given talents are almost always double-edged, both their saving grace and their undoing: Othello's imagination, Hamlet's introspection, Lear's imperious-ness. This is a Sophoclean irony, but also a Christian one.) Like Hamlet, Macbeth is honest enough to realize the supernatural message uncannily focuses his own thoughts and self-interest, and hence prompted to wonder whether the visions he has seen are demonic or heavenly in origin – indeed, whether his ambitions can even be called his own. A loyal and accom-plished subject, he recognizes that achieving his desire will require violating ethical codes he has long honoured: 'this Duncan / Hath borne his faculties so meet, hath been / so clear in his office, that his virtues / Will plead like angels, trumpet tongued against / The deep damnation of his taking off' (1.7.16–20). He has no illusions about the nature of deed or the effects on his identity: 'I have bought / Golden opinions from all sorts of people/Which would be worn now in their newest gloss, / Not cast aside so soon . . . I dare do all that may become a man' (1.7.32–47). Like the witches, however, his wife voices the other side of the argument that bedevils him: 'What beast was't then / That made you break this enterprise to me? / When you durst do it, then you were a man; / And to be more than what you were, you would / Be so much more the man' (1.7.47–51). While in becoming king he largely seems persuaded by the voices of others, and compliant to his apparent fate, his own initiative and determination come to the fore in striving to stay king, a struggle against the remainder of the witches' prediction that his sovereignty (like anyone's) will be limited to the term of his own life.

The play's equivocal representation of Macbeth as alternately pawn and master of his fate paints a portrait of evil's corrosive effects, but it also raises a disturbing question: if a human being is damned, why must he be forced to endure the further insult of a conscience? If he has indeed been marked out by a supreme being for regicide, a monster among men, why has he also been, superfluously, endowed with the capability to understand his evil but not to resist it? What is life like for the chaff of history, those persons who serve as mere grist for a greater good (in this case, the lineage of kingship leading to James I)? Is his ability to discern good from evil a dram of grace ignored by Macbeth, or a gratuitous cruelty on God's part? What kind of power do we possess to be good, or bad, in a world where all our conclusions are written for us? To complicate matters further, Macbeth possesses an ethical sensibility (and command of poetry) more nuanced and brave than any other character in his world. We can find ourselves disconcertingly in the position of silently urging him on in his terrible goals, feeling compassion and admiration for a man trapped, like any of us, in a divinely wrought web.

Finding a home for our sympathies in *King Lear* is a more difficult task. The king himself is a difficult man to defend. Even for those of us with only a passing notion of kingdoms, dividing one seems untoward if not outright imprudent. Lear's violent rejection of what literary convention tells us must be his good child and his stalwart counsellor verges on the tyrannical, even allowing for the latitude we afford title characters, majesty or the respect due to age. While even in Act 1 we sense Goneril and Regan are not to be trusted, it is difficult given the evidence before us to dispute their assessment of Lear's 'grossly' 'poor judgement', and it may well be likely that 'he hath ever but slenderly known himself' (1.1.90–3). It is not necessarily clear that his knights aren't indeed as unruly as his temper, and his curses of his daughters are virulently immoderate. The other father on display, for his part, is a self-professed adulterer and (given what we may know of all literary bastards) an easy gull.

It is not long before pity for these two overcomes our distaste – Lear's self-righteousness, unlike Goneril and Regan's, is at least intermittent and not without irony. Self-recognition comes early, and simply: 'I did her wrong'

(1.5.23). While not one for sustained public introspection, Lear is not, it seems, without the ability to know himself or others, no matter how unpleasant the knowledge. As the play grinds on, his abdication can seem in retrospect less rash than the attempt of a man to strip himself of worldly comforts, valiantly (albeit hubristically) trying to meet death without flinching, but then forced, like some still-breathing version of the ghost of Hamlet's father, to experience his own irrelevance.

Our sympathies for such figures notwithstanding, the competition for our loyalties in this play is between degrees of sinners and the lesser of evils: we must choose between the imprudent and the indecent. And while evil may well be cartoonish, that is no impediment to its success. Indeed, the efforts of the 'less evil' characters appear overweening and self-regarding (Edgar's) or belated (Albany's) or well-intentioned but misguided (Kent's) – but with the exception of Cordelia and Cornwall's nameless servant, to call them good may be going too far. Even the scruples that lead Cordelia to refuse to stand on ceremony can seem, given what havoc they unleash, like another kind of ostentation. Cordelia is made of sterner stuff than Desdemona, Ophelia, or even Lady Macbeth (good requires more courage than evil), but she remains subject to the tragic law by which the good die first; such deaths would seem to figure the expiatory logic of the crucifixion, were they not so utterly without reason or redeeming value. Unlike the vaguely pre-Christian universe in which the play is set, Christianity insists on the loving-kindness of its own deity, and the necessity (if impossibility) of emulating divine charity in human society; *King Lear* would be an unbearable play, even an unbelievable one, were there no Cordelia. But it is precisely because such visions are dangled before us that having them snatched away pains so intensely.

With most of Shakespeare's plays, we know what to wish for on behalf of the characters: that they achieve their heart's desire. Tragedy, admittedly, can complicate this longing: sometimes, as with Macbeth, their desires are bad ones (although Shakespeare's nuanced representation of ethics coupled with our intellectual craving for the completion of an action can cover a multitude of sins). But with *King Lear* it is hard to know what to long for, apart from a general convention at Dover (but then what?). Do we want, as Kent seems to, Lear back on his throne, or at least in possession of the military force that seems necessary to secure an old man some kindness? That the bad guys receive their comeuppance - a desire for vengeance not much different from their own? By the play's end, Shakespeare has us longing for the mercy of death purely for its virtue as a cessation of mortal being. Kent's desire for a recognition scene with his master, or Edgar's insistence on the orchestration of his father's despair and his brother's shame, seem puny human fussings over a world they think important, when we know Lear's existence prolonged, were it in heaven itself, would be cruelty.

My focus here on *Macbeth, King Lear, Hamlet* and *Othello* is not meant to indicate that religion is not a factor in other of Shakespeare's tragedies. Issues of knowledge and knowing, or providence, for instance, pervade all his plays. It is, however, their handling in the tragedies that has earned Shakespeare a critical opinion as the heroic progenitor of scepticism, a scepticism that will flower in the Enlightenment and result in his plays' own eventual enshrinement as the scripture of secular humanism (the belief that humane values can be anchored in non-transcendent terms, leading the same social estate that once debated how many angels could dance on the head of a pin to now devote the same energies to literary criticism). This reputation may owe no small debt to secular humanism's amnesia about its own debt to Christian norms and practices; the habit of turning to a text to underwrite the tenets of human experience was invented by Protestant exegetes, and Protestantism originated in scepticism about belief practices. Shakespeare was (and remains) a Christian writer, but the nature of his relation to Christianity can be difficult to grasp, both because of the degree to which his plays are saturated by Christian thought, and also because of the degree to which post-modern culture continues to be informed by Christianity. We can all agree that Shakespeare thought *with* Christianity; but what did he think *of* Christianity?

Scholarship that does enquire into the plays' religious dimensions has in recent years tended to pursue the question of confessional allegiance, searching his plays for clues to particular doctrinal opinions and Shakespeare's opinions of those opinions.[11] These efforts are fuelled and stymied by Shakespeare's discretion on matters confessional; friars abound in Shakespeare's plays, as one might expect given their frequent Italian and medieval English settings. But like all other characters they appear in both complimentary and unflattering lights. The foundational critic of the tragedies, A. C. Bradley, interpreted this ecumenism to mean that religion per se was incidental to Shakespeare's process, and that 'the Elizabethan drama was almost wholly secular; and while Shakespeare was writing he practically confined his view to the world of non-theological observation and thought'.[12] Such an absence of opinion is not true of other writers in this period, such as Herbert or Milton, or even those like Donne or Jonson who made their change from one brand of Christianity to another a matter of record. Shakespeare's discretion has been read as ecumenism or agnosticism or even recusant-like discretion: did the man who wrote with seeming sympathy of 'bare ruined choirs' (Sonnet 73) and exposed the psychic costs of predestined existence dissent from the state religion? Or did he revel in the possibilities for personal enquiry and the English language that Protestantism ushered into existence? These enigmas notwithstanding, Shakespeare's plays, in their vocabulary, plot structures and imagery engage more visibly with religious questions than his contemporaries' do – Marlowe's *Dr Faustus* alone excepted.

This is a debate that will no doubt prove as eternal as the truths religion espouses. That we would consider evidence of a given brand of Christianity evidence of religion per se is in part due to the partisanal habits of the Reformation. Explanations for Shakespeare's circumspection range from elusiveness to indifference to religion's ultimate irrelevance: it could be due to that equivocation shapes drama; or due to the fact that the businessman Shakespeare, ever-conscious of the legal constraints governing theatrical performance and profits, was prudently avoiding controversy. Perhaps if he was an advocate of the 'old' religion, he disguised his opinions as deep as any priest hole. Perhaps scholars, in attending to the most vocal members of the early modern population, have overestimated the difference between confessions as well as the extent to which regular folk took religion itself to heart.[13] Or perhaps the reason it can be difficult to identify religious concerns is that the kind of questions that fall under the heading of 'religion' in this period are inseparable from all storytelling, whose concerns include the nature of human actions and ethics; how to live and how to die.

Notes

1. *The Book of Common Prayer*, 1559, ed. John E. Booty (Washington, DC: Folger Books), p. 16.
2. *Documents of the English Reformation*, ed. Gerald Bray (Minneapolis: Fortress Press, 1994), p. 345.
3. See Huston Diehl, *Staging Reform, Reforming the State: Protestantism and Popular Theater in Early Modern Drama* (Ithaca, NY: Cornell University Press, 1997).
4. For an interpretation of the social costs of the Reformation rather than its triumphs, see Eamon Duffy, *The Stripping of the Altars: Traditional Religion in England, 1400–1580* (New Haven, CT: Yale University Press, 1992).
5. David Kastan, *Shakespeare After Theory* (London: Routledge, 1999), p. 200.
6. See Michael O' Connell, *The Idolatrous Eye: Iconoclasm and Theater in Early Modern England* (Oxford University Press, 2000).
7. See Jeff Knapp, *Shakespeare's Tribe: Church, Nation and Theater in Shakespeare's England* (University of Chicago Press, 2002).

8. *Puritan Manifestos*, ed. Frere and Douglas (London: SPCK, 1954), p. 22. On this point see Ramie Targoff, *Common Prayer: The Language of Public Devotion* (University of Chicago Press, 2001).

9. See, for instance, Martha Tucker Rozett, *The Doctrine of Election and the Emergence of Elizabethan Tragedy* (Princeton University Press, 1984), and Peter Kaufmann, *Prayer, Despair, and Drama* (Bloomington: University of Illinois Press, 1996).

10. *Documents of the English Reformation*, ed. Bray, p. 295.

11. See, for example, Richard Dutton, Alison Gail Findlay and Richard L. Wilson, eds., *Lancastrian Shakespeare: Region, Religion and Patronage* (Manchester University Press, 2004).

12. A. C. Bradley, *Shakespearean Tragedy: Hamlet, Othello, King Lear, Macbeth* (London: Macmillan, 1960), p. 25.

13. For this interpretation see Christopher Haigh, *The Plain-Man's Pathway: Kinds of Christianity in Post-Reformation England, 1570–1640* (Oxford University Press, 2007).

CHAPTER 6

Tragedy and political authority

Michael Hattaway

Shakespeare's tragedies are usually remembered for the central characters for whom they are named. However, the fact that all of their heroes are what Renaissance writers called 'princes', occupying the power centres of their realms, means that these narratives of usurpation and death are also anatomies of political crises. In setting out contexts for his tales of woe or wonder Shakespeare reveals himself to have been as curious about the make-up of courts and kingdoms as he was about the psychology of individuals. The sufferings of great men and women in Shakespearean tragedy derive from conflicts, the analysis of which inevitably entails a consideration of 'the properties of government'[1] – its characteristics and its proprieties. In 1589, at about the time Shakespeare was beginning to write, George Puttenham observed that 'poets ... were the first lawmakers to the people, and the first politicians, devising all expedient means for th'establishment of commonwealth'.[2] Although in his tragedies Shakespeare may concentrate far more on rulers than on the ruled, 'commonwealth' interests are inevitably invoked by the fact that any act on the part of a king is *de facto* what, in *Hamlet*, Claudius terms 'sovereign process' (4.3.65).

This theatrical scrutiny of sovereignty and rule, also practised by contemporaries like Kyd, Marlowe, Chapman, and Jonson, discomforted court, church, and City. In the context of the century of political division engendered by religious difference that followed the Reformation of Henry VIII, 'matters ... unfit and undecent ... handled in plays', including 'both Divinity and State', were, according to the Privy Council, likely to be incitements to rebellion and therefore of concern to both magistrates and ministers.[3] Likewise, in the City of London, the Common Council was vexed by playhouse 'examples or doings of ... unchastity, sedition, [and] suchlike unfit and uncomely matter'.[4] Almost all of Shakespeare's tragedies have central characters who take arms against legitimate or established rulers. So although the actions of the plays were historically remote, the appointment of officers to 'allow' texts before they were performed as well as conventions of theatrical representation – performances were in 'modern' dress – reveal that performances and publication of tragedies were regularly construed as potentially seditious interventions in the political life of the nation.[5]

The very fact of placing a tragic action at court was, because of the particular decorum of English tragedy, likely to demystify the authority of prince and courtiers. Tragedies of the English Renaissance, unlike most from continental Europe, mingle kings and clowns, and comic scenes in the tragedies provide not just comic relief but occasions for popular voices to baffle or scoff at their 'betters'. The Clown's jokes about deflated bagpipes in *Othello* (3.1) hint at the windiness of the rhetoric of the grandees of Venice. When the Gravedigger hands Hamlet the skull of a nameless courtier, he reflects that it is 'now my Lady Worm's, chopless, and knocked about the mazard [head] with a sexton's spade. Here's fine revolution', he continues, 'and we had the trick to see't' (5.1.75–6). (This is one of the first uses of the word 'revolution' to designate the overthrow of a political regime.) Moreover, David Scott Kastan's argument about the oppositional nature of playing the king in a history play holds true for a tragedy: 'Whatever their overt ideological content, history plays inevitably, if unconsciously, weakened the structure of authority: on stage the king became a subject – the subject of the author's imaginings and the subject of the attention and judgement of an audience of subjects.'

We might segue from Kastan's formulation to note that the author's heroes, particularly if they are racked by ambition as is Macbeth, often themselves realize that their particular imaginings have failed to create an 'ethically adequate object'.[6] These are likely to overwhelm any moral obligation towards what was often invoked as 'the commonweal'. Macbeth suppresses his image of King Duncan who, even in his own mind, possesses mystical virtues that '. . . , plead like angels against / The deep damnation of his taking-off' (*Macbeth*, 1.7.19–20). In the play's 'English' scene, Macbeth's antagonist Malcolm, in a kind of moral symmetry, fears that he will be unable to withstand his own lurid imaginings, of sexual depravity, 'staunchless avarice', and a wanton desire to 'Pour the sweet milk of concord into hell' (*Macbeth*, 4.3.78 & 98). Bullingbrook, at the beginning and end of *Richard II*, is revealed as a man who professes a concern for the commonwealth but who exposes flashes of ambition to seize the throne and, probably, then kill the king.[7]

Robert Weimann has argued that theatrical representation is a symptom of a long-running post-Reformation 'crisis of authority'.[8] Even if, as we watch the regime changes at the end of *Titus Andronicus, Hamlet,* or *Macbeth,* some public calm or *moral* order is restored, the representation of 'carnal, bloody, and unnatural acts' (*Ham.* 5.2.360) is likely to have destabilized our confidence in the *social* order on which the new order is based. Torture might have been more acceptable as a political instrument or punishment than it is now, but audiences are scarcely invited to rejoice when Lodovico deputes Cassio, once more Governor of Cypress, to proceed to the torture of Iago at the end of *Othello*. This is state-sponsored revenge, and when, as is so often the case earlier in the action of these plays, individuals cannot find what is fair or just because the court, the fount of justice, is itself polluted, in pursuing revenge they are likely to achieve power but lose authority, become confused, crazed, even monstrous. Were revengers like Titus, Hamlet, or Edgar vindicating a public good or re-establishing their family honour? Two wrongs do not make a right.[9] The plays in which they play out their roles demonstrate that the morality of tyrannicide or revolution is seldom grounded entirely on the rights of the disempowered or oppressed.

In his own lifetime Shakespeare's tragedies were not set apart from other genres that opened more obviously on to political life: the categorization of texts by the editors of the Folio as comedies, histories, and tragedies raises critical and historical problems. The Roman plays, which portray historical figures and which are so obviously concerned with issues of power, author-ity, and empire, are placed among the tragedies. Conversely, the 'history' plays are often designated as 'tragedies' in their titles (or in their quarto versions), and they share as sources the chronicles of Hall and Holinshed with plays like *Macbeth* and *King Lear. King Lear* is designated as a history on the title page of its quarto version and as a tragedy in the Folio, and the full title of Shakespeare's most famous play in both its curtailed (Q1) and most extended form (Q2) is *The Tragical History of Hamlet*. Chains of causation that create tragedy in Shakespeare derive as much from situation – the feud in *Romeo and Juliet*, the unexpected love-test that goes wrong at the beginning of *King Lear* – as from what actors or readers deem to be the personality of the hero.[10] (A situation is often what is designated in the texts by 'fortune'.)

Shakespearean tragedy, moreover, is the tragedy of groups as much as of individuals. Conflicts of class or gender, contests between generations or within the family, unresolvable moral dilemmas, accidents (sometimes designated as 'fate') are as important to the unfolding of the tragic action as the consequence of the 'hero's' choice. This is what A. C. Bradley in 1904 described as 'action issuing from character' – a notion that encapsulated

Romantic readings of the plays and set a restricting critical agenda centred around accounts of the 'characters' (in the sense of 'personalities') of Shakespeare's tragic heroes that endured for about eighty years.[11] Confronted with momentous events often magnified by supernatural portents, caught up in political change, or immersed, as most of them are, in rites of passage that mark a change in the nature of the self, it is just as likely that characters in tragedy will act 'uncharacteristically' as 'characteristically'. The fact that tragedies may derive from uncharacteristic actions on the part of their protagonists is what sets them apart from moral fables where 'good' but 'flawed' individuals come to just but unhappy ends.

In his studies of the degradation of powerful men and women Shakespeare inevitably engaged not only with morality but also with the nature of political power and authority. Nearly all early modern discussions of these topics refer to the famous assertion of St Paul that secular power derives from divine authority: 'Let every soul [person] be subject unto the higher powers; for there is no power but of God, and the powers that be are ordained of God' (Romans 13:1 [Geneva version]). That text stands not just as an 'idea' that individuals could choose to believe or disbelieve but as an ideological instrument: it is glossed in the Geneva Bible (1560) as '*The obedience to the rulers*' and in the Authorised Version (1611) as '*Subjection, and many other duties we owe to the magistrates* [those in authority]'. The passage was useful to princes who could claim that any attack on their person was a violation of a divinely sanctioned order. The homily or official sermon 'Against Disobedience and Wilful Rebellion' which, after the Northern Rebellion of 1569 and a Papal Bull of 1570 that excommunicated Elizabeth and absolved her subjects from allegiance,[12] was added to the collection of homilies issued in the reign of Edward VI, argued that rebellion was 'an abominable sin against God and man'. Moreover, given that the person of the monarch was held to be a manifestation of the timeless spiritual body of the kingdom (see below), any attack on the monarch could be construed, as the homily indicates, as an attack on the nation: 'the wrath of God is kindled and inflamed against all rebels, and . . . horrible plagues, punishments, and deaths, and finally eternal damnation . . . hang over their heads'.[13] We hear of prodigious disasters from the Old Man in *Macbeth* (2.4). Regicide was akin to deicide: both crimes were essentially different from homicide. In *Hamlet* Claudius argues that divine authority even offers protection to the monarch:

> What is the cause, Laertes,
> That thy rebellion looks so giant-like? –
> Let him go, Gertrude. Do not fear our person.

> There's such divinity doth hedge a king
> That Treason can but peep to what it would,
> Acts little of his will.   (4.5.120–5)

However, towards the beginning of the sixteenth century, political historians, most famously Niccolò Machiavelli, had begun to anatomize the
constitution of the states of Europe and Asia, past and present, and
showed that authority derived not from God but from the constitution
of the state as well as from the means whereby a monarch had obtained the
crown. The power of a consul holding office for only one year in the
Roman republic was different in nature from that of a king who reigned
for life, and the authority of a ruler who had seized power by force was
different from that of a prince who had inherited authority upon the death
of a relative. Pragmatic comparisons between different political systems
revealed that authority might be secular rather than divine in origin. A
prince, as Machiavelli pointed out, had to create an image for himself,
take care about the ways in which he was perceived by his subjects. Even if
he could not have the wisdom of a fox and the boldness of a lion he should
imitate those who did:

> It is not . . . necessary for a prince to have . . . the above named qualities, but
> it is very necessary to seem to have them. I would even be bold to say that to
> possess them and always to observe them is dangerous, but to appear to
> possess them is useful. Thus it is well to seem merciful, faithful, humane,
> sincere, religious, and also to be so; but you must have the mind so disposed
> that when it is needful to be otherwise you may be able to change to the
> opposite qualities.[14]

We can see why Hamlet inveighs against 'seeming' and why the Player King
is not just a strolling actor but also a figure for all those with authority in
Denmark. Moreover the roles politicians had to assume in order to protect
their standing could take over their 'selves'. Richard III recognized this
when, at the end of the play, he found his self-fashioned fictive self had
taken over his essential or 'natural' self:

> What? Do I fear my self? There's none else by.
> Richard loves Richard, that is I am I.   (*R3* 5.3.185–6)

Hamlet's 'antic disposition' (1.5.172) not only provided in feigned madness a
fool's cover for the truth-telling of a malcontent but also created out of a
sweet prince something of a monster, careless of the lives of those about
him. ('Antic' in the period had connotations of grotesquerie and monstros-
ity as well as of clownage, and could designate figures that were half-man
and half-beast.)

Moreover, if a prince did not reign by the consent of his or her subjects, it was apparent that might was a more necessary adjunct for rule than right. Alternatively it could be expedient to derive authority from *ragione di stato* or political necessity rather than from moral legitimacy. This kind of political analysis seemed dangerous, and the word 'politician', newly imported from France according to Puttenham, rapidly acquired a pejorative meaning.[15] In the gravedigger scene Hamlet reflects over another skull: 'This might be the pate of a politician ... one that would circumvent God, might it not?' (5.1.66–7). So it may not be surprising that, in *Julius Caesar*, Cassius, although convinced that the cause of the state and specifically the freedom of the Roman citizenry is threatened by the quasi-divinity of Julius Caesar, feels it necessary to legitimate his insurrection by drawing the noble Brutus into his conspiracy.

Materialist and 'Machiavellian' analyses of power gradually came to stand alongside those that pronounced it divine in origin. In a work that used to be ascribed to Sir Walter Ralegh, a certain T.B., in *Observations Political and Civil*, described 'authority' as 'a certain reverend impression in the mind of subjects and others touching the prince's virtue and government. It resteth chiefly in admiration and fear ... [Authority] is reinforced and enlarged by power, without which no prince can either defend his own or take from others ... Power and strength is attained unto by these five ways, viz., money, arms, counsel, friends, and fortune.'[16] This makes no reference to a divine origin for power and matches the radical claim made at the beginning of *1 Henry VI* when a messenger points out that English misfortunes in battles against the French derive not from the moral sin of treachery, which would conventionally provoke condign punishment from God, but from 'want of men and money'.[17]

Now the endings of *Hamlet*, *Macbeth*, *King Lear*, and, eventually, *Romeo and Juliet* turn in part on the outcome not only of battles but also of duels or judicial combats. A duel was a species of trial, a demonstration that a claim to honour was authentic or divinely ordained. It could also destabilize the authority of the king, since duels operated by a code of honour that he might not be observing himself and sought a judgement that was not under his control. Yet, in most performances of these struggles, there seems little evidence of a divinely ordained outcome, the playing out of what Hamlet, following Calvin, termed 'special providence' (5.2.192). In a playhouse these are, and can only be, like wrestling matches, feats of physical violence, and any claim by interested parties that in these broils hazard plays no part, that they are theodicies or justifications of the ways of God to men, seems highly dubious.

It had, however, pleased Sir Thomas More, as well as the chroniclers Edward Hall and Raphael Holinshed who followed him, to read the battle of Bosworth (where Elizabeth's grandfather, Henry Tudor, the future Henry VII, defeated the last Plantagenet, Richard III) as a theodicy. But, given the obvious precariousness of those who had seized power, it is not surprising that, while Shakespeare was writing his tragedies, Tudor and Stuart monarchs claimed to hold authority primarily by virtue of inheritance. During the reign of Elizabeth, subjects were reminded of this constantly, particularly in the iconology of royal pageants and at the tilts held every year on the anniversary of the Queen's succession. Yet the claim of the later Tudors to authority by inheritance was weak: Elizabeth herself had been declared a bastard by parliament in 1536 and came to the throne only because of the early death of her half-brother Edward VI and the childlessness of her half-sister Mary I. The mother of King James, Mary Queen of Scots, had been executed by Elizabeth. So, although the story had long been exposed as a myth, it pleased English monarchs to be celebrated as descendants of Brutus, grandson of Aeneas, a prince of Troy.[18] In some respects, Shakespeare's chronicles of the usurpation of the throne of Richard II by Henry Bullingbrook and, at the beginning of his career, of the Wars of the Roses (when the lineal descent of King Henry VI, scion of the House of Lancaster, proved a weak weapon against the forces of the House of York), must have appeared exceedingly provocative. When, in what its first edition calls *The Tragedy of King Richard II* (1595), Bullingbrook ascends his throne as Henry IV there is no sign of divine displeasure. The play seems to have appeared so threatening to the regime – Elizabeth on several occasions identified herself with Richard – that it was not until its fourth edition (1608) that the deposition scene was printed, although in the meantime it may have been performed.[19] Macbeth assassinated his way to the throne of Scotland: his comrade in arms Banquo, whose rectitude contrasts with that of the hero, was ancestor to King James (before whom the play may have been performed in 1606) and bore testimony to his descendant's moral legitimacy.[20] (James had recently escaped assassination in the Gunpowder Plot of 1605.)

The tragedies of Shakespeare and his contemporaries, moreover, reminded their audiences that kings could become tyrants. Kyd's *Spanish Tragedy* displayed the plight of Hieronimo, who was crazed by his inability to find justice at court, supposedly the fount of justice, but in this case irredeemably contaminated. (Hieronimo's predicament resembles that of Hamlet.) The emergence of princes as obviously evil as Saturninus in *Titus Andronicus*, Richard III, Macbeth (or Jonson's Sejanus) turned rebellion from sin to sanctioned political action. In fact, St Thomas Aquinas had argued that subjects had a right to depose a king who became a tyrant,[21] and texts that emerged during the French Wars of Religion (which lasted roughly forty years from 1562), notably the *Vindiciae contra tyrannos* (1579) probably written by the French 'politique' historian Philippe Duplessis-Mornay, contested the assumption of the Tudor *Homilies* that all rebellions are sins against God. The surge of interest in the 1590s in the writings of Tacitus, who exposed the corruption of imperial Rome, along with the chronicling of violence and excess in the tragedies of Seneca, demonstrated that rebellion by subjects could be the correct course of action. In 1600 William Barclay generated the word 'monarchomachist' to designate any writer who justified the right to resist, although it does not imply a denial of the validity of monarchy.

A subject had to be certain that it was his conscience and not ambition that incited him to take arms against an erring prince. Even then the end might not justify the means. Saturninus and Tamora had brought about the rape and mutilation of Lavinia, daughter to Titus Andronicus. The banquet at the end of *Titus Andronicus* in which Titus serves Tamora the flesh of her sons in a pie in imitation of the way Atreus revenged himself upon Thyestes for seducing his wife – the subject of Seneca's *Thyestes* – reveals that, although the morality of Titus's revenge may be understandable, albeit fired by misogyny or an obsessive need to contain female authority,[22] the quaintness of its manner is repulsive. Cases of conscience were made more intricate if rebellion was fomented by revenge upon the private person of the king. Hamlet, finding his own situation mirrored in that of Fortinbras of Norway, had to consider whether to move against Claudius:

> Rightly to be great
> Is not to stir without great argument,
> But greatly to find quarrel in a straw
> When honour's at the stake. (4.4.52–5)

His quizzical juxtaposition of a 'great argument' and a 'straw' exposes the sometime contradiction between acting morally or legally and acting honourably. Hamlet's decision to stand firm for family honour, to avenge the cuckolding of his father by his uncle, generates the pile of corpses at the end of the play which to many may reveal that vengeance indeed ought to be the prerogative of God (see Romans 12: 19).

Authority figures in Shakespeare's time may have been particularly open to criticism because they were perceived as the fountainheads of power and justice: their actions were not yet subject to checks and balances by parliament or an independent judiciary, nor was the royal household or the court designed to function as a civil service. Indeed, an English 'state', defined according to Quentin Skinner as 'a form of public power separate from both the ruler and the ruled, and constituting the supreme political authority within a certain defined territory',[23] had not come into being. This was made explicit by Sir Thomas Smith in 1583: 'To be short, the prince is the life, the head and the authority of all things that be done in the realm of England.'[24] In his tragedies Shakespeare indicates that the actions have their origins not in divine providence but in a decision of the king.

However, although, as we have seen, monarchical power theoretically derived from God, and although 'early modern Englishmen were more used to thinking in terms of duties than of rights',[25] few Elizabethans would have believed that a monarch had an absolute right to do whatever he or she liked. While popular maxims such as 'The king can do no wrong' and 'What the king wills, that the law wills' are recorded from the 1530s, throughout the period 'ancient rights' of subjects and parliament (often unspecified) were frequently invoked: authority needed to be legitimated.[26] Certainly what emerges from an attentive reading of Shakespeare's tragedies is that they place as much emphasis on the duties as on the rights of kings. At the time Shakespeare was writing his tragedies Richard Hooker was arguing that the king had to be subject to the law:

> where the law doth give dominion, who doubteth but that the king who receiveth it must hold of it and under the law according to that old axiom *Attribuat rex legi quod lex attribuit ei potestatem et dominium* [May the king attribute to the law that power and dominion that the law attributes to him] and again *rex non debet esse sub homine, sed sub Deo et lege* [the king ought not to be subject to a man but to God and the law].[27]

These historical realities notwithstanding, many critics of Shakespeare have invoked concepts of 'divine right'. It is worth noting that the phrase occurs in no Shakespearean text, and it is crucially important to distinguish between a divine right to rule (i.e., to reign as an anointed king) and a divine right to act – perhaps against the interests of church and people. The notion of divine right had really been brought into being by Henry VIII's claim to be entitled to appoint bishops in place of the Pope. It is generated by the presence within one political system of both secular and religious powers. Hooker insists that an English king does not have a divine right to meddle in ecclesiastical affairs[28] – although this is not really a topic in Shakespearean tragedy. In a speech to parliament on 21 March 1610 King James set out an 'axiom of divinity':

> That as to dispute what God may do is blasphemy ... so is it sedition in
> subjects to dispute what a king may do in the height of his power. But just
> kings will ever be willing to declare what they will do if they will not incur the
> curse of God. I will not be content that my power be disputed upon, but I
> shall ever be willing to make the reason appear of all my doings and rule my
> actions according to my laws.[29]

In fact James's analogy between himself and God subverts his power
because he concedes that his authority is not absolute but subject to his
ruling justly under the law. In Shakespeare there is always an implicit appeal
from the political to the moral or the spiritual – his kings are not possessed
of an absolute and unquestionable 'divine right'. (Hooker concludes, 'unto
kings by human right honour by very divine right is due'.[30])

Some of Shakespeare's tragedies went further and implicitly questioned
whether inherited monarchy was the best or 'natural' form of government.
Neither the word 'republic' nor its derivatives appears in any Shakespearean
text: the *OED*'s earliest citation of the word dates only from 1603 (although
the word was common in Renaissance Latin texts). Yet *Julius Caesar* (1599)
invokes the virtues of republicanism, hinting that the conversion of Rome
into an empire under Caesar might bring back the excesses of monarchical
tyranny. These had been displayed in Shakespeare's *Rape of Lucrece*, the
'Argument' of which notes how the rapist, the son of the last of the Roman
kings, Tarquinius Superbus, had been rooted out of Rome by Junius
Brutus, ancestor of the Brutus in *Julius Caesar*. It was obvious that
Machiavelli favoured the liberty and self-government of the Roman republic over any other form of state, and his contemporary, Sir Thomas More,
chancellor to Henry VIII, owed far greater allegiance to a *res publica
Christiana* than to any monarch.[31] In Shakespeare the word 'commonwealth' signals analogous secular values, although among the tragedies the
word appears only in the Roman plays.

It is especially notable that in four of his tragedies, *Titus Andronicus*,
Julius Caesar, *Hamlet*, and *Coriolanus*, Shakespeare shows political authority
emerging from forms of election rather than inheritance or *coups d'état*. The
fact that Hamlet's Denmark had a hybrid constitution, an elective monarchy, is central to the political and moral concerns of the play. Claudius,
who, it turns out, was a regicide and probably an adulterer was, arguably, a
'good' king. He was above all a peacemaker, exercising diplomatic powers
to deflect invasion from Norway while maintaining a strategic deterrent.
The electors of Denmark, it is hinted, while ignorant of his crimes, may
have done well to choose him in preference to his nephew, whose threats
to his companions – 'By heaven, I'll make a ghost of him that lets me'

(1.4.85) – reveal a nature as choleric as it is melancholic. Even after he has encountered the warlike Fortinbras, who was prepared to sacrifice 'twenty thousand men' (4.4.60) in order to avenge his family's honour, Hamlet lends his dying voice to the election of the Norwegian to the throne of Denmark. In many productions of the play Fortinbras is portrayed as a belligerent monster whose accession will harm the commonweal. Election, as Shakespeare implies and Thomas Starkey had argued in about 1530, provides no simple remedy against tyranny.[32]

George Chapman was to write poems and plays about whether great men could or ought to be good men: Hamlet was 'good' by virtue of agonizing over the moral choices open to him but, arguably, showed few of the 'great' qualities necessary for strong and peaceful rule. Machiavelli and his contemporaries had investigated the relation between goodness and greatness; their writings indicate a challenge to the pieties of Christian humanism, which held that only a good man could be a great man.

The action of *King Lear* is defined by polarities of goodness and greatness, power and authority. Lear's intention is to abdicate, surrender his monarchical power to his daughters and their husbands. It may well be that the division of the kingdom was regarded by the play's first audiences as an act of folly likely to destabilize England's political order. An academic play, Thomas Norton and Thomas Sackville's *Gorboduc*, performed at the Inner Temple in 1562, had chronicled the miseries of civil war caused by King Gorboduc's decision to divide his realm between his sons. Eubulus, whose role resembles that of Kent in Shakespeare's text, speaks out:

> Pardon I crave, and that my words be deemed
> To flow from hearty zeal unto your grace
> And to the safety of your commonweal:
> To part your realm unto my lords your sons
> I think not good for you, ne yet for them,
> But worst of all for this our native land.
> Within one land one single rule is best:
> Divided reigns do make divided hearts.   (1.2.253–60)[33]

Even if Lear's abdication in favour of three putative heirs was not self-evident folly, the play conducts a subtle examination of the relationship between power and authority. Having handed over his power to Albany and Cornwall, the King, now politically impotent, seeks to retain authority. His authority is recognized by his faithful retainer Kent but denied by Oswald, who, along with Goneril and Regan, finds Lear's conspicuous display of authority, in particular his retinue of knights, superfluous to his new station. Any director of the play is going to have to decide how riotously these knights should behave: if their conduct matches the nuisance that Goneril describes (1.3.6), an audience is likely, for the moment at least, to sympathize with the daughters against the patriarch. The implications are clear: a king may owe his power to his office rather than to any virtue or moral strength. The *reductio ad absurdum* is that any evil person may be invested with a form of legitimated power by virtue of the ceremonies of office – in Elizabethan English the word 'ceremony' could designate not just ritual practices but regalia. A famous story of Queen Elizabeth's chief minister, Lord Burghley, makes the point: 'At night when he put off his gown, he used to say, lie there, Lord Treasurer',[34] an anecdote in which the separation of man from mantle may signify the separation of authority from power. When Lear cries 'Off, off, you lendings' (3.4.102) he is seeking to rid himself of the trappings of a power which at that moment he sees as able to lead only to corruption.

In this play one of the functions of Edmond is to expose the impotence of those who claimed that the stability of the state rested upon ancient custom and a system of civic law that was validated, as Richard Hooker argued in 1593, by being derived from 'natural law', which itself derived from divine law.[35] Edmond worships an opposing kind of nature (*Lear* 1.2.1–22), a goddess of force and self-interest or 'commodity'. By contrast Lear, in his conversation with Gloucester when the latter thinks he has been miraculously saved from suicide, reveals that, having put off the 'lendings', he may have internalized a kind of moral authority:

> LEAR ... Thou hast seen a farmer's dog bark at a beggar?
> GLOUCESTER Ay, sir.
> LEAR An the creature run from the cur, there thou mightst behold the great
> image of authority. A dog's obeyed in office.
> > Thou rascal beadle, hold thy bloody hand.
> > Why dost thou lash that whore? Strip thy own back.
> > Thou hotly lusts to use her in that kind
> > For which thou whip'st her. The usurer hangs the cozener.
> > Through tattered clothes great vices do appear;
> > Robes and furred gowns hide all. Plate sin with gold,
> > And the strong lance of justice hurtless breaks;
> > Arm it in rags, a pygmy's straw does pierce it.
> > None does offend, none, I say none.   (4.5.147–60)

At moments like this we might consider that Lear has achieved what Aristotle considered to be central to the tragic experience, *anagnorisis* or recognition, in this case a recognition that emerged from his suffering.

In *Measure for Measure* an articulate woman, Isabella, demolishes the authority of Angelo by the use of a conceit that matches the anecdote about Burghley:

> But man, proud man,
> *Dressed in a little brief authority,*
> Most ignorant of what he's most assured,
> His glassy essence, like an angry ape
> Plays such fantastic tricks before high heaven
> As makes the angels weep, who, with our spleens,
> Would all themselves laugh mortal.   (2.2.121–7, emphasis added)

Her indictment swirls out to include not only all magistrates but also all
males. In the tragedies the claims to moral authority by men are exposed
time and again. The treatment of Ophelia by Hamlet and by her father
turns her mad. If the nineteenth century saw Ophelia as a chaste and sweet
victim of circumstance, more recent productions have given us Ophelias
whose madness is fuelled by a misandry engendered by righteous anger that
is the obverse of Hamlet's misogyny shaped by inchoate desire. In the mad
scene she sings of a maid whose honour was lost to a man:

> By Gis [Jesus], and by Saint Charity,
>   Alack, and fie for shame,
> Young men will do't if they come to't –
>   By Cock, they are to blame.
>
> Quoth she, 'Before you tumbled me,
>   You promised me to wed.'
> He answers –
> 'So would I ha' done, by yonder sun,
>   An thou hadst not come to my bed.'   (4.5.58–66)

The song may refer to herself and Hamlet, or, possibly, to a stage in the
relationship between Gertrude and Claudius before the murder of Hamlet's
father. But what is significant is its exposure of the double standard: a man
gains honour among his own sex by virtue of sexual conquests, while by the
same activity a woman loses hers. (Earlier Hamlet had claimed that the need
to revenge himself had made him 'like a whore, unpack [his] heart with
words' [2.2.538] – just like Ophelia?)

Utterances of this kind, spoken in madness, led to George Orwell's
famous observation that Shakespeare was 'noticeably cautious, not to say
cowardly, in his manner of uttering unpopular opinions . . . Throughout his
plays the acute social critics, the people who are not taken in by accepted
fallacies, are buffoons, villains, lunatics or persons who are shamming
insanity or are in a state of violent hysteria . . . And yet', Orwell continues,

'the fact that Shakespeare had to use these subterfuges shows how widely his thoughts ranged. He could not restrain himself from commenting on almost everything, although he put on a series of masks in order to do so.'[36]

It was clear that Tudor kings had to rule within the law – perhaps as a consequence of the spread of rationalist political history that exposed the material bases of monarchical power, part of a movement described by Max Weber as 'the disenchantment of the world'.[37] This meant that, in reaction, emphasis continued to be laid on the mystical status of monarchy. In *Henry V* the king reflects that kings are 'twin-born with greatness' (4.1.222), a reference to the fiction that a king had 'two bodies', the 'body politic', a sacramental and immortal body that partook of divinity, and the 'body natural', his body as a man. Shakespeare played with the notion in *Richard II* and made of the emblem of doubleness a figure for self-division within his heroes.[38] It generates Hamlet's quibble to Rosencrantz and Guildenstern who are seeking the body of Polonius:

> HAMLET The body is with the king, but the king is
>   not with the body. The king is a thing –
> GUILDENSTERN A thing, my lord?
> HAMLET Of nothing.   (4.2.24–4)

Hamlet implies that iniquity has cost Claudius the mystic body of kingship, and implies that it ought now to be his – but he, of course, has been neither elected nor crowned.

The coronation had a sacramental dimension, which is perhaps why Shakespeare and his contemporaries mostly refrained from including coronations in their plays: to have done so would have invited censorship. As Hooker wrote:

> Our kings therefore, when they take possession of the room they are called into, have it pointed out before their eyes, even by the very solemnities and rites of their inauguration, to what affairs by the said law their supreme authority and power reacheth. Crowned we see they are, and inthronized, and anointed: the crown a sign of military, the throne of sedentary or judicial, the oil of religious or sacred power.[39]

Macbeth's attack on the body of King Duncan appears to Macduff as 'sacrilegious murder [which] hath broke ope / The Lord's anointed temple and stole thence / The life o'th'building' (2.3.59–61). Later Malcolm describes the goodness of King Edward of England, an obvious contrast with the degradation of Macbeth, manifest in Edward's ability to cure scrofula by touch – the disease was known as 'the King's Evil':

> 'Tis called the Evil.
> A most miraculous work in this good king,
> Which often since my here-remain in England
> I have seen him do. How he solicits heaven
> Himself best knows, but strangely visited people,
> All swoll'n and ulcerous, pitiful to the eye,
> The mere despair of surgery, he cures,
> Hanging a golden stamp about their necks
> Put on with holy prayers; and 'tis spoken,
> To the succeeding royalty he leaves
> The healing benediction. With this strange virtue
> He hath a heavenly gift of prophecy,
> And sundry blessings hang about his throne
> That speak him full of grace.   (4.3.148–61)

King James touched sufferers brought to him by the royal physician, although it was reported by the Duke of Saxe-Weimar that 'the ceremony of healing is understood to be very distasteful to the King, and it is said that he would willingly abolish it'.[40] By the time of the Commonwealth the habit was seen as a pseudo-miracle and representative of monarchical fraud.[41]

The Greek word *charisma* meaning a 'gift of grace'[42] only entered English in the 1640s when it designated a 'miraculous gift of healing'.[43] Julius Caesar enjoins his barren wife Calpurnia to touch Mark Antony when running through the streets of Rome as part of the feast of Lupercal (1.2.6–9), a ritual to ensure fertility that is reported by Plutarch.[44] But it is obvious that Caesar himself evinced what commentators after Max Weber now also call 'charisma', a capacity for inspiring devotion or enthusiasm through power of leadership. In the history plays kings acquire charisma through military valour, as do Othello and Coriolanus. However, the charisma of Othello is not sufficient for this noblest of Moors to be accepted into an exclusive Venetian family. Cominius thus describes the progress of Gaius Marcus, later graced with the cognomen Coriolanus:

> He bestrid
> An o'erpressed Roman, and, i'th'consul's view,
> Slew three opposers. Tarquin's self he met,
> And struck him on his knee. In that day's feats,
> When he might act the woman in the scene,
> He proved best man i'th'field, and for his meed
> Was brow-bound with the oak. His pupil age
> Man-entered thus, he waxèd like a sea,
> And in the brunt of seventeen battles since

> He lurched all swords of the garland. For this last
> Before and in Corioles, let me say
> I cannot speak him home. He stopped the fliers,
> And by his rare example made the coward
> Turn terror into sport. As weeds before
> A vessel under sail, so men obeyed
> And fell below his stem. His sword, death's stamp,
> Where it did mark, it took. From face to foot
> He was a thing of blood, whose every motion
> Was timed with dying cries. Alone he entered
> The mortal gate of th'city, which he, painted
> With shunless destiny, aidless came off,
> And with a sudden reinforcement struck
> Corioles like a planet.   (*Cor.* 2.2.87–109)

The growth of man into an icon of magnificence is enhanced by the reference to the wounding of 'Tarquin', who, as we have seen, was a byword for tyranny. The celebration of this 'thing of blood' remembers not only Macbeth but also another set-piece description of a type of valour. This is the description of Pyrrhus, avenging son of Achilles, that crowds into Hamlet's mind's eye when he is contemplating revenge upon his own father's murderer:

> The rugged Pyrrhus, he whose sable arms,
> Black as his purpose, did the night resemble
> When he lay couchèd in the ominous horse,
> Hath now this dread and black complexion smeared
> With heraldry more dismal. Head to foot
> Now is he total gules, horridly tricked
> With blood of fathers, mothers, daughters, sons,
> Baked and impasted with the parching streets,
> That lend a tyrannous and damnèd light
> To their lord's murder. Roasted in wrath and fire,
> And thus o'er-sizèd with coagulate gore,
> With eyes like carbuncles the hellish Pyrrhus
> Old grandsire Priam seeks.   (*Ham.* 2.2.410–22)

For Hamlet at this moment Pyrrhus seems to be a monster, a figure of a man without conscience or remorse. In the *psychomachia* (or struggle between good and evil) for the soul of the hero he stands as the antagonist of the Ghost who encourages his son to sweep to his revenge.

But if charismatic authority could be gained by valour, it was, when translated to the life of civil society, vulnerable. Shakespeare's tragedies often focus on the ability or otherwise of warrior princes to rule successfully as kings of peace: Titus, Julius Caesar, Othello, Macbeth, Antony, and

Coriolanus. In *Coriolanus* there is an important reflection on the loss of political authority by the tragic hero that is worth dwelling upon. Aufidius is reflecting on both the ability of Coriolanus to capture Rome and his previous inability to maintain authority there.

> I think he'll be to Rome
> As is the osprey to the fish, who takes it
> By sovereignty of nature. First he was
> A noble servant to them, but he could not
> Carry his honours even. Whether 'twas pride,
> Which out of daily fortune ever taints
> The happy man; whether defect of judgement,
> To fail in the disposing of those chances
> Which he was lord of; or whether nature,
> Not to be other than one thing, not moving
> From th'casque to th'cushion, but commanding peace
> Even with the same austerity and garb
> As he controlled the war: but one of these –
> As he hath spices of them all – not all,
> For I dare so far free him – made him feared,
> So hated, and so banished. But he has a merit
> To choke it in the utt'rance. So our virtues
> Lie in th'interpretation of the time,
> And power, unto itself most commendable,
> Hath not a tomb so evident as a chair
> T'extol what it hath done.
> One fire drives out one fire, one nail one nail;
> Rights by rights falter, strengths by strengths do fail.   (4.6.33–55)

The speech stands as an important corrective to simplistic ascriptions of 'tragic flaws' to tragic heroes and readings of their stories that insist upon their consequent loss of authority, thus turning tragedies into moral fables. Aufidius does conjecture that Coriolanus might have been tainted with pride, but it is important to remember that 'tainted' in the period means 'infected' (*OED*, taint, vb. 4a): he does not say that Coriolanus was, in the words of Dickens's Mr Hubble, 'naterally wicious'.[45] The word from Aristotle that generated the notion of 'tragic flaw' is *hamartia*. Etymologically the word means 'missing the mark with a bow and arrow', an error but not necessarily a culpable one. It designates an action – an error or mistake – rather than a flaw in character. However, by the time of the translation of the New Testament from Greek, five hundred years after Aristotle, the word had changed its meaning to 'sin'.[46] Yet Aufidius, in his second stab at fixing Coriolanus's personality, does not insist upon wicked intent, simply on 'defect of judgement' and a failure to control events ('chances').

He then turns to what he calls 'nature': it is apparent from the context that the word here means 'role' or 'fictive self'. Coriolanus was unable to move 'from th'casque to th'cushion', translate his authority from the battlefield to the senate house. (Earlier in the play the hero made a boast: 'I play / The man I am' (3.2.14–15).) The indictment is even-handed: Coriolanus is worthy of merit, and Aufidius insists that men's virtues (here meaning 'strengths' [*OED*, virtue 1a]) are inevitably trans-lated ('interpreted') in different ways at different periods and in different situations. A man whose rule is based on valour will not be highly regarded in time of peace, his authority (the meaning here of 'power') will be as fragile as a wooden chair (with a hint of a throne of office). He ends by refusing to moralize: tragedy derives not from a contest between good and evil, as the moralists would have it, but from a conflict between right and right, a notion that adumbrates Hegel's model of tragedy as conflict between two self-validating ethical substances. (In Sophocles' *Antigone* it was right for the heroine to wish to bury her brothers who had rebelled against Thebes – she owed a duty to her family. It was equally right for Creon to insist that their bodies be left unburied – he owed a duty to the city.) It is right for Hamlet to seek to avenge his father, equally right for Claudius to seek to continue to occupy the throne of Denmark and save the country from the ravages of retaliation.

By now we realize how complex are the meanings of the word that concludes the following passage:

LEAR   What art thou?
KENT   A very honest-hearted fellow, and as poor as the king.
LEAR   If thou be'st as poor for a subject as he's for a king, thou'rt poor enough.
        What wouldst thou?
KENT   Service.
LEAR   Who wouldst thou serve?
KENT   You.
LEAR   Dost thou know me, fellow?
KENT   No, sir; but you have that in your countenance, which I would fain call
        master.
LEAR   What's that?
KENT   Authority.   (1.4.16–27)

Although poets, politicians, and moralists might dispute about the author-ity of monarchy and the nature of kingly power, the power of particular princes depended upon the way they could stage themselves to men's eyes, upon their ability to generate authority through performance. It is com-paratively easy to establish ironical perspectives upon the monarchs and magistrates who people Shakespeare's plays, and yet experiences of charismatic performances by players of great 'countenance' (bearing or demeanour) may suggest something of the way in which princes of the early modern period could instil love and loyalty by their own roles in those rituals and ceremonies that constituted the theatre of the nation. Theatricality was an immensely important mechanism for sovereignty in a period that, as we have seen, was yet to see the development of state institutions.

Richard Burbage, the greatest of the player kings and the man for whom Shakespeare's tragic roles were contrived, inspired an anonymous funeral elegy when he died on 13 March 1619:

> He's gone, and with him what a world are dead,
> Which he revived, to be revivèd so
> No more: young Hamlet, old Hieronimo,
> Kind Lear, the grievèd Moor, and more beside
> That lived in him, have now forever died.
> Oft have I seen him leap into the grave,
> Suiting the person, which he seemed to have,
> Of a sad lover, with so true an eye
> That there I would have sworn he meant to die.
> Oft have I seen him play this part in jest
> So lively that spectators, and the rest
> Of his sad crew, whilst he but seemed to bleed,
> Amazèd, thought even then he died in deed.[47]

In terms of the opening conceit of the passage, the authority of Burbage created a 'world' just as the authority of a 'real' monarch created an order, of fairness, of law, and of justice, which would shape the realm. If authority could, to sceptical spectators, seem to reside in robes of office, a great player upon the stage of the world could 'suit himself' to his 'person' (here meaning 'role'), grow into the part to such a degree that he became himself what he conveyed, an icon of authority. Even if spectators realized that this role was false, played 'in jest', a 'lively' (here meaning 'energetic' as well as 'lifelike') kind of 'monarchising'[48] could create its necessary effect upon the onlookers. We spoke of actors making kings their subjects: princes who played their parts in as lively a manner as Burbage could, contrariwise, turn spectators into subjects.

Notes

1. *Measure for Measure*, 1.1.3.
2. George Puttenham, *The Arte of English Poesie* (London, 1589), pp. 4–5.

3. *English Professional Theatre, 1530–1660*, ed. Glynne Wickham, Herbert Berry and William Ingram (Cambridge University Press, 2000), p. 74; for Henrician precedents, see Greg Walker, *Writing Under Tyranny: English Literature and the Henrician Reformation* (Oxford University Press, 2005).

4. *English Professional Theatre*, pp. 94–5.

5. Richard Dutton, *Mastering the Revels: The Regulation and Censorship of English Renaissance Drama* (University of Iowa Press, 1991).

6. Stephen Greenblatt, 'Shakespeare and the Ethics of Authority', *Shakespeare and Early Modern Political Thought*, ed. David Armitage, Conal Condren and Andrew Fitzmaurice (Cambridge University Press, 2009), pp. 64–79.

7. See Michael Hattaway, *William Shakespeare: King Richard II* (Tirril, Humanities-Ebooks, 2008) www.humanities-ebooks.co.uk/book/Shakespeare_Richard_II.html

8. David Scott Kastan, '"Proud Majesty Made a Subject": Shakespeare and the Spectacle of Rule', *Shakespeare Quarterly* 37 (1986): 459–75; Robert Weimann, 'Representation and Performance: the Uses of Authority in Shakespeare's Theatre', *Materialist Shakespeare: A History*, ed. Ivo Kamps (London: Verso, 1995), pp. 198–217.

9. Linda Woodbridge, *English Revenge Drama: Money, Resistance, Equality* (Cambridge University Press, 2010), pp. 22–58.

10. For an analysis of the failure of authority figures in *Romeo and Juliet*, see Peter C. Herman, 'Tragedy and the Crisis of Authority in Shakespeare's *Romeo and Juliet*', *Intertexts* 1–2 (2008): 89–109.

11. A. C. Bradley, *Shakespearean Tragedy* (London: Macmillan, 1957 edn), p. 7.

12. The hypothesis that Shakespeare was brought up a Catholic and was therefore possibly unconvinced of the later Tudors' right to rule, see E. A. J. Honigmann, *Shakespeare: The 'Lost Years'* (Manchester University Press, 1985).

13. Cited in Robin Headlam Wells, *Shakespeare, Politics and the State* (Basingstoke: Macmillan, 1986), pp. 93–4; the author conveniently assembles extracts from many texts pertinent to this essay together with a useful commentary.

14. Niccolò Machiavelli, *'The Prince' and the 'Discourses'*, ed. Max Lerner (New York: Modern Library, 1950), chap. 18, p. 65.

15. Puttenham, *The Arte of English Poesie*, p. 122.

16. BL Add. MS 27320, ff.23–4; modernized from Tuck's citation of the passage in Richard Tuck, '*Power* and *Authority* in Seventeenth-Century England', *The Historical Journal* 17 (1974): 43–61.

17. See *1 Henry VI*, 1.1.69. I am using 'power' and 'authority' in their modern senses: in Renaissance texts the use of the words is not clear-cut. Either could be used, for example, to translate the Latin *potestas*: see Tuck, '*Power* and *Authority*'.

18. Patrick Collinson, 'History', *A New Companion to English Renaissance Literature and Culture*, ed. Michael Hattaway, 2 vols. (Oxford, Wiley-Blackwell, 2010), vol. 1, pp. 55–73. at p. 68.

19. William Shakespeare, *King Richard II*, ed. Andrew Gurr (Cambridge University Press, 1984), pp. 6, 9–10; for a reminder of the provocative nature of the play as

written (if not performed), see Emma Smith, 'Richard II's Yorkist Editors', *Shakespeare Survey* 63 (2010): 37–48.

20. See 1.3.65, 4.1.111–23 and William Shakespeare, *Macbeth*, ed. A. R. Braunmuller (Cambridge University Press, 1997), pp. 8–9.

21. See the passage from *On Kingship*, cited in Wells, *Shakespeare, Politics and the State*, pp. 91–2.

22. See Liberty Stanavage, '"I fear she cannot love at all": Unnatural Female Sexuality in the Revenge Tragedy', *Genre: An International Journal of Literature and the Arts* 28 (2008): 125–43.

23. Quentin Skinner, *The Foundations of Modern Political Thought: The Age of Reformation*, 2 vols. (Cambridge University Press, 1978), vol. II, p. 353.

24. Sir Thomas Smith, *De republica anglorum [1583]*, ed. L. Alston (Cambridge University Press, 1906), pp. 62–3; Smith, however, must be read in the context established in Patrick Collinson, *De republica anglorum, or, History with the Politics Put Back* (Cambridge University Press, 1990); see also John F. McDiarmid (ed.), *The Monarchical Republic of Early Modern England: Essays in Response to Patrick Collinson* (Aldershot: Ashgate, 2007).

25. Kevin Sharpe, *Remapping Early Modern England* (Cambridge University Press, 2000), p. 54.

26. M. P. Tilley, *A Dictionary of the Proverbs in England in the Sixteenth and Seventeenth Centuries* (Ann Arbor: University of Michigan Press, 1950), k61 and 72.

27. Richard Hooker, *Of the Laws of Ecclesiastical Polity*, ed. Arthur Stephen Mc-Grade (Cambridge University Press, 1989), Book vii, p. 40; see also Torrance Kirby, '"Law Makes the King": Richard Hooker on Law and Princely Rule', *A New Companion to English Renaissance Literature and Culture*, ed. Michael Hattaway, 2 vols. (Oxford, Wiley-Blackwell, 2010), vol. I, pp. 274–88.

28. Hooker, *Laws*, pp. 141–2.

29. King James, *Political Writings*, ed. Johann P. Sommerville (Cambridge University Press, 1994), p. 184; with this compare the discussion of John Donne's conception of royal prerogative in Sharpe, *Remapping Early Modern England*, p. 53.

30. See Kirby, '"Law Makes the King"', at p. 286; see also McDiarmid, *Monarchical Republic, passim*, and Roger Ludeke and Mahler Andreas, 'Stating the Sovereign Self: Polity, Policy, and Politics on the Early Modern Stage', *Solo Performances: Staging the Early Modern Self in England*, ed. Ute Berns (Amsterdam: Rodopi, 2010), pp. 209–27.

31. J. H. Hexter, *More's 'Utopia': The Biography of an Idea* (New York: Harper and Row, 1952), pp. 93, 122.

32. Thomas F. Mayer, *Thomas Starkey and the Commonweal: Humanist Politics and Religion in the Reign of Henry VIII* (Cambridge University Press, 2002), pp. 110–11; contrast Woodbridge, *English Revenge Drama*, p.140.

33. *Minor Elizabethan Tragedies*, ed. T. W. Craik (London: J. M. Dent, 1974), p. 12; the play is well discussed by Andrew Hadfield, 'Tragedy and the Nation

State', *The Cambridge Companion to English Renaissance Tragedy*, ed. Emma Smith and Garrett A. Sullivan (Cambridge University Press, 2010), pp. 30–43.

34. *English Professional Theatre*, pp. 74 and 94–5, cited in William Shakespeare, *The Tempest*, ed. Stephen Orgel (Oxford University Press, 1987), 1.2.24–5n.

35. See Hooker, *Of the Laws of Ecclesiastical Polity*, Book 1.

36. George Orwell, 'Lear, Tolstoy, and the Fool' [1947], *Collected Essays* (London: Secker and Warburg, 1961), pp. 415–34, at p. 430.

37. Max Weber, 'The Evolution of the Capitalistic Spirit', *General Economic History*, trans. F. H. Knight (London: Weber, Allen and Unwin, 1928), pp. 352–69.

38. See Ernst H. Kantorowicz, *The King's Two Bodies: A Study in Mediaeval Political Theology* (Princeton University Press, 1957).

39. Hooker, *Of the Laws of Ecclesiastical Polity*, Book VIII, p. 147.

40. W. B. Rye, *England as Seen by Foreigners in the Days of Elizabeth and James the First* (London: John Russell Smith, 1865), p. 151.

41. See the passage from Arthur Wilson's *History of Great Britain* (1653), p. 289, cited in *Macbeth*, ed. Braunmuller, p. 244.

42. See *OED* 'charisma', a citation from 1644; for a general study see Raphael Falco, *Charismatic Authority in Early Modern English Tragedy* (Baltimore, MD: Johns Hopkins University Press, 2000).

43. William Barclay, *De Regno et Regale Potestate adversus Buchananum, Brutum, Boucherium, & reliquos Monarchomachos* (Paris, 1600).

44. Cited in William Shakespeare, *Julius Caesar*, ed. Marvin Spevack (Cambridge University Press, 1988), pp. 156–7.

45. Charles Dickens, *Great Expectations*, chap. 4.

46. W. K. Wimsatt and Cleanth Brooks, *Literary Criticism: A Short History* (New York: Alfred A. Knopf, 1957), p. 39.

47. *English Professional Theatre*, p. 182.

48. See *Richard II*, 3.2.165.

CHAPTER 7

Gender and family

Catherine Belsey

A family dinner

The sound of trumpets ushers in the dinner guests. Dressed as a cook, an old soldier brings in the food. He greets the Emperor Saturninus and his wife with courtesy and encourages them to begin. The former Roman general's costume elicits a question, but since the guests already suspect that Titus Andronicus is not in his right mind, they do not press the point.

Over dinner, Titus turns the conversation to an episode in Roman history, when Virginius killed his daughter because she had been raped. Was this right, he wonders? Decidedly, the emperor assures him: she should not outlive the deed that shamed her. The old man takes this for authority, rounds on his own daughter and kills her then and there.

Self-evidently, this is *not* how families are expected to behave, and Saturninus says as much. However patriarchal Shakespeare's culture, or ancient Rome, come to that, this is 'unnatural and unkind' (5.3.4). But Lavinia too was raped, Titus explains, and begs his guests not to interrupt their meal, as if the summary execution of his daughter were no more than incidental. Her rapists, he discloses with apparent reluctance, were the empress's sons, Chiron and Demetrius. Surprised, Saturninus calls for the offenders to be brought before him at once. That will not be necessary, however, Titus laconically informs him:

> Why, there they are, both baked in this pie,
> Whereof their mother daintily hath fed,
> Eating the flesh that she herself hath bred. (5.3.59–61)

Drawing on the radical incongruity between cookery and carnage, the proprieties of hospitality and cannibalism, this scene represents a double horror: a father killing his own child; the spectacle of a mother devouring the sons that in nature she herself would once have once fed.

These days, perhaps only film in a line of descent from Martin Scorsese or Quentin Tarantino is equally stylized and sardonic in its treatment of the unthinkable. Julie Taymor's brilliant *Titus*, released in 2000, draws on the work of both to create a movie independent of either. But possibly our epoch has also become more receptive to the painful realization that the family often shelters remarkable cruelty, if not usually on quite this scale, between parents and children and, indeed, between parents themselves. The Victorians were not impressed by *Titus Andronicus*, but then the Victorians, officially at least, believed unequivocally in family values. We may want to, and most politicians tell us we should, but the emerging statistics for domestic violence and child abuse are making it harder to preserve our innocence.

Titus Andronicus is a play about two families, each unhappy in its own way. Oddly enough, the same observation applies in different terms to several of Shakespeare's tragedies. It fits, for instance, *Romeo and Juliet*, where the violence between Montagues and Capulets destroys the children of both; *Macbeth*, where the character of the hero's tyranny is thrown into relief by a direct contrast with the innocence of the Macduff family it destroys; or *Hamlet*, where the process of the hero's struggle to identify his own filial duty has direct implications for the family of Polonius, with tragic consequences for the prince himself.

Families, as we now know, construct positions for their members to occupy, including gender positions, but the family can be made to obscure the construction process itself by rooting it in 'nature'. Marriage, the cornerstone of the family, 'natural-izes' certain modes of behaviour: parental responsibility, sexual fidelity, heterosexuality itself.

We are the direct heirs of four hundred years of family values. But Shakespeare was not. Romantic courtship, marrying for love, and the loving socialization of children by two caring parents were new enough in his day not to pass for nature. Indeed, we might see Shakespeare's plays as contributing directly to the early modern process of naturalizing the affectionate nuclear family. But because this was a moment of change, they also make apparent to us now the anxieties provoked by the values themselves and the gender-models they construct.

It could be argued that this change in the understanding of the family can be traced within Shakespeare's work. His earliest tragedy raises some of the questions about the family and gender that the later tragedies will also address, but will answer differently in certain respects. As its climactic dinner party indicates, *Titus Andronicus* is a play about the appropriation of women, patriarchal power and family feuds; it is also, however, if more marginally, about domestic concord and familial love.

Courtship

The courtship practices the play depicts are remarkably perfunctory. As Titus Andronicus returns in triumph from the war against the Goths, he finds a contest between Saturninus and his younger brother Bassianus for the imperial throne. Saturninus wins with the help of Titus, and announces that, as a reward, he will marry Titus's daughter:

> Titus, to advance
> Thy name and honourable family,
> Lavinia will I make my empress,
> Rome's royal mistress, mistress of my heart.   (1.1.242–5)

This is a strategic move for Saturninus: an alliance with the Andronici will secure the general's future loyalty. And, strategically too, Titus agrees to the match: in a world where names mean titles, and titles in turn are entitlements to property and influence, the family will surely benefit from the patronage of the emperor. No one consults Lavinia. She does not protest.

But Bassianus does. In a warrior society women are possessions. Rome, as many in Shakespeare's audience would know well, was founded on the appropriation of women, when Roman soldiers in quest of wives simply took them by force from their Sabine neighbours. Bassianus declares a prior claim to Lavinia:

> BASSIANUS Lord Titus, by your leave, this maid is mine.
> TITUS How, sir? Are you in earnest, then, my lord?
> BASSIANUS Ay, noble Titus, and resolved withal
> To do myself this reason and this right.
> MARCUS *Suum cuique* is our Roman justice:
> This prince in justice seizeth but his own.   (1.1.280–5)

Titus's brother Marcus usually represents the voice of sanity in this play: we take him seriously. Lavinia is already betrothed to Bassianus and Marcus confirms that she therefore belongs to him. The younger generation support this. Still no one consults Lavinia, though this time we may assume that she has given her consent to the betrothal. But the words used to claim her are proprietary, not romantic.

Cheated of one option, meanwhile, Saturninus promptly embraces another. He has already noticed the charms of the chief prisoner-of-war, Tamora, queen of the Goths. Briefly complimenting her with a comparison to Diana, goddess of chastity, he proposes to Tamora, acknowledging that this is a 'sudden choice', but no less determined for that (1.1.323). As a prisoner, Tamora has a great deal to gain by marriage to the emperor. The wedding is held without delay, though events will show that the new empress is no Diana.

Conversely, the short married life of Bassianus and Lavinia is apparently a happy one, though evidently not given over to sexual extravagance. When the next morning Saturninus makes a joke about young wives wanting to sleep late, Lavinia stoutly insists that she has been wide awake for two hours already.

Romance

How different, then, the story Shakespeare dramatizes in *Romeo and Juliet*, where the heroine is ready to call a lark a nightingale in order to keep her husband in her bed a little longer. Here the courtship process is intense, lyrical, passionate – and (almost) equal. At their first meeting, the lovers' exchanges compose a sonnet, in which Romeo speaks the first quatrain, Juliet the second. The remaining lines are evenly divided between them, and if Romeo initiates the dialogue here, while Juliet displays a degree of conventional coyness, she reveals her love to him without knowing it in the orchard, and then teasingly offers to stand on form and play hard to get, but only if it will intensify his courtship: 'I'll frown and be perverse and say thee nay, / So thou wilt woo; but else, not for the world' (2.2.96–7).

Moreover, in this play, where the lovers defy their parents and convention by their secret marriage, it is Juliet whose surprisingly eager and explicit expectations enable the audience to imagine their wedding night, as she appeals to the darkness that will cover them to

> learn me how to lose a winning match
> Play'd for a pair of stainless maidenhoods.
> Hood my unmanned blood, bating in my cheeks,
> With thy black mantle, till strange love grow bold   (3.2.12–15)

Here, Juliet's father does his best to arrange a strategic alliance, but in vain. In this play it is the world of family feuds and the masculine obligation to avenge a wrong, precisely the values that seem to inform *Titus Andronicus*, which destroy a marriage based on love and reciprocity, made precious in the eyes of the audience by the idealizing intensity of the poetry the lovers produce together.

Perhaps the most romantic of all Shakespeare's marriages is the elopement of Othello and Desdemona. Challenged to give a public account of her behaviour to the Senate, Desdemona does so fluently and without apology, explaining that, while she recognizes what she owes her father, she must now, like her mother before her, 'prefer' her husband (1.3.187). And when the Duke suggests that Othello should leave her at home on his journey to Cyprus, she takes part in the discussion to affirm her commitment, including her sexual commitment, to her new husband:

> That I did love the Moor to live with him
> My downright violence and scorn of fortunes
> May trumpet to the world. My heart's subdued
> Even to the very quality of my lord:
> I saw Othello's visage in his mind,
> And to his honours and his valiant parts
> Did I my soul and fortunes consecrate,
> So that, dear lords, if I be left behind,
> A moth of peace, and he go to the war,
> The rites for which I love him are bereft me,
> And I a heavy interim shall support
> By his dear absence. Let me go with him.   (1.3.249–60)

The plain style of the speech ('I did love the Moor to live with him', 'Let me go with him') lays implicit claim to an equality with the Senate she addresses. Calm, authoritative, measured, Desdemona's rhetoric draws attention to the nature of the choice she has made between love and convention, passion and wealth. By marrying him, she has already dedicated to Othello her 'soul' and her fate; but left behind, she would lose the erotic 'rites' (or conjugal 'rights': the difference is not audible on the stage) which are her motive for loving him.

This is a strong statement, and some commentators have had difficulty with it, not least, no doubt, because Othello is black. The quarto text of the play, the first to be published, but after Shakespeare's death, intensifies the sexual component of Desdemona's speech. There lines 251–2 read, 'My heart's subdued / Even to the utmost pleasure of my lord.' Since the Folio version a year later has 'Even to the very quality', most editors have opted for this softened version. M. R. Ridley, however, the editor of Arden 2 (1962), not otherwise notable for his racial progressiveness, defied convention and gave the quarto reading.[1] But the most recent Arden reverts to the Folio version, on the grounds that 'utmost pleasure' 'might suggest sexual pleasure' (line 252n.). Yes, indeed it might. Since it also scans better, and has an equal claim to authority, we might well prefer it.

Whichever reading we choose, both Juliet and Desdemona display a sexual frankness which is evidently not inconsistent with early modern propriety. It was the Enlightenment that would increasingly oblige virtuous women to exemplify indifference to desire.[2] But Shakespeare was not a

Victorian, and the polarized alternatives of demure virgin or voracious whore are not helpful in making sense of the plays. Evidently, early modern women were not expected to be sexless, though they were required to be faithful. Domestic conduct books of the period recommend that married sex should be pleasurable for both husband and wife.

Past and present

How should we explain the radical differences between *Titus Andronicus* and these two later plays? *Othello* is usually dated 1604, or a year or two earlier; *Titus* was probably first performed at least a decade before. Do the differences 'reflect' a cultural change in the understanding of love, marriage, and the place of women in both? A case could be made for this view. But cultural change on such a scale, especially in a world without television to bring the new values into every household, usually takes a little longer. (Every night on television fiction equates true happiness with reciprocal love between a heterosexual couple.) Meanwhile, *Romeo and Juliet* was probably staged only a few years after *Titus*.

There is a difference of genre, of course: *Titus* is usually thought of as a revenge play, in a line of descent from Kyd's *Spanish Tragedy*. It concerns the power relations in a warrior society, while the later plays are love stories centred on the home. But *Titus* locates its revenge plot in the relationship between two families, and the family is a prominent issue within it. Could there be an additional way of accounting for its apparent indifference to romantic love?

Everyone knows that Shakespeare's plays are hopelessly anachronistic. The clock that strikes in *Julius Caesar* is a classic instance. But have we, perhaps, allowed this knowledge too much sway? *Titus Andronicus* places strong emphasis on its Roman setting. In Act 1 alone there are no fewer than sixty-eight references to 'Rome', 'Roman', or 'Romans'. Locating the action in this way is helpful to the audience, of course, the equivalent of an establishing shot in the cinema, but it might be supposed that even the most inattentive would have taken in a mere setting rather more easily. All the literary references in this highly allusive play are to classical literature. The text is full of Latin tags, like the one Marcus invokes ('*Suum cuique* is our Roman justice'). And in a disarming touch, the play makes clear that Chiron the Goth learned Latin as a foreign language, just like any Elizabethan schoolboy, so that he is able to recognize (though not to interpret) the Latin quotation sent by Titus (4.2.20–8). The religion invoked is also Roman – the dead 'hover on the dreadful shore of Styx' until they are buried (1.1.91) – though in one unexpected lapse Roman suddenly means Roman Catholic (5.1.76–7).

The last instance apart, or, indeed, included, since popery had been outlawed (if inconsistently) for more than half a century by the 1590s, is it possible that *Titus* deliberately sets its horrifying events in an alien culture, and that the society it depicts is defined precisely as archaic in respect of its domestic relationships, as well as in its invocation of the human sacrifice that seems to be required by Roman custom, the Stoical endurance of suffering with dignity and reticence, the tyranny of imperial rule, and the final regression to cannibalism? If this is a fictitious Rome, a conflation of Republican austerity, imperial decadence and a tribal culture that probably never existed at all, it is nonetheless coherently imagined, and a long way in most regards from Elizabethan London. If so, we may see its marriage customs as archaic too, though not, perhaps, so archaic that they were unintelligible to many in Shakespeare's audience, whose values did not necessarily match their actual habits. Arranged marriage was probably still the norm in practice, even while marrying for love becomes the ideal on the stage.

For that reason, *Titus Andronicus* offers a useful point of reference, an indication of what Shakespeare's culture felt it was in the process of leaving behind. Our difficulty now is to see just how much of what has become 'obvious' to us was less obvious then and, conversely, to distinguish between different moments of the West's cultural past, so that we are able to see what sense (or senses) these plays might have made in their own time.

Cultural subjects

However we read *Titus*, two separate sets of values were evidently available to its original audience. Each of these distinct worlds offers different modes of behaviour for men and women to enact. In one, men are expected to be proprietary and easily roused to violence; by contrast, women, or good women, at least, are silent and submissive. In the other, both men and women are rendered eloquent by love; their relationships are intimate, private, no one's concern but their own, if only others would leave them in peace. Different social arrangements involve different values as the condition of their existence, and virtuous conduct varies from one cultural moment to another.

The implication seems to be that human behaviour is not given in advance by identities prior to culture, but that, on the contrary, identity itself is to a high degree shaped by cultural values. Each relies on the other.

There is no patriarchy without patriarchs, and no romance without romantics. New values do not come into existence unless people subscribe to them, reproduce them in their own understanding of themselves and their relationships. It follows, then, that the spread of new values entails, perhaps over generations, new forms of subjectivity. At the same time, new values do not circulate themselves without inscription in cultural practices, including fiction. Arguably, if people had not seen romantic courtship at the theatre, or read about it in romances, they would never have thought of it on their own. Plays do not necessarily reflect behaviour; instead, perhaps they help to inculcate it.

If cultures both depend on and generate the subjects who reproduce them, so too, of course, do fictional genres. Love stories require protagonists who talk and act like lovers, not warriors. In Shakespeare's comedies love civilizes – or perhaps 'feminizes' – young men, turns them into poets and dreamers, and distracts them from the world of violence. Romeo fights Tybalt only with the greatest reluctance. The polar opposition between passive femininity and male violence depicted so sharply in *Titus* gives way to a degree of symmetry or even similarity between Romeo and Juliet so noticeable that in the nineteenth century the hero's part was sometimes played by women.

Ironically, on Shakespeare's own stage the parallel is achieved by other means, since Juliet would, of course, have been played by a boy. The effect of this convention on the development of female roles in the period, and on audiences who took the convention for granted, is matter for speculation. The conclusions we reach will depend on our assumptions about the experience of watching a fictional performance. The identity of the actor, like the Epilogue or the Chorus, is both inside and outside the fiction. Perhaps it assumes a priority at certain moments, and seems a matter of indifference at others?

By focusing on the young, and not their fathers, *Romeo and Juliet* and *Othello* both depict and help to bring about a moment of cultural change, when the older generation takes for granted the obligation of parents to arrange the marriages of their children, and the younger generation perceives this practice as oppressive. But the change of values in society at large was not purely the result of fiction, nor was it simply the result of what we perceive as progress towards greater human happiness. On the contrary. The social project, diligently promoted by the church, Reformers and moralists, was to stabilize the institution of marriage itself as the cornerstone of a more stable society. If couples married for love, so the story went, they would live together in harmony, and bring up their children in the fear of

God and obedience to social convention. The loving family, Milton would later affirm, was 'the fountain and seminary of good subjects'.[3] And in this he echoed Shakespeare's contemporary, the Reformer William Perkins, who saw the family as 'the fountain and seminary of all sorts and kinds of life', since 'this first society is as it were the school wherein are taught and learned the principles of authority and subjection'.[4] But if, like society, the theatre had an investment in romantic courtship, tragedy brought out, as the moralists did not, the capacity of the close-knit family for abusive relationships in *Hamlet*, *Macbeth*, *Othello* and *Lear*. In each of these plays it is precisely the intensity of the ties between family members that promotes suffering or evil.

Extra-marital love

In accordance with the ideal of the loving family, strategic alliances designed to serve the interests of dynasty or the state were coming to be perceived as distinctly unstable. While Shakespeare's comedies were deeply influenced by the tradition of popular romance, where a happy ending meant lovers united in mutual love and marriage,[5] the grand, tragic narratives of medieval love, including Chaucer's *Troilus and Criseyde*, had dwelt on extra-marital passion. Stories that formed a point of reference for early modern tragedy linked it with disorder: the irresistible desire of Paris for Helen led to the catastrophe of the Trojan war; Dido very nearly succeeded in deflecting Aeneas from his duty to found Rome. At the same time, such love was heroic in its intensity. Did the practice of arranged and often loveless marriage offer an excuse for extra-marital liaisons?

Titus would suggest not. Tamora's marriage to Saturninus does not interrupt her sexual relationship with Aaron the Moor. The very next morning, she seeks him out alone in a secluded place, and invites him to emulate with her the secret pleasures of Dido and Aeneas in the cave. But for all the lyrical echoes of her speech (2.2.10–29), this is no romance. Aaron is presented as a devil (5.1.40, 45; 5.3.5, 11) who gladly claims responsibility for the rape and mutilation of Lavinia and for tricking Titus into chopping off his own hand. And he adds proudly,

> when I told the empress of this sport,
> She sounded [swooned] almost at my pleasing tale
> And for my tidings gave me twenty kisses.   (*Tit.* 5.1.118–20)

The liaison between Aaron and Tamora constitutes a minor episode in a play crammed with appalling incident. But extra-marital sex is a central issue in *Antony and Cleopatra*, where the sympathies of the audience are harder to assess. Here too Dido and Aeneas offer a precedent. Preparing to kill himself, Antony foresees his reunion with Cleopatra in the Elysian underworld:

> Where souls do couch on flowers we'll hand in hand
> And with our sprightly port make the ghosts gaze.
> Dido and her Aeneas shall want troops,
> And all the haunt be ours.   (4.14.52–5)

This strange and delicate conjunction of the sensual (flowers and hands) with the insubstantial ('souls', 'ghosts', 'haunt') idealizes the passion it promises to seal at last in a spectral future. It also evokes the theatrical image of Cleopatra in the barge, which forms the prelude to their first meeting. Then too, she drew all eyes to her,

>   and Antony,
> Enthroned i'th'market-place, did sit alone,
> Whistling to th'air, which, but for vacancy,
> Had gone to gaze on Cleopatra, too,
> And made a gap in nature.   (2.2.224–8)

This time Antony is alone. In Elysium, however, the lovers are together.

It would surely be difficult not to succumb to this, or to resist the power of this story of forbidden love, relating *Antony and Cleopatra* back to the earlier romances of doomed and tragic passion. And yet, when we look more closely, there are certain ironies here. Aeneas forsook Dido, who killed herself in despair. When they met in the underworld, she turned away. Misled or self-deceived, Antony radically rewrites the well-known narrative.[6] Indeed, at this moment, he is literally misinformed, convinced by Mardian's false report of Cleopatra's death, her last and fatal seductive stratagem. The woman Antony imagines he will overtake in death (4.14.45) is at this moment hiding from his anger in her monument.

Compared with Cleopatra, 'Kingdoms are clay!', Antony declares (1.1.36). But in the very next scene news of trouble in kingdoms of the empire changes his mind: 'These strong Egyptian fetters I must break', he now insists (1.2.112). Fetters are iron shackles for the feet, designed to prevent prisoners from moving. Throughout the play, Antony oscillates between Egypt and Rome, desire and politics, while Cleopatra, who has her own political interests, lies, cheats, and throws tantrums.

On the other hand, the poetry consistently invests them with mythic status. Cleopatra in her barge outdoes paintings of the goddess of love herself, 'O'erpicturing that Venus where we see / The fancy outwork nature'

(2.2.210–11). Even here, however, there is an implication that the picture improves on the thing itself, or that the spectacle Cleopatra herself creates is an effect of fantasy, not truth. In one sense, of course, it is: this woman who personifies the feminine is played by a boy, as the text itself obliquely reminds us (5.2.218–20). Antony is repeatedly compared with Mars, god of war (2.2.6; 2.5.117), but in the first instance the parallel is set in his heroic past, while his present condition is defined as 'dotage' (1.1.1–4).

Ovid tells the story of Venus and Mars in *The Metamorphoses*, one of the books used to teach little boys Latin. The goddess's husband, Vulcan the smith, skilful in metalwork, made a net of bronze as fine as a spider's web and spread it over their couch. When Mars and Venus next made love, they were caught by the net and held in position. Then Vulcan opened the doors to let in the other gods, who laughed, and entertained each other with the story for a long time to come (4.171–89).[7]

Does *Antony and Cleopatra*, which scales the heights of tragic poetry, also ask its audience to laugh at the lovers it depicts, caught in their own self-deceiving passion? Perhaps the continued fascination of the play for us now depends on the undecidable character of its attitude to adultery. Is this the greatest love story ever told, or a record of reciprocal misrecognition – or both? (Doesn't love always involve a degree of overvaluation?) Is Cleopatra, as she finally claims, a wife in all but name (5.2.286–7) or a remarkably accomplished courtesan – or both?

Masculinity

Meanwhile, what are the alternatives for Antony? Cleopatra's rival is not primarily another woman, but the power-struggles of imperial Rome. Antony's strategic marriage to Octavia is intended to cement his relationship with Caesar, his partner and rival in the government of Rome. It fails to do so, of course, because the world of masculine competition is no substitute for the pleasures of Egypt, and the redoubled insult to Caesar's family when Antony betrays Octavia only deepens the hostility between them.

Left to their own devices, it would appear, men quarrel. Bassianus and Saturninus contend for the throne; Chiron and Demetrius are ready to do battle over Lavinia. Montagues and Capulets fight as a matter of habit. Edmund is prepared to go to any lengths to get Edgar's inheritance; Claudius kills Old Hamlet for his.

Relations between men are commonly grounded in emulation. The word carries two apparently antithetical meanings, both appropriate, both intimately connected. It indicates, on the one hand, admiration and imitation, and on the other, rivalry. The person you want to excel is the one you respect most. It is because Caesar acknowledges Antony's heroism that he competes with him; a similar relationship develops temporarily between Cassius and Brutus in *Julius Caesar*. Iago hates Cassio because 'He hath a daily beauty in his life / That makes me ugly' (*Oth.* 5.1.19–20). Macbeth has Banquo murdered for fear of his virtue – 'and under him / My Genius is rebuked; as, it is said, / Mark Antony's was by Caesar' (3.1.54–6). Coriolanus has to beat Aufidius because he is the best.

In a world that sees war as heroic, true masculinity also means the ability to bear pain. If Titus is stoical in the face of almost unbearable emotional suffering, Antony's physical defeat of famine was once the admiration of the world. Despite his delicate upbringing, Antony, it seems, exceeded the animals in their ability to survive in hostile nature:

> Thou didst drink
> The stale of horses and the gilded puddle
> Which beasts would cough at.
>
> . . .
>
> On the Alps,
> It is reported, thou didst eat strange flesh
> Which some did die to look on.   (*Ant.* 1.4.62–9)

And this without ever showing any distaste, or even losing weight (69–72)!

If women are to become consenting partners for men, perhaps one condition is that they too must endure pain without protest. Ironically, it is to prove herself a fit wife for Brutus, his friend and companion, able to share fully in his political secrets, that Portia has deliberately wounded her own thigh in *Julius Caesar*. Portia's act is usually read as a concession to Roman Stoicism, but isn't it as a perverse version of the same project that Cleopatra insists on fighting alongside Antony at Actium? Surely a corruption of this companionate ideal also drives Lady Macbeth when she urges evil spirits to 'unsex' her, to make her capable of taking an equal part in Duncan's murder, blocking all natural scruples, turning her life-giving milk bitter, 'That my keen knife see not the wound it makes, / Nor Heaven peep through the blanket of the dark, / To cry, "Hold, hold!" ' (1.5.40–54).

Lady Macbeth also perverts the meaning of manhood as a way of taunting her husband with cowardice. 'I dare do all that may become a man', he insists. 'Who dares do more, is none' (1.7.45). 'When you durst do it, then you were a man', she retorts (1.7.49). The challenge works, and Macbeth agrees to murder the king. 'Bring forth men children only!' he exclaims, in response to the ingenuity of her plan for the crime (1.7.73).

Lady Macbeth is wrong: masculinity is not by nature criminal, and it is not without feeling. When Macduff laments the slaughter of his family, Malcolm urges, 'Dispute it like a man' (4.3.220). Macduff replies, 'I shall do so; / But I must also feel it as a man' (4.3.224–5). The feeling, we are invited to believe, is what motivates his action.

And yet, strangely enough, the version of manhood urged by Lady Macbeth is not so far from the kind the play appears to endorse. The first words of the saintly Duncan are, 'What bloody man is that?' (1.2.1). The man is, it turns out, a soldier fresh from the battle, who recounts the exploit that so gratifies the king, Macbeth's combat with the traitor Macdonwald:

> brave Macbeth (well he deserves that name),
> Disdaining Fortune, with his brandished steel,
> Which smoked with bloody execution,
> Like Valour's minion, carv'd out his passage,
> Till he fac'd the slave:
> Which ne'er shook hands, nor bade farewell to him,
> Till he unseamed him from the nave to th'chops,
> And fixed his head upon our battlements.   (1.2.16–23)

The sword 'smokes' with warm blood in the cold air; Macbeth 'carves' his way through the ranks, like a butcher; and he slits his enemy open, as if he were severing a row of stitches, upwards from the navel to the jaw. The difference between this and the murder of Duncan, apart from the fact that this is more bloodthirsty, is that the battle is legitimate. 'O valiant cousin! worthy gentleman' (1.2.24), comments the king, and promptly promotes him.

How are we to read this play, where the feminine is exiled or killed, witches should be women but have beards (1.3.44), Macbeth's wife demands to be unsexed in order to be a better partner in crime (1.5.39), and masculinity exceeds its own bounds – but only just – and becomes tyranny? What, in other words, are the proper limits of manhood?

'It will have blood, they say: blood will have blood', mutters Macbeth (3.4.122). Does he refer only to the murder of Banquo, or to the violence that prevails from the beginning? Would this proverb, in other words, serve as an epigraph to the whole play? Is Macbeth speaking simply of his plan to kill Duncan, when he reflects, 'we but teach / Bloody instructions, which, being taught, return / To plague th'inventor' (1.7.8–10)? Should we, perhaps, see killing, lawful and apparently heroic on the one hand, and criminal on the other, as in a way continuous? If so, though it differentiates between a good cause and a bad, perhaps the play also foregrounds the tragic potential of the militaristic values that require a real man to devote his energies to making 'Strange images of death' (1.3.95).

Values in conflict

This issue is directly engaged in the revenge tradition, where law and the readiness to act in what looks, in some ways, like a good cause, come into direct conflict with each other. Titus Andronicus, who has no hesitation in killing his own son when he violates his father's code of conduct, defers vengeance against the legitimate ruler until he is at least half crazed with grief. His 'piety' (1.1.118) impels him to obey the law. As Marcus explains, despite his sorrow, Titus is 'so just that he will not revenge'. And he appeals to the gods, 'Revenge the heavens for old Andronicus!' (4.1.128–9). If the heavens act at all, however, it is only to send him Tamora and her sons in disguise, and this looks more like an intervention from hell.

Here, the patient endurance of suffering replaces unlawful violence, at least in the first instance. In this light, it seems unlikely that Hamlet is contemplating suicide when he wonders which of his options is *nobler*:

> Whether 'tis nobler in the mind to suffer
> The slings and arrows of outrageous fortune,
> Or to take arms against a sea of troubles
> And by opposing end them. To die –   (*Ham.* 3.1.57–60)

What the Ghost demands is the murder of Hamlet's uncle and his king. Which is right, unlawful masculine violence, or equally masculine endurance? But suffering what fortune sends is hard to distinguish in practice from cowardice, as Hamlet knows well:

> it cannot be
> But I am pigeon-livered and lack gall
> To make oppression bitter, or ere this
> I should ha' fatted all the region kites
> With this slave's offal.   (2.2.529–33)

On the other hand, if this image of violence is repulsive, the consequences are still more so so: 'To die – '. Revengers almost always die. But death, Hamlet reflects, is not the problem: to die is to sleep, no more than that. Who would not be willing to die, to escape the miseries of life, were it not that the murder of an uncle and a king, if not justified, also incurs punishment in the next life? In consequence, 'the dread of something after death . . . puzzles the will' (3.1.78–80). 'Thus', Hamlet inconclusively concludes, 'conscience does make cowards of us all' (83).

Feminization

Nineteenth-century writers and artists regarded Hamlet with profound ambivalence. Surely, they reasoned, a young man ought to obey his father? And surely, too, a proper man would polish off a bad king in no time? Laertes, after all, would cheerfully have broken sanctuary to get at the murderer and 'cut his throat i'th'church' (4.7.125). But they also admired Hamlet's intellectual engagement with the issues and his philosophical range. We, with less conviction that fathers are always right, and more reservations about violence as the solution to all problems, might be inclined to admire more than we condemn.

In the nineteenth century Hamlet's hesitation was widely regarded as 'feminine', and like Romeo, he was often played by women. More recently, we might prefer to see a contradiction in the ideal of masculinity. An early modern man should both endure, like Titus, and act, like Macbeth. Both are noble. But even Macbeth needs considerable encouragement to kill a king. 'I do fear thy nature', his wife observes. 'It is too full of the milk of human kindness' (1.5.16–17). Only thirty lines later, she will repudiate the milk of her own 'woman's breasts' (1.5.47–8).

In a brilliant article which suddenly made obvious what we ought to have seen all along, Stephen Orgel explained that men in Shakespeare's time were in perpetual fear of feminization.[8] When Galenic physiology, and especially midwifery, thought of women as less perfect versions of men, possessing the same sexual organs, but with less heat to push them outwards,[9] there was, it seemed, always a danger that men would slide back towards imperfect femininity.

It's true, of course. This is what happens to Antony: the effect of his 'dotage', and his devotion to love's 'soft hours' (*Ant.* 1.1.45), is that he loses the masculine will to war and, in consequence, at Actium he follows Cleopatra from the battle, yielding the day to Caesar. Romeo in love is unwilling to fight his new cousin Tybalt, and Mercutio incurs his own death doing it for him:

> O sweet Juliet,
> Thy beauty hath made me effeminate
> And in my temper soften'd valour's steel.   (3.1.104–6)

But my own doubt is whether this feminization is offered, even in its own period, as cause for alarm, or instead as a relief from the remorseless demands of male aggression. The feud in *Romeo and Juliet* is made to seem particularly pointless and, as Romeo points out, street brawling is against the law

(3.1.87–8). Hamlet reproaches himself because all he does is talk and curse, like a whore or a kitchen-maid (2.2.538–40), but would we really expect the audience to find him less sympathetic than Laertes because he deliberates?

The test case must surely be Coriolanus, brought up by his mother, a woman who, ironically, out-Romes Roman military values, to personify all that is most violent in masculinity, at the expense of the civil virtues that courtship and marriage are seen to inculcate elsewhere. When his upbring-ing leads Coriolanus to join the Volscians and threaten war against Rome itself, only his family can dissuade him: two women and a child. He tries to hold out against his own natural impulse to give way to the 'woman's tenderness' they elicit in him (5.3.129):

> But out, affection!
> All bond and privilege of nature break!
> Let it be virtuous to be obstinate.   (*Cor.* 5.3.23–5)

It would not be virtuous, however, but perverse, and his words make clear that Coriolanus knows that. It is hard to imagine spectators who would not sigh with relief when he relents, even though the text also makes clear that the Volscians will not let him outlive this betrayal of their cause (5.3.187–9).

In the event, what happens is worse: his rival, Aufidius, calls Coriolanus a 'boy of tears' (5.6.100). For the hero, this is unbearable, but for the audience? The spectacle of Aufidius emblematically standing in triumph on his dead body surely elicits, perhaps for the first time, our sympathy for a figure who has loved one aspect of masculine values not wisely, but too well.

Homoeroticism

A warrior society, which thinks heterosexual love softens heroism, depends on close ties of loyalty between men, and the values of such a society were evidently still part of the fabric of early modern culture. The relationship between Antony and Enobarbus is presented as jocular, but close. Hamlet trusts Horatio, much as knights must have trusted their friends to drag them off the field of war when things went badly, and promises to 'wear' him 'In my heart's core, ay, in my heart of heart' (3.2.72–3).

Were these friendships understood as including a homoerotic element? This question is extremely difficult to answer accurately at this distance of time, not least because it depends on access to what was implicit rather than explicit in what is said. What we know, or think we know, is that, while homosexual acts undoubtedly took place, early modern culture did not identify individuals as gay or lesbian. Those identifications, which classify a person rather than a practice, and imply a fixity of preference unknown to earlier epochs, belong to the eighteenth-century 'science' of sexuality. We also know that, while 'sodomy' was defined in the statutes as an appalling crime, prosecutions for sodomy were extremely rare.

The main areas of interest for homoerotic criticism of Shakespeare are probably the Sonnets and the comedies. There are indications in *The Merchant of Venice*, for instance, of a possible conflict between friendship and marriage, especially now that wives were themselves becoming their husbands' best friends. The homosocial world of the warrior Coriolanus, however, knows no such contests. The hero, who addresses his wife, in public, at least, as 'My gracious silence' (2.1.148), is much more effusive in the excitement of military triumph towards his friend, Cominius:

> Oh, let me clip ye
> In arms as sound as when I woo'd; in heart
> As merry as when our nuptial day was done,
> And tapers burned to bedward.   (1.6.29–32)

But how should we interpret this? From one perspective, the comparison affirms the heterosexual intensity of his marriage night. From another, it transfers the eroticism of that moment to an embrace with another man.

There is an exact parallel here with Aufidius's welcome to Coriolanus himself: 'More dances my rapt heart / Than when I first my wedded mistress saw / Bestride my threshold' (4.5.113–15). Their relationship follows the pattern of tragic love: hostility gives way to intensity and, in betrayal, a bitter disappointment that issues in lawless violence.

'Race'

Aufidius is a Volscian. Is he therefore less 'civilized' than the Romans? Cleopatra is Egyptian, a 'gipsy' (1.1.10), 'tawny' (1.1.6), or (possibly) 'black' (1.5.29); Tamora is white, but a Goth and therefore barbaric; Aaron is black. Does their foreignness, their otherness, compound their threat, and in particular, their danger to family values?

There can be no doubt that early modern England, with its developing sense of national identity, and an emerging white racism as the legitimation of a growing slave trade, regarded with mounting suspicion other 'races', who palpably subscribed to different values from their own. Cultural difference is easily frightening – to the degree that it demonstrates that there are other ways of ordering people's lives. And what is frightening is readily demonized. Aaron in particular, while a Moor, is also clearly a descendant of the Vice of the moral plays, the dashing, witty, calculating figure who seduces the representative human hero to his own damnation. The Vice, like the devil, his 'father', had long been represented as black, the traditional colour of inhabitants of the darkness of hell.

How, then, should we understand the irruption of racial otherness into the heart of the family in *Othello*? There can be no doubt that Othello's blackness is a significant component of the play. The first act alone is pervaded by hate-speech. Othello is identified as 'the thick lips' (1.1.65); 'an old black ram ... tupping' the white ewe, Desdemona (1.1.87–8); a 'Barbary horse' who will give Brabantio's family 'nephews to neigh to you' (1.1.110–11). Desdemona is imagined in 'the gross clasps of a lascivious Moor' (1.1.124). Her father tells Othello he cannot believe that his daughter would voluntarily leave her home for 'the sooty bosom / Of such a thing as thou' (1.2.70–1).

This is not, of course, the whole story. The speakers are Iago, who hates him, Roderigo, who himself wanted to marry Desdemona, and Brabantio, the absurd father who would more properly belong in comedy (compare Egeus in *A Midsummer Night's Dream*) if the consequences were not so tragic. At his first appearance, Othello utterly fails to live down to his reputation. And the Senate will hear none of Brabantio's racist slurs. Convinced by Desdemona, who 'saw Othello's visage in his mind' (1.3.253), the Duke affirms, 'If virtue no delighted beauty lack / Your son-in-law is far more fair than black' (1.3.290–1).

But this proto-liberal colour-blindness is no match for the super-subtle Venetian racism of Iago. Gradually, all the main characters in the play become his dupes, until Othello himself comes to fear that his blackness makes him unlovable (3.3.267). The 'ocular proof' of Desdemona's infidelity that Othello demands (3.3.363) is, of course, as much an illusion as Iago's widely recognized honesty. Othello's own blind innocence (1.3.398–400) is matched by Desdemona's and Cassio's. Ironically, it is Iago's wife, who knows him best, who finally perceives the truth.

In my view, this play uniquely values the partnership it depicts with such idealism. But a marriage founded on passionate, idealizing love is correspondingly vulnerable to imagined betrayal. What destroys this one is not so much, I think, an instability intrinsic to an inter-racial marriage, as the shaping fantasies of white racism itself.

Parents and children

Othello and Desdemona do not live long enough to have children. Titus Andronicus, by contrast, has had twenty-six. He has lost twenty-one sons in five military campaigns; he himself kills another, when Mutius defends his sister's marriage to Bassianus. Of those that remain, two more are executed and the last banished in the course of Tamora's revenge; Lavinia is raped and mutilated by the Goths, Chiron and Demetrius. This is the insupportable sequence of wrongs Titus finally avenges when he induces the empress to dine on her own children.

But the story of Tamora's revenge begins when Titus ignores her plea to spare her eldest son, whose life the 'cruel, irreligious piety' of Rome demands as a blood sacrifice (1.1.133). 'And if thy sons were ever dear to thee, / O, think my son to be as dear to me' (1.1.110–11). But were his children dear to Titus? And in what sense? Titus's austere ethical code, the play repeatedly makes clear, comes first. He loves his children, but on condition that they reproduce his own values. (Is there a parody of this idea in Aaron's passionate love of his baby? It is, he claims, 'Myself, / The vigour and the picture of my youth' (4.2.109–10).)

The Andronicus family is dynastic: Titus backs lineage. Although Bassianus would make a better emperor, Titus supports the claim of the elder brother. His own children expect to kneel to him (1.1.164, 374 s.d.). If there is a glimmer of hope at the end of the play, it lies with the accession of Lucius, the surviving Andronicus, and the innocence of young Lucius, his son. (The survival of Aaron's baby, conversely, implies the continuation of evil in the world.)

At the same time, a new set of values is evident in the play. The younger generation are right to defend Bassianus, and Titus belongs to a vanishing order. Paradoxically, as a grandfather, he himself prefigures the new one, dancing young Lucius on his knee, singing to him and telling him stories (5.3.159–65). The new family will make children more precious, and idealize the love between parents and children as unconditional.

In that sense, *Titus Andronicus* anticipates *King Lear* more than a decade later. In both plays fathers expect the obedience of their children, and do not find it. The young inhabit a different world. But in *Lear* the tragedy is the outcome of an emotional intensity the dynastic family cannot sustain. What Lear wants is not just obedience, but unconditional love. Sadly, the family is not able to accommodate the exorbitant demands now placed on it. That way, the tragedy will demonstrate, madness lies.

Notes

1. William Shakespeare, *Othello*, ed. M. R. Ridley (London: Methuen, 1962). For a discussion of the story to this point, see Anthony Barthelemy, 'Introduction', *Critical Essays on Shakespeare's 'Othello'* (New York: G. K. Hall, 1994), pp. 3–4.

2. Faramerz Dabhoiwala, *The Origins of Sex: A History of the First Sexual Revolution* (London: Allen Lane, 2011), pp. 141–233.

3. John Milton, *The Complete Prose Works*, 8 vols., vol. ii, ed. Ernest Sirluck (New Haven, CT: Yale University Press, 1959), p. 447.

4. William Perkins, *Christian Oeconomie, Works*, vol. iii (Cambridge, 1618), p. 671, Epistle Dedicatory (n.p.).

5. Helen Cooper, *The English Romance in Time: Transforming Motifs from Geoffrey of Monmouth to the Death of Shakespeare* (New York: Oxford University Press, 2004), pp. 218–68.

6. Coppélia Kahn, *Roman Shakespeare: Warriors, Wounds and Women* (London: Routledge, 1997), p. 131.

7. Ovid, *Metamorphoses*, with an English translation by Frank Justus Miller (Cambridge, MA: Harvard University Press, 1984).

8. Stephen Orgel, '"Nobody's Perfect", or, Why Did the English Stage Take Boys for Women?', *South Atlantic Quarterly* 88 (1989): 7–29.

9. See Thomas Laqueur, *Making Sex: Body and Gender from the Greeks to Freud* (Cambridge, MA: Harvard University Press, 1990).

CHAPTER 8

The tragic subject and its passions

Gail Kern Paster

The poet John Dryden, writing near the end of the seventeenth century, criticized Shakespeare for failing to respect the unity of character in his tragedies: 'The last property of manners is, that they be constant, and equall, that is, maintain'd the same through the whole design: thus when Virgil had once given the name of *Pious* to *Aeneas*, he was bound to show him such, in all his words and actions through the whole Poem.'[1] According to Dryden, the playwright is bound by the canons of realism – rules that characters as represented in literary works ought to manifest a high degree of psychological and behavioural consistency. Thus for Aeneas *to be himself* – to have the identity of Aeneas – he should be pious in mind as in deed. For Dryden, this artistic requirement is grounded in a conviction that real human beings *are* psychologically consistent and, as such, the autonomous source of their meanings. Self-sameness in a person's behaviours flows from an invisible self-identity. This inner identity is the product of a disembodied consciousness that sees the world as the objectified instrument of its own willed designs. The 'I' with which an individual represents him- or herself to the world is fully present to itself and thus can be held accountable for its words and deeds.[2]

This essay will argue that Dryden's demand for unity (or self-sameness) of character in Shakespeare is anachronistic, based on a conceptual distinction between emotions and the body, between psychology and physiology, that is foreign to early seventeenth-century conceptions of an inward self.[3] Dryden does not use the term 'psychology', a term that entered the English language only at the end of the seventeenth century and referred at that point to the philosophical study of the soul (psyche). But there can be little doubt that he would understand the psychological properties of 'human nature' in more or less modern, post-Enlightenment terms as instruments of a sovereign self, a disembodied consciousness.[4] They are immaterial and incorporeal – hence cumulative and consistent in outward expression over time.

But Shakespeare is unlikely to have imagined the workings of self or its near-synonym, subjectivity, in such disembodied terms or to have imagined that the emotions of his tragic protagonists occurred anywhere but in and through their bodies or that they occurred otherwise than materially. This does not mean Shakespeare and his contemporaries lacked a conception of inwardness. On the contrary, as Katharine Maus has argued, the idea of a 'socially visible exterior and an invisible personal interiority' – the idea of an own self – has 'a long history in the Western philosophical tradition'.[5] The problem is how to understand that inwardness in terms other than the disembodied ones of post-Enlightenment modernity. The difference arises because 'in vernacular sixteenth- and early seventeenth-century speech and writing, the whole interior of the body – heart, liver, womb, bowels, kidneys, gall, blood, lymph – quite often involves itself in the production of the mental interior, of the individual's private experience'.[6] Selfhood then, in early modern terms and as used in this essay, refers to a form of self-experience intensely physical in kind and expression.[7] Indeed it is hard to overstate the implications of the period's persistent materialism of thought where conceptions of selfhood are involved. Even Hamlet's famous state-ment – 'But I have that within which passes show' (1.2.85) – refers not to an incorporeal site where a disembodied self might be located but, as David Hillman suggests, 'to a realm of specifically *corporeal* interiority contrasted with mere outward signs'.[8] Thus the language of self-experience in Shakespeare's plays expresses an understanding of the sources of self in which the modern separation of the psychological from the physiological had not yet happened. In the Galenic physiology, 'self' in behavioural terms was the product of invisible, mysterious interactions between an immaterial soul and its material instruments. These instruments included the faculties of reason, imagination, and will, the five senses, and the body itself. Experience of self arose through a baby's early identification with its body, but the culture's idea of bodiliness included much that we now designate as non-bodily. In this paradigm, emotions were transformative bodily events emanating from the heart as seat of the affections. The body and its emotions were understood to be functionally inseparable, with change in one realm producing change in the other.

An assumption that emotional change produces bodily alteration under-lies Desdemona's reaction to the transformation in Othello: 'My lord is not my lord', she tells Cassio and Iago, 'nor should I know him, / Were he in favour as in humour altered' (*Oth.* 3.4.118–19). Her distinction between Othello's countenance and his mood is between two aspects of physical being – his unchanged face (which she can see) and his changed bodily disposition or 'humour' (which she cannot). 'Something sure of state', she goes on, '. . . Hath puddled his clear spirit' (3.4.134–7). Her imagery of the puddled spirit represents powerful feeling as a fluid changing in colour from clear to dark and in motion from flowing to stopped. It defines the onset of Othello's jealousy as the onset, literally, of physical disease. The physical model underlying ancient and early modern psychology is 'a simple hydraulic one, based on a clear localisation of psychological function by organ or system of organs'.[9] In other words, the bodily fluids that flowed from and to different bodily organs were thought to affect mood, disposition, desires, and emotions – sources of the self.

Desdemona's belief in the functional coexpressiveness of body and emotions suggests that Shakespeare would not have felt himself obligated, like Dryden, to equate character with the disembodied properties of constancy and equality. Desire for constancy is often the wish of Shakespeare's heroes, a hallmark of neo-Stoic behaviour that they aspire to but often fail to achieve. But constancy is desired because these heroes see themselves as vulnerable to passions having the power to transform or even dissolve them. Emotions were understood in the early modern period, as they are now, to be essential for survival – God-given equipment for producing the right responses of hate and love, fear and desire, fight or flight. But they were also thought, again as they often are now, to cloud the judgement, corrupt the will, and seduce the reason. The power accorded to the passions helps to explain why Stoicism, which advocated the suppression or transcendence of the passions altogether, was an important ethical counterforce in the period. As the English moral philosopher Thomas Wright explains, the passions are able to effect an almost metamorphic change in cognition, judgement, and behaviour:

> By this alteration which Passions work in the Wit and the Will we may understand the admirable Metamorphosis and change of a man from himself when his affects are pacified and when they are troubled; Plutarch said they changed them like Circe's potions, from men into beasts. Or we may compare the Soul without Passions to a calm Sea; with sweet, pleasant, and crispling streams; but the Passionate, to the raging Gulf swelling with waves, surging by tempests, menacing the stony rocks, and endeavouring to overthrow Mountains; even so Passions make the Soul to swell with pride and pleasure; they threaten wounds, death and destruction by audacious boldness and ire; they undermine the mountains of Virtue with hope and fear, and, in sum, never let the Soul be in quietness, but ever either flowing with Pleasure or ebbing with Pain.[10]

In Wright's account, passions are powerful forces whose role in the body is analogous to the role of weather in the natural order.[11] For the early moderns, believing strongly in a universe structured through analogy, such a correspondence was deeply meaningful. As the French philosopher Nicolas Coeffeteau explained, 'there were some which have believed that as there were four chief winds which excite divers storms, be it at land or sea; so there are four principal *Passions* which trouble our *Souls*, and which stir up divers tempests by their irregular motions'.[12] In a model of the human body expressing the cosmos, emotions cross the bodily interior as winds cross the earth. They are part of the material substance of a self continually moved and threatened with change by forces within and without the body.

Wright's vivid vocabulary here is easily applicable to Shakespeare's tragic protagonists. Wright describes a man as being 'himself' when his 'affects are pacified' and presumably under the control of his reason. Proper selfhood, then, involves reason, and reason helps to guarantee that self will be the same from one moment to the next. But the hyperbolic terms that Wright uses to describe the workings of the great passions – pride, pleasure, boldness, and ire – belong to the weather-tossed realm of tragic action. That tragic protagonists are souls moved by great passions is true almost by definition thanks to their position at the centre of worlds in crisis; their passions are oceanic as a matter of social scale no less than of immediate circumstances. Such figures do not avoid being changed by their great passions, but such change necessarily brings about change to others. This is true especially, as M. L. Lyon and J. M. Barbalet have shown, because 'emotion is best regarded not as an "inner thing" but as a "relational process"' because 'emotion is not only embodied but [is] also essentially social in character'.[13] The social character of emotion is particularly true for the figures of Shakespearean tragedy. The passions of love and hatred, hope and fear, boldness and shame act like winds and tides within and upon the tragic hero because those passions are strong enough to cause changes of mood and disposition in his inward self and hence in his outward behaviour. But such emotions are relational because they cannot be understood by the tragic hero (or by us) apart from the particularized dramatic worlds in which they occur.

It is because of the emotions' transforming power that Shakespearean tragic heroes have to struggle so mightily to achieve self-control and the Stoic constancy that self-control helps to produce. Hamlet reserves a special praise for his neo-Stoic friend Horatio as one 'whose blood and judgement are so well commeddled, / That they are not a pipe for Fortune's finger / To sound what stop she please' (*Ham.* 3.2.59–61).[14] (Blood is metonymic here for emotion, the substance embodying the significance.)[15] In a corrupt kingdom such as Claudius's Denmark, the 'time' is politically 'out of joint' for Horatio just as for Hamlet because they are both subjects of the Danish state. Shakespeare signals this by having Horatio among the watch awaiting the Ghost and speculating about the political problems that have provoked its visitation. 'A mote it is to trouble the mind's eye', says Horatio calmly of the state's disorders (1.1.112). Because of his rationality and trustworthiness, it is Horatio whom Hamlet asks for help in interpreting Claudius's response to 'The Murder of Gonzago'. But Horatio is an onlooker of the tragic action. His constancy and rationality are easily attained – even in such troubled times. For Hamlet, such constancy signifies mostly as a behavioural ideal that he can only admire from a distance. Thus, if Horatio is an exemplar of Renaissance Stoicism, Hamlet himself stands as critique of Stoicism's political relevance and viability in a state founded on usurpation through murder. The passionlessness so admired by the Stoics does not serve as the springboard to action for a son obligated to feel and revenge his father's murder. For in this time out of joint, Hamlet knows himself 'born to set it right' (1.5.190); the son who bears the name of the father is the real target of the Ghost's midnight stalking and stern invocation to remember filial duty. After he has raged against her as representative woman in the nunnery scene, Ophelia bemoans his transformation from a self-possessed prince to a madman: 'O what a noble mind is here o'erthrown!' (3.1.144). But we as audience have not seen much evidence of the self-possession that she remembers as characteristic. Or we have seen it only in brief flashes – in the moments before Hamlet has learned to distrust his old friends Rosencrantz and Guildenstern, for example, or when he greets the visiting players. On the contrary, the disarray in Hamlet's clothing and appearance that Ophelia particularizes in her report to Polonius suggests the linkage thought to exist between inner turmoil and its socially visible manifestations. He was 'pale as his shirt, his knees knocking each other, / And with a look so piteous in purport / As if he had been loosèd out of hell / To speak of horrors' (2.1.79–82).

Because of the challenges entailed by his position, then, no less than of what an early modern audience might, like Ophelia, presume to be his innate nobleness, Hamlet sees himself with shame as Horatio's temperamental opposite – emotionally volatile, swinging wildly between melancholic lethargy and ineffectual rage. In Hamlet himself, this oscillation produces a self-portrait fuelled by contempt because control of one's emotions was a trait ostensibly belonging to the male elite and justifying their right to the mastery of others.[16] Loss of self-control threatens loss of social identity. Thus, in the bitter second soliloquy beginning 'O what a rogue and peasant slave am I!' Hamlet calls himself 'a dull and muddy-mettled rascal' (2.2.502, 519). The scornful phrasing represents the kind of abuse that would be directed from a high- to a low-born man. The descriptors link the rascal's sluggish and ineffectual disposition, his 'muddy' mettle, to his base birth. In such a one (in contrast to Horatio), blood and judgement are not equally co-meddled (or co-'mettled'). Thus Hamlet, perplexed by his continuing lethargy, berates himself for being one whose cognitive faculties are literally darkened (muddied) and slowed by the workings of the melancholy humours bred of grief, lethargy, disappointment, misogyny, and thwarted ambition. His lack of purpose and inner strength – his lack of worthy 'mettle / metal' – is degrading for a king's son; hence it is a form of psychological servitude, transforming him from prince to 'rogue and peasant slave'.

In Hamlet, self-reproach expresses itself as the perception of mental and bodily defect – a cold and bloodless liver, a lack of bitter choleric humour: 'it cannot be / But that I am pigeon-livered, and lack gall / To make oppression bitter' (2.2.529–31). Reasoning inductively from behaviour to the body, Hamlet rationalizes his lack of purposive activity, his seeming inability to rouse himself to a murderous revenge. In the depressed interaction between a grief-laden, 'muddy' mind and a body physiologi-cally unproductive of the heat and blood required for action against the usurper-king, Hamlet finds a diagnosis, though not an excuse, for his inconstancy. Given what Hamlet sees as his reasons for failing to exact revenge, it is not surprising that his efforts to change himself and his situation take the indirect form of putting on a play. The depressed prince requires the mimetic actions of others – professional players unin-volved in the political crisis and merely eager for patronage – to stimulate himself and Claudius into direct confrontation. (And, even then, direct confrontation does not happen until the final moments of the play when Hamlet is already dying from the poison received at the tip of Laertes's foil.)

When, after startling Claudius into a display of guilt and alarm during 'The Murder of Gonzago', Hamlet begins to feel instilled with purpose, he perceives his momentary sense of triumph as a transformation in bodily self-experience, in temperature, and in emotional appetite: 'Now could I drink hot blood, / And do such bitter business as the day / Would quake to look on' (3.2.390–2). Perhaps some of this new energy prompts the stab through the arras that kills Polonius in the closet scene. But Hamlet's sense of purpose and motive carried within the body remains unsteady and tenta-tive, as when he implores the Ghost not to look reproachfully at him,

> Lest with this piteous action you convert
> My stern effects. Then what I have to do
> Will want true colour: tears perchance for blood.   (3.4.127–29)

It is as if the energy – the blood – required to stab Polonius has been expended with the deed, leaving Hamlet still open to the Ghost's rebukes about his 'almost blunted purpose' (3.4.110). Yet, even in this volatile scene, it is always self-assessment of his bodily state that Hamlet relies on to express his emotions. Here, having impulsively committed murder, raged against his mother's choice of husbands, and spoken imploringly to a paternal ghost invisible to Gertrude, Hamlet nevertheless seeks to reassure his alarmed mother of his overall sanity. He compares the regular, even harmonious movement of his body's blood-flow to hers: 'My pulse as yours doth temperately keep time, / And makes as healthful music. It is not madness / That I have uttered' (3.4.141–3). And Hamlet is not alone, of course, in seeking bodily expression for the emotions. His wild, inconstant behaviour produces the symptoms – metaphoric and literal both – of hot bodily diseases in others: 'Do it England', Claudius exclaims in apostrophe after sending Hamlet off to execution abroad, 'For like the hectic in my blood he rages, / And thou must cure me' (4.3.61–3). Here, too, emotions are represented as both embodied and relational – even contagious – in nature.

Though Hamlet may be among the most volatile of Shakespeare's tragic heroes, others too demonstrate the materiality of early modern selfhood in verbal representations of their inward experience. Othello, convinced of Desdemona's infidelity, feels suddenly incapable of participating in any of the martial actions that formerly defined his place in the world:

> Farewell the neighing steed and the shrill trump,
> The spirit-stirring drum, th'ear-piercing fife,
> The royal banner, and all quality,
> Pride, pomp, and circumstance of glorious war!
> . . . Farewell! Othello's occupation's gone   (3.3.352–8)

His transformation from soldierly calm to jealous anxiety renders him unfit in his own eyes for military command of warfare. Later, resolved upon murder, he imagines all the afflictions he could have borne with constancy – sores and shames, total poverty, imprisonment, even scorn – all the afflictions, that is, other than the idea, graphically brought to him by Iago's images of Desdemona 'topp'd', of his wife's infidelity. He comes to feel that the decay of his love for Desdemona and his sense of her moral corruption are stored in the great receptacle of affections that is his heart.[17] Such an agonized self-perception renders him psychologically alienated from his own bodily substance, the substance in which his love for Desdemona was stored. His relation to himself is no longer a properly self-possessed interior 'here' but an alienated elsewhere, a 'there':

> But there where I have garnered up my heart,
> Where either I must live or bear no life,
> The fountain from the which my current runs
> Or else dries up – to be discarded thence
> Or keep it as a cistern for foul toads
> To knot and gender in! (4.2.56–61)

His sense of bodily foulness in this passage is a strong version of Hamlet's self-contempt as 'muddy-mettled rascal'. It follows logically from a grief and jealousy so strong that their workings have rendered the once-eloquent Othello wildly inarticulate, shouting to the bewildered Venetian visitor, 'You are welcome, sir, to Cyprus. Goats and monkeys!' (4.1.254). In the moments before her murder, Desdemona is alarmed to see the self-possessed man she had married gnawing his 'nether lip' and shaking with 'bloody passion' (5.2.43–4). In this circular logic, Othello's passion is 'bloody' because it is a violent one; and it is a violent one because jealous rage has literally heated his heart's blood, darkened and polluted his spirits, and readied him to prompt such a violent deed as murdering his new wife.

Indeed it is precisely the early modern belief in the continual interaction between emotions and the body that validates Iago's description of his plot against Othello as a poisoning. From this point of view, Othello's acceptance of Iago's insinuations against Desdemona is ingestion, a bodily incorporation of powerfully aversive words and images. They move from the ear to the mind to the rest of his body and work to change him, emotionally and physically. Spoken words, while not material entities themselves, were thought to produce material changes in the mind – and hence in the self that receives them. But the changes in Othello's emotions, cognition, and behaviour were transported by blood. 'The Moor already changes with my poison', Iago remarks:

> Dangerous conceits are in their natures poisons,
> Which at the first are scarce found to distaste
> But, with a little act upon the blood,
> Burn like the mines of sulphur. (3.3.327–30)

Given the effect of such a poisoning on Othello's embodied self – the sulphurous burning of his blood, the agitation of his spirits – it is not surprising that loss of consciousness would mark one of the first stages of Othello's psychological journey from contented new husband to wife-murderer. 'Work on, / My medicine, work!' Iago gloats (4.1.42–3), having added to the poisonous effect of verbal images on Othello the psychological impress of the lost handkerchief, an image of the object whose loss and misunderstood recovery is also material to Othello's transformation by passion.

It would be reductive to read Shakespeare's tragic protagonists merely in terms of a struggle between reason and passion, as some early critics have done.[18] But this struggle did in fact preoccupy the moral philosophers of early modern Europe and helped to set the terms for their understanding of human choice and agency.[19] Wright, one of the most influential of such philosophers in England (at least to judge by the success and later editions of his 1604 *Passions of the Mind in General*), describes passions, in league with the senses, engaged in a continual struggle against rational self-government. Most men, says Wright, 'feeling this war so mighty, so continual, so near, so domestical that either they must consent to do their enemy's will, or still be in conflict resolve never to displease their sense or passions, but to grant them whatsoever they demand'.[20] But, as we have seen with Hamlet, tragic heroes are set apart from the ordinary run of men – by dint of hereditary rank, accomplishment, life experience, strength, bravery, ruthlessness, or some combination of these. The tragic hero's exceptionality is a dramatic given so that it may be tested, that it may fail, that it may triumph, that it may inspire in us such self-dissolving and self-forgetting emotions as admiration, pity, or even (as with heroes such as Macbeth, Antony, Coriolanus, or Timon of Athens) complex mixtures of contradictory emotions. Such figures are set apart further by the suffering reserved for them. The reasoning here sounds and is circular, if tragic actions, by definition, represent the extraordinary life circumstances of exceptional figures whose obligation to be self-controlled and whose capacity to act and suffer is accepted as greater than that of ordinary people. And the reasoning is notoriously masculinist as well, in that it tends to exclude women as historically significant agents in tragic actions, with rare exceptions (Shakespeare's Cleopatra being one, John Webster's Duchess of Malfi being another). Classic tragedy asks the ordinary men and women in a theatre audience to ratify this social selectivity and gender exclusion even as it requires them to identify with the tragic hero and feel the tragic emotions of pity and fear at his downfall.

In these tragic male protagonists, the struggle between reason and passion takes on a representative or exemplary character. In *Antony and Cleopatra* Caesar remembers the young Antony as a model of Stoic constancy and physical endurance:

> Thou didst drink
> The stale of horses and the gilded puddle
> Which beasts would cough at. Thy palate then did deign
> The roughest berry on the rudest hedge . . .
>
> . . . all this
> – It wounds thine honour that I speak it now –
> Was borne so like a soldier that thy cheek
> So much as lanked not.   (1.4.62–72)

The young Antony conquered physical appetite, according to this memorial narrative, by an act of will that put bodily need in service to the long-range goals of the Roman state with which he identified. His was a triumph of self-control, here over an aversion so profound that it was shared, Caesar asserts, by animals and men alike. Such Stoicism differs from the more ordinary brand of passionlessness that Hamlet praises in Horatio as almost a gift of nature because Antony's is achieved, is precisely *not* natural.[21] In such an attained self-control Caesar recognizes the mark of personal greatness and exceptional masculinity – here given military modelling ('borne so like a soldier'). Self-control earned the younger Antony his reputation ('honour') and justified his control over others.

What matters desperately now for Caesar, given what the Romans diagnose as Antony's anti-Stoic pursuit of pleasure with Cleopatra, is that their long-standing psychic and cultural investment in him as the exemplar of human dignity has come into question. For Caesar, Antony's affair with Cleopatra signifies an immersion in the present moment and irrational surrender to the demands of the body. John Gillies argues that 'at the simplest level, Egypt attacks Antony through his senses' while 'at another level, Antony's judgment is bewitched' by Cleopatra herself.[22] To accept Renaissance psychology in its own terms, however, means that we can understand these two 'levels' functioning as one – the sensory transformation in Antony's physical and emotional environment overwhelming his once-rational control and effecting profound changes in his behaviour and his response to the world. His immersion in temporality, too, represents a form of inconstancy, a trait synonymous with woman and justifying women's exclusion from historical process. It is only logical, then, that Caesar finds Antony hopelessly – perhaps irrevocably – feminized: he 'fishes, drinks, and wastes / The lamps of night in revel'. By doing so, he 'is not more manlike / Than Cleopatra, nor the queen of Ptolemy / More womanly than he'. He is 'the abstract of all faults / That all men follow' (1.4.5–7, 9–10), a man regressing into the ungendered state of boys who, 'being mature in knowledge, / Pawn their experience to their present pleasure / And so rebel to judgement' (1.4.31–3). His affair with Cleopatra thus threatens to destabilize the great organizing binaries (here represented by the difference of male and female, man and boy) by which Rome knows its dominant place in the world.

Much in the imagery and action of *Antony and Cleopatra* resists the disparaging reading of the lovers' story that Rome finds it necessary to promulgate. The play's triumphant representation of the Egyptian queen's 'infinite variety' which 'age cannot wither', 'nor custom stale' (2.2.245–6) serves to question Rome's reductive binarisms of West–East, male–female, reason–passion, discipline–pleasure, constancy–inconstancy. Convinced of her lover's personal greatness and her own, wilfully defiant of Roman behavioural codes, Cleopatra exempts him from any obligation to Stoic impassivity. For her, immersion in pleasure and present time is a privilege granted to those who rule, a sign not of ignoble subjection but of the scope of their command of others, even of the natural world. She differs powerfully from Caesar in regarding emotional display in Antony as in effect validated by his greatness, not destructive of it: 'Be'st thou sad or merry', she says to him in affectionate apostrophe, 'The violence of either thee becomes, / So does it no man else' (1.5.62–4). It is nevertheless true that Antony's oscillation between service to Rome and allegiance to Cleopatra works like an oscillation between incompatible identities that are produced behaviourally in response to the demands and values of others.[23] As Linda Charnes has argued, 'the real battle in this play, then – that between Caesar and Cleopatra – is staked out across the terrain of Antony's "identity": the set of representations, images, and narratives he needs to recognize himself as "Antony" '. She adds, 'Both Octavius and Cleopatra understand how susceptible Antony is to attacks on his "manhood".'[24] This is why Cleopatra can try to shame him by interpreting his emotions as reactions to Rome: 'As I am Egypt's queen, / Thou blushest, Antony, and that blood of thine / Is Caesar's homager' (1.1.31–3). After his and Cleopatra's final defeat by Caesar's legions and having been told erroneously that Cleopatra has killed herself rather than surrender to Caesar, Antony feels suddenly lost and insubstantial, as if his body were dissolving into air. He asks his boy Eros a question which sounds not at all rhetorical: 'Eros, thou yet behold'st me?' (4.14.1). He goes on to express the sensation of self-dissolution and loss of personal boundaries in a comparison of his bodily self to the clouds. Asking Eros to think about the motions of clouds changing from 'bear or lion, / A towered citadel, a pendent rock' (4.1.3–4), Antony comments:

That which is now a horse, even with a thought
The rack dislimns and makes it indistinct
As water is in water.

                    . . .

My good knave Eros, now thy captain is
Even such a body. Here I am Antony,
Yet cannot hold this visible shape   (4.14.9–14)

This speech is usually valued for its pathos and eloquence as Antony faces
the shame of loss and the challenge of suicide. Yet this speech is also –
perhaps paradoxically – a good example of the early modern self's sense of its
physicality and embeddedness in the natural world. Antony's disidentifica-
tion with his body comes through a contrasting identification with the
clouds. The shaming comparison of himself to clouds tells us that he has lost
the capacity for the sustained, self-same, willed action synonymous with
heroic masculinity, becoming as inconstant in his motions as they are. The
clouds are Antony's body dissolving, his self-sameness melting away: 'black
vesper's pageants', they betoken death imagined as vanishing into insubstantiality (4.14.8).

Yet the speech is equally extraordinary for what it represents as the agency
within natural forces even as those forces – represented by clouds – symbolize Antony's loss of agency and of sustainable identification with a fixed
bodily self. This paradox becomes clear in the degree of almost purposive
power that Antony's verbs – 'dislimns', 'makes' – give to the clouds
themselves. In them, continual self-obliteration is also continual refashioning; the clouds *make* their indistinction as an expression of their essential
nature. The clouds mirror the continual remaking – 'even with a thought' –
of embodied consciousness but in a way that mocks – even as it expresses –
the self's longing for fixity. For Antony comes to realize that identity
requires what the clouds do not – the 'firmness of identity provided by
unwavering allegiance to a particular place'.[25]

We too may feel such evocative reciprocity between clouds and embodied consciousness to be problematic here as Antony seeks to reassure the boy
Eros (and himself) that he retains faculties of personal agency. But his more
powerful sense of self-loss and insubstantiality makes his capacity for self-
murder questionable. Only when Eros summons his own will and kills
himself rather than hold the sword for Antony is Antony able to take such
'brave instruction' (4.14.98). Even then, he bungles the job and ends up a
living dead-weight, becoming so firmly identified with his body that he
needs to be hoisted clumsily by Cleopatra and her women up into the

monument in order to die there. As Cynthia Marshall suggests, 'wounded, bleeding, and lacking agency, Antony takes on a typically feminine position [and] ... troubles an audience's notions of what it means to be a (masculine) hero'.[26]

Rather than being sovereign (hence incorporeal) selves, then, we need to see Shakespeare's tragic heroes as beings in whom psychology and physiology have yet to be pried apart conceptually. Their behaviours express a physical, emotional, and psychological embeddedness in fictive worlds structured and made meaningful by correspondence between inner and outer, body and cosmos, emotions and weather. We need to define those worlds broadly enough so that we can place the natural as well as the cultural and social dimensions of those worlds in a historical frame. Once we have done so, then the intentions of the materialized self may be mirrored by such objects in the landscape as Othello's befouled cisterns or Antony's clouds in motion. In these more precise terms, the 'inwardness' of a Shakespearean tragic hero is neither an internal psychological space hollowed out by language nor merely a function of rhetoric, but a collection of the embodied faculties, capacities, intentions, and passions that together constitute individual agency. What we should expect, then, from such a reconstituted notion of tragic selfhood is not disembodied constancy and equality of manners, in Dryden's terms, nor even the unified selfhood so dear to humanistic thought, but a self in which continuousness of psychological identity is put under severe stress by psychological and physiological openness to a complex and painful environment.

By using the terms of Renaissance behavioural thought to reconceptualize the tragic self as a permeable and hence changeable one, we are able to see Shakespeare's tragic heroes moved, and even transformed, by passions understood as 'psycho-physiological' events embedded in an environment both natural and cultural. Self is not a condition of disembodied inwardness independent of the material world that it inhabits. Self is rather inhabited reciprocally by that world, shaped by its elements.[27] In the extreme cultural environments of Shakespeare's tragedies, such permeation can lead to radical displacements of agency and interiority, rendering the self nearly unrecognizable as the site of ordinary emotions, desires, and motivations.

In *Titus Andronicus*, for example, it is Titus's role at the beginning of the play to represent a mythically exaggerated version of Roman imperial will. Phallicly potent, Stoic, sacrificially public-spirited, Titus is first presented to us less as an interiorized self than as the stern embodiment of Roman militarism, an allegory of iron will. His merit, he announces to the public assembled for his return, consists of forty years of military service and the fathering of twenty-five sons, all but four of whom have died in battle. When Titus greets the opened family tomb as 'sacred receptàcle of my joys, / Sweet cell of virtue and nobility' (I.I.92–3), Titus's hailing of the tomb functions to ratify Rome's successful ideological 'hailing' of him: he is the faithful scion and arm of the state, his past and future identity equated with the city's. The link between rule of others and rule of self, so key to the action in *Hamlet, Othello,* and *Antony and Cleopatra,* is here established in mythic terms, rather than psychological or even social ones, because it is linked to a sequence of events which lead to Titus's fatally illogical renunciation of the crown. Rome turns to Titus to 'help to set a head on headless Rome' (I.I.186). When Titus refuses to take up the imperial crown on the manifestly weak grounds that 'a better head her glorious body fits / Than his that shakes for age and feebleness' (I.I.187–8), he is setting aside the logic of his own identity and imperilling that of the civil body from which his own earliest experience of self and masculine agency arose.

It has not been usual among critics to see Titus's abdication here as an abdication of reason, a surrender to passion. Yet it may be productive to do so, because Titus's renunciation of patriarchal duty is like a renunciation of the will. His refusal of the crown not only signifies a slackening of his lifelong vigilance as guarantor of Rome's physical and moral wholeness but also leads directly to the dismemberments visited first upon Lavinia and Titus and then, in the boomerang logic of revenge tragedy, on the bodies of the surviving Gothic brothers. Katherine Rowe has suggested that 'Titus's actions in the opening scene make him as dangerous and unfit as Saturninus.'[28] Certainly, it is as an embodiment of overweening will that Titus himself initiates the play's cycle of dismemberment and revenge that will lead to his family's downfall and suffering. The play's action suggests that Titus has been too severe in his execution of military authority, much too rigid a guardian of Rome's boundaries. He mercilessly insists upon the ritual sacrifice of a Gothic prince, whose 'limbs are lopped, / And entrails feed the sacrificing fire' (I.I.143–4) as payment for his sons' lives. This insistence, so early in the play, has the effect of reconfiguring Titus's Stoic self-control as a species of primitive vengefulness, a displacement of the pain he has endured on to those held responsible for it. In the predatory calculus of this tragedy, it is as if Titus had decided that integrity of self (construed to include Rome's corporate body no less than his own and that of his family) could only be guaranteed by a dismemberment of others rationalized as Roman piety. This may be why he refuses to accept any principle of equivalence between the public service of Roman and of Gothic warriors even though the Gothic queen Tamora argues powerfully for one:

But must my sons be slaughtered in the streets
For valiant doings in their country's cause?
O if to fight for king and commonweal
Were piety in thine, it is in these   (1.1.112–15)

For John Gillies, Titus commits a gross disregard of what Elizabethans
might have regarded as 'natural piety'.[29] Titus's failure to recognize the
possibility of heroic agency in the Other and decision to locate it solely in
himself and by biological extension in his family lead directly to the vengeful
acts of the Gothic princes – their rape and mutilation of Lavinia, the murder
of her husband Bassianus, and the execution of two of Titus's sons. In
Titus's self-interested figuration, the suffering Andronici remain human
while their enemies render themselves bestial. He describes the city for
which the Andronici have fought so stoically as a beast-infested wilderness
lacking the traces of human ordering: 'Rome is but a wilderness of tigers? /
Tigers must prey, and Rome affords no prey / But me and mine' (3.1.54–6).
But for Titus to see himself and his family, the tiger's prey, as victims in
these naturalized terms is effectively to de-politicize the meaning of his
suffering – hence that part of his own complex responsibility for it. If Rome
is a wilderness, he has helped to make it so – by denying the reality of
Tamora's maternal suffering, by sacrificing her children for his own, by
murdering his defiant son Mutius ('What, villain boy, / Barr'st me my way
in Rome?' (1.1.290–1)), by choosing Saturninus over Bassianus as new
emperor of Rome, and by allowing the stranger queen Tamora through
marriage to be 'incorporate in Rome' (1.1.462). Though, as Douglas Green
has argued, the play tries to deflect its criticism of Titus through exaggeration of the evil represented by Tamora and her male entourage, Titus's
extreme wilfulness as patriarch, soldier, and elector is hard to overlook given
the magnitude of the horrors that it inspires.[30]

   The extremes of his subsequent suffering (passion in its literal sense from
the Latin verb 'patior', to suffer, to endure) take Titus into an altered
cognitive state, into a form of madness. Here too, as we have seen before in
Othello, the body's sufferings work changes in the mind. Reality appears
nightmarish – a 'fearful slumber' (3.1.251) – and Titus's own responses to it
become wildly inappropriate. 'Why dost thou laugh?' his brother Marcus asks
in bewilderment as Titus reacts with 'Ha, ha, ha!' to the soldiers' presentation
of the executed heads of his sons (3.1.265, 264). He gives way to the passion of
revenge in spectacular fashion – feeding the Gothic queen Tamora a dish
baked from the heads of her sons. But to do so, we soon realize, is to become a
mirror version of his enemies and to collapse the binaries of Roman–Goth,

human–bestial, pious–vengeful that constitute the play's symbolic vocabulary. It also suggests that extreme suffering collapses the overwhelmed self back into its mutely expressive environment. This is what Titus seems to recognize in describing the handless, tongueless Lavinia as a 'map of woe' (3.2.12) who 'drinks no other drink but tears, / Brewed with her sorrow, mashed upon her cheek' (3.2.37–8).

As Elaine Scarry has suggested of the practice of torture, the reduction of the suffering body only to its experience and recognition of extreme pain entails an unmaking of the world. In political torture, the interactivity that constitutes normative social intercourse is radically dislocated. Agency devolves wholly to the torturer, suffering wholly to his victim. For the tortured, the basic faculties of self-articulation are lost to pain and dread; social identity as constituted by loyalties to others becomes an axis of extreme vulnerability; and identification with one's own body as anything other than the location of pain is no longer possible.[31] Given his partisan account of suffering as the exclusive property of the Andronici, Titus could not recognize himself as torturer, only as the tortured. Yet what he and all his enemies share is a grotesque affirmation of hypertrophied will as the locus of agency, and of suffering as the locus of bodily self-experience. Lavinia begs Tamora to be killed rather than raped by her sons. The bodily punishments they do inflict on her – rape and the mutilation of her tongue and hands – constitute a display of agency on their part as merely killing her could not. Their power is not merely over her body or even her will to resist, but over the male relatives entrusted with a personal and social obligation to protect her. As Green comments, Lavinia's 'mutilated body "articulates" Titus's own suffering and victimization'; she becomes the mirror in which he sees and thus remakes self.[32] For Titus and Lavinia, pain and mutilation institute an unmaking of the world which they counter with a mirror unmaking – tricking their enemies into their own undoing. For Lavinia does not, in the end, display merely the agential power of her father's enemies nor serve as eloquently mute symbol of her family's passion in suffering. By finally communicating the story of her rape and its perpetrators, by carrying her father's severed hand offstage in her mouth, even perhaps by being wilfully murdered by Titus himself at the end of the play, Lavinia signals a resumption of agency both for herself and her father – though on terms a modern audience finds difficult to countenance or understand except as a tragic action parodying its own tendency towards excess. What Lavinia and her father concoct – literally – is a cannibal feast which they describe to their victims just before killing them: 'Hark, villains', Titus tells Chiron and Demetrius with unmistakable glee, 'I will grind your bones to dust, / And with your blood and it I'll make a paste' (5.2.186–7). He insists not only on Tamora consuming her sons' flesh and blood, but being made to know it before she too is killed. If Shakespeare makes it almost impossible for us to sympathize with Tamora, he also lets us see her undergo, in horror, the climactic unmaking of *her* world.

The mutilations visited upon the bodies of the Andronici and the cannibal savagery that Titus's family visits upon the family of Tamora enact a grotesque version of the dissolution of the body which figures Antony's self-loss in the mirroring clouds in *Antony and Cleopatra*. In both tragedies, however, and indeed in all the tragedies discussed in this chapter, the experience of self entails identification with a suffering body at a moment in intellectual history when bodies were open and porous, when bodily substances were thought to be psychologically both formative and expressive, when fluids could express the full weight of a character's destiny. What I have sought to emphasize here is the materiality of embodied consciousness in Shakespeare's tragic heroes – a condition not peculiar to them of course but peculiarly significant in them as the central representatives of subjectivity in their plays. In this sense, my neglect of the representation of female subjectivity in these plays is almost more inevitable than accidental, for the masculinist bias in all these tragedies – not excepting *Antony and Cleopatra* – presupposes the centrality as well as the representativeness of the embodied consciousnesses of the male protagonists. (To recognize this is not, of course, to agree with it.) Finally, to recognize the embodiment of consciousness matters in Shakespeare's tragedies because a prior generation of critics and the many students who still read such criticism today have tended to see the 'tragic self' in transhistorical and essentialist terms. What this chapter has sought to demonstrate instead is the importance of understanding the dramatic construction of self historically, in a period before psychology and physiology had divided conceptually. The representation of subjectivity in Shakespeare's tragedies represents a way of thinking about inwardness in many ways fundamentally different from our own.

Notes

1. John Dryden, 'The Grounds of Criticism in Tragedy', in *Troilus and Cressida, or Truth Found Too Late, A Tragedy,* Dryden, *The Dramatic Works,* ed. Montague Summers, 6 vols. (London: Nonesuch Press, 1932), vol. v, p. 19.
2. For a cogent presentation of this position, see Catherine Belsey, *The Subject of Tragedy: Identity and Difference in Renaissance Drama* (London and New York: Routledge, 1985), pp. 33–42.

3. *Discourse on Method* in *Philosophical Writings of Descartes*, 4 vols., trans. John Cottingham, Robert Stoothoff and Dugald Murdoch (Cambridge University Press, 1985), vol. 1, p. 127.

4. Dryden does not use 'psychology' because it had not yet come into general usage. The *OED* records the first use in 1653 in William Harvey's *Anatomical Exercises*, in which Harvey describes psychology 'as a doctrine which searches out mans Soul, and the effects of it' (sig. H8v).

5. Katharine Eisaman Maus, *Inwardness and Theater in the English Renaissance* (Chicago and London: University of Chicago Press, 1995), p. 12.

6. *Ibid.*, p. 195.

7. Timothy Reiss has described this distinctly early-modern form of self-experience as one of 'passibility', by which he means 'experiences of being whose common denominator was a sense of being *embedded in and acted on* by [circles or spheres] – including the material world and immediate biological, familial and social ambiences'; see *Mirages of the Selfe: Patterns of Personhood in Ancient and Early Modern Europe* (Stanford University Press, 2003), p. 2.

8. David Hillman, 'Visceral Knowledge: Shakespeare, Skepticism, and the Interior of the Early Modern Body', *The Body in Parts: Fantasies of Corporeality in Early Modern England*, ed. David Hillman and Carla Mazzio (New York and London: Routledge, 1997), p. 91. For a fuller discussion, see David Hillman, *Shakespeare's Entrails: Belief, Scepticism and the Interior of the Body* (Basingstoke: Palgrave Macmillan, 2007), pp. 1–57.

9. Katharine Park, 'The Organic Soul', *The Cambridge History of Renaissance Philosophy*, gen. ed. Charles B. Schmitt (Cambridge University Press, 1988), p. 469. On this passage in *Othello*, see Gail Kern Paster, *Humoring the Body: Emotions and the Shakespearean Stage* (Chicago and London: University of Chicago Press, 2004), pp. 60–4.

10. Thomas Wright, *The Passions of the Mind in General*, ed. William Webster Newbold (New York: Garland, 1986), pp. 133–4.

11. See Andrew Wear, 'Medicine in Early Modern Europe', *The Western Medical Tradition 800 BC to 1800 AD*, ed. Lawrence I. Conrad *et al.* (Cambridge University Press, 1995), pp. 255–64.

12. See Nicolas Coeffeteau, *A Table of Humane Passions*, trans. Edward Grimeston (London, 1621), p. 31.

13. M. L. Lyon and J. M. Barbalet, 'Society's Body: Emotion and the "Somatization" of Social Theory', *Experience and Embodiment: The Existential Ground of Culture and Self*, ed. Thomas J. Csordas (Cambridge University Press, 1994), p. 57.

14. Michael C. Schoenfeldt, *Bodies and Selves in Early Modern England: Physiology and Inwardness in Spenser, Shakespeare, Herbert, and Milton* (Cambridge University Press, 1999), pp. 15–17.

15. This phrase borrows from Charles Taylor, *Sources of the Self: The Making of the Modern Identity* (Cambridge, MA: Harvard University Press, 1989), p. 189.

16. Schoenfeldt, *Bodies and Selves*, pp. 90–1. Ewan Fernie writes that 'the language of the play is … thoroughly imbued with shame's imagery'; see *Shame in*

Shakespeare (London and New York: Routledge, 2002), pp. 107–35, especially p. 113.

17. On the heart as receptacle of feelings, see Robert A. Erickson, *The Language of the Heart, 1600–1750* (Philadelphia: University of Pennsylvania Press, 1997), pp. 11–15.

18. Lily Bess Campbell, *Shakespeare's Tragic Heroes: Slaves of Passion* (Cambridge University Press, 1930).

19. See Susan James, *Passion and Action: The Emotions in Seventeenth-Century Philosophy* (New York: Oxford University Press, 1997).

20. Wright, *Passions of the Mind in General*, p. 96.

21. John Gillies suggests that Shakespeare has several models besides Plutarch for Antony's Stoic control here, 'any number of literary journeys in which Stoic virtue is measured against exotic perils'. See *Shakespeare and the Geography of Difference* (Cambridge University Press, 1994), p. 118.

22. *Ibid.*, p. 119.

23. As Cynthia Marshall has written, 'Antony is always someone else's version of Antony, never himself.' See 'Man of Steel Done Got the Blues: Melancholic Subversion of Presence in *Antony and Cleopatra*', *Shakespeare Quarterly* 44 (1993): 387.

24. Linda Charnes, *Notorious Identity: Materializing the Subject in Shakespeare* (Cambridge, MA: Harvard University Press, 1993), p. 112.

25. *Ibid.*, p. 113.

26. Marshall, 'Man of Steel Done Got the Blues', p. 403.

27. See my 'The Body and Its Passions', in 'Forum: Body Work', ed. Bruce R. Smith, *Shakespeare Studies* 29 (2001): 44–50.

28. Katherine A. Rowe, *Dead Hands: Fictions of Agency, Renaissance to Modern* (Stanford University Press, 1999), p. 77.

29. Gillies, *Shakespeare and the Geography of Difference*, p. 104.

30. Douglas E. Green, 'Interpreting "Her Martyr'd Signs": Gender and Tragedy in *Titus Andronicus*', *Shakespeare Quarterly* 40 (1989): 321–2. For a contrasting argument that Titus actually represents moderation in action, see Christopher Crosbie, 'Fixing Moderation: *Titus Andronicus* and the Aristotelian Determination of Value', *Shakespeare Quarterly* 58 (2007): 147–73.

31. Elaine Scarry, *The Body in Pain: The Making and Unmaking of the World* (New York: Oxford University Press, 1987).

32. Green, 'Interpreting "Her Martyr'd Signs"', 322.

CHAPTER 9

Tragedies of revenge and ambition

Robert N. Watson

Revenge and ambition, past and present

Revenge and ambition had meanings in Shakespeare's world significantly different from what they mean now. Yet we can still easily recognize them in Shakespeare's plays, allowing us both an emotional connection to the human past and an intellectual perspective on it.

Shakespeare's brilliant contemporary Francis Bacon called revenge 'a kind of wild justice',[1] and it provided an important supplement to official justice in an era of limited police powers and severely enforced social hierarchy. The Tudor monarchies made some progress in controlling lawlessness, but there must have been some basis for the persistent jokes in Elizabethan comedy about incompetent constables and watch-squads. With so many crimes unsolved, so many criminals immune to punishment, and so many outrages against women, the poor, and ethnic and religious minorities not even considered crimes, it is hardly surprising that the public developed an appetite for revenge fantasies.[2] A prime example is Thomas Kyd's *The Spanish Tragedy* (1587?), which showed Hieronimo feigning madness in order to uncover and punish the secret murder of his son by his social superiors. The huge commercial success of that story led to Shakespeare's *Hamlet* and dozens of other revenge plays in the period.

Ambition, too, was a particularly alluring and dangerous sin in Shakespeare's society, where radical economic, technological, and theological changes had unsettled people from hereditary roles that dated back to medieval feudalism. For the many who migrated to urban centres, there was neither a safety-net to prevent starvation nor a glass ceiling to prevent social climbing – only a scramble for money from the gullible and favours from the powerful. While the subtle refashioning of inward identity provoked soliloquies, the rapid refashioning of outward identity provoked civil authorities – desperate to preserve traditional order – to punish upstarts and innovators (even high-ranking ones such as the throne-hungry Earl of

Essex). The conservative tendency of human culture must have been similarly punitive, in less official but more pervasive ways: during unsettled times, people reflexively conspire to ridicule new styles and penalize opportunists, and Elizabethan and Jacobean comedies (especially those of Ben Jonson) showed people doing so. Those trying to get ahead deserved punishment, while those trying to get even deserved sympathy and sly complicity; where to draw the line depended on where the viewer stood in the class system. Furthermore, in a society where status was so unstable, ambition often led to violent revenge, as duels over honour became an epidemic among the aristocratic elite.

In a broader sense, this period seems to have invented a new and inexhaustible kind of ambition – and defined it as fundamental to human nature. Against a classical and medieval notion of desire as finite, seeking its own end in satisfaction, Renaissance culture promoted a Romantic and modern notion of desire as insatiable, willing to invent further goals in order perpetually to forestall its own demise in stasis.[3] Christopher Marlowe's great overreachers, such as Tamburlaine and Faustus, explored the tragic implications of this discrepancy between what the aspiring mind could imagine and what the mortal body could accomplish. A similarly relentless desire propels Shakespeare's Macbeth into crime after crime, tomorrow and tomorrow, and discontented into death. These tragic instances reflected a Christian warning, amplified by Protestantism, that nothing in the material world could ever satisfy the needs of the soul.

Yet, important as understanding the immediate social and philosophical contexts may be, Shakespeare's tragedies of revenge and ambition have applications and resonances far beyond the historical circumstances of his culture. Impulses like the ones fuelling these tragedies are visible from the earliest recorded human histories to the most recent. Indeed, these impulses are easily visible in many non-human animals, as they punish those who have hurt or insulted them, and compete for dominance over the others of their species and gender. While much can be learned about Shakespeare's tragedies by learning the history of Shakespeare's society, and vice versa, these plays seem almost supernaturally capable of speaking to fundamental questions. Neither an essentialist belief in universal human truths immune to cultural difference nor a constructivist claim that all human reality is produced by local ideological conditions therefore allows Shakespeare's tragedies their full stature and intricacy.

Unlike even the best of the other tragedians of revenge and ambition in this period – from the strong Elizabethan roots in Marlowe to the decaying Jacobean blossoms in John Webster – Shakespeare looks inside not only the psychological workings of his characters, but also the complex ethical transactions of revenge and ambition. He offers not merely the grand cautionary spectacle of falling greatness, not merely the gruesome cautionary spectacle of escalating vengeance, but insight into the ways different individuals manage, and are managed by, some primal desires for power and redress. By staging the collisions of such desires, Shakespeare can provide an indispensable acknowledgement of moral complexity – and thereby a means of understanding and forgiving – that law itself cannot provide, that Christianity (condemning both ambition and revenge) resists, and that not even such subtle and powerful philosophers as Kant (with his determination to make punishments fit crimes) and Hegel (with his reliance on punishment to negate all negations of the moral order) have been able to generate.

Shakespeare's philosophy of revenge and ambition

Characteristically, Shakespeare's observation of human behaviour enables him to trace patterns for which science would provide a rationale and a vocabulary centuries later. He can therefore answer a question that troubles readers of history, not just of history plays: what makes kingship so desirable that a man will destroy the peace of both his land and his mind in order to acquire it? This is a theological question as well as a political and psychological one: 'What is a man profited, if he shall gain the whole world, and lose his own soul?' (Matthew 16:26). In the case of Macbeth, the implicit answer lies in an innate craving for dominion and progeny that the ambitious man himself cannot fully understand, that drives him even against his own better reason. The irony is that Macbeth, in pursuing that goal so desperately, in a selfishly mechanical rather than co-operatively humane way, destroys his own chances for a place in the human future. Seemingly driven by instincts from an evolutionary phase when only the dominant male had reproductive privileges, reading both Scottish history and (like some crude Darwinians) the survival of the fittest in too narrow a sense, Macbeth overlooks the complex, collective aspect of a social species.

No less characteristically, Shakespeare takes very ordinary human situations and impulses, magnifies them to the highest dramatic scale, looks for their deepest implications, and offers no simple moral. His plays reflect a persistent myth of ambition, a myth that entails a tragic paradox. The desire to transcend oneself, to become something greater than one was born to be, is a natural and seemingly noble human tendency; yet it becomes a means of self-destruction, a betrayal of nature and origins that invites primal punishment. Even where – as for Leontes in *The Winter's Tale* – the aspirations (towards purity and timelessness) are noble, and some of the resulting losses miraculously repaid, the tragic potential of ambition and the vengeful potential of the natural order remain painfully obvious.

One version of Shakespeare's philosophical myth looks pragmatic and political: his history plays insist that anyone who takes the throne without inheriting it will always be vulnerable to new usurpers, and will have trouble passing it on to his own offspring, but can never safely relinquish that throne, either. Another, parallel version of this myth seems Freudian (which is not really an anachronism, since Sigmund Freud derived it largely from reading classical and Shakespearean tragedy): as the psychoanalytic theories about oedipal conflicts would suggest, the son attempts to outdo the father, perhaps attempts (like Coriolanus) to reconceive himself through a sym-bolic courtship of a maternal figure. Ambition takes the form of a desire to be reborn in some chosen ideal form, autonomous and powerful, unlimited by inherited identity or social taboo. The father (or some trace of him) punishes the son, specifically by destroying the son's procreative powers (a kind of castration). Shakespeare's ambitious men rarely succeed in generating heirs, perhaps as a poetically just punishment for disdaining the condition of their own births; and they exist in a perpetual state of anxiety and self-alienation, able neither to make their achieved identity perfect and permanent, nor to retreat safely back to their humbler natural condition. The effort to expand the self instead ends up dividing it.

Beyond these frustrating reactions of the political and psychological systems, there remains the fact that changes made by force of individual human will and action are erased in geological time, which allows nature to erode all efforts back to ground level, by something like the laws of entropy. In a culture already strained by the long view back to the re-discovered classical past – Hamlet traces 'the noble dust of Alexander, till he find it stopping a bunghole' (5.1.172–3) – Shakespeare offers glimpses of an even longer view: Macbeth gazes towards infinite tomorrows that will reabsorb the strongest castle into the eternal forest (5.5.19–51). The world goes on, and on. Tragedies of ambition thus often become stories in which the natural or social order becomes the avenger. Except in cases where lovers are immortalized in each other's eyes, which becomes implicitly the only view that matters, the focus of Shakespearean tragedy on unique individuals dissolves into a deep field of anonymity.

The dual mandate of this chapter thus has some compensating explan-atory value. These two types of tragedy are reciprocal: one depicting the will to superior power, the other depicting an unwillingness to be overpowered.

Tragedies of ambition depend on the protagonist's illusion that an exception can endure, that no mindless or jealous reflex in the social system, or in nature beneath it or the heavens above it, will produce a reaction equal and opposite to the heroic action, recapturing exertion as merely lost heat. Tragedies of revenge depend instead on the protagonist's illusion that things can and must be made even (an eye for an eye, a humiliation for a humiliation). The plays suggest that Shakespeare often thought of ambition as a doomed effort to rise above a position of equality, and of revenge as a doomed effort to restore equality. Aristotle thought of tragedy itself in a similar way: as a cathartic treatment designed to restore equilibrium. This does not mean, however, that Shakespeare's tragedies of ambition and revenge are inherently reactionary. Their superficial endorsement of a final return to normality co-exists – in a typical Shakespearean paradox – with a deep acknowledgement of the loss of human greatness, and the betrayal of an implied human essence, in the protagonist's inevitable fall from ambitious heights.

One dynamic definition of tragedy, derived from Hegel, describes it as a dramatic story in which the protagonist receives imperative but contradictory instructions from two superior forces, and is therefore doomed to destruction by whichever one he or she disobeys. These forces need not be deities, as they often are in classical literature; they can reflect the inconsistencies of a mixed culture. The local Anglo-Saxon warrior tradition and the recovered traditions of classical antiquity (except in Platonic and Stoic philosophy) endorsed the instinctive desire to repay injuries, and to seek power and status over our fellow creatures. Yet the Christian ethos at the core of Renaissance culture praised pity, love, humility, and the turning of the other cheek, exalting as the greatest hero a sacrificial lamb who chose to abdicate his heavenly palace to suffer among the lowliest.

Tragic contradictions were everywhere in Shakespeare's London, provoking exalted ambitions and then taking revenge on those who pursued such ambitions. Protestant theology – the most obviously pressing cultural innovation – at once told Christians to aspire to direct communication with God, and told them to despair of ever knowing anything about Him; told them to focus obsessively on their prospects for eternal salvation, and to recognize that those prospects were beyond their power to control or even comprehend; to seek desperately, and yet to mistrust utterly, an inner conviction of divine favour. The terrifying instability of the new urban capitalist economic system – whose essence was to encourage but also punish ambition – was matched by the terrifying instability of this new belief system, which left many true believers vacillating wildly between a faith that God's love would exalt them beyond all comprehension, and a fear that God's just anger at such presumptuous sinners would damn them beyond any redemption. Nor were Catholics spared from the painful dialectic of ambition and revenge. Protestant spokesmen portrayed Catholicism (to which many of the English continued to subscribe) as allegiance to ambitious foreign political powers, justifying violent official retribution; and as an overweening attempt to control God and earn heaven, deserving punishment here in anticipation of punishment here-after. Especially in the emerging urban settings of which Shakespeare's London was a prime example, old tribal systems that controlled by shame had ceased to function, and no fair and efficient system of official policing had yet arisen to take its place, only a tacit and hugely complicated system of power (including civil and canon law-courts) radiating down-wards from a court that must, to most, have seemed hardly less mysterious, inaccessible, and arbitrary than the Reformation God. The earthly version of Star Chamber – originally designed to enable punishment of high-ranking criminals, but later seen as a tool for secret extra-legal control by the monarchy – offered some uncomfortable parallels with Calvinist theology.

Under all these circumstances, both ambition and revenge were extra-ordinarily tempting and risky – perfect material for tragedy. Plays on those topics would have been deeply ambivalent experiences for Shakespeare's audience, whose loyalty would have remained divided between old and new models of heroism, which had shifted from warrior to sufferer, but also (arguably the opposite direction) from knowing one's place to overreaching it, and (depending on whether one looks at 'natural philosophy' or Calvinist theology) either from believing to inquiring or vice versa. The nascent conquest of nature by empirical science (including astrology and alchemy, as well as more modern-seeming navigational and medical technologies) could look at one moment like glorious achievement, at the next like foolish or evil presumption, and at the next like mere fraud (the magic of Marlowe's Faustus sometimes seems to be all three at once). And the persistent bad seasons of flood and plague and famine in Shakespeare's England were not only harsh implicit rebukes to the promise that science would allow human-ity to comprehend and rule the created world, but widely and explicitly preached as divine punishment of that ambition.

The remainder of this chapter will explore the relationships between classical and Renaissance tragedy, and the range of Shakespearean tragedies of revenge and ambition, before turning to two famous examples – *Macbeth* and *Hamlet* – to show how a culture's ambivalence about these topics can grow into tragic agony, as Shakespeare combines the historical and transhistorical aspects of the vengeful and ambitious impulses.

The functions of tragedy and Shakespeare's development

Cultures exist largely to channel the infinite possibilities of the creative and self-conscious human mind into safely limited and shared channels, so that individuals can sustain sanity and communities can sustain co-operation. This is work better suited to myth-makers than law-makers; and when cultures cannot manage to resolve, or even afford to acknowledge, their internal inconsistencies, they delegate those tasks to tragedians. Art – a seemingly self-contained ritual form in which nothing material such as money or power is obviously at stake – provides a relatively safe territory for negotiating the contradictions. Indeed, this may explain why the only period of great tragic drama comparable to Elizabethan and Jacobean England was classical Greece, which was comparably beset by 'a growing discontinuity between forms of social mobility ... and the precarious consequences of that mobility which can result in destruction'.[4] Greece was also, like England, a naval power, and therefore regularly exposed to the diseases of pluralism.

Classical stories of ambition were generally tragedies of revenge, in which the gods (or their reflections in nature) punished *hubris*, the excessive pride of protagonists such as Arachne, Oedipus, or Pentheus. Under Christianity, this transaction reappears as the Fall, in which God punishes the presumption of humanity's quest, both as individuals and as a species, for knowledge and immortality. In the Renaissance, tragedies of revenge often partake of ambition, since the avenger – from Kyd's Hieronimo to Middleton's Vindice to Webster's Bosola – is often seeking to overcome his powerlessness against a higher-ranking miscreant.

Seneca's tragedies, written during the first century AD and translated into English during Shakespeare's adolescence, were the chief classical source for Elizabethan revenge plays. In an exalted rhetorical style, Seneca told passionate, violent stories in which the furious indignation of the revenger – often provoked (as in *Hamlet*) by a ghost or vision of a beloved victim – took aim at the perpetrator and his kin. This vengeance (again as in *Hamlet*) often required elaborate deception by the revenger, and finally provided some kind of poetic as well as practical justice.

Because Seneca probably wrote his plays to be read rather than staged, he could describe sensationally gruesome acts without worrying about how they could be performed by actors or endured by spectators. His

Elizabethan imitators blithely put the same kind of violence into visible action. The resulting horrors are nowhere more obvious than in Shakespeare's earliest surviving tragedy, *Titus Andronicus*. The play is neglected enough, and the story remarkable enough, to merit a brief retelling here. Titus is a great Roman military hero of old-fashioned patriotic values who, to appease the spirits of his many sons killed battling the Goths, ritually executes a Gothic prince. The prince's younger brothers then ambush Titus's virtuous daughter Lavinia, slay her husband, toss his body into a pit, then rape her, cutting off her tongue and both her hands so that she can neither speak nor write to accuse her attackers. When her brothers go looking for her, they fall into the pit with the corpse and, discovered there, are accused of murder. A villainous Moor named Aaron tells Titus that he can save these sons only by cutting off one of his hands and sending it to the emperor, as a gesture of good faith, but the hand is promptly returned to him along with the heads of his sons. So he sadly carries one head offstage in his remaining hand, while his mutilated daughter carries off the severed hand in her teeth.

This all provides satisfactory revenge for Tamora, the queen of the Goths, but it provokes a massive counter-revenge, in which Titus finally traps the rapist princes and slices their throats while his daughter holds a bowl with the stumps of her arms to catch the blood, which he then mixes with a paste of their bones and (in a zany disguise as a chef) serves (in an echo of the classical Philomel myth) as a stew to their mother and imperial stepfather at a glorious banquet where Titus fatally stabs his daughter and Tamora, and is fatally stabbed in turn by the emperor, who is in turn fatally stabbed by Titus's surviving son, Lucius, who blurts the talionic formula:[5] 'Can the son's eye behold his father bleed? / There's meed for meed, death for a deadly deed!' (5.3.64–5).

The sheer amplification of violence in *Titus Andronicus* tends to preclude subtle modulations of voice, or of moral thought. Letting the good guys do what the bad guys did is an easy source of emotional gratification, but a peculiar way to celebrate ethical distinctions. Much of Shakespeare's subsequent career was shaped by his efforts to solve that problem – a problem especially tricky for a dramatist whose renowned ability to see all sides of a situation with equal clarity precluded the distortions that conveniently disguise the amoral mirroring function of so many feuds. By turning the competing accusations into mere echoes of each other, Shakespeare (like a modern sound engineer) arranged for these justifications to cancel each other out, to make audible the cries of pain behind the claims of moral justification.

In his first group of history plays, Shakespeare seems already to feel the limitations of revenge as a symmetrical, political practice:

> QUEEN MARGARET Thou hadst a Richard, till a Richard killed him.
> DUCHESS I had a Richard too and thou didst kill him;
> I had a Rutland too, thou holp'st to kill him.
>
> . . .
>
> QUEEN MARGARET Bear with me. I am hungry for revenge,
> And now I cloy me with beholding it.
> Thy Edward he is dead that killed my Edward;
> The other Edward dead to quit my Edward;   (*R3* 4.4.42–64)

This is obviously a bad social system, and not so good as drama or poetry either (the scene is crammed with this kind of forced parallelism).

Even in *Romeo and Juliet* a few years later, the older-fashioned speakers and situations produce this kind of revenge-rhyme:

> LADY CAPULET I beg for justice, which thou, Prince, must give:
> Romeo slew Tybalt, Romeo must not live.
> PRINCE Romeo slew him, he slew Mercutio;
> Who now the price of his dear blood doth owe?
> [LORD CAPULET] Not Romeo, Prince, he was Mercutio's friend;
> His fault concludes but what the law should end . . .   (3.1.171–6)

Notice, however, that this exoneration is offered by Juliet's father rather than Romeo's, suggesting that rational perception and psychological dynamics – here Lord Capulet's established preference for Romeo's character over Tybalt's – can break the vicious cycle of familial vendetta. Juliet's assumption to the contrary is yet another of the play's narrowly missed opportunities for the tragedy to turn comic – ironically replicated by the fact that nearly all modern readers miss it also, because editors are so attached to the symmetrical model of vengeance that they overrule the First Folio and the best early quartos by attributing this speech to Lord Montague. As the play continues, Shakespeare pursues more complex motives and a more complex rhetoric to express them. Juliet tries to find a way out of a potentially unstoppable cycle of talionic violence, seeking somehow to replace it – as the play itself flirts with an escape from tragedy into comedy – with a rhetoric of love and acceptance.

The diplomatic delicacy of this shift is exquisitely delineated just after Romeo departs into exile. Juliet shows her wit by choosing words that simultaneously satisfy her mother's expectation that she would want to murder Romeo (for killing her cousin Tybalt), and her own need to express a different sort of desire for him. She tells Lady Capulet,

> JULIET God pardon him, I do, with all my heart:
> And yet no man like he doth grieve my heart.
> LADY CAPULET That is because the traitor murderer lives.
> JULIET Ay, madam, from the reach of these my hands.
> Would none but I might venge my cousin's death!

When her mother promises to satisfy what she assumes is Juliet's desire for 'vengeance' by having Romeo poisoned, Juliet answers,

> Indeed I never shall be satisfied
> With Romeo, till I behold him – dead –
> Is my poor heart, so for a kinsman vex'd.
> Madam, if you could find out but a man
> To bear a poison, I would temper it,
> That Romeo should upon receipt thereof
> Soon sleep in quiet. O, how my heart abhors
> To hear him named, and cannot come to him
> To wreak the love I bore my cousin
> Upon his body that hath slaughtered him!   (3.5.82–102)

This breathtaking piece of verbal tightrope-walking is possible only because the line between death-wishing and love-desire – between unrequited wrongs and unrequited love – is so blurred by this play's passions. Love does not simply negate revenge here; it steers the energies of revenge into the thinly veiled violence of sexual appetite. Juliet will convert the poisonous humours that elicit death into the fluids that love-making elicits, leading to sleep, and to another kind of bearing and feeding.[6]

Shakespeare himself perfects this ambivalence, and provides closure to this topic, near the end of his career, by writing *The Tempest*, which appears to be a revenge tragedy that renounces its own genre. The hero Prospero decides not to enforce punishment on the traitors he has finally captured: 'At this hour / Lies at my mercy all mine enemies', he announces at the end of Act 4 (4.1.264–5). Yet, at the start of Act 5, in conversation with the spirit Ariel, Prospero declares, 'The rarer action is in virtue, than in vengeance. They being penitent, / The sole drift of my purpose doth extend / Not a frown further' (5.1.27–9). He moves the story from tragedy to comedy, from a story of death to a story of marriage, focusing on matching his daughter Miranda joyfully with Ferdinand – a project hardly compatible with taking brutal revenge on Ferdinand's father. In a sense, Prospero achieves what Romeo and Juliet died attempting: the conversion of vendetta – the merciless Italian morality of revenge – into wedding, into a morality of forgiveness and community. He is able to 'requite' Ferdinand's father for the restoration of his dukedom with new life, instead of for the usurpation of that kingdom with enforced death (5.1.169). Revenge is notably forsworn in other late plays also: in *The Winter's Tale*, King Leontes's falsely accused wife and friend, Hermione and Polixenes, have good cause for vengeance and good positions from which to impose it, but finally allow the king's penitence to take the place of punishment. The Christian associations of these redemptive shifts spoke for themselves, with only a little prompting. Pain and mortality – which comprised God's revenge for the ambitions of Adam and Eve – do not disappear, but they are mitigated by forbearance, forgiveness, and the promise of a better future.

From the first plays to the last, then, the revenge motive is everywhere in Shakespeare. Even in his comedies, characters such as Shylock in *The Merchant of Venice*, Oliver de Boys in *As You Like It*, and Malvolio in *Twelfth Night*, are ambitious and vengeful figures against whom some combination of virtue, nature and women's wisdom takes a poetically just counter-revenge, imposing humiliation. For tragic villains such as Aaron in *Titus*, Iago in *Othello*, or Cornwall in *King Lear*, revenge often seems merely a rationalization by an already malign spirit. These villains – who are generally at least superficially ambitious – set out to punish what we are asked to see as goodness; sometimes they do so precisely because they too see it as goodness, as an innocence and lovingness they cannot match, and can therefore only destroy. John Milton's Satan is the great inheritor of this Shakespearean syndrome.

An important sub-category of revenge tragedy is the malcontent plot – made famous by Shakespeare's contemporaries such as Marston and Webster, but clearly shaping Iago and Edmund – in which someone with frustrated ambitions, unappreciated by the royal court, decides to show the world his abilities in a destructive mode instead. Hamlet arguably flirts with this role; Macbeth plays it; Don John in *Much Ado About Nothing* is a minimalist caricature of it. The ambitions of Shakespeare's Richard III reflect some of this same resentment, a resentment which turns his political career into an act of vengeance against a world that cannot love him, and – in a psychological turn typical of Shakespearean drama – against a deformed self he himself cannot love.

Heroes can be vengeful as well, though rarely at their best moments. Henry IV and Henry V both skilfully disguise their political tactics as causes of honourable vengeance. In *Julius Caesar*, Antony is certainly an avenger, with Caesar's ghost as his guiding and aiding spirit. Romeo becomes one, briefly but disastrously, in killing Tybalt. King Lear seeks revenge against his bad daughters, Timon against his fair-weather friends, Coriolanus against his Roman banishers, Othello mistakenly and effectually against his wife, then legitimately but futilely against Iago for causing that terrible mistake, and finally against the erring part of himself. In *Hamlet*, Shakespeare provides us with his most explicit and extended exploration of heroic revenge, producing the most self-conscious and morally intricate revenge tragedy in the long, lively history of the genre.

The history of *Hamlet* and the functions of revenge

Hamlet has long stood as the most famous revenge tragedy in Western civilization. The entire history of that fame is a lesson in the tension between locality and universality in the reading of Shakespeare. The play's opening words – 'Who's there?' (1.1.1–2) – make a claim on every audience that orders this ghostly play to 'Stand, and unfold yourself.' Hamlet the character says that the purpose of drama is to hold 'the mirror up to nature'. *Hamlet* the drama holds up a mirror in which even the most sophisticated viewers have trouble seeing beyond their own reflections. So *Hamlet* is universal, in that each individual or historical period tends to see it as the story of all humanity; but local, in that each individual or historical period thereby defines the story in its own terms.

The reception of *Hamlet* thus provides a kind of core sample of cultural eras. The Romantics who commented on Shakespeare in the early nineteenth century were often morbidly sensitive intellectuals (such as Coleridge and Hazlitt in England, Goethe and Schlegel in Germany) trapped in the world of brutal action: poet-philosophers with too much brain-power and emotional delicacy for their own good. They perceived Hamlet as much the same, with Claudius's usurpation standing in for the French Revolution in particular and the Industrial Revolution in general. The problem with revenge, from this perspective, is that it is a dish best served stupid. Hamlet repeatedly condemns himself for getting caught up in analysing vengeance instead of performing it:

> Now, whether it be
> Bestial oblivion, or some craven scruple
> Of thinking too precisely on th' event –
> A thought which quartered hath but one part wisdom,
> And ever three parts coward – I do not know
> Why yet I live to say, 'This thing's to do,'
> Sith I have cause, and will, and strength, and means
> To do it.   (4.4.39–46; cf. 2.2.550–86)

Yet Hamlet may well have been right to hesitate. How can anyone rouse the moral certainty to commit murder, however compelling the cause may appear, if he suspects that 'nothing is good or bad, but thinking makes it so' (2.2.239–40) – let alone if he suspects that innocent people, including his own school-friends, sweetheart, and mother, will likely be killed also in the process?

Furthermore, Shakespeare provides us with perspective – almost a scientific control-group – by including two other sons also seeking to avenge their fathers' slayings. Fortinbras (whose father was killed by Hamlet's father in single combat) seems too cold, sending 'twenty thousand men' to die fighting an otherwise pointless cause (4.4.60–5). Laertes (whose father was killed by Hamlet himself) seems too hot to notice that his honour is being destroyed by the effort to preserve it. Warfare itself – killing provoked by a sense of duty to ghosts of our fathers in armour – is brought into moral question, along with all the smaller-scale forms of revenge. *Macbeth* raises similar questions about ambition by showing that the same kind of brutal violence which makes Macbeth the greatest of heroes in the play's opening scene makes him the worst of villains a few scenes later. Is revenge any better an excuse for killing than ambition is, or vice versa? What excuse is good enough?

When another Germanic cultural wave washed over England and America a century after Romanticism – psychoanalysis – it again stared into the Hamlet mirror and saw itself. In his unsophisticated but influential book *Hamlet and Oedipus*, Ernest Jones – a student of Freud's – argued that Shakespeare and Sophocles were drawing on the same sources and patterns of psychic energy. Hamlet cannot kill Claudius because he identifies with him too strongly. All Claudius has done is fulfil precisely Hamlet's own oedipal fantasies: his guilt-ridden, subconscious desire to murder his father and then marry his mother, the ambition that (in Freud's tragic myth of the nuclear family) provoked the revenge of castration. So, Hamlet's task entails revenge against his own ambitions, and thus becomes inextricable from suicide. 'To be or not to be' may not mean (as most people assume it does), 'Should I kill myself?', but rather the question Hamlet goes on to consider: should he survive by stoically accepting injustice, or die performing revenge? If Claudius is essentially an expression of Hamlet's deepest ambitions, however, then the deaths of Hamlet and Claudius will necessarily coincide in the psychological allegory as well as the plot.

Now, another century later, Hamlet again seems to mirror the latest cultural revolution, and becomes a study of information systems at their limits: the problems of communicating data and perfecting equations amid realities that may never be more than virtual. The biggest theoretical questions currently haunting literary critics and historians and psychotherapists and Web-surfers cluster around the multiplicity and instability of truth. In an age obsessed with moral relativism and recovered-memory syndromes and deconstruction and multiculturalism, how can we know each other, or ourselves, or reality – especially through language, which programmes us in ways we can never get outside of? Now the problem with revenge is that – as the play keeps reminding us – we cannot understand ourselves, recognize our enemies, calibrate our actions, define morality, or intuit divine purposes surely and precisely enough to trust that our revenge will constitute absolute justice.

Hamlet's task of revenge appears fairly neat: his target is high but not out of reach, he has multiple kinds of evidence convicting Claudius, and his own plausible claim to the throne gives his efforts legitimacy as well as a supplementary motive of ambition. But, as so often in Renaissance drama, revenge tends to overflow, inflicting collateral damage on by-standers, ruining the logic of redressed grievance and the aesthetic of restored symmetry. Long before he finally strikes down 'that murderous, that adulterate beast' (1.5.42), Hamlet has turned bitterly vengeful against several other people: not just his mother (briefly) for her supposed complicity, but against several members of his own generation who he feels have become disloyal to him, allowing themselves to be manipulated by the powerful elders. His fatal anger turns against the lovelorn Ophelia, against the ambitious Rosencrantz and Guildenstern, and against the proud Laertes. That anger also nearly becomes deadly against himself; before he can even undertake violence against Claudius, his speech and actions are markedly suicidal.

Drawing on a scholarly tradition that associated revenge with impiety, excess, and madness in Renaissance culture,[7] Eleanor Prosser argues that Shakespeare would not have approved of Hamlet's extreme vengefulness, even against Claudius, and would not have assumed approval from the audience. Against the long tradition of Hamlet criticism that wonders why he is so hesitant to take revenge, this argument suggests he should (by all recorded Elizabethan norms) have been even more hesitant, leaving vengeance to God and never seeking to damn another human soul.[8]

In fact, the divine injunctions against human retaliation ('Vengeance is mine, saith the Lord' in the Old Testament, 'turn the other cheek' in the New) were widely quoted – and even more widely ignored. Hamlet expresses concern that God has forbidden 'self-slaughter', but not that God has forbidden revenge. In any case, Hamlet's situation is ambiguous, since he pursues not only a personal vendetta on behalf of his family, which Elizabethan commentators condemned, but also official justice as a prince of the state, which they tended to approve. Shakespeare employs such ambiguities to prevent the audience from seizing on a simplistic moral view of the protagonist's dilemma, which must be irresolvable if it is to be fully tragic. Something similar occurs with the laws of succession in *Macbeth*, where Macbeth's ambition may or may not be legitimate, since Shakespeare carefully avoids specifying whether Duncan's son has any presumptive claim on the throne, or whether (as a kinsman and leading general of the king) Macbeth deserved a chance at the 'election'.

The platitudinous father Polonius advises Laertes, 'to thine own self be true' (1.3.78). That advice only highlights what a strange new world Shakespeare – and Hamlet, and Macbeth – actually inhabited. The legacy of paternal identity was often rendered irrelevant by socio-economic changes that drove people into cities where they had to make a living or make a name for themselves, rather than simply inheriting both; yet, as in the play, the abandonment of that legacy was always haunted by guilt. The revenge of Hamlet, by which he seeks to claim his inheritance, thus becomes an especially interesting case. Since the emphatic public discourses of church and state alike condemned it, the practice of revenge seems to mark a moment of individual and/or instinctual resistance to official influence[9] – perhaps an exception to theories (still popular among followers of Foucault) that depict the self as entirely constructed by social authority, and that dismiss individuality and instinct as delusive myths when applied to human beings, who are in the encompassing grip of their historical moment with its ideologies and epistemes.[10] Another current strand of scholarly critique reaches similar conclusions from the opposite side of the culture/ nature debate, through evolutionary theory, whereby both revenge and ambition become genetic imperatives rather than personal choices.

If we combine these observations with the tendency (also strong in recent scholarship) to credit this play with the invention of modern inwardness, of unique personal subjectivity, we find *Hamlet* breaking both Renaissance orthodoxy and modern academic orthodoxy about that Renaissance orthodoxy. We find ourselves again focused on the character's unprecedented autonomy – his freedom of agency, his ability to explore inwardly. And yet, when called upon to act, he feels himself very far from free, as his soliloquies make painfully clear. Revenge is tragic because (like ambition) it divides the protagonist against himself, casting him in incompatible roles, and because it is philosophically as well as practically difficult; the drama of moral choice complicates and deepens the drama of active suspense.

While the task of blood-revenge was discouraged by Elizabethan authorities, it may have been stimulated by Elizabethan theology, less directly but no less forcefully, because vengeance was suddenly about the only thing mourners could do on behalf of the dead.[11] The Catholic tradition of praying and paying to redeem loved ones from purgatory was outlawed and ridiculed by the Reformation (which got its start at Wittenberg, where Shakespeare tells us Hamlet has been educated); and promptly the Elizabethan stage began depicting characters using worldly revenge to redeem tormented ghosts. Laertes's vengeful fury is amplified by his resentment that neither Polonius nor Ophelia can be buried with the full traditional rites. If prayers for the dead were discouraged in churches, then revenge on behalf of a ghost would be performed in theatres; diplomacy with God would give way to war on human villains, who became the satisfyingly localized and assailable scapegoats for the crime of mortality. Beneath the surface horror of Renaissance revenge tragedy (and modern detective fiction) lies the reassuring implication that death is a contingent event – the strange result of crime rather than the normal result of time – and the consoling idea that death can in some sense be refuted by destroying its immediate cause. This version of homeopathic medicine, by which death cures death, partly explains the renewed appeal of the classical drama of blood-revenge. It also explains why – acutely, in the case of Hamlet – revenge seems to hover between the mimetic and the memorial, as it strives to cancel the losses of the past.[12]

It may also explain why blood-revenge often becomes almost comically extreme in Jacobean tragedy, as avengers seek a dosage adequate to achieve the desired cure; and why audiences tend to side with such avengers despite all the official admonitions to the contrary. It doesn't take a murdered beloved, only a dead one, to make us share the sense of betrayal and futility that generates dramatic avengers. As in Shakespeare's great cluster of tragedies of 1605–8 – *King Lear*, *Macbeth*, *Coriolanus*, and *Antony and Cleopatra* – what looks like a tragedy about a particular political crime at a particular historical moment proves to be also a tragedy about the painful contradictions of ordinary human life, full of high aspirations, but subservient to both nature and culture, and limited by mortality.

Coriolanus provides a revealing instance: a character whose huge ambitions manifest themselves in vengefulness against both his own common bodily needs and the commoners of his body-politic, which conspire to resist his claim to be the perfect embodiment of Rome's martial ideal, purified in blood, fasting and fire. Shakespeare here stages a historical incident, closely based on Plutarch, with clear links to the history of

Shakespeare's own time: the rebellion of the ambitious Essex, the Midlands grain uprisings of 1606–7, and emerging anxieties about representative government. But the play takes on a mythical rather than a historical aura. The factual background and political analysis coexist synergistically here with an archetypal study of the costs and limits of ambition itself. Clearly the revenge taken against Coriolanus is at once that of a social underclass against aristocratic arrogance, and that of fundamental elements of his birth against the superhuman soldier he aspired to become. The mob finally destroys him on behalf of slain kinsmen ('He kill'd my son! – My daughter! – He kill'd cousin Marcus – he kill'd my father!' (5.6.121–2)), but also on behalf of the shared nature he insisted on transcending: Coriolanus is executed for crimes against his own humankindness. Taking his mother and his son each by a hand, hearing the honorary name he achieved reduced back to his patronymic, Coriolanus is fatally obliged to acknowledge his identity as merely one link in a chain of mortal generations. In this, Coriolanus's tragedy most clearly resembles Macbeth's: a story of nature and its norms taking revenge on ambition.[13]

Macbeth and nature's revenge on human ambition

Macbeth tells the story of a man whose ambitions (abetted and personified by his wife) lead him into 'unnatural' deeds, deeds for which nature, society, and the psyche all exact a vivid and systematic revenge. At the beginning of the story, Macbeth understands that ambitious crimes invite retribution:

> ... we but teach
> Bloody instructions, which being taught, return
> To plague th' inventor. This even-handed justice
> Commends th' ingredience of our poisoned chalice
> To our own lips.   (1.7.8–12)

When the murderous couple receive a taste of their own bitter medicine, they discover that its side-effects are more pervasive than the dangerous precedent a king-killer sets for his own kingship. Ambition – rebelling against the nation's divinely given hierarchy – entails a series of violations of natural order, all of which return to haunt Macbeth as relentlessly as Banquo's ghost does. Macbeth embodies normal human competitiveness, but he does so in a situation which converts that impulse into a terrible and irredeemable reality, and in a universe that takes massive revenge on those who overstep the natural and traditional boundaries.

Shakespeare goes to considerable trouble, not only to make the crimes vividly brutal, but also to show that Macbeth gets just what he deserves – what, in fact, he asks for. Macbeth's crime *is* his punishment. He forfeits precisely the regenerative functions that he violated in murdering Duncan. To seize the throne, Macbeth must violate the healthy, orderly cycles of nature, and in each case he discovers that he cannot survive without the aspects of nature his ambitions obliged him to shatter. Having murdered sleep, he and his Lady endure an endless night of insomnia. Having tried to rob the next human generation of life and inheritance, they die prematurely and childless. Having blighted the agricultural health of their nation by murdering its life-giving figurehead, the desiccated 'yellow leaf' Macbeth finds his castle walls swarmed by an instantly resurgent forest – the same forest human ambitions had presumably cleared from that place to build the castle long ago. The real avenger here appears to be nature itself, with the biological heir Malcolm as merely its stalking-horse.

The immediate result of yielding to ambition, of forcibly disturbing the hereditary order, of making himself into something he was not born to be, is that Macbeth becomes disastrously divided against himself. His manliness erases his humanity; his senses contradict each other; his hand and eye, face and heart, become deceptively discrepant. Ambition provokes an inward as well as an outward civil war. The boundary between self and other blurs nightmarishly; his 'single state of man' loses its 'better part of man' (1.3.140, 5.8.18); and 'all that is within him does condemn / Itself for being there' (5.2.24–5).[14] A similar syndrome of disorder and division pulls down his ambitious wife.

Macbeth's decision to indulge the ambitious appetite reads like a Freudian allegory. The hapless ego is restrained by the super-ego, the rules ingrained in conscience to make social existence possible. Macbeth's soliloquy (in 1.7) catalogues those rules: protect sleeping guests, benefactors and kin; never make the question of hierarchy into a bloody free-for-all; listen to the angels, who will reward virtues while exposing and punishing crimes. At the end of the soliloquy, he recognizes that he has no valid reason to proceed, 'Only vaulting ambition, which o'erleaps itself / And falls on th' other'; Macbeth here compares himself to a man leaping proudly up on to horseback, only to discover that his momentum carries him inevitably towards a painful and humiliating fall off the other side. Ambition is as impractical as it is immoral, provoking a retribution as certain as inertial physics. Lady Macbeth refutes this conscientious argument in the voice of the conscienceless id. She mocks him for 'Letting "I dare not" wait upon "I would"' (1.7.44); then she proves that a little wine and sexual provocation can wash away conscientious resistance. In this sense, the portrayal of Macbeth's fate as poetic justice lacks tragic complexity. He is not caught between conflicting imperatives: if he can ignore some obviously sinister advice, he can look forward to the sociable, contented old age he envisions (5.3.24–6).

Yet this play has continued to haunt audiences in ways no facile moral admonishment could, because (as so often in Shakespeare's work) it also harbours a contrary morality, a revisionist fairy tale which turns into a horror movie: the face of dear old Mother Nature blurs and reconfigures itself as an ugly witch who promised us glory, but in fact always had us trapped in a deterministic labyrinth. Virtue triumphs at the expense of *Homo sapiens* and *Homo faber*, criminalizing our ability to imagine something better and plan towards it, our practical need for tools and clothing and housing to supplement the bodies we are given.

That may be one reason why this play puts so much symbolic weight on weapons and garments and castles.[15] The individualistic philosophy infiltrating England from Renaissance Italy, as prominently articulated by Petrarch and Pico della Mirandola, argued that human beings were authorized to alter their given world, and to aspire above their given place in that world, by the fact that they were created without claws or fur or exoskeletons, and so needed artificial equivalents in order to survive. The human species defines itself – at considerable ecological cost – by the way it distances itself from nature. 'Human nature' is an oxymoron, a contradiction full of tragic potential. Hamlet says, 'What is a man, / If the chief good and market of his time / Be but to sleep and feed? A beast, no more' (4.4.34). King Lear registers a similar complaint: 'Allow not nature more than nature needs / Man's life is cheap as beast's' (2.4.267–8). The advancing Birnam Wood evokes, in a dramatically accelerated form, the mindless relentless organic processes that eventually will swallow up everything human pride – or the human genome – has provoked us to build. Akira Kurosawa's superb Japanese film adaptation of *Macbeth* (*Kumonosu-jō*, often called *Throne of Blood*) emphasizes exactly this demoralizing moral.

There are certainly other ways to slant the moral of this story. If it had been told by an ordinary Elizabethan author, susceptible to conventional thought and eager to please the government, it would have been a simple celebration of rightful power triumphing over diabolical ambition. Told by a more openly rebellious and Promethean spirit such as Christopher Marlowe or George Chapman, this might have been the story of a great soul's repression by a narrow and mechanical physical world. Shakespeare, as usual, tells it both ways at once, leaving us to decide whether we want to excavate a human tragedy out of a didactic tale about the rise and fall of two evil-doers. Underneath his depiction of nature's vivid revenge against ambition lies a vision of entropy's ponderous nullification of human enterprise.

Macbeth is thus broadly psychological and philosophical in its treatment of ambition and revenge. It suggests that, in a conservative universe – one where God, or a reactionary society, or the stubbornness of intentionless physics limits human freedom – ambitious desires invite a tragic confrontation with what Freud calls the reality-principle, which demands 'the abandonment of a number of possibilities of gaining satisfaction and the temporary toleration of unpleasure as a step on the long indirect road to pleasure'.[16] *Macbeth* is a tragedy of ambitions which override that principle, choosing short-term, selfish satisfactions ('be it thought and done') over the compromises which sustain collective human life. That collectivity then exacts revenge.

Macbeth is also insistently historical. Even if we take the 'weird sisters' more as allegory than as a commentary on Renaissance witchcraft, we can still see them either as agents of *wyrd* – fate – or more locally as an embodiment of contradictions in the organization of a Renaissance English society that repeatedly aroused high aspirations and then took vengeance on those who pursued them. The changes in Shakespeare's world, like the witches in Macbeth's, generated a foggy, confusing moral landscape, and then destroyed people for not finding the same old path through them. They tempted people to ambitious activity with glorious prophecies – rule the world, know the universe – and then brutally punished them for not passively accepting their given conditions. The glorious aspirations of humanism, even the ordinary aspirations of humans, are hard to reconcile with Christian and monarchical principles that demanded not only humility, but even unquestioning acceptance of the word, will and world of God and kings.

The world hardly needed Shakespearean tragedy to suggest that ambition was a dangerous violation of some benevolent and divinely ordained order which conveniently included the established hierarchies. Moralists were only too willing to send that message, and authorities (who had the most to lose in any breakdown of established hierarchies) made sure that was the message which appeared in print and echoed through churches.

Macbeth appears to participate in that process of ideological control, but may also offer a critique of it. As in much government propaganda about the value of accepting subjugation (by race, class, and gender) and of following conventional practices (in sexuality, work, and belief), tradition is here equated with nature, and hence with justice and divine intention.[17] We witness a wise and powerful force, comprising God and nature and political legitimacy, taking poetically just revenge on Macbeth for transgressions against the pious and natural and political orders.

Shakespeare also reminds us, however, that those orders rarely stay so perfectly aligned except in propaganda. Coded into that moralistic story is a story of moral ambiguity, less obvious but no less powerful, that acknowledges the paradoxes entangling human beings generally and Shakespeare's contemporaries in particular. Here again, Shakespeare voices a human problem that stretches across the range of civilizations in time and space, but was amplified and inflected by circumstances local to his experience and his audience.

Renaissance artists, scientists, and explorers heard a temptress's voice, a witch's voice, a Lady Macbeth voice, telling them that conquest and glory were within their reach, if they were only bold and manly enough to grasp them. Those same aspirations were then smothered by Protestant doctrines that insisted on humanity's helpless depravity, and by the stubborn limitations of ignorance, traditionalism, and mortality. Versions of Macbeth's seducers – equivocal forces that provoked and then betrayed ambition, that 'palter with us in a double sense' (5.8.20) – were constantly being conjured by the rapidly shifting economic, scientific, and theological conditions of the people for whom Shakespeare was writing his plays. Like Marlowe's *Doctor Faustus*, Shakespeare's *Macbeth* often looks like an old-fashioned story about the olden days, a story of sinful ambition and holy revenge. But, even more craftily than *Faustus*, Shakespeare's great tragedy of ambition comports a warning about the ethical contradictions produced by ordinary living in the emerging modern world, and a mourning for its countless, helpless victims.

This sympathetic view of ambition rarely extends to women in Shakespeare's tragedies. On the contrary, Shakespeare's women who seek more than momentary corrective power appear generally monstrous and destructive, lacking the redemptive aspiration to some higher ideal that qualifies the implied condemnation of male pride. The initial element of maternal justice-seeking evident in Tamora is corrupted by her rise to power. Gertrude and Ophelia are tainted and destroyed by their enmeshment in statecraft, uncertain whether, how, and against whom to seek revenge. The cases of Lear's unctuous daughters, Coriolanus's icy mother and Macbeth's fiery wife – all seeking high political power – show only too clearly Shakespeare's willingness to endorse his culture's mistrust of female sovereignty.

In cases of comic reprisal, however, Shakespeare seems less complicit in his misogynistic culture than corrective towards it. As the male-centred tragedies reveal the admirable, even indispensable aspect of ambition, the female-centred comedies suggest that, even if revenge is 'wild justice', it may be justice nonetheless. Vengeance becomes a reparative rather than a destructive form, a real rather than an illusory solution to social (if not existential) problems – especially as engineered by clever women. The successes of Portia in *The Merchant of Venice*, Maria in *Twelfth Night* and Mistress Ford in *The Merry Wives of Windsor* suggest the way Shakespearean comedy often associates women with the restoration of commonsensical norms that sustain community.[18]

The imaginative and verbal power of Shakespeare's tragic masterpieces conceals the fact that the pattern of ambition provoking revenge is fundamentally comic, if viewed from the perspective of a community happy to share survival rather than an individual hoping to achieve transcendence. In many comedies, the insecure braggart or social climber or would-be seducer strikes a lofty pose, and then is jeered back down to the common level when his cowardice or his lies are exposed, and he is revealed as merely another mortal body thinly clothed with verbal pretensions. Malvolio in *Twelfth Night* is a perfect example; but he exits vowing to be 'revenged on the whole pack of you', like a Coriolanus or Timon in training. The cycles of retaliation evoked by the symmetries of Shakespeare's early tragic rhetoric take on an even more pervasive and implacable form in his later tragedies, which may still tell the stories of famous historical figures doomed to fatal errors, but which make those stories into allegories for the painful paradox of human nature, the cry of protest implied by the very act of speech, which can end only in the silence of the grave.

Notes

1. This is the opening sentence of Bacon's 'Of Revenge', in his *Essayes* (London, 1625).
2. Linda Woodbridge, *English Revenge Drama: Money, Resistance, Equality* (Cambridge University Press, 2011), explores this function across the legal, political, economic and social realms. On the legal realm especially, see Lorna Hutson, *The Invention of Suspicion* (Oxford University Press, 2007).
3. William Kerrigan, '*Macbeth* and the History of Ambition', *Freud and the Passions*, ed. John O'Neill (University Park: Pennsylvania State University Press, 1996), pp. 13–24, outlines this argument vividly.
4. George Thompson, *Aeschylus and Athens* (1941; rpt London, 1980), p. 2; paraphrased by John Drakakis, *Shakespearean Tragedy* (London: Longman, 1992), p. 7. Thompson is remarkably foresighted about the necessary balance between historicism and essentialism.
5. The law of the talion is the principle of symmetrical repayment: an eye for an eye. And another eye for that one: René Girard, *Violence and the Sacred*

(Baltimore, MD: Johns Hopkins University Press, 1977), argues that breaking such cycles of mimetic violence is an essential function of tragedy.

6. Lady Macbeth will attempt the opposite transformation, turning her milk to gall, and the milk of her husband's humankindness into bloody murder (1.5.48, 17).

7. Many classic works on English Renaissance drama have acknowledged a powerful Elizabethan orthodoxy against private vengeance; see Lily Bess Campbell, *Shakespeare's Tragic Heroes: Slaves of Passion* (Cambridge University Press, 1930), pp. 3–24; Willard Farnham, *The Medieval Heritage of Elizabethan Tragedy* (Berkeley: University of California Press, 1936), pp. 343–51; and Fredson Bowers, *Elizabethan Revenge Tragedy, 1587–1642* (Princeton University Press, 1940), pp. 3–61. For a brief summary of this tradition that also acknowledges an unabashed counter-tradition – 'Drake named the sea vessel he led against the Armada not *Forgiveness* or *The Turned Cheek* but *The Revenge*' – see Harry Keyishian, *The Shapes of Revenge* (Atlantic Highlands, NJ: Humanities Press, 1995), pp. 1–14. Woodbridge also sees revenge as (in the popular mind if not the official moralizations) primarily corrective rather than destructive.

8. Eleanor Prosser, *Hamlet and Revenge* (Stanford University Press, 2nd edn, 1971). This argument is helpfully revisited in Roland Mushat Frye, *The Renaissance Hamlet* (Princeton University Press, 1984), pp. 22–37.

9. Catherine Belsey, *The Subject of Tragedy* (New York: Routledge, 1985), pp. 115–16.

10. The latter term, meaning the vocabularies of possible knowledge at different historical moments, is developed by Michel Foucault in *Les mots et les choses* (Paris: Gallimard, 1966).

11. Robert N. Watson, *The Rest is Silence* (Berkeley: University of California Press, 1987), p. 5; the point was later explored extensively in Stephen Greenblatt, *Hamlet in Purgatory* (Princeton University Press, 2002).

12. On Hamlet's transition from the common eye-for-an-eye project of revenge to an emphasis on commemoration, see John Kerrigan, *Revenge Tragedy: Aeschylus to Armageddon* (Oxford: Clarendon Press, 1996).

13. Robert N. Watson, *Shakespeare and the Hazards of Ambition* (Cambridge, MA: Harvard University Press, 1984), pp. 83–221, makes this argument about Coriolanus and Macbeth at greater length.

14. Cf. Sigmund Freud, *Civilization and its Discontents* (New York: Norton, 1961), p. 13, which explores 'states in which the boundary lines between the ego and the external world become uncertain or in which they are actually drawn incorrectly. There are cases in which parts of a person's body, even portions of his own mental life . . . appear alien to him.'

15. See, for example, the classic studies by Cleanth Brooks, 'The Naked Babe and the Cloak of Manliness', from his *The Well-Wrought Urn* (New York: Harcourt Brace, 1947), and Caroline Spurgeon, *Shakespeare's Imagery and What it Tells Us* (1935; rpt Boston: Beacon Hill Press, 1958).

16. Freud, *Beyond the Pleasure Principle*, trans. James Strachey (New York: Liveright, 1961), p. 4.

17. Two prominent examples are 'An Exhortation Concerning Good Order, and Obedience to Rulers and Magistrates' and 'A Sermon on Disobedience and Willful Rebellion', *Sermons or Homilies Appointed to be Read in Churches in the Time of Queen Elizabeth of Famous Memory* (London: C. and J. Rivington, 1825), pp. 114–15; also Richard Hooker, *Of the Laws of Ecclesiastical Polity* (1594), Everyman's Library (London: J. M. Dent, 1907), p. 157.

18. Marguerite A. Tassi, *Women and Revenge in Shakespeare: Gender, Genre, and Ethics* (Cranbury, NJ; Associated University Presses, 2011), makes this argument perceptively.

CHAPTER 10

Shakespeare's tragedies of love

Catherine Bates

'Tragedy of love' is to some extent a contradiction in terms. Love is the great force that unites and binds. It is, to cite a statement that if nothing else has all the force of tradition behind it, what prompts a man to leave his father and mother and cleave to his wife.[1] Celebrated conventionally in romantic comedy, love is the divine bond that leads to marriage and the creation of a new family. In forming the basic building block of the social group, love is, in this definition, not only a beneficial but also a fundamentally creative force and as such it is opposed to the forces of destruction. Love not only creates society, moreover, but it seeks to preserve what it has made. It is therefore the great civilizing force, the energy that counters anarchy and chaos with order and degree (in primitive societies, marriage is always the first law). Love makes for civil conversation, courtesy, and good manners. It oils the wheels of social functioning and mitigates aggression and selfishness. When, in literature, love does encounter the forces of destruction it is generally in order to meet them head on and reverse them in a glorious moment of redemption. When Hero appears to die in *Much Ado About Nothing*, for example, or Hermione in *The Winter's Tale*, their later appearance alive, well, and, surprisingly, still loving is made all the more poignant for the fear that they have been lost. Tragedy is averted as love's redemptive force wins out. Strictly speaking, the sleeping potion that Juliet takes in order to feign death should fall into this category too. It is a classic comic device, designed to flirt with tragedy only to defeat it the more triumphantly in the end. When, instead, she wakes up not in Romeo's arms but in the family vault with her lover dead at her side it is a sign that things have gone doubly wrong. The forces of death have not only wrought destruction: they have, in destroying love, killed creativity itself. In tragedy things by definition go wrong but in love tragedy what goes wrong are the very best things – goodness, mercy, and love. The forces of redemption are shown to be inferior to the forces of death, as if God had lost out in the struggle against darkness and evil. The result is a degree of nihilism and despair that often surpasses that of the grimmest tragedy. Tragedies of love can leave us with a sense of generic outrage, as if something deep in the order of things has gone wrong and the comedic will towards forgiveness and redemption has been diabolically reversed. The death of Cordelia is a case in point. In the many versions of the Lear story available to Shakespeare, love and goodness finally triumph and the life of Cordelia is spared. It is his version alone that wrenches the story out of this comedic pattern, and the resulting sense of emotional and literary vandalism continues to make this one of the most painful scenes in the Shakespeare canon. 'Civilization', wrote Freud in a famous essay,

> is a process in the service of Eros, whose purpose is to combine single human individuals, and after that families, then races, peoples and nations, into one great unity, the unity of mankind. Why this has to happen, we do not know; the work of Eros is precisely this. These collections of men are to be libidinally bound to one another. Necessity alone, the advantages of work in common, will not hold them together. But man's natural aggressive instinct, the hostility of each against all and of all against each, opposes this programme of civilization. The aggressive instinct is the derivative and the main representative of the death instinct which we have found alongside of Eros and which shares world-dominion with it. And now, I think, the meaning of the evolution of civilization is no longer obscure to us. It must present the struggle between Eros and Death, between the instinct of life and the instinct of destruction, as it works itself out in the human species.[2]

For Freud, human civilization is nothing less than an ongoing struggle between the forces of life and the forces of death, and it is only because his words capture so well the subject matter of Shakespeare's love tragedies that I quote them here at such length. Love sponsors the forces of life, creating human families and social groups in the teeth of man's instinct for destruction – both self-destruction and the destruction of the other. It is the perpetual struggle between these two forces that creates that tense, uneasy and fragile achievement that in Freud's characterization constitutes human civilization, and Shakespeare's tragedies of love are both a product of that civilization and a profound, not always comfortable, reflection on it.

Romeo and Juliet

Usually dated around 1595, *Romeo and Juliet* is Shakespeare's first proper tragedy of love, and from the opening lines of this early play it is clear that man's incivility to man is to be the drama's key issue:

> Two households, both alike in dignity,
> In fair Verona, where we lay our scene,

> From ancient grudge break to new mutiny,
> Where civil blood makes civil hands unclean.   (Prologue, 1–4)

Shakespeare plays on the intrinsic instability of the word 'civil'. It is when the citizens' hands are turned against themselves that civility turns to civil war, the worst kind of strife, and we soon learn of three 'civil brawls' which have disturbed the city's streets (1.1.89). Shakespeare puns on the word throughout the play as if to emphasize that the precariousness of human civilization is embedded in language itself.[3] There is no word for 'civil' that does not contain the seeds of its own destruction.

Indeed, the world into which the play opens is one where the chaos caused by the internecine squabbling of the Capulets and the Montagues is matched by a linguistic disorder in which the pun is king. The play's first four lines of dialogue toss puns around like loose change – 'coals ... colliers ... choler ... collar' – for here language is evidently a currency so light that even servants can be free with it (1.1.1–4). This is not the world of the humanistic 'golden sentence' in which word is tied securely to thing but a mercantile free-for-all in which the true masters are the linguistic prodigals.[4] Where words have lost their value, characters can afford to be profligate with them – like the garrulous Nurse whose flood and tumble of unedited utterance is only one step above mere noise. At the beginning of the play Romeo puns incessantly and not very well – 'You have dancing shoes/With nimble souls, I have a soul of lead' (1.4.14–15) – but it is Mercutio who tops the bill as a 'gentleman ... that loves to hear himself talk, and will speak more in a minute than he will stand to in a month' (2.4.147–9). An inveterate punster, Mercutio is playing with words right up to the end – 'you shall find me a grave man' (3.1.98). His Queen Mab speech is an exercise in spinning something out of nothing:

> ROMEO Peace, peace, Mercutio, peace!
> Thou talk'st of nothing.
> MERCUTIO   True, I talk of dreams,
> Which are the children of an idle brain,
> Begot of nothing but vain fantasy,
> Which is as thin of substance as the air   (1.4.95–9)

Dazzling and mercurial, Mercutio's speech bursts with an inventiveness and delight in words that makes him the true heir to Spenser's Phantastes, the character who represents both the poet's greatest asset and his major liability – the imaginative faculty of the brain. Housed in a chamber that is painted in rainbow colours and which reverberates to the ceaseless buzz of flies, Phantastes is monarch of all 'idle thoughts and fantasies,/Deuices,

dreames, opinions vnsound,/Shewes, visions, sooth-sayes, and prophesies;/
And all that fained is, as leasings, tales, and lies'.[5]

In a world where words are, as here, loose, detached, potentially mean-
ingless and by implication debased, it is hardly surprising that, as the Prince
complains, the civil brawls that disturb his city are born of a single 'airy
word' (1.1.89). Indeed, the fatal fight between Tybalt and Mercutio which
sets what should, properly speaking, have been a romantic comedy lurching
irretrievably in the direction of tragedy is generated by little more:

TYBALT Gentlemen, good den, a word with one of you.
MERCUTIO And but one word with one of us? Couple it with something, make it a
    word and a blow.   (3.1.38–40)

In Shakespeare's time, a lack of respect for language was equivalent to a
lack of respect for authority. 'Wheresoever manners, and fashions are
corrupted', wrote Ben Jonson, 'Language is. It imitates the publicke
riot. The excesse of Feasts, and apparell, are the notes of a sick State;
and the wantonnesse of language, of a sick mind.'[6] According to the tenets
of Renaissance humanism, linguistic disorder and social disorder were
effectively one and the same. If language were allowed to decline, the long-
term effects were sure to be dire. History provided the lesson. 'When apt
and good words began to be neglected and properties of those two tongues
[Greek and Latin] to be confounded', noted Roger Ascham, Queen
Elizabeth's own schoolmaster,

> then also began ill deeds to spring, strange manners to oppress good orders,
> new and fond opinions to strive with old and true doctrine, first in philos-
> ophy and after in religion, right judgment of all things to be perverted, and so
> virtue with learning is contemned, and study left off. Of ill thoughts cometh
> perverse judgment; of ill deeds springeth lewd talk.[7]

As the prop of civilization, language had the power to civilize the savage
by teaching him how to speak (or to curse, in the case of Caliban). Since
language was the vehicle for reason, it was able – in theory, at least – to
subdue the barbarian and bring him to good order. 'Suche force hath
the tongue', wrote Sir Thomas Wilson in his *Arte of Rhetorique* (1553),
'and such is the power of eloquence and reason, that most men are forced
even to yelde in that, whiche most standeth against their will.'[8]
Renaissance literature and humanist education in logic and rhetoric
aimed at nothing less.

It is appropriate, therefore, that the love of Romeo and Juliet – which has
the potential, at least, to reconcile the warring families and so to civilize a

disordered state – should express itself above all by the effect that it has on words:

> ROMEO If I profane with my unworthiest hand
> This holy shrine, the gentle sin is this,
> My lips, two blushing pilgrims, ready stand
> To smooth that rough touch with a tender kiss.
>
> JULIET Good pilgrim, you do wrong your hand too much,
> Which mannerly devotion shows in this,
> For saints have hands that pilgrims' hands do touch,
> And palm to palm is holy palmers' kiss.
>
> ROMEO Have not saints lips, and holy palmers too?
>
> JULIET Ay, pilgrim, lips that they must use in prayer.
>
> ROMEO O then, dear saint, let lips do what hands do:
> They pray, grant thou, lest faith turn to despair.
>
> JULIET Saints do not move, though grant for prayers' sake.
>
> ROMEO Then move not while my prayer's effect I take.   (1.5.92–105)

This is the lovers' first exchange. At the Capulet feast, with Romeo still in disguise and the pair not yet aware of each other's identity, the wondrous immediacy of their love expresses itself in a sonnet – one of the most condensed, rich and complex literary forms of the period. 'Is it not most delightfull', wrote Samuel Daniel, praising the sonnet form in *A Defence of Ryme* (1603), 'to see much excellently ordred in a small roome or little, gallantly disposed and made to fill vp a space of like capacitie?'[9] Shakespeare alters the standard rhyme scheme of his own sonnets to repeat the B rhyme, partly in order to condense the rhyme still further and partly to spell out quietly the action in which the sonnet culminates: 'this kiss, this kiss'. Surrounded by the bustle of the feast, the action of the scene is momentarily put on hold, crystallizing into a moment of suspension, of stillness, before it erupts into drama again with that fateful meeting of lips. And, although Juliet accuses Romeo of kissing 'by th'book' (110), this is manifestly not a staid, copy-book Petrarchism but rather a living moment, the intensity of which suddenly exposes as empty rhetoric Romeo's now scarce-remembered passion for Rosaline. By comparison with the holy words he exchanges with Juliet, Romeo's earlier protestations of 'devout religion'

(1.2.88) for his 'saint' (1.1.214) now seem nothing but idolatry. The experience of real love massively expands the signifying power of words. The old Romeo was akin to Spenser's scorned courtier who 'himselfe doth [n]ought esteeme, / Unlesse he swim in love up to the eares'.[10] In such a world it is not only language but poetry that is debased. For Mercutio it is enough 'to pronounce but "love" and "dove"' to be a poet (2.1.10) or to copy 'the numbers that Petrarch flow'd in' (2.4.38–9). But now Romeo is coming to the experience of love from the inside and the effect is dramatic. The language of the play – heightened, lofty, and poetic – has long been commented on.

At the lovers' next rendezvous, the balcony scene (2.2), the atmosphere is so charged that the smallest gesture is loaded with significance. Juliet need not even speak in order to communicate to her beloved. 'She speaks, yet says nothing', comments Romeo, 'what of that? / Her eye discourses' (12–13). Transmuted into a purely visual emblem, a 'speaking picture', Juliet has become in herself the embodiment of pure poetry.[11] In the exchange that follows, language is further distilled down to its most essential. 'I take thee at thy word' (49) is Romeo's response to Juliet's offer of love and she replies in kind: 'Dost thou love me? I know thou wilt say, "Ay", / And I will take thy word' (90–1). As the affirmative and the first person singular coincide here in a single syllable, not only do the two lovers converge into one (one word, one flesh, so to speak), but we also see punning from, as it were, the opposite angle: not as the debased result of language's fall from grace but as an instance of that ideal, originary state in which words were grounded in a divine Logos, the principle of their intelligibility confirmed, and any connectedness between them not the outcome of some empty, fortuitous coincidence but proof, rather, of a deep and underlying meaningfulness. Under this aura, affirming one's love and affirming one's identity 'really' are, at origin, one and the same. And one must, of course, include Juliet's eloquently discoursing 'eye' here as a further pun in the series. The effect of love is so profound that it eliminates the need for words altogether: it is enough for the eye to proclaim the Ay of the I.[12] How different this is from the earlier 'airy word' of the warring parties' empty provocations. By the end of the lovers' exchange, 'Three words' are sufficient to propose, accept, and arrange their hasty marriage (142).

It is during the balcony scene, of course, that Juliet famously meditates on the relation of meaning to words:

> 'Tis but thy name that is my enemy;
> Thou art thyself, though not a Montague.

> What's Montague? It is nor hand nor foot,
> Nor arm nor face, nor any other part
> Belonging to a man. O be some other name!
> What's in a name? That which we call a rose
> By any other word would smell as sweet (38–44)

Juliet resists nominalism – the argument that convention alone (and arbitrarily) links words to things. Against the potentially unrooted play of signifiers Juliet sets an altogether more conservative theory of language: one in which the inherent property of a thing – its *quidditas* – articulates its true nature and not any arbitrarily imposed name. Inspired by her experience of love, Juliet adopts the position of Socrates who, in Plato's dialogue *Cratylus*, goes behind the shifting surface of language to the Forms in order to locate there the permanent and unchanging truth of things.[13]

Juliet's tendency to summarize, hone, and distil meaning down to some essential core surfaces again in 2.6, the scene in which she and Romeo are married at Friar Lawrence's cell. An ecstatic Romeo urges *copia*, encouraging her to 'blazon' forth their mutually 'heap'd' joy and 'Unfold' it to the air (26, 25, 28), but instead Juliet moves in the opposite direction. Rhetoric can be a surfeit. For her, a telescoping process makes the smallest unit better express the greatest experience. In place of expansiveness, therefore, Juliet's lapidary words argue rather for compression and conciseness as they strain towards epitome, *sententia*, and closure:

> Conceit, more rich in matter than in words,
> Brags of his substance, not of ornament;
> They are but beggars that can count their worth,
> But my true love is grown to such excess
> I cannot sum up sum of half my wealth. (30–4)

Again, Juliet is adopting the conservative position that it is *materia* or substance which properly grounds human language. In a divinely governed universe where human words are guaranteed by a God-given and truth-giving Word, a distinct hierarchy of values comes into view. In the process of education, the 'knowledge of words comes earlier', as Erasmus admitted, 'but that of things is the more important'. And for Ben Jonson, too, there was no doubt about the proper ordering of priorities: 'Words, aboue action: matter, aboue words'.[14]

In *Romeo and Juliet* the miraculous effect that love has on words promises to restore a debased language and with it a whole system of values. It is all the more tragic, therefore, that this redemptive move towards meaning and integrity should founder. By a cruel irony of fate, the lovers' ability to concentrate meaning in a single word turns mockingly against them. After Romeo's murder of Tybalt and subsequent flight one word comes to sum up the whole awful situation: 'That "banishèd", that one word "banishèd",/ Hath slain ten thousand Tybalts' (3.2.113–14). In the following scene, the word is spoken over and over again by Romeo with the sonority of a tolling bell. In the face of tragedy language retreats into repetition and empty formulae, like the chorus of wails that goes up around the bed of the supposedly dead Juliet:

> LADY CAPULET Accurs'd, unhappy, wretched, hateful day! . . .
> NURSE O woe! O woeful, woeful, woeful day! . . .
> PARIS Beguiled, divorcèd, wrongèd, spited, slain! . . .
> CAPULET Despised, distressèd, hated, martyred, killed! . . .
>
> (4.5.43, 49, 55, 59)

After love's intensification of meaning it is as if language has been let loose again to be piled up indiscriminately in great catalogues of cliché.

It is the tragedy of Romeo and Juliet that their experience of love is, for all the glimpse of its potentially redemptive capacity, not enough to save them. On the contrary, they remain victims of that same messy, prodigal world in which the play began – a world of illiterate servants and an inefficient postal system. It is significant that what first sets the play in motion is Romeo's reading of something that he is not supposed to read – the Capulets' guest-list – for what brings the tragedy round full circle is his failure to read something that is most definitely intended for his eyes: Friar Lawrence's explanatory letter. As in *King Lear*, tragedy is brought about by something as banal as a message not arriving in time. Given the demonstrable effect that love has had on their words, it is the more poignant that things 'not nice but full of charge,/Of dear import' like the Friar's missive should ultimately suffer the same fate as the emptiest of words (5.2.18–19). Love's great enrichment and refinement of language counts for nothing in the end. Only in the golden effigies, which are erected by the two grieving and belatedly reconciled families, do Romeo and Juliet ever approximate again to the speaking picture of love they experienced all too briefly in life. But, silent, cold, and metallic – with no chance, like Hermione, of ever living and loving again – these statues belie any optimistic hope that such loss might be redeemed, made good by art.

Othello

Similar issues were preoccupying Shakespeare when, a decade or so later, he once more turned to love tragedy, this time with *Othello* (c. 1604). Again, love is portrayed as the great binding force, only here uniting not the warring elements within a single society but, more dramatically, two quite disparate cultures – the Moorish and the Venetian – symbolically encoded as black and white. And, once again, the vehicle of love's civilizing power is shown to be language. Shakespeare makes it clear that Othello wins Desdemona's love, and indeed the ultimate acceptance of the Venetian state, through his words. We are first introduced to Othello as a great military general who is 'Horribly stuff'd with epithets of war' (1.1.14), a man who is, by his own self-deprecating account, rude in speech 'And little bless'd with the soft phrase of peace' (1.3.82). Yet Othello is most effective not in the field (where, in fact, we never see him) but in the gentler warfare of persuasive speech. Tamburlaine brings all down before him with a heady mixture of verbal and physical violence in Marlowe's play (1587), but Othello's best sword is in his words.

Accused by Brabantio of having made off with his daughter, Othello defends himself by telling the Senate the 'round unvarnish'd tale' (1.3.90) of all his dealings with Desdemona and, as he does so, he visibly captivates his listeners:

> Her father loved me, oft invited me;
> Still questioned me the story of my life
> From year to year – the battles, sieges, fortunes,
> That I have passed.
> I ran it through, even from my boyish days
> To th'very moment that he bade me tell it . . .
> . . . These things to hear
> Would Desdemona seriously incline;
> But still the house affairs would draw her thence,
> Which ever as she could with haste dispatch,
> She'ld come again, and with a greedy ear
> Devour up my discourse.   (1.3.128–33, 145–50)

If Othello's story is capable of mesmerizing the hardened heads of the Venetian Senate when, as here, retold at second hand, then how much the greater its unmediated effect upon the susceptible heart of Desdemona. It is a story that, as the impressed Duke comments, 'would win my daughter too' (1.3.170). Indeed, Othello's gift as a raconteur is akin to that of the poet who, in Sidney's phrase, 'cometh unto you, with a tale which holdeth children from play, and old men from the chimney corner'.[15] When seen as the understandable response to such a tale, Desdemona's choice is accepted as decisive and irreversible by all except Brabantio, the only character in the scene who closes his ears to Othello's rhetorical charms:

'But words are words; I never yet did hear/That the bruised heart was pierced through the ear' (1.3.216–17). Yet even this formidable father, who by Iago's calculation 'hath in his effect a voice potential/As double as the Duke's' (1.2.13–14), is successfully 'out-tongue[d]' by his opponent (19). It is Othello's conquering words that carry the day.

Othello is like the orator who, in countless Renaissance emblem and commonplace books, is depicted as leading his hearers with a golden chain: 'with his golden chaine/The Oratour so farre men's harts doth bind,/That no pace else their guided steps can find,/But as he them more short or slacke doth raine'.[16] And yet it is Othello's fate to become entangled, in turn, by just such a chain of another's devising and to be as tenderly 'led by th'nose/As asses are' (1.3.384–5). For, if Othello conquers Desdemona with the sheer irresistibility of his tale, so he falls victim to the sly suggestions and expert handling of Iago. A number of literary symmetries make it clear that Othello's miraculously effective words find their demonic counterpart in Iago, whose storytelling, though equally effective, works to conversely deadly effect. An expert raconteur himself, Iago catches Othello's ear with a skilful weaving of narrative cliché and readerly expectation. He presents the story of Desdemona's adultery with Cassio in the terms of a hackneyed city play whose plot is just waiting to happen: 'the knave is handsome, young, and hath all those requisites in him that folly and green minds look after. A pestilent complete knave; and the woman hath found him already' (2.1.231–5). Cassio's actions are presented by Iago as 'an index and obscure prologue to the history of lust and foul thoughts' (2.1.243–4) giving rise to a narrative logic which, in time, Othello's 'unbookish jealousy must conster' (4.1.99). Utterly taken in, Othello gazes on while Iago 'begins the story' (4.1.127), and he is so convinced by what he sees and hears that ultimately he too rewrites his wife: 'Was this fair paper, this most goodly book,/Made to write "whore" upon?' (4.2.70–1).

'That Cassio loves her, I do well believe't', Iago comments to himself; 'That she loves him, 'tis apt and of great credit' (2.1.266–7). The credibility of his lies rests, in other words, on the force not of truth but of probability and plausibility. Indeed, these are all that are required of the literary workman in order to evoke in his readers the most piteous response and emotional identification. In his essay *On the Composition of Comedies and Tragedies* (1543), Giraldi Cinthio discusses the traditional distinction, drawn from Aristotle, between comic and tragic plots. The comic is generally taken from 'actions that occur in the ordinary life of citizens' if not from contemporary events, while the tragic is generally drawn from the more public and well-known narratives of history. But, he goes on to say, it is just as possible for a poet to make up or 'feign' a tragic plot from his own imagination, provided he obeys the law of probability:

> it is in the power of the poet to move at his wish the tragic feelings by means of a tragedy of which he feigns the plot, if that plot is in conformity with natural habits and not remote from what can happen and often does happen.[17]

In essence, what Cinthio is doing here is describing the craft of Iago, who relies on the plausibility of Desdemona's liking for her own kind – 'Whereto we see in all things nature tends' (3.3.233) – in order to persuade Othello of her adulterous liaison with Cassio. Iago, that is to say, is merely putting into practice the literary advice of his own inventor, Cinthio also being, of course, the author of the novella that Shakespeare closely followed as the source for his play. And Othello's (in literary terms, quite proper) response to the tragedy that he's been told – 'O Iago, the pity of it, Iago!' (4.1.184–5) – shows just how effective Iago has been in being able to move tragic feelings in another at will; in being, that is to say, a perfect tragic poet.

In *Romeo and Juliet* the lovers fall victim to external circumstance, but there is nothing demonstrably wrong with their love in itself. In *Othello*, however, Shakespeare deepens the tragic potential considerably. Here love is not merely a good in an evil world. It is shown to contain the seeds of evil within itself. Love's civilizing power is displayed in all its positive, creative effect in Othello's persuasive speech, but it also finds its diabolic double in Iago who operates the same persuasive speech to an utterly destructive end. The symmetry between the two lends a tragic irony to Othello's fate. As it is his propensity to love that makes him jealous, so it is his propensity to persuade others that, tragically, makes him all too persuadable himself. Renaissance humanists rested their case on the ability of rhetoric to make 'of wilde, sober: of cruel, gentle: of foles, wise: and of beastes, men'.[18] Yet Iago shows that all that rhetorical training could just as easily be turned in the opposite direction. The effect is to undermine confidence in a well-established and much-theorized educational practice. If civilization's principal tool can be used against itself in order to barbarize what has been refined, then what becomes of civilized values? The play plants a dark uncertainty at the heart of civilization itself, searchingly probing the slippery semantics of civility, liable to shift from a shared set of social values to civil war at a moment's notice.[19]

'What meane you by that woord, Civile?', asks Stefano Guazzo in *La civile conversatione*, a courtesy-book translated by George Pettie and

Bartholomew Young between 1580 and 1586. His interlocutor, one Annibale, replies as follows:

ANNIBALE If you meane to know my meaning of it, I must first aske if you know any citizen which liveth uncivilly?
GUAZZO Yes mary doe I, more then one.
ANNIBALE Now let me aske you on the contrarie, if you know any man of the countrey which liveth civilly?
GUAZZO Yea very many.
ANNIBALE You see then, that we give a large sense and signification to this woorde (civile) for that we would haue understoode, that to live civilly, is not sayde in respect of the citie, but of the quallities of the minde.[20]

Simply living in the city and being a denizen of its polite practices guarantees nothing. Civility is rather an inner virtue, an individual human quality that owes nothing to breeding or class (much scope for anti-court satire here). In Book VI of *The Faerie Queene* (1596), Spenser similarly extends the meaning of 'courtesy' beyond any narrow etymological derivation. 'Of Court it seemes, men Courtesie doe call', he sardonically writes, 'For that it there most vseth to abound', but in the course of Book VI it becomes apparent that true courtesy is to be found less in any social location than, as for Guazzo, 'deepe within the mynd'.[21]

In the concluding notes to his edition of Shakespeare's plays (1765), Samuel Johnson wrote of *Othello* that 'had the scene opened in Cyprus, and the preceding incidents been occasionally related, there had been little wanting to a drama of the most exact and scrupulous regularity'.[22] Shakespeare's decision to flout the classical unities by setting his first act in Venice thus seems designed to dramatize the contrast between the two locations. In Shakespeare's day, the great trading city of Venice was a byword for civilization and luxury, and the play opens with its citizens' comfortable assurance of that fact just about still intact. 'This is Venice!', cries Brabantio, called up in the middle of the night by the rowdiness of Iago and Roderigo: 'My house is not a grange' (1.1.106–7). It is only the gravity of the occasion – Desdemona's elopement with the Moor – which, Roderigo assures him, licenses their otherwise unwarrantable disturbance of the peace:

> Do not believe
> That, from the sense of all civility,
> I thus would play and trifle with your reverence.   (1.1.129–31)

As the play progresses the parameters of the word 'civility' grow ever more extenuated and strained, and particularly after the scene has shifted to

Cyprus. In contrast to the refinement of the city, Cyprus – the legendary birthplace of Aphrodite – is a wild, chaotic place, the more so as the island is, on the arrival of Othello and Desdemona and with the unlooked-for dispersal of the Turkish fleet, given over to revelry and carnival: 'It is Othello's pleasure . . . [that] every man put himself into triumph; some to dance, some to make bonfires, each man to what sport and revels his addiction leads him' (2.2.1–5). Against this backdrop the mincing manners of an over-educated elite begin to look rather different. When Desdemona first arrives on the Cytherean shore she brings her city manners with her in the pleasantries and courtly *questioni d'amore* that she exchanges with Iago and Cassio. But in time this Venetian politesse and finger-kissing begin to have the thin and nervous feel of a foreign import. Indeed, it is precisely the free and easy manners of city living that Iago uses to entrap his victims: 'With as little a web as this will I ensnare as great a fly as Cassio. Ay, smile upon her, do; I will gyve [trap] thee in thine own courtship' (2.1.164–5). With its sense of menace, of love run to bestiality and madness, Cyprus has hints of Circe's isle, a nightmare version of the dream-like 'green world' to which the company traditionally repair in Shakespearean comedy.[23] In plays like *A Midsummer Night's Dream* or *As You Like It*, the forest provides a foil to courtly manners and introduces the characters to their true feelings. But in *Othello* Cyprus distorts to the point of grotesqueness the norms of civil breeding such that it is Desdemona's very accomplishments and cultivated habits which finally indict her:

OTHELLO So delicate with her needle! an admirable musician! O, she will sing the
    savageness out of a bear. Of so high and plenteous wit and invention!
IAGO She's the worse for all this.
OTHELLO O, a thousand, a thousand times.   (4.1.177–81)

It is a sign of how far things have gone that, by the time Ludovico arrives in Cyprus in Act 4, Othello's violent behaviour towards his wife is, to the Venetian, frankly unrecognizable: 'this would not be believed in Venice' (4.1.232).

Translated to Cyprus where they are out of context and isolated from the supporting habitus of social and cultural assumptions, the civilized manners of Venice begin to look unnatural and strange.[24] Shakespeare's decision to visualize and thus dramatize the contrast not only emphasizes the juxtaposition between the two but drives home the dialectical nature of cultural self-definition. Notions of wildness, madness, otherness and heresy are not moral absolutes but concepts that serve to confirm the value of their dialectical antitheses: civilization, rationality, identity, and orthodoxy.

The self-esteem of a given group rests upon the security and unquestion-ability of such definitions, with the result that any unwanted libidinal desires or inadmissible aggressive urges classically get projected out upon the Other. 'In times of sociocultural stress', writes Hayden White, 'when the need for positive self-definition asserts itself but no compelling criterion of self-identification appears, it is always possible to say something like: "I may not know the precise content of my own felt humanity, but I am most certainly *not* like that."'[25]

In *Othello*, the first and most obvious target for such projection is, of course, Othello himself, Desdemona's passion for whom is designated by her fellow citizens as downright unnatural:

> BRABANTIO   A maiden, never bold;
> Of spirit so still and quiet that her motion
> Blush'd at herself; and she, in spite of nature,
> Of years, of country, credit, everything,
> To fall in love with what she feared to look on!
> It is a judgment maimed, and most imperfect,
> That will confess perfection so could err
> Against all rules of nature.   (1.3.94–101)

By a process of synecdoche, Othello's tales of the 'Anthropophagi, and men whose heads/Do grow beneath their shoulders' (1.3.142–3) cast an aura of the monstrous and the unknown over their teller and help the Venetians to locate the Other comfortably elsewhere in thrillingly distant and exotic lands. But as the play develops Shakespeare treats such projections with increasing scepticism. For, as the Venetians gradually discover to their cost, the Wild Man lurks not in his traditional haunts of the desert, the forest, or the wilderness but, more disconcertingly, at home, right at the heart of civilization itself. The Venetian state is, in fact, less imperilled by the Other – the Turkish barbarian against whom Othello is engaged to fight, or indeed by the Moor himself – than it is by its own kind, a super-subtle Venetian whose evil is the more invidious for being homegrown. Iago is a perfect picture of that unsettling contradiction – the 'citizen which liueth vnciuilly' – who reveals civilization's claims to natural order and cultural superiority to be nothing but a sham.

In his essay 'On Cannibals' (1603), Montaigne writes that 'men call that barbarisme which is not common to them' and reports briefly on some of the more bizarre degustatory practices of primitive peoples as recounted by ancient and modern travellers. But he resists the occasion to prop his own culture's practices upon such projections. 'I am not sorie we note the barbarous horror of such an action, but grieved, that prying so narrowly into their faults we are so blinded in ours', he writes, for, turning his attention to the apparently civilized Europeans, Montaigne finds that they in fact exceed the cannibals 'in all kinde of barbarisme'.[26] Here, as throughout his sceptical philosophy, Montaigne's object is to force his own people to reconsider their unexamined assumptions and to recognize the degree to which their civilization hides a deeper, more horrifying barbarity. The savage exists in a state of nature that, in itself, is neither good nor bad. But for Montaigne it is infinitely preferable to civilization's *perversion* of nature – its attempt to naturalize its fictions as truths, its parochial categories as moral absolutes.

The most unsettling thing about Iago, therefore, is his unblushing separation of being from seeming. For him Venetian culture is but a whited sepulchre in which 'our country disposition' is not a natural gentility or courtesy but a merely seeming so: 'In Venice [women] do let God see the pranks/They dare not show their husbands', he urges (3.3.204–5). The charge of hypocrisy undermines the conservative attempts of a Guazzo or a Spenser to locate the true source of civility 'deepe within the mynd', for it merely runs into the old Catch 22: the more natural, the more feigned. It is this that enables Iago cynically to treat civility as mere show – like the 'flag and sign of love' (1.1.155) he displays to the trusting Othello – and which makes it easy for him to accuse the suave Cassio of 'putting on the mere form of civil and humane seeming' (2.1.226). It is only a small step from this to insinuating that Othello's cultivated wife is equally capable of giving out 'such a seeming' (3.3.211). As a purely artificial construction – that can be bent to self-advantage at will – civility loses at a stroke its pretensions to order, superiority, or goodness. To the extent that *Othello* scrutinizes the contradictions embedded at the heart of civilization, therefore, it shares in the larger question posed by Shakespeare's tragedies and history plays as a whole: what is it that makes a civilization or a nation state collapse in upon itself and descend from civil practice to civil war?

Antony and Cleopatra

The issue receives perhaps its grandest treatment in Shakespeare's next and last tragedy of love, *Antony and Cleopatra* (1606–7). For the civilization that is held up to scrutiny here is none less than that great repository of learning and (for the Renaissance in particular) model of civilized values – imperial Rome. The contrast between Venice and Cyprus in *Othello* expands to the wider political and geographical sweep of a play that tilts not once but continually between those two great historical symbols of cultural difference, Egypt and Rome. In this play, Rome is depicted as the home of austerity and *virtūs* – the manly vigour that draws its strength from the self-assured and stable identity of the Roman self. The qualities of Rome are characterized, furthermore, by a linguistic propriety of which Octavia's 'holy, cold, and still conversation' is a typical example (2.6.120). When Lepidus endeavours to bring the disgruntled Caesar and Antony together in common cause against Pompey, he knows that the success of the meeting depends upon 'soft and gentle speech' all round (2.2.3). It is a Roman trait to try to put aside mutual recriminations and to contain conflict in diplomatic language: 'Touch you the sourest points with sweetest terms' (26). The guarding of the tongue is an exercise in self-control, one in which the two sides just about succeed – ''Tis noble spoken', 'Worthily spoken, Maecenas' (105, 109). When the plain-speaking Enobarbus bluntly cuts through the careful rhetoric, it is not the content but only 'The manner of his speech' to which Caesar objects (119). For the Romans, as for the Renaissance human-ists who drew their cherished precepts from the handbooks of Roman rhetoric and oratory, the control of words was a first step in the control of the world.

By comparison with such staid and ponderous procedure, however, Egypt represents everything that is alien and strange. Indeed, Rome defines its own reputation for due measure, order, proportion, and degree against the quality that it projects out most insistently upon Egypt – a country whose presiding genius is, as for Spenser's Bower of Bliss, Excess.[27] Egypt's great symbol and metonymic centrepiece, 'the o'erflowing Nilus' (1.2.46), metaphors the gush and flow that characterize the landscape, language, and everything else in Egypt. Egypt melts, stretches, bursts, swells, spills over – the dialectical antithesis of the political, sexual, and rhetorical restraint of Rome. To the critical eye of Rome any encounter with such difference can only be met with blank incomprehension. Antony's proper 'self' compro-mised by the perceived lust and luxury of the East, he can only be described as 'transform'd', as 'not Antony' (1.1.12, 59). The failure of one culture to define difference in terms more imaginative than simply what it is not was never so starkly indicated. Antony's dotage, like everything else Egyptian, 'O'erflows the measure' (2). A single blanket epithet makes do to character-ize the culturally different, reducing its heterogeneity to the bland and partial statements of 'the common liar' (61), 'the general tongue' (1.2.101), or 'the world's report' (2.3.5).

The play obliges us, however, to redraw the parameters of civilization and to question Rome's self-appointed role as the great world-civilizing power. For it is not in Rome or in Octavia's cold bed that love flourishes, and yet love is the creative force whose mission is to unite individuals, harmonize the group, and temper the forces of destruction. Love, of course, flourishes in Egypt where its effect, as in the other plays we have looked at, is a marvellous enrichment and expansiveness of human experience and language. For the besotted Antony, the experience of love redefines the contours of the civilized world and indeed totally redraws the map. For him, Cleopatra is his new empire, his new America, his new-found-land:

> Let Rome in Tiber melt, and the wide arch
> Of the ranged empire fall! Here is my space.   (1.1.33–4)

The spirit of excess extends to human speech and has the natural effect of making hyperbole the common currency in Egypt. Here men do not search, as in Rome, for an etiolated *mot juste* but for words that overgo the limits of convention. 'We cannot call her winds and waters sighs and tears', remarks a jocular Enobarbus of Cleopatra, 'they are greater storms and tempests than almanacs can report' (1.2.144–5). The Romans naturally put such expansiveness down to an Egyptian excessiveness which has rubbed off on and bewitched their Antony, rather as Brabantio assumes that his daughter must have been seduced by magic and witchcraft as nothing else could explain her actions.

Egypt wonderfully expands the limits of human experience and leaves Rome looking increasingly fusty and hidebound. This move towards expansiveness and amplification finds one famous example in Enobarbus's description of the Nile-borne Cleopatra:

> The barge she sat in, like a burnish'd throne,
> Burnt on the water. The poop was beaten gold,
> Purple the sails, and so perfumed that
> The winds were love-sick with them; the oars were silver,
> Which to the tune of flutes kept stroke, and made
> The water which they beat to follow faster,
> As amorous of their strokes. For her own person,
> It beggared all description: she did lie
> In her pavilion – cloth of gold, of tissue –
> O'er-picturing that Venus where we see
> The fancy outwork nature.   (2.2.201–11)

Enobarbus is describing a privileged moment here – Antony's first sight of the Egyptian queen – and his words conjure the sheer visual impact of the scene which, like a great painting, captivates all who see it. Through the artfulness of her self-presentation, Cleopatra outdoes the famous painting of Venus by Apelles in which the painter's art was said to transcend nature. Art outdoes art. 'The *istoria* which merits both praise and admiration will be so agreeably and pleasantly attractive that it will capture the eye of whatever learned or unlearned person is looking at it and will move his soul', writes Leon Battista Alberti in his treatise *On Painting* (1435–6); 'that which first gives pleasure in the *istoria* comes from copiousness and variety of things'.[28] In the same way, Cleopatra's 'infinite variety' (2.2.246) captivates the gaze (and the soul of the gazer), drawing for its power on a subtle blending of the natural with the artificial. As Erasmus writes in *De Copia* (1512), one of the best-known Renaissance schoolbooks instructing youth in the arts of rhetorical embellishment and amplification, 'Nature above all delights in variety; in all this huge concourse of things, she has left nothing anywhere unpainted by her wonderful technique of variety.'[29] For Erasmus, *copia* properly used is the art of bending a great natural resource to one's own use, simply imitating the artfulness or 'painting' of nature itself in order to enhance one's own literary style. If taken to extremes, he concedes, *copia* can assume an excessiveness or 'Asian exuberance' (touches of Rome here) but at its best *copia* is, like the Nile itself, 'a golden river, with thoughts and words pouring out in rich abundance'.

It is the tendency of love to expand and fill all the available space. The sight of Cleopatra in her barge was so extraordinary, enthuses Enobarbus, that had nature not abhorred a vacuum the air itself had gone to gaze on her and 'made a gap in nature' (2.2.228). Cleopatra endures Antony's absence as an empty void, a 'great gap of time' (1.5.5), for where the beloved is the world is and where the beloved is not there is nothing: 'O, my oblivion is a very Antony' (1.3.91). Love's expansiveness does not only move centrifugally, however, pressing out to the limits of the known universe. It also works in the opposite direction, rolling the universe up into a ball and creating language and experience of high intensity. Indeed, the two tendencies are, as Erasmus noted, intimately related for 'who will speak more succinctly than the man who can readily and without hesitation pick out from a huge army of words, from the whole range of figures of speech, the feature that contributes most effectively to brevity?'[30] Here, therefore – as in *Romeo and Juliet* – love also sponsors a move towards epigram and closure. The largest is expressed by the smallest, the greatest by the least – or better still by silence. Antony cannot tell Cleopatra how much he loves her – 'There's beggary in the love that can be reckoned' (1.1.15) – exactly as Juliet refuses Romeo's invitation to blazon their love abroad: 'They are but beggars that can count their worth' (2.6.32). And, again as in *Romeo and Juliet*, *Antony and Cleopatra* demonstrates the same drift from verbal to visual, iconic representation being the most economic form of representation. The play opens with Demetrius and Philo describing Antony as 'the bellows and the fan/To cool a gipsy's lust' (1.1.8–9) to give way immediately to a visual picture of the same: *Enter Antony and Cleopatra . . . with eunuchs fanning her* (stage direction). The exhortations to 'Look', 'Take but good note', 'Behold and see' (10, 11, 13) remind us that the theatre is, before it is anything else, a 'place for seeing' (from θέᾱτρον). In Enobarbus's famous speech, the royal barge that 'Burned on the water' (2.2.202) likewise becomes a word-picture, a visual paradox equivalent to Donne's epigram of the burning ship: 'They in the sea being burnt, they in the burnt ship drown'd'.³¹ It is the same privileged vision of Cleopatra that we finally come to see for ourselves, moreover, when, staging her own death in the play's closing moments, she is 'again for Cydnus' (5.2.227), arrayed once more as Antony eventfully saw her for the first time.

Love thus enriches experience and refines and intensifies human language. As such, it is the world's great civilizing force, showing human society the best of which it is capable and forcing us to extend our definition and to reconsider what 'civilization' means. Yet, this being a tragedy, love does not triumph. In the end, love's expansiveness proves unsustainable and its redemptive power too weak for the forces of death. As in *Othello*, furthermore, love is not the innocent victim of circumstance or an uncaring world but, rather, is shown to be compromised, to be the vehicle of its own destruction. The surrounding world 'Shines o'er with civil swords' as Antony notes (1.3.45), but love is not enough to save it because it is not exempt from such internal struggles itself. Love's ability to civilize the world falls victim to its own civil wars, in other words, making battles rage not only around but within the individual and causing self-destruction all round.

Antony and Cleopatra is full of characters who figure the state of civil war within themselves. Octavia is the very picture of predicament. She first appears standing between Caesar and Antony (2.3), an icon of betweenness who becomes increasingly desperate as the parties it was hoped her marriage would bind together only split further apart:

> A more unhappy lady,
> If this division chance, ne'er stood between,
> Praying for both parts . . .
> . . . no midway
> 'Twixt these extremes at all. (3.4.12–14, 19–20)

Enobarbus is another such emblem of dilemma, the once-loyal soldier who turns against Antony, sickened by the latter's apparent folly and indecisiveness at the battle of Actium, only to turn back to him again,

pricked by remorse at his master's magnanimity. As with Octavia, however, there is no resolution for such divided loyalties, only a state of total
impasse: 'I fight against thee? No, I will go seek/Some ditch wherein to
die' (4.6.38–9).

The archetype of such self-destructiveness, of course, is Antony himself.
In the course of the play Antony comes for many characters to stand as an
emblem or summation of particular qualities. He is 'th'abstract of all faults'
for the high-minded Caesar (1.4.9). His mere name – 'That magical word of
war' (3.1.32) in which lay 'a moiety of the world' (5.1.19) – is enough to spell
out a whole universe of ideas and values. Like the Egyptian crocodile that, as
Antony jokes, 'is shaped . . . like itself' (2.7.38), Antony has no point of
reference outside himself. He becomes his own metaphor – for Cleopatra,
her 'man of men' (1.5.75) or 'Lord of lords' (4.8.16) – since the superlative
can have no other point of comparison, no false compare. Metaphor thus
devolves upon itself to become mere tautology – an extreme example of the
trend towards epitome or distillation that we have seen elsewhere in the
play. Ultimately, however, such magnificent economy and self-reference
implodes and collapses in upon itself. Cursing himself for losing at Actium
by blindly following Cleopatra's fleeing boats, Antony's once-stable Roman
identity breaks apart altogether: 'I have fled myself . . . My very hairs do
mutiny' (3.11.7, 13). Caesar works such self-destructiveness to his own
advantage, putting Antony's deserters in his own front line so that when
Antony encounters his troops in battle he 'may seem to spend his fury/
Upon himself' (4.6.9–10). In the end Antony comes to symbolize what
Sidney styles the 'wretched state of man in self-division' and, like the chief
characters in the *Arcadia*, he proves incapable of resolving this terrible
internal conflict.[32] As with Enobarbus, suicide is the only way out, an end
that provides both an economical and a logical conclusion to love's bitter
civil wars:

> ANTONY Not Caesar's valour hath o'erthrown Antony,
> But Antony's hath triumphed on itself.
> CLEOPATRA So it should be, that none but Antony
> Should conquer Antony, but woe 'tis so!
>
> (4.15.14–17)

Antony and Cleopatra thus takes Shakespeare's tragedies of love to their
final point of paradoxical resolution – a resolution in self-cancellation and
death. Freud's 'struggle between Eros and Death' has been decisively
called, and, where the civilizing forces of life and love collapse in upon
themselves, woe is indeed the only properly tragic response that is left
to us.

Notes

1. Genesis 2.24.
2. Sigmund Freud, *Civilization and its Discontents* (1930), in *The Standard Edition of the Complete Psychological Works of Sigmund Freud*, ed. and trans. James Strachey, 24 vols. (London: The Hogarth Press, 1960), vol. XXI, p. 122.
3. For example: 'I will be civil with the maids; I will cut off their heads' (1.1.22); 'Come, civil night,/Thou sober-suited matron all in black' (3.2.10–11); see also the punning exchange between Mercutio and Romeo on the meaning of 'courtesy' (2.4.50–7).
4. 'Wisdom is better than wealth, and a golden sentence worth a world of treasure', a typical humanist view as expressed in Thomas Lodge, *Rosalynde* (1590), ed. Donald Beecher (Ottawa: Dovehouse Editions, 1997), p. 100. For an alternative view of words as nothing but small change, contrast Thomas Nashe, *Christs Teares Over Jerusalem* (1594), *The Works of Thomas Nashe*, ed. R. B. McKerrow, 5 vols. (Oxford: Blackwell, 1966), vol. II, p. 184: 'Our English tongue of all languages most swarmeth with the single money of monasillables, which are the onely scandall of it. Bookes written in them and no other seeme like Shop-keepers boxes, that containe nothing else saue halfe-pence, three-farthings, and two-pences.'
5. See Edmund Spenser, *The Faerie Queene* (1590), ed. A. C. Hamilton (London: Longman, 1977), II. ix.51.
6. Ben Jonson, *Discoveries* (1640), *Ben Jonson*, ed. C. H. Herford and Percy and Evelyn Simpson, 11 vols. (Oxford: Clarendon Press, 1925–52), vol. VIII, p. 593.
7. Roger Ascham, *The Schoolmaster* (1570), ed. Lawrence V. Ryan (Charlottesville: University of Virginia Press, 1967), p. 115.
8. Sir Thomas Wilson, *The Arte of Rhetorique* (1553), ed. Thomas J. Derrick (New York: Garland, 1982), pp. 18–19.
9. Samuel Daniel, *Poems and A Defence of Ryme* (1603), ed. Arthur Colby Sprague (Chicago and London: University of Chicago Press, 1930), p. 138.
10. Spenser, *Colin Clouts Come Home Againe* (1595), lines 781–2, *The Yale Edition of the Shorter Poems of Edmund Spenser*, ed. William A. Oram *et al.* (New Haven, CT: Yale University Press, 1989), p. 555.
11. The concept of poetry as a speaking picture – *ut pictura poesis* – derives from Horace's *Ars Poetica*, paragraph 361. See also Sir Philip Sidney, *An Apology for Poetry* (1595), ed. Geoffrey Shepherd, revised and expanded by R. W. Maslen (Manchester University Press, 3rd edn 2002), p. 101.
12. Compare Shakespeare's sonnet 78 in which the beloved's very being and the poem itself merge, for a sublime moment, into a single word: 'thou art all my art'. Again, an idealized love relation manifests itself in an idealized semantic relation in which meaning and sound perfectly coincide. That this integrative ideal is ultimately unsustainable becomes evident in the second part of the sequence: contrast Juliet's loving eye with sonnet 152 in which the speaker's 'perjur'd eye' expresses precisely the disjunction between what it sees and what it knows. That idealized models of love and language are, at bottom, illusory and prone to tragic

disintegration is treated at length in Joel Fineman's *Shakespeare's Perjured Eye: The Invention of Poetic Subjectivity in the Sonnets* (Berkeley: University of California Press, 1986).

13. See Plato, *Cratylus*, in *Plato: Complete Works*, ed. John M. Cooper (Indianapolis: Hackett, 1997), pp. 101–56.

14. Desiderius Erasmus, *De rationi studii* (1512), *Collected Works of Erasmus*, vol. XXIV, ed. Craig R. Thompson (University of Toronto Press, 1978), p. 666; Ben Jonson, *Cynthia's Revels* (1601), Prologue, line 20, in *Ben Jonson*, ed. Herford and Simpson, vol. IV, p. 43.

15. Sidney, *Apology*, p. 113.

16. Sidney, *Astrophil and Stella*, 58, in The *Poems of Sir Philip Sidney*, ed. W. A. Ringler (Oxford: Clarendon Press, 1962), pp. 193–4.

17. Giraldi Cinthio, *On the Composition of Comedies and Tragedies* (1543), selections reproduced in *Literary Criticism: Plato to Dryden*, ed. Allan H. Gilbert (New York: American Book Co., 1940), these quotations pp. 252–3.

18. Thomas Wilson, *Arte of Rhetorique*, p. 18.

19. In *Tragic Conditions in Shakespeare: Disinheriting the Globe* (Baltimore, MD: Johns Hopkins University Press, 2009), Paul A. Kottman suggests that, while 'tragic representation becomes central to civic discourse in moments at which the city seeks to question its own value or sustainability, as in fifth-century BCE Athens' (p. 21), Shakespeare's plays advance on – if not radically break with – this classical tradition by compelling us 'to regard the social bonds on which we depend for the meaning and worth of our lives together as being, in spite of that total dependence, fully dissolvable' (p. 4). Kottman's recent article, 'Defying the Stars: Tragic Love as the Struggle for Freedom in *Romeo and Juliet*', *Shakespeare Quarterly* 63 (2012): 1–38, goes considerably further than the very brief reading of the play offered here. However, I remain deeply sympathetic to his argument that Shakespeare deconstructs the claims of 'civilization' to promote a continuing, sustainable, and heritable order, particularly in the later plays.

20. Stefano Guazzo, *La civile conversatione*, translated by George Pettie and Bartholomew Young as *The Civile Conversation of M. Steeven Guazzo (1580–6)*, ed. Charles Whibley, 2 vols. (London: Constable, 1925), vol. I, p. 56.

21. Spenser, *The Faerie Queene* (1596), VI.I.I, VI. Pro. 5.

22. Samuel Johnson, *The Yale Edition of the Works of Samuel Johnson*, ed. Allen T. Hazen *et al.*, 16 vols. (New Haven: Yale University Press, 1958–90), vol. VIII, p. 1048.

23. See Harry Berger, *Second World and Green World: Studies in Renaissance Fiction-Making* (Berkeley: University of California Press, 1988).

24. For a discussion of the social *habitus*, see Pierre Bourdieu, *Outline of a Theory of Practice*, trans. Richard Nice (Cambridge University Press, 1977).

25. Hayden White, 'The Forms of Wildness: Archaeology of an Idea', in *The Tropics of Discourse* (Baltimore, MD: Johns Hopkins University Press, 1978), pp. 150–82, this quotation p. 151.

26. Michel de Montaigne, *Essays*, translated by John Florio (1603), 3 vols. (London: Dent, 1910), I. 219, 223, 224.

27. Spenser, *The Faerie Queene*, II. xii. 55–7.
28. Leon Battista Alberti, *On Painting*, ed. and trans. John R. Spencer, rev. edn (New Haven, CT: Yale University Press, 1966), p. 75.
29. Desiderius Erasmus, *On Copia of Words and Ideas, Collected Works*, vol. XXIV, ed. Thompson, p. 302, the following two quotations pp. 301, 295.
30. *Ibid.*, p. 300.
31. Donne, 'A burnt ship', line 6, *The Complete English Poems of John Donne*, ed. C. A. Patrides (London: Dent, 1985), p. 128.
32. Sir Philip Sidney, *The Countess of Pembroke's Arcadia (The Old Arcadia)*, ed. Jean Robertson (Oxford: Clarendon Press, 1973), p. 63.

Further reading

Fineman, Joel, *Shakespeare's Perjured Eye: The Invention of Poetic Subjectivity in the Sonnets* (Berkeley: University of California Press, 1986).
Kottman, Paul A., *Tragic Conditions in Shakespeare: Disinheriting the Globe* (Baltimore, MD: Johns Hopkins University Press, 2009).
'Defying the Stars: Tragic Love as the Struggle for Freedom in *Romeo and Juliet*', *Shakespeare Quarterly* 63 (2012): 1–38.

CHAPTER II

Shakespeare's classical tragedies

Coppélia Kahn

As twenty-first-century readers, when we approach the five tragedies that Shakespeare set in the Greco-Roman world – *Titus Andronicus, Julius Caesar, Antony and Cleopatra, Coriolanus,* and *Timon of Athens* – we must negotiate among several kinds of cultural and historical differences.[1] A striking moment in *Antony and Cleopatra* exemplifies the challenge these plays pose for us. In the wake of Antony's death and the victory of his arch-rival Octavius, Cleopatra imagines herself a captive in Rome, chief trophy amongst the victor's spoils:

> The quick comedians
> Extemporally will stage us and present
> Our Alexandrian revels; Antony
> Shall be brought drunken forth, and I shall see
> Some squeaking Cleopatra boy my greatness
> I'th'posture of a whore. (5.2.215–20)

The Egyptian queen pictures this public display in the terms of Elizabethan theatre, her feminine role performed by a boy; strictly speaking, Shakespeare has created an anachronism. Her theatrical imagery also peers into the future, as it were, reminding us that this play has in fact been staged countless times since Shakespeare penned these lines. His play lives on in our own cultural present, in film and popular culture as well as onstage. The events on which it is based took place from 41 to 30 BC, and were fraught with political controversy that was debated in the Renaissance and is still argued over by scholars today. That controversy moulded the views of Antony and the Egyptian queen that came down to Shakespeare through his main source, Plutarch, who wrote nearly a century after Octavius won the empire from Antony. Various perspectives on Antony and Cleopatra criss-cross the centuries, then, none more objective than another. Thus it isn't possible to read directly back in time from Shakespeare to what 'really' happened in Rome, or forward from Shakespeare to 'modern' revisions.

'The classics' doesn't designate an apolitical realm of transhistorical values but rather, like any body of literature, a discourse always open to reinterpretation and even reconstruction, as critical tastes and historical understanding change through the centuries.[2]

Inevitably we bring our own notions of 'the classics' to these plays, and Shakespeare – notwithstanding his own original perspective – gives us not the Romans we think we know, but rather 'the Elizabethan Romans'.[3] Yet because the Elizabethans carried on continuous reassessment of ancient heroes, events, and authors, no single classical tradition existed even then. Thus the category that inspires this essay, '*the* classical tragedies', is somewhat misleading, as is our term 'Greco-Roman'. To us, Greeks and Romans are closely linked, equally honoured, and knowable mainly through the work of erudite scholars. Quite differently, in Shakespeare's day Rome was a sort of cultural parent and ever-present model, and Greece a less familiar, often disparaged distant relative of Rome. We honour Greece for creating tragedy and epic, our most valued literary genres, but few if any links between English Renaissance tragedy and epic and the Greek originals have been demonstrated.

In Shakespeare's day, Rome took precedence over its predecessor Greece for several reasons. First, in English chronicle histories, the founding of Britain was connected to the founding of Rome through Brutus, the grandson of Aeneas, founder of Rome. Richard Grafton, writing in 1569, declares: 'When Brute ... first entred this Island and named it Briteyne: there beginneth mine history of this Realme.'[4] In 55 BC, Julius Caesar had invaded Britain, and Roman troops occupied it for several centuries: legend had it that he had built the Tower of London. Indeed, the old Roman wall still defined the boundaries of the city of London, and Hadrian's wall in the north was a well-known landmark linking Britain's past to Rome's.

Second, in the humanistic culture of England, as of Europe generally, reading, writing, and speaking Latin was the key to privilege and authority, and Rome the model of civilization itself. Since the reign of Henry VIII (1509–47), a state-authorized curriculum of Latin authors had trained men, village parsons as well as princes, to govern England, while only well-connected and especially ambitious gentlewomen might, for their own pleasure, learn Latin from tutors at home. Progressing from Terence through Plautus, Virgil, Horace, Cicero, Caesar, and Sallust, generations of schoolboys translated back and forth from English to Latin, memorized passages, and acquired a *copia* (store) of rhetorical figures they could wield to defend any proposition, or flaunt to impress any patron or mistress. They wrote compositions on such themes as 'Vituperate Julius Caesar' or

'That ... Cicero ... should not accept the condition offered by Antony',[5] engaging in the clash of viewpoints that had shaped Roman history and its historians. As I will argue throughout this essay, Shakespeare brought these ambiguities and contradictions into his classical tragedies, so that 'the conflict of interpretation that the audience brings to the theater becomes part of the play'.[6]

Finally, the Latin curriculum shaped habits of reading and thought long after formal schooling. The ruling elite sought political and ethical models in Latin authors, extracting *sententiae* (mottoes) from them to copy down in their commonplace books, or writing marginalia in their Latin texts to work out analogies between the politics of republican Rome and of the English court. Elizabethans read the Latin historians in particular as a source of military strategy and models for government. William Fulbecke, for example, finds a homely moral for Englishmen in the fall of Rome, which in his eyes was due solely to ambition, and advises his countrymen to a 'humble estimation of ourselves'.[7] In the character of Fluellen, the Welsh captain in *Henry V* blindly devoted to 'the disciplines of the pristine wars of the Romans' (3.2.82–3), Shakespeare mocks infatuation with the ancients as models for the present. Near the end of Elizabeth's reign, the question of whether it was right to rebel against a tyrant was being discussed under the cover of whether Julius Caesar was a tyrant.

Though humanist educators promoted the study of Greek, and praised the ancient Greeks enthusiastically,[8] Greek was only introduced midway in the grammar school curriculum, and rather than studying Greek 'classics', students read the New Testament in Greek. Editions of Latin texts and translations of Latin texts into English far outnumbered those of Greek: even by 1640, for example, none of Aeschylus's tragedies had been translated, and only one of Aristophanes' comedies. Furthermore, a Roman and medieval tradition of denigrating the Greeks persisted in the Renaissance: 'merry Greeks' were held to be typically 'licentious, luxurious, frivolous, bibulous, venereal, insinuating, perfidious, and unscrupulous'.[9] This widespread cultural valorization of Latin over Greek, then, partly accounts for the fact that Shakespeare wrote four tragic dramas and a tragic poem (*The Rape of Lucrece*) based on Roman legend and history, and only one tragedy (which has often been called a satire) drawn from Greek materials, though he used Greek settings in other genres (Hanna, pp. 107–28). For all these reasons, then (in addition to its own artistic peculiarities), *Timon of Athens* stands apart from the four Roman tragedies, as it will to some extent in this essay.

Shakespeare probably learned his Latin (and possibly some Greek) in the local grammar school of Stratford-upon-Avon, beginning at about the age of seven. We don't know how long his formal training may have lasted, but we do know that he read Latin because he sometimes appropriates or echoes the wording of Latin authors, even when an English translation is available. Ever since Ben Jonson asserted, in the tribute he wrote for the 1623 Folio edition of Shakespeare's works, that the poet knew 'small Latine and lesse Greeke', scholars have tried to determine just how learned Shakespeare was. Whether he read his favourite Latin authors in the original or in translation, or whether he knew Greek at all, however, matters less than what he found in his reading and how he used what he found. Besides, in addition to a fair selection of translations, Shakespeare had access to the ancient world through contemporary abridgements, digests, anthologies, dictionaries, encyclopaedias, and handbooks that organized what the educated person should know about the Greeks and Romans: 'the classical presence was ubiquitous'.[10]

Just as important as what Shakespeare read about the ancient world, however, is what he saw and heard of it in his workplace, the great city of London. Royal entries and coronation pageants and the annual Lord Mayor's pageants, open to all, linked Rome to the political order of Britain. For example, on 24 November 1588, to celebrate the defeat of the Armada, Elizabeth imitated the ancient Romans by riding in triumph in a symbolic chariot and, on his accession to the throne, James was welcomed to London in 'imperial style', triumphal arches decked with Roman gods and Latin inscriptions proclaiming him 'England's Caesar'.

When Shakespeare began writing about Rome in the early 1590s, a tradition of plays drawing on Roman history and legend was already well established. Frequent onstage representations of the senate and the capitol, tribunes and triumphs, Caesar and Pompey in the theatre made Rome seem less strange. In fact, Rome in the theatre was as much assimilated to an English scene and an English sensibility as it was distanced to the antique past. This all too comfortable familiarity produced some jarring aesthetic disjunctions, though. For example, in Thomas Lodge's *The Wounds of Civil War* (1587), two 'burghers' with English names talk in comic *double-entendres* like Dogberry and Verges in Shakespeare's *Much Ado About Nothing*. In Thomas Heywood's *The Rape of Lucrece* (1609), a courtier turned balladeer who sings bawdy songs in a thoroughly English idiom rubs shoulders with the noble Romans of Livy's sombre narrative.

Because the public theatre had no established canon like the one on which the Latin curriculum was founded, playwrights picked up material for plays from every conceivable source. Roman history and legend competed with Italian novellas, medieval romances, and English histories as matter for the stage, and often combined with them in the same play. Here, Rome didn't command the priority it enjoyed in elite culture. Both the anonymous *Caesar's Revenge* (printed 1607) and Thomas Lodge's *Wounds* owe as much in structure and convention to the revenge play and the *de casibus* tragedy as they do to Roman history. Though many in the audience might have recognized the quotations, allusions, appropriations, and parodies of the ancients that could pop up in any play, many others knew little more than the names of a few famous classical 'worthies'. This popular milieu, eclectic and improvisational, freed Shakespeare to find his own perspective on the Greeks and the Romans. He could approach venerable figures of the ancient world in the opportunistic spirit of a popular playwright, a cultural entrepreneur hoping to make a profitable entertainment.

Even Plutarch's *Lives of the Noble Greeks and Romans*, 'Englished' by Thomas North in 1579, Shakespeare's major source for the Roman tragedies, offered no coherent account, or even a vague idea, of the course of Roman history. Writing near the end of the first century AD, Plutarch could assume that his readers knew the institutions, mores, political issues, and events of Roman history, and plunge into the circumstantial details of each biography without explicitly contextualizing it. Shakespeare, in contrast, had to evoke the workings of a republic or an empire and make them intelligible to the subjects of a monarchy. Succeeding brilliantly, he created credible playworlds by drawing not just on Plutarch's highly anecdotal and digressive narratives, but on any source that served his purposes.

Yet in contrast to the mingle-mangle of English and Roman styles in Heywood or Lodge, Shakespeare makes his Roman and Greek tragedies coherent and probing representations of the dilemmas and struggles of life in the city, the republic, or the empire. His famous anachronisms – clocks in *Julius Caesar* and billiards in *Antony and Cleopatra* – help dramatize the underlying logic of interests, ideologies, and personalities in those tragedies. The entertainments he produces are of a different order from those of Heywood or Lodge because he takes his ancient materials seriously: he makes Rome, or Athens, the testing-ground rather than the backdrop of heroic virtue. In other Roman plays, ethical or psychological questions arising from the heroes' actions are often subsumed into the overarching *de casibus* motif of Fortune's turning wheel. As Cassius declares of Caesar in the anonymous *Caesar's Revenge*, 'Thou placed art in top of fortunes wheele,/Her wheele must turne, thy glory must eclipse.'[11] In contrast, Shakespeare's hero turns that wheel himself. What he does brings about his fate, and his commitment to the ethical and political ideas of his community determines what he does.

As Timothy Hampton explains, 'The promotion of ancient images of virtue as patterns that aim to form or guide readers is a central feature of almost every major text in the Renaissance . . . The heroic or virtuous figure offers a model of excellence, an icon . . . [who] can be seen as a marked sign that bears the moral and historical authority of antiquity.' These exemplars were widely disseminated in the Renaissance, as a key motif in the humanistic programme of emulating the ancient world. The exemplar's name served as a sign that contained 'the entire history of the hero's deeds'[12]. Not only educated people but unlettered common folk could recognize the great exemplars from Greek and Roman history. 'Julius Caesar' or 'Pompey' signified a puissant conqueror who commanded vast foreign territories and enjoyed universal fame, only to be brought down by a fellow Roman who had been his ally; 'Lucrece' stood for a narrative of rape, revenge, and revolution that culminated in the founding of the republic. Three heroes of Shakespeare's Roman tragedies – Brutus, Julius Caesar, Mark Antony – are renowned exemplars, and the fourth, Titus Andronicus, is modelled on exemplars of the early republic. The heroine of his tragic poem *The Rape of Lucrece* is an exemplar of chastity for women. Plutarch's *Lives of the Noble Greeks and Romans* was a treasury of such exemplars, which in Elizabethan and Jacobean England embodied an ethical image of Rome particularly: 'a set of virtues, thought of as characterizing Roman civilization – soldierly, severe, self-controlled, self-disciplined'.[13]

Because Rome was a patriarchal society, Romanness *per se* was closely linked to an ideology of masculinity. Though the Roman plays include vivid, complex female characters, they no less than the male characters are configured in terms of the overriding cultural ideal of *virtus*, a word for manliness or manly virtue that is derived from the Latin word for man, *vir*. In the fiercely martial Rome of *Coriolanus*, courage in battle is the essence of manliness; in *Julius Caesar*, it is shaped by the idea of the republic, in *Titus Andronicus*, by *pietas* – or devotion to family honour. Whatever its specific content, Roman manliness is characterized by service to the state: all Shakespeare's Roman heroes are first and foremost public men whose family ties and personal relations don't exist in what we would call a 'private' realm, but rather are conceived and pursued as part of the hero's public identity.

This compelling idea of Roman manliness is dramatized in three central motifs: emulation, wounds, and chastity. These motifs will be explained briefly here, to be fleshed out as each play is discussed. First, emulation: derived from the Latin *aemulari*, to rival, the word itself is defined in the *OED* as 'to copy or imitate with the object of equalling or excelling'. The cultural pattern it describes originated in Greek society as a one-on-one rivalry or *agon* through which a hero wins his name by pitting himself against his likeness or equal in contexts of courage and strength. Like Hector and Achilles in the *Iliad*, in the Roman plays pairs of evenly matched heroes act out a mixture of admiration, imitation, and domination that ends in the destruction of one rival and the triumph of the other. Second, wounds are a central, recurring image that is the sign both of *virtus* and of its instability. The Latin word for wound is *vulnus*, the root of 'vulnerability'. In an obvious sense, wounds image a bodily vulnerability that, in patriarchal cultures, is easily associated with women: they show that flesh can be penetrated and bleed, they make apertures in the body. But when Roman heroes, armed with 'soldierly, severe' traits of self-control and self-discipline, seek, endure, and surmount wounds, they demonstrate their manliness and their Romanness. Third, though women seem 'socially peripheral' to the patriarchal Roman state, they are actually 'symbolically central' to it, by means of their chastity.[14] Chastity isn't a freely willed practice or a trait natural to women; rather, it arises from their acculturation to patriarchal control over their reproductive power – their wombs. Through the national cult of Vesta, virgin goddess of the hearth, Rome made such control sacred and identified it with the very continuity of the state.

Titus Andronicus

Shakespeare was about thirty in 1594 when *Titus Andronicus* was published, but this sensational revenge tragedy is marked by the bravura of a younger poet who wants to show off both his knowledge of classical authors and his mastery of a crowd-pleasing popular genre. Weaving the Ovidian tale of Philomel into a Senecan revenge tragedy that culminates in a Thyestean banquet of parent eating child, seeding allusions to the *Aeneid* in nearly every scene, Shakespeare even seems to compete with his Latin predecessors, making the horrors of his source-tales more horrible: 'Not one rapist but two, not one murdered child but five, not one or two mutilated organs but six, not a one-course meal but a two.'[15] Yet a serious purpose underlies its sensationalism. Shakespeare generates his main action from versions of Roman *virtus* and *pietas*, making this play a serious critique of Roman ideology and institutions that resonates with contemporary English concerns. He fashions his hero's character along the lines of the great exemplars from the republic while placing him in a milieu of imperial decadence. The play insists on an antithesis between civilized Rome and the barbaric Goths, only to break it down: the real enemy lies within Rome, in its extreme, rigid conception of manly virtue, personified in Titus.

The play opens in high Roman fashion by staging two public ceremonies, an election and a funeral. A general returning victorious from a ten-year campaign against the Goths, Titus is declared the new emperor, but final rites for his two sons slain in battle take precedence over public office. His surname 'Pius' recalls the epithet describing Aeneas, founder of Rome. Titus's form of *pietas*, however, trips off the revenge mechanism that drives the play to its savage denouement. Deaf to the pleas of his prisoner Tamora, queen of the Goths, he insists on sacrificing her eldest son so that his own two sons can rest in peace. Ironically alluding to his surname, Tamora brands his action 'cruel irreligious piety' (1.1.130).

Once her son's limbs are 'lopp'd', Tamora becomes Titus's enemy, and once she conspires against his children, he becomes the injured, avenging father on the model of *The Spanish Tragedy*. The play can be seen as the story of Titus's transformation from pious Roman to revenge hero, a transformation he accomplishes by struggling through the tangled matrix of outrages that Tamora perpetrates. One crime spawns another, and the ultimate source of all is the offended, alienated mother who has escaped patriarchal control. As a *quid pro quo* for her murdered son, Tamora engineers the rape and mutilation of his daughter Lavinia, who then becomes the focus of action in the middle part of the tragedy, and the most shocking of its many images of bodily violation. Not only is she violated by the queen's two surviving sons: her tongue is cut out and her hands are cut off.

The audience is privy to the knowledge of Lavinia's rape, which leaves no outward mark. It is her all too obvious mutilations that capture the attention of her male kin, but hinder them from realizing that she has been raped. In a painful sequence of scenes (2.3, 3.1, 3.2, 4.1), first Titus's brother Marcus, then Titus and the remaining Andronici try to interpret Lavinia's signs, but project on to them their own mistaken meanings. Because we know Lavinia's hidden truth, however, these scenes ironically serve to dramatize the erasure of the female voice in the Roman patriarchy; to destabilize the language in which women are customarily figured as objects of exchange or vessels of reproduction; and to bring obliquely to light what has been censored.

Lavinia finally tells her story by rifling the pages of Ovid's *Metamorphoses*, one of the master texts of Latin culture, to cite the tale of Philomel. Then, in a gesture as ironic and ambiguous as that of the handmaiden, she takes her uncle's staff in her mouth, guides it with her stumps, and scratches the Latin word for rape and the names of her attackers in the earth (4.1). Thus she figures the double bind of women, who must either speak in the language of the fathers or improvise other means of communication in its interstices. Once Lavinia has made the rape known, the task of avenging it passes into the hands of her father, who is now positioned between the injured daughter and Tamora, the avenging mother, whose rampant evil (she has, meanwhile, given birth to Aaron's bastard child) he must contain. In terms of the play's gender politics, Titus repossesses the initiative illicitly seized by the mother, and re-establishes patriarchal control over her.

He does so in a clever, supremely fitting denouement typical of revenge tragedy. Tamora attacked his progeny by supervising the murder of his sons and the rape of his daughter; she raided his treasury and mocked the sign of his power, his daughter. Now he insults her womb (the word also means stomach), the site of her power, by making her 'swallow her own increase' (5.2.191). Then, citing as 'pattern, precedent, and lively warrant' Verginius's murder of his daughter in Livy's history of Rome, he kills Lavinia. Both murders are intended to assert the social and ideological centrality of the father's guardianship of his daughter's chastity. Thus despite the inconceivable wounds Titus has endured with heroic strength, he remains unchanged in his adherence to the central precepts underlying Roman patriarchy. What has changed, in the course of this daring, clever, and moving tragedy, is our awareness of the destructiveness inherent in the manly virtue it produces.

Julius Caesar

In Anglo-American culture, *Julius Caesar* more than any other literary work has created a lasting image of public duty, political idealism, ringing oratory, and patrician Stoicism as keynotes of the classical world. It is surely Shakespeare's most 'classical' tragedy. This popular image, however, is belied by the textual reality, for in fact it is an enigmatic play, representing the assassination of Caesar from shifting perspectives that frustrate any certain judgement of either the victim or his assassins. Cicero's statement, 'But men may construe things after their fashion,/Clean from the purpose of the things themselves' (1.3.34–5), better suggests how we experience the play, for though it poses many questions it provides no clear answers, leaving us to 'construe things' for ourselves. Was Caesar a tyrant who deserved to die, or a ruler whose greatness provoked the envy of lesser minds? Was Brutus 'the noblest Roman of them all', or a misguided idealist? How can we tell? By making the motives and the personalities of Caesar,

Brutus, and Mark Antony so richly ambiguous, Shakespeare involves us in their political dilemma as if it were our own.

Because an extensive critical literature explores these questions concerning the play's main characters, this essay will focus instead on the conception of 'Rome' (mentioned thirty-two times in some form, more than in any other play): that, I suggest, from which both characters and action are generated. The Rome of *Julius Caesar* is specifically the republic, and it is the mysticized ideal of the republic that impels Brutus to lead the conspiracy against Caesar, that compels the conspirators' belief in their cause, that generates a discourse endowing them and Caesar as well with identity, agency, and manly virtue. Most of all it is the 'public' style of the play that makes its Rome a republic. The major scenes take the form of public debates. Even in private, characters speak formally, in lofty abstractions, and refer to themselves in the third person ('illeism'), as though they are spectators and audience of themselves as public figures.

This construction of the self as a public entity emanates from the patrician reverence for ancestry and public service so prominent in Roman social practice as in literature. In the words of Leo Braudy,

> the political history of Rome was clearly written in the genealogies of its great families for all to see. *Nobilis* in Latin originally means someone who is *known*. The upper class, the political class, was therefore by definition a class whose families were known for their public adherence to the public good . . .[16]

Yet, as Gary Miles remarks, 'It is . . . precisely the public dimension of his Romans' lives that is most problematic for Shakespeare', because he is at the same time deeply engaged in revealing 'the interior life of his characters'.[17] It isn't the predominance of the public realm, but rather the dilemma of how public and private are related to each other that is central to the play's conception of Rome. In the course of the conspiracy, the ethos of the republic demands that Brutus and his comrades separate their inner worlds from the public domain, by placing the public good above any personal consideration. It is this separation that constitutes them as Romans. More specifically, the republic makes them men, infuses them with manly virtue, because the public realm is associated with Roman 'firmness' and the private realm with 'the melting spirits of women' (2.1.122).

It is already evident from the play's first scene, however (and becomes even clearer as the roar of the crowd punctuates their conversation), that even though the *idea* of the republic governs patrician mentality, in actual practice the republic has already ceased to exist. The tribunes rebuke the plebs for transferring their allegiance from Pompey to Caesar – from one strong man to the next – not for transgressing against the republic. Allusions to Pompey run through the play to remind us that, before Caesar, another charismatic leader bypassed Rome's 'noble bloods' to gain a plebeian power base. Though in person Caesar may fall short of the mystique he generates, like Pompey he knows how to use 'the tag-rag people', as Casca calls them, but for Brutus and Cassius they hardly exist (1.2.252). These patricians imagine themselves the ethical and political heartbeat of the republic, while in reality they have lost power to a constituency they despise. Thus the republic is for them, in the sense proposed by the post-Marxist philosopher Louis Althusser, an ideology, an imaginary conception of their actual relation to the Roman state.[18] As Sigurd Burckhardt argues, Brutus and the conspirators aren't guilty of treachery, nor is their conception of the republic 'right' or 'wrong': in a deeper sense than clocks or billiards, it is an anachronism.[19]

In another sense as well, the republic of *Julius Caesar* can be understood in terms of ideological contradiction. It is intricately bound up with the basically agonistic, highly competitive practices of the Roman ruling elite institutionalized in the sequence of electoral contests for state office known as the *cursus honorum*. At the top level, the level at which a Caesar or a Pompey wins or loses, the *cursus* is based on emulation, 'an unstable combination of identification and rivalry, love and hate'.[20] But how can emulation coexist with 'the general good'? Cassius and Brutus believe that all Romans are brothers, united by their shared belief in the republic. But emulation is equally Roman, as the shifting allegiances in the play suggest. Caesar and Pompey were allies before they were rivals, and Brutus first supported Pompey, then became Caesar's favourite when Pompey fell. Even Brutus and Cassius, friends and confederates profoundly united by shared ideals, quarrel bitterly at the end of the play. When Brutus, genuinely dedicated to the common good, ponders whether Caesar would be king, he imagines Caesar as climbing 'ambition's ladder', attaining 'the upmost round', and then 'scorning the base degrees by which he did ascend' (2.1.21–7). It is this vision of being trampled on by a rival that enables Brutus to 'fashion it thus' despite the admitted lack of evidence, to make the leap beyond proof and logic to kill Caesar.

Yet Brutus is at the same time reluctant to murder Caesar, and it is precisely his reluctance that gives rise to the second scene, a conversation with Portia on the eve of the assassination (2.1). The scene depends on our prior knowledge that, as she suspects, Brutus does have 'some sick offence within his mind'. Just before the conspirators arrived, in two brief soliloquies he admitted that his 'genius' (immortal spirit) and his 'mortal instruments' (his powers as a man) were at war as he contemplated 'the acting of a dreadful thing' – the assassination (2.1.61–9, 77–85). Then, in taking leadership of the conspiracy, he repressed his doubt and fear. But they return when Portia urges him to confide in her by declaring,

> Tell me your counsels, I will not disclose 'em.
> I have made strong proof of my constancy,
> Giving myself a voluntary wound
> Here, in the thigh: can I bear that with patience,
> And not my husband's secrets?   (2.1.298–302)

Women – untrained in reason, dwelling in the *domus* (household) and excluded from the forum, susceptible in the extreme to the affections – lack access to constancy: control over the affections, adherence to rationally grounded principles like those of the republic, firmness. It is men who are firm, and women who are 'melting spirits'. The constancy to which Portia lays claim through self-wounding can be traced to Stoic philosophy, well known in England through translations of Boethius, Cicero, Seneca, and Justus Lipsius, and a hallmark of Romanness as presented on the English stage. Not surprisingly, its leading postulates are framed in the same terms as the opposition of masculine to feminine: reason and opinion, soul and body, constancy and inconstancy.[21]

For the sake of 'the general good' as the republican ethos defines it, individual moral scruples must be overcome. If such scruples are voiced by a woman, in the private sphere of the *domus*, all the more reason to disregard them (as Caesar also does, in the following scene). Portia's urgings allow Brutus's scruples to be feminized, privatized, and discarded as he embarks upon the conspiracy, but nonetheless, those urgings underpin his construction as a tragic hero who must embrace a man's duty and repress his 'feminine' fears. On the other hand, Portia's wound also denaturalizes constancy, suggesting that it can be learned, and isn't necessarily native to the male gender. Furthermore, the site of the wound, in her thigh, hints ambiguously at a genital wound, which psychoanalysis would take to be the wound of castration, signifying that as a woman, she lacks the phallus, symbol of power in patriarchal society. In the words of Madelon Sprengnether, 'she reveals the underlying paradox of the play, which equates manliness with injury, so that the sign of masculinity becomes the wound'.[22]

Mark Antony eulogizes Brutus as 'the noblest Roman of them all', because 'He only, in a general honest thought/And common good to all' murdered Caesar (5.5.68–72). Voicing the same cherished ideal of the republic that Brutus stated when he reasoned his way into the conspiracy, the vengeful and ambitious Mark Antony sees him as he saw himself. The triumvirate of which he is a member rules by fiat and terror. Yet he too affirms the republic as a government of and for 'the common good'. But perhaps it is more significant that he envisions one man only in that republic who triumphs – in virtue – over all the rest.

Antony and Cleopatra

Antony and Cleopatra, published in 1608 nine years after *Julius Caesar* was first performed, is Shakespeare's most daring and original classical tragedy. Actually, the play refuses to confine itself to a single genre: it is tragedy, comedy, history, and romance all at once. As a 'love tragedy', in Renaissance terms it is an oxymoron, and probably better classified as 'a tragic experience embedded in a comic structure' (Adelman, *Common Liar*, p. 52). Still, no generic category can explain its disjunction between realism and romance, personified in the hero and heroine, who are petty and grand by turns, who declaim and then squabble. Michael Neill identifies hyperbole (called 'the overreacher' by the Renaissance rhetorician George Puttenham) as the play's basic rhetorical and structural principle. Aiming high, this tragedy often tumbles into anticlimax, creating the 'perceived gap between expectation and performance' that is the leitmotiv of so much interpretation.[23]

Perhaps in reaction to this stylistic and generic hybridity, many have read the play in terms of binary oppositions under the general headings 'Rome' and 'Egypt'. War and love, public and private, duty and pleasure, reason and sensuality, male and female then make up the framework of the play's meaning.

From the beginning, however, when Octavius and Mark Antony became rivals for rule of the empire, the opposition of Rome to Egypt was politically motivated and crafted. Writers under Octavius's patronage who were later venerated as 'Augustan' – Virgil, Ovid, Horace – fused xenophobia with patriarchal ideology in order to demonize Cleopatra as Rome's most dangerous enemy, a foreigner and a woman whose power was fatally inflected by her sexuality. They made Cleopatra and Egypt the Other, at the same time portraying Antony as a traitor to Rome corrupted and alienated by his love for her. In this discourse, Octavius seemed the only true Roman fit to rule. This play, then, isn't only *about* two super-heroes competing for sole dominance over an empire; in a historical sense, the literary and historical materials on which it draws *constitute* part of that struggle. Shakespeare draws on Plutarch even more closely here than in *Julius Caesar*, and though Plutarch – a Greek writing more than a century after the events in question – makes Cleopatra more complex and ambiguous than his predecessors do, he too sees her as the cause of Antony's downfall.

Understandably fascinated by Cleopatra, generations of critics have focused on her, viewing the play primarily as a 'love tragedy'. But the contest for mastery between Antony and Octavius is at least as important as the love affair, and much of the continuity between this play and those before and after it resides in the agonistic relationship of two heroes. Despite the obvious contrasts of character between Antony and Octavius, they mirror each other in a blinding desire for *imperium*. Early in the play, when Antony asks the soothsayer, 'Whose fortunes shall rise higher, Caesar's or mine?', it is clear that Antony, like Brutus with Julius Caesar or Coriolanus with Aufidius, is locked into the Roman cultural pattern of emulation (2.3.15). For his part, eulogizing Antony at the end, Octavius Caesar admits, 'I have followed thee to this . . . We could not stall together / In the whole world' (5.1.36, 39–40). 'If thou dost play with him at any game', the Soothsayer warns Antony, 'thou art sure to lose,' explaining that Antony's 'high, unmatchable' guardian spirit will always be overpowered if Caesar is near (2.3.25–30). Significantly, the Soothsayer doesn't advise Antony to abandon Cleopatra but rather, to preserve his 'lustre' – his charisma, fame, authority – by keeping his distance from Caesar. Thus not only Antony's pleasure but also his advantage lies in the East, in Egypt. His genuine fascination with Cleopatra notwithstanding, she also serves as an alibi for gaining the distance from Caesar that can enable his 'unmatchable' spirit to triumph in the end.

Yet, however typically Roman Antony is in emulation, in another sense he fails to fit the mould. In his passion for Cleopatra, he 'o'erflows the measure', crosses the boundary between Rome and Other, and violates the cultural codes in which manly virtue is written. His passion for her shakes the foundations of that virtue and reveals its fragility in relation to the feminine Other, while his rivalry with Caesar enables him to shore up his masculine identity. Repeatedly, Cleopatra draws Antony to her, dividing him from Caesar and all that is Roman; repeatedly, he spins back into Caesar's orbit, to the familiar, fatal game of emulation. Thus his passion, rather than simply feminizing him in service to her lust as the Romans believe, actually enters into the dynamics of rivalry.

In the dizzying succession of defeats and victories, quarrels and reconciliations that follow Antony's defeat at Actium, he undergoes an experience of self-loss triggered not so much by defeat at Caesar's hands as by his sense of betrayal at Cleopatra's: not defeat *per se*, but what he perceives as domination by a woman, is what unmans Antony.[24] 'O, thy vile lady!', he cries to the eunuch who serves her, 'She has robbed me of my sword' (4.14.22–3). Defeated and believing Cleopatra dead, through suicide he seeks to regain his manly virtue and Roman identity. Almost invariably, critics call Antony's attempt to kill himself 'bungled' or 'botched', and consider it a theatrical and moral disaster. But on the English stage and in humanistic studies, suicide was a well-established marker of the Roman exemplar's dignity. Many were familiar with the deaths of Lucrece, Cato, and Brutus as signifying their rationality and free will. Moreover, the hero who died *sua manu* – by his own hand – robbed his rival of victory over him, avoided the shame of defeat, and retained his own name and honour untarnished. Though this secular rationale clashed with well-ingrained Christian prohibitions, still, because defence of one's honour was as central to the ethos of the ruling elite in England as it was to the Roman patricians, suicide served as a marker of nobility and commanded a certain respect. Finally, the prospect of being led in triumph as Caesar's captive, twice anticipated by both hero and heroine in four vivid descriptions of some length, and often referred to by others, makes suicide more urgent: it is Antony's last gesture in the contest that has defined him, the only means left to him of besting his rival.

Coriolanus

Gail Kern Paster astutely remarks that *Julius Caesar* and *Coriolanus* both 'enact a central urban paradox: the social mandate for heroic self-sacrifice collides with the heroic mandate for self-realization conceived in civic terms'.[25] With some qualifications, the same might be said of *Timon of Athens*. In all three tragedies, the city turns against heroes who seemingly embody its fundamental values, and in both *Coriolanus* and *Timon* the paradox is doubled when the hero in turn becomes the city's enemy and sets out to destroy it. Though this harsh, violent play has never enjoyed the popularity of other Shakespearean tragedies, in recent decades it has gained respect: feminist critics especially have unpacked the logic underlying its profound critique of Rome's militaristic ethos.[26] That critique focuses on the paradoxical position of mothers in patriarchy, for it is the hero's relationship to his mother, Volumnia, that accounts for both his greatness and his downfall.

In *Coriolanus*, Shakespeare follows Plutarch's biography in leaving the father's place vacant, thus focusing on Volumnia's power as a mother, which she gains by fusing her nurturance with the masculinist ideology of Rome. 'Thy valiantness was mine', she says to her son: 'thou suck'st it from me' (3.2.130). In this Rome of the early republic, 'Valour is the chiefest virtue' (2.2.78). Here Shakespeare plays on words by identifying valour as the essence or virtue of *virtus*.[27] Volumnia uses nursing as a metaphor for her role in forming her son's temperament and value system, but that role doesn't end when she sends him, still only 'a man-child', to war. Though he has become Rome's most honoured warrior, he remains 'bound to his mother'. He seeks his wounds obsessively, for two contradictory reasons: to please his mother and to assert his supremacy in valour – precisely as a defence against that emotional dependency on her, which in fact impels his hyper-masculine immersion in blood and wounds. Furthermore, on a social and political level, the corollary of his valour is his unflinching contempt and blistering anger towards whatever he sees as deviation from his patrician warrior code, notably, the hungry, mercurial proletarian mob.

Coriolanus is Shakespeare's least inward hero: he has little if any self-knowledge, and only one soliloquy. Rather, through the play as a whole, Shakespeare makes the psychological and political dimensions of his tragedy deeply coherent through the fusion of emotionally resonant imagery with highly charged, often brutal action. For example, in the seven battle scenes (1.4–10) dramatizing Rome's siege against the city of Corioli, the hero re-enacts his dilemma of trying to be at once a man and his mother's boy. He enters the quasi-feminine enclosure of the city alone to fight an entire army, then emerges victorious, 'mantled', 'smeared', and 'masked' in blood (1.6.29, 69, 1.8.10). Despite his contempt for the cowardly soldiers who refuse to follow him, 'They all take him up in their arms' as he shouts, 'Make you a sword of me!' (1.6.75–6).

The play begins at a political turning point in the history of Rome: the creation of tribunes to represent the interests of the proletarians. Though the patricians retain political supremacy, the election ritual is designed to reflect the newly won power of the people: the candidate must don humble garb and show his wounds to them as proof that his service to the state makes him worthy of their votes. Coriolanus, nominated to stand as candidate for consul, cannot refuse the honour. This ritual demands of him, however, precisely what he cannot perform: he must beg the people for their votes and show his wounds to them.[28] Because both wounds and people represent for him the hidden reality of his dependency on Volumnia, any social recognition he wins as man, warrior, or office-holder also rein-scribes him as her nursling. He cannot force himself, despite her urgings, to dissemble his scorn for the mob, and so when he lashes out at them, he is banished from Rome. 'Like to a lonely dragon', Coriolanus stalks into exile – but immediately allies himself with Aufidius, his enemy rival, and vows to destroy Rome. In the bonding of the two warriors, Shakespeare represents Roman emulation with more explicitly erotic intensity than in any of the classical tragedies. When Aufidius embraces Coriolanus as a new-found ally, he confesses that ever since being defeated by him, he has 'Dreamt of encounters 'twixt thyself and me – / We have been down together in my sleep, / Unbuckling helms, fisting each other's throat –' (4.5.120–3), and compares his joy to that of a bridegroom. Yet in the end his rivalry, less noble-minded than Coriolanus's, will lead him to devise the hero's death.

The play's tragic denouement stages a contradiction between the patrician warrior ethos Volumnia inculcated in Coriolanus and the kind of pity and tenderness she has, it seems, rooted out of him. On the one hand, to pursue his revenge would indeed be to 'stand as if a man were author of himself / And knew no other kin' (5.3.35–7), the most extreme denial of his bond to a matrix both social and emotional. It would also be completely congruent with the relentless, narrowly defined integrity she instilled in him in the name of valour. On the other hand, to relent as he finally does means to feel pity and love for the first time, to be more of a man and yet, paradoxically, less than ever his mother's son. He relents as she asks him to, but on grounds that she has never allowed him to recognize. And ironically, though she is hailed as the saviour of Rome, the power that the state invested in her as a mother also locked her son into the kind of manly virtue that turned him into its enemy. The mother who has lived only through her son survives, but he is sacrificed so that she and the state with which she is identified may live. Surely *Coriolanus* constitutes Shakespeare's most trenchant critique of Rome.

Timon of Athens

Three of the Roman plays are set in the city itself, and though *Antony and Cleopatra* ranges far and wide in locale, it consistently counters Egyptian sensuality with Roman measure. The Athens of *Timon of Athens*, in contrast, lacks monuments such as the capitol to signify that it is a seat of government, landmarks like the Tiber, or the carpenters and cobblers of *Julius Caesar*'s first scene to evoke daily urban life. When Timon turns his back on the city walls to exile himself, an archetype of the city as marker of civilization itself is invoked, rather than any specific sense of Athens as the city in which democracy began. Like the comedies and romances with Greek settings or sources (*The Comedy of Errors* or *Pericles*, for example), this play is ec-centric rather than centred in the *polis*: it moves outwards, beyond the wilderness in which Timon digs for roots, to 'the very hem o'th'sea' (5.4.66).

Similarly, its hero is eccentric, veering from boundless generosity to single-minded misanthropy, each stance absolute and uncompromising. His extremes give the play its distinctive bi-polar structure, the first three acts dramatizing Timon's mysteriously indiscriminate, obsessive giving that inevitably collapses when resources run out; the last two acts, his rejection of Athenian society and failed attempt to raze it to the ground. We are even more disengaged from Timon than from Coriolanus, because whether he demonstrates love or hatred for mankind, he is set apart: he has no family, holds no office, and is equally estranged from women and from politics. Though his alienation from society has been compared to Lear's, Timon's venomous diatribes take the form of a satirist's anatomizing catalogues rather than of cries from the heart.[29]

Clues to the play's coherence reside both in the emotional resonances of its imagery and in the similarity of Timon's giving to Jacobean practices of patronage and credit finance.[30] In the first scene, a poet describes his depiction of the goddess Fortuna in a work he will present to Timon in hope of remuneration. A colossal, maternal presence, she first nurtures a crowd of beneficiaries, then singles out Timon for her favours while 'translating' his rivals to 'slaves and servants' (1.1.73–4). In the following scenes, Timon's bounty is similarly grandiose and magical: in his eyes, it needs no replenishment, it cannot be depleted, it has no limits. In the final movement of the poet's *paragone*, however, 'Fortune in her shift and change of mood/Spurns down her late beloved' (1.1.86–7). Similarly, Timon experiences the loss of his fortune (of which his steward Flavius often warns him) and of the friends gained through lavish gifts and hospitality (whose hypocrisy the cynic philosopher Apemantus frequently points out) as a sudden, brutal, and unmerited transformation of his world. Thus the play hints at the hero's infantile fantasy of identification with a maternal presence that ultimately betrays him.

Timon's peculiar generosity violates normal social exchange: by refusing any reciprocity, he makes everyone his inferior as well as his dependant. Yet he imagines that he presides over an idealized community of 'brothers':

> We are born to do benefits; and what better or properer can we call our own than the riches of our friends? O what a precious comfort 'tis to have so many like brothers commanding one another's fortunes. (1.2.101–3)

In this speech, Timon portrays friendship as a bond that ambiguously entails helping, needing, and 'using' friends. Thus he conflates two registers of social exchange that actually conflict with each other: an ethos of disinterested friendship and reciprocity among peers, drawn from Cicero and Seneca, and the widespread practice of loaning money at interest known pejoratively as use or usury. Actually, Timon's 'friends' do make use of him. For example, a senator preparing to call in his loans when he sees the great man's credit failing refers to the gifts he gave Timon as investments: 'If I want gold, steal but a beggar's dog / And give it Timon – why, the dog coins gold' (2.1.5–6).[31]

It cannot be said, however, that the misanthrope of the play's second half commands more sympathy or credibility than the universal benefactor of its first half. Both his states of mind seem rooted in primitive fantasy rather than being rational responses to reality. The loyalty of his steward and the gratitude of his other servants belie his categorical denunciation of 'All feasts, societies, and throngs of men' (4.3.21). Yet the very extremes of his situation and his language lend themselves to pungent theatrical effects. When his friends refuse to loan him money, thus reducing him to destitution, Timon invites them to one last banquet, fills the covered dishes with warm water, and after delivering a caustic grace, intones, 'Uncover, dogs, and lap' (3.6.82). Upon leaving the city, he reverts to a primitive, pre-social existence supposedly free of Athenian corruption. Muttering 'Earth, yield me roots', he scratches the ground and in the play's boldest stroke, instead finds gold, the root of all evil (4.3.23–6). Neither these moments of mordant humour nor his last-act encounters with Alcibiades, who 'testifies to ... a more complex sociopolitical world than the one we witness for most of the play', allow us to see Timon's descent into misanthropy as tragic rather than curious or perverse.[32] Nonetheless, a pathos that resonates with his betrayal by Fortuna clings to the imagery of his demise. Described four times and then shown onstage, his tomb is located 'Upon the beached verge of the salt flood', where, he says to himself, 'the light foam of the sea may beat/Thy grave-stone daily' (5.1.215, 4.3.381–2). The quasi-maternal, rhythmic embrace of the sea suggests regression towards a primal state preceding the separation of self from world, a surrogate for the human bonds he never established in life.

Notes

1. Parts of this essay have been adapted from my books *Man's Estate: Masculine Identity in Shakespeare* (Berkeley and Los Angeles: University of California Press, 1981) and *Roman Shakespeare: Warriors, Wounds, and Women* (London: Routledge, 1997).

2. In the last decade, to take criticism of *Titus Andronicus* as an example of ongoing reinterpretation, scholars have interpreted the play in the light of trauma theory (Deborah Willis, '"The gnawing vulture": Revenge, Trauma Theory, and *Titus Andronicus*', *Shakespeare Quarterly* 53, 1 (2002): 21–52); Renaissance constructions of race (Emily C. Bartels, *Speaking of the Moor: from Alcazar to Othello* (Philadelphia: University of Pennsylvania Press, 2008); Reformation controversy over the legitimacy of violence in defence of Christianity (Nicholas R. Moschovakis, '"Irreligious piety" and Christian History: Persecution as Pagan Anachronism in *Titus Andronicus*', *Shakespeare Quarterly* 53, 4 (2002): 460–86); Aristotelian moderation, including concepts of equity, exchange, gratitude and justice (Christopher Crosbie, 'Fixing moderation: *Titus Andronicus* and the Aristotelian Determination of Value', *Shakespeare Quarterly* 58, 2 (2007): 147–73).

3. T. J. B. Spencer, 'Shakespeare and the Elizabethan Romans', *Shakespeare Survey* 10 (1957): 27–38. More recently, in her book *The Cultural Uses of the Caesars on the English Renaissance Stage* (Aldershot and Burlington, VT: Ashgate, 2008), Lisa Hopkins argues that to the Elizabethans and Jacobeans, 'Rome' meant the seat of Catholicism, and referred to the Ottoman Empire and Russia as well, imperial states that inherited Roman power structures.

4. Richard Grafton, *A Chronicle At Large and Meere History of the Affayres of England and Kinges of the same . . .* (London, 1569), p. 31.

5. T. W. Baldwin, *William Shakespere's Small Latine and Lesse Greeke*, 2 vols. (Urbana: University of Illinois Press, 1944), vol. I, pp. 88, 89.

6. Janet Adelman, *The Common Liar: An Essay on 'Antony and Cleopatra'* (New Haven, CT: Yale University Press, 1973), p. 53.

7. William Fulbecke, *An Historical Collection of the Continuall Factions, Tumults, and Massacres of the Romans and Italians . . .* (London: William Ponsonby, 1601), sig. A2.

8. Sara Hanna, 'Shakespeare's Greek World: the Temptations of the Sea', *Playing the Globe: Genre and Geography in Renaissance Drama*, ed. John Gillies and Virginia Mason Vaughan (Madison, WI: Fairleigh Dickinson University Press, 1998), pp. 107–28.

9. T. J. B. Spencer, '"Greeks" and "Merrygreeks": a Background to *Timon of Athens* and *Troilus and Cressida*', *Essays on Shakespeare and Elizabethan Drama in Honor of Hardin Craig*, ed. Richard Hosley (Columbia: University of Missouri Press, 1962), pp. 223–33.

10. Robert S. Miola, *Shakespeare's Rome* (Cambridge University Press, 1983), p. 9.

11. Anon., *The Tragedie of Caesar and Pompey. Or Caesar's Revenge . . .* (London: imprinted for Nathaniel Fosbrooke and John Wright, 1607).

12. Timothy Hampton, *Writing From History: The Rhetoric of Exemplarity in Renaissance Literature* (Ithaca, NY: Cornell University Press, 1990), pp. 5, i, xi, 25.

13. G. K. Hunter, 'A Roman Thought: Renaissance Attitudes to History Exemplified in Shakespeare and Jonson', *An English Miscellany: Presented to W. S. Mackie*, ed. B. S. Lee (Capetown and New York: Oxford University Press, 1977), p. 94.

14. Barbara Babcock, ed., *The Reversible World: Symbolic Inversion in Art and Society* (Ithaca, NY: Cornell University Press, 1978), p. 32.

15. Leonard Barkan, *The Gods Made Flesh: Metamorphosis and the Pursuit of Paganism* (New Haven, CT: Yale University Press, 1986), p. 244.

16. Leo Braudy, *The Frenzy of Renown: Fame and Its History* (New York: Oxford University Press, 1986), p. 59.

17. Gary B. Miles, 'How Roman are Shakespeare's "Romans"?', *Shakespeare Quarterly* 41.3 (1989): 279.

18. Louis Althusser, 'Ideology and Ideological State Apparatuses', *Lenin and Philosophy and Other Essays* (New York: Monthly Review Press, 1971), pp. 164–5.

19. Sigurd Burckhardt, 'How Not to Murder Caesar', *Shakespearean Meanings* (Princeton University Press, 1968), p. 9.

20. Wayne A. Rebhorn, 'The Crisis of the Aristocracy in *Julius Caesar*', *Renaissance Quarterly* 43.1 (1990): 77.

21. In the last decade, several critics have elaborated on the play's construction of masculinity: Eugene Giddens, 'Honorable Men: Militancy and Masculinity in *Julius Caesar*', *Renaissance Forum* 5, 2 (2001): 1–16; Lloyd Davis, 'Embodied Masculinity in Shakespeare's *Julius Caesar*', *EnterText* 3, 1 (2003): 161–82; Amy Scott, '"Romans, Countrymen, and Lovers": Performing Politics, Sovereign Amity, and Masculinity in *Julius Caesar*', *Renaissance Papers* (2003): 99–117.

22. Madelon Sprengnether, 'Annihilating Intimacy in *Coriolanus*', *Women in the Middle Ages and the Renaissance*, ed. Mary Beth Rose (Syracuse University Press, 1986), p. 96.

23. Michael Neill, 'Introduction', *The Tragedy of Antony and Cleopatra* (New York: Oxford University Press, 1994), p. 68.

24. Richard P. Wheeler, '"Since First We Were Disseered": Trust and Autonomy in Shakespearean Tragedy and Romance', *Representing Shakespeare: New Psychoanalytic Essays*, ed. Murray Schwartz and Coppélia Kahn (Baltimore, MD: Johns Hopkins University Press, 1980), *passim*.

25. Gail Kern Paster, *The Idea of the City in the Age of Shakespeare* (Athens: University of Georgia Press, 1985), p. 58.

26. See Janet Adelman, '"Anger is My Meat": Feeding and Dependency in *Coriolanus*', *Representing Shakespeare*, ed. Schwartz and Kahn, pp. 129–49.

27. Phyllis Rackin, '*Coriolanus*: Shakespeare's Anatomy of *Virtus*', *Modern Language Studies* 13, 2 (1983): 68–79.

28. Regarding this crucial, quasi-theatrical moment of performance, see Eve Rachele Sanders's interpretation of Coriolanus as tracing a trajectory 'from anti-theatrical ideologue to shape-shifting actor' ('The Body of the Actor in *Coriolanus*', *Shakespeare Quarterly* 57, 4 (2006): 387–412).

29. For a radically new reading of both Timon's giving and his misanthropy as a religious quest to render himself up to the wholly other, to God, by escaping the circle of economic exchange through making an absolute, non-reciprocal gift, see Ken Jackson's extraordinary '"One wish" or the Possibility of the

Impossible: Derrida, the Gift, and God in *Timon of Athens*', *Shakespeare Quarterly* 52, 1 (2001): 34–66.

30. See Coppélia Kahn, '"Magic of Bounty": *Timon of Athens*, Jacobean Patronage, and Maternal Power', *Shakespeare Quarterly* 38.1 (1987): 34–57.

31. As Louis Adrian Montrose has shown, in Shakespeare's England, on a scale comparable to Timon's, royal gift-giving was likewise 'a tacitly coercive and vitally interested process predicated on the fiction that it [was] free and disinterested' ('Gifts and Reasons: the Contexts of Peele's *Arraynement of Paris*', *ELH* 47 (1980): 433–61); see also Lawrence Stone, *The Crisis of the Aristocracy 1558–1641*, abridged edn (London: Oxford University Press, 1967).

32. Katharine Eisaman Maus, 'Introduction' to *The Life of Timon of Athens*, The Norton Shakespeare, gen. ed. Stephen Greenblatt (New York: W. W. Norton, 1997), p. 2250.

CHAPTER 12

Why think about Shakespearean tragedy today?

Paul A. Kottman

... what virtue lies in the distinctions Tragedy, Comedy, History, Pastoral, Tragical-Historical or Historical-Pastoral, Pastoral-Comical or Comical-Historical-Pastoral? And were we to shuffle those ... a hundred times, what insight would we have in the end?
Johann Gottfried Herder, 'Shakespeare' (1773)[1]

A peculiar feature of the humanities is that we devote so much time to thinking about art objects and practices that were not created with this kind of thinking in mind. We study paintings commissioned by kings and popes; Greek plays that were composed for religious festivals; dramas by Shakespeare that were written for commercial purposes; liturgical music; not to mention Hollywood films and so forth. At the same time, although we perhaps agree than an educated person should at least be acquainted with the works of Shakespeare, the Bible, Sophocles and others, we no longer devote attention to such things simply because our society requires some people to be experts in these matters – the way the study of Latin, Greek and the Bible were once thought essential to an authoritative, coherent transmission of our history and culture. As a result, the motive for sustained humanistic study can sometimes seem unclear.

To complicate matters further, we have almost no agreement on *how* best to study or think about these works. On the one hand, this has led many schools and universities to adopt a *laissez-faire* approach – giving humanists broad discretion regarding what to study, and how to study it. On the other hand, the anxiety provoked by the disappearance of traditional justifications for the humanities has led humanists to retreat into quasi-scientific approaches that would allow us to amass truths about or around artworks (historical facts, concrete cultural-anthropological evidence, linguistic analyses and so on). Sometimes our approaches even become scientific outright – appeals to neurology or biology or psychology in order to explain why a certain literary character acts a certain way, why a painting moves us, why poems give us pleasure and so on.

I will not dwell on the limitations or virtues of such approaches here. Instead, in this chapter I want to explore the need for humanistic inquiry, once it is no longer restricted to the task of simply transmitting cultural authority. More specifically, I want to show how Shakespearean tragedy has – over the past two and half centuries – become a central touchstone for articulating this need.

Shakespearean tragedy, after all, has helped bring into focus questions that the humanities are best equipped to help us tackle – normative questions that scientific knowledge or theological tenets cannot fully decide, such as 'what ought we do?' Or, to extrapolate further: what is it to *lead* a life, rather than merely suffer what happens or feel oneself pushed along by natural or historical forces beyond one's control? What does it mean to live and interact as an individual in an increasingly fractured, complex society? Should political communities be permitted to coerce their members with violence? How should a text be interpreted? As this chapter will show, the reception of Shakespearean tragedy over the past three centuries or so – starting with the so-called 'Shakespeare cult' of the Romantic age – has taught us to see these kinds of questions as unavoidable.

The Shakespeare cult

The phrase 'Shakespeare cult' is often used to describe the intense attention paid by German writers and philosophers to Shakespeare's drama – starting, especially, with writings by Gotthold Ephraim Lessing (1729–81), Johann Gottfried Herder (1744–1803) and Johann Wolfgang Goethe (1749–1832), extending to writings by Friedrich Schiller (1759–1805), the brothers August Wilhelm and Friedrich Schlegel (1767–1845 and 1772–1829), and G. W. F. Hegel (1770–1831). The birth of the Shakespeare 'cult' also corresponds, in ways I will explore in the following pages, to the emergence of a philosophy of the tragic – as distinct from a poetics of tragedy.[2] Because Shakespeare was venerated, especially, for his contribution to thinking about the tragic, his work as a tragedian also earned him special attention.

Interestingly, in spite of the term 'cult,' the Germans' appeal to Shakespeare invites us to see any veneration (or condemnation) of Shakespeare as responding to precisely the wrong sorts of questions – such as, 'How are we to judge Shakespeare's achievement?' or 'What are the right generic criteria for assessing Shakespeare's work?' Herder, a key figure in this movement, urges us to ask instead: 'How does Shakespeare force us to look at ourselves differently?' 'How do *we* look by the lights of Shakespearean drama?' For Herder, to engage Shakespeare is to better grasp *one's own* historical situation – rather than the other way around. Herder in fact devoted much of his career to making academic pursuits more critically self-aware in this regard, calling for an anthropological turn in the study of philosophy – by which he meant not only the expanded study of distant cultures, but above all the critical exposure of our own prejudices with respect to such far-off horizons.

How, then, does Shakespeare help us better to grasp our own historical situation?

Consider the prejudices that Herder seeks to expose in his essay on Shakespeare. Herder's first target was the rigid neo-classicism of his day – namely, the view that artistic practices are graspable in terms of ahistorical rules and guidelines. Such a view was prevalent not only in the workshops of Renaissance Europe, wherein artists learned a craft by following time-honoured principles of composition; it was visible as well in the influence of Aristotle's *Poetics* over the understanding of artistic practices. (Although Aristotle's direct influence was less evident in sixteenth-century England than in Italy – Sir Philip Sidney's *Defense of Poetry* (1595) is probably the first appearance of Aristotelian ideas in English – proto-Aristotelian attempts to develop generic definitions of tragedy were increasingly visible in late sixteenth-century England.)[3] In the *Poetics*, Aristotle had set forth rules for composing tragedies – rules that were rooted in what Aristotle saw as the goal or *telos* of poetic or artistic works. The primary rule for tragedy, according to Aristotle, is that it should be organized around a plot-structure, a *mythos*.[4] Tragic plots, according to Aristotle, are the most refined kinds of plots – more refined than epics, chronicles or histories (like those of Herodotus).[5] Like history or epic, tragedies portray a sequence of human actions; but unlike history or epic, tragedies condense that sequence – by 'unifying' time and place, for instance – in such a way as to most fully contain, and therefore intensify and reveal, the significance and consequentiality of what human beings might do to and with one another.[6] In this way, Aristotle suggests, tragic plots furnish insights into human actions and their social conditions that are not to be gained outside of tragedy. Tragedies are set in motion by specific deeds and transgressions – Oedipus's slaying of his father, Antigone's burial of her brother – whose consequences (and, therefore, whose meaning) come to light only later. This temporal interval between the deed and what Aristotle calls the 'recognition' that follows is central to tragic structures, to 'plots' in which 'events occur contrary to expectation yet on account of one another'.[7] What Aristotle is developing, in short, is the thought that it is only through a retrospective view or 'recognition' of this unexpected consequentiality that we learn something about the social, ethical, political or personal stakes of the actions themselves.

At any rate, to make a long story short, by the early seventeenth century Aristotle's influence had coalesced into a broadly shared view according to which artworks conform to standardizing descriptions of their form and content. To study artworks meant striving for the right definitions for different *kinds* of art – definitions that ended up being criteria for artistic genres. The continued reference, in Shakespeare's day and afterwards, to a genre called 'tragedy' is, in this sense, a direct consequence of Aristotle's influence and proto-Aristotelian efforts to 'define' tragedy and other poetic genres. Like all the arts, tragedy was thought to be an ahistorical, rule-governed activity.

Herder's essay on Shakespeare represents the first forceful challenge to this understanding of tragedy as an ahistorical artistic genre – and to the view that human activities can be grasped in this way. 'Oh,' cries Herder, 'if Aristotle were alive today and saw the false, perverted use of his rules in dramas of a wholly different kind!'[8] Of course, Herder's point was that Aristotle did not live to see a Shakespeare play – that Aristotle's philosophy was, like any philosophy, expressive of its own time and place. So in Herder's view, what his contemporaries (and Shakespeare's earliest critics) mistook to be universal 'rules' for tragedy had simply been – for Aristotle, Sophocles and the Greeks – their 'view of the world, [of] their customs'.[9] Instead of being read as providing ahistorical rules for drama, then, Aristotle's *Poetics* should be seen as 'theorizing according to the great tendency of his time'. Aristotle 'is in no way to blame for the restrictive and childish follies which have turned him into the paper scaffolding of our modern stage'.[10]

And this tumbles into the second prejudice tackled by Herder: our blindness to our own historical situation, our blindness to the historicity of our production and reception of dramatic works. To counter this, Herder first points out that Aristotle's emphasis on plot-structure in tragedies was 'deeply embedded in what was called the deeds of ancient times'; and, moreover, that in the years that separate us from Greek antiquity 'the material for plots vanished', along with 'the opportunities for their use, the incentive for using them'.[11] In other words, Herder is pointing out, first, that the concerns of ancient legends no longer implicate our (or even Shakespeare's) whole culture in the way that, say, the Oedipus myth captured deep anxieties about the delicate balance of matrilineal family and the *polis* in the Greek world; and, second, that plot-structures as such – sequences of actions built around reversals and recognitions – no longer always reveal the meaning of our actions. For Herder, this fact explains Shakespeare's sheer inventive energy in drawing upon all kinds of 'story' material – native, Roman, Greek, biblical and so forth – in wholly new ways. Although plot-structures may once have been, as Aristotle maintained, an appropriate way to unveil the meaning of human actions through the display of their unintended consequences, the very possibility of such a plot-based revelation vanishes in the context of a complex, modern social world. The relationship between our actions and their consequences is now far more complicated, and hence less easily traced or narrated. As Herder put it: 'Shakespeare's age offered him anything but the *simplicity* of national customs, deeds, inclinations, and historical traditions which shaped Greek drama.'[12] Given the sheer complexity of the socio-historical world in which Shakespeare wrote (and *of* which he wrote), a tight plot-structure of the Aristotelian–Sophoclean sort could not but have been false to Shakespeare's age. And we today are – as Herder said – 'closer' to Shakespeare than to the Greeks.

The broader point, then, is this: because the conditions for human activity – social, political, economic, physical – have been radically transformed over time, and must therefore be seen as transformable still, our dramatic representations of our activities (*our* dramatic art) must also be seen as transformable in ways that no 'rules' can govern.

Indeed, this transformability no doubt characterizes the way that Shakespeare's drama – as historical artefact, literary text and theatrical canon – looks to Herder, as well as to us today. It explains the sheer variety and quantity of critical responses occasioned by Shakespeare's drama in schools, playhouses and popular culture since the eighteenth century. Taking our historical mutability seriously, therefore, means that there can be no 'poetics' of Shakespearean tragedy in the classical or neo-classical sense, because of our very understanding of what drama is, or of what is dramatic, is itself subject to deep revisions in the social conditions of our activities. Any understanding of Shakespeare to which we can aspire must therefore start by tracking such revisions – a task from which no new audience is immune – both in Shakespeare's work and in our own activities and their changing conditions.[13]

Herder's way of explaining this is to point out that the historical world in which Shakespeare writes knows no Aristotelian 'unity of time and place'. Such a unity is no longer part of our contemporary lived experience – given all the distracting, competing demands on our attention. Nor was it part of the complicated social worlds that Shakespeare depicted four centuries ago. Consider, as one example, that Hamlet must figure out for himself the meaning of Claudius's coronation, or of his mother's remarriage to his uncle, or of his dead father's call for revenge – all the while trying to grasp what, exactly, being prince or 'son' or 'courtier' is supposed to entail.

As further evidence for this, Herder notes an obstacle that every student of Shakespeare encounters, and which was the source of neo-classical complaints about Shakespeare: namely, that Shakespeare's plays simply do not lend themselves to easy 'plot summary' the way that *Oedipus the King* can be recounted in a few sentences. In fact, formal rules for storytelling are of no help for a body of drama – like Shakespeare's – that has to solve for itself, again and again with each new play and performance, what a drama *is* and what it might become. In Shakespeare's creative and varied output, we are shown 'history in the widest sense' in all of its complexity and disunity. 'O God,' effuses Herder describing Shakespeare's plays, 'what vicissitudes of times, circumstances, tempests, climes, ages!'[14]

With this Herder puts his finger on the source and significance of neo-classical anxiety about Shakespeare. It is not only Shakespeare's unravelling of plot-structure that provokes worries; it is also the way in which this unravelling reveals a crisis in our understanding of our own actions, their consequences and implications. Shakespeare forces us to confront – again and again, with each new audience – the opacity of our own social world.

And this also means – as my epigraph suggests – that generic categories are useless when it comes to Shakespeare. Shakespeare exposes tragedy-as-a-genre to a tragic downfall of its own.

Modern humanistic study, first-personal questions

Not only, then, does coming to terms with Shakespearean tragedy mean giving up the search for generically adequate definitions of 'tragedy' (Shakespearean or other). At stake is a more far-reaching problem, to which the humanities have sought to respond.

We have had to give up on securing a generic, universal, standardizing view – a 'God's eye' view from 'the outside' – of the relation between individual human beings and the natural or historical world in which they act. Instead, what Shakespeare provides are multiple views 'from the inside'. That is, Shakespeare shows us how different situations look from the standpoint of particular individuals (Hamlet, for instance) – as well as from other standpoints *on* those individuals and that situation (Claudius, Gertrude, Polonius, Ophelia, each of whom has a world-view of their own) – without ever showing how or whether these individual points of view truly coincide.

In fact, the action of a Shakespearean drama is invariably motivated by the non-coincidence of these multiple points of view – the sheer lack of an objective view of things. Think, for example, of the way that differing perspectives on Hamlet's behaviour drive much of what actually occurs in the play *Hamlet*. Or, of the way that what an audience perceives – about Macbeth's response at the banquet to the murder of Banquo, for instance – does not correspond to how others in the play see things. Or, of how the worlds of Theseus and Oberon encounter one another in *A Midsummer Night's Dream*, highlighting the distinctions between their (and our) perceptions of events in the forest. Or, of how the Friar's retelling of the lovers' actions at the end of *Romeo and Juliet* necessarily misses so much of what mattered to the audience – the balcony scene, the morning aubade and so on.

Recall, by contrast, that to compose an Aristotelian plot meant grasping the 'unity' of an individual's time and place; it meant comprehending the whole of someone's relation to the natural or social world of which he is a part. Sophocles, for instance, saw – *had* to see – that Oedipus was both king of Thebes (hence, Jocasta's husband) and Jocasta's son (hence, Laius's murderer) in order to show how Oedipus himself was brought to 'see' the whole picture, by means of the reversals and recognitions of which Aristotle spoke. So, while Oedipus's view of things at the outset of Sophocles's play is partial and subjective – *he* thinks that he is Jocasta's husband, even as he is blind to the fact that he is also her son – events force him to see the whole picture, to come to know everything that Sophocles (not to mention the audience, or the soothsayer Tiresias) already knows from the outset. And by finally surveying the entirety of his relation to his social world – the same way that ancient mythologies regarded the cosmos as bounded by comprehensible horizons – Oedipus is brought to ruin, and the tragedy concludes. To compose a drama of this sort is thus to present a God's-eye, ahistorical view on the spectacle of human beings in action – a perspective that allows us all (playwright, protagonists, audience) to perceive whether such-and-such a situation is tragic or comic, by coming to know the relationship between (subjective) individuals and their (objective) world.

Shakespeare, however, forces us to regard any perspective on human actions as deeply provisional, historically bounded and contextually determined. Indeed, the most probable reason that Shakespeare (the dramatist) has seemed so wise to audiences around the world is that – even at the conclusion of a play – Shakespeare the playwright invariably seems to know more than what any individual protagonist *in* the play, or any particular audience, comes to know. Which is to say that no character in Shakespeare – and no audience of a Shakespeare play – ever learns the 'whole truth', or gains a panoptic perspective on human actors in the world. Quite the contrary: in *King Lear*, for instance, Lear's or Gloucester's blindness to the standpoints of their respective children is never subsequently 'reversed' (to use Aristotle's term) into insight by the unintended consequences of their deeds. Instead of moving from blindness to insight, we see how and with what implications an ongoing (and worsening) blindness can replace insight. Even when events seem to be cleared up at the end of a Shakespearean drama – the way, for instance, that revelations come tumbling one after the other at the close of *Cymbeline* – we are left not with a sense of clarity and insight, but with more questions than ever. 'Nor the time nor place / Will serve our long inter'gatories,' admits the baffled King Cymbeline at the play's close (5.5.391–2).

Our sense of 'closure' at the conclusion of a Shakespeare play is routinely belied by our sense that the fate of one or more of the characters remains deeply unresolved, or unexplained, by the actions we have witnessed. Even our clarity about what is wrong or broken is diminished. Whereas in Greek tragedy, it matters tremendously – to the city that watches, above all – that at least the terms of the crises, if not of solutions, are clear, in Shakespeare we are denied even that clarity. What will Malvolio do next? Is Shylock really 'content', and will he actually perform the acts he has pledged to perform? What does Jaques go on to do in the Forest of Arden? Will Iago confess once back in Venice? What will become of the broken kingdom at the end of *King Lear*? Even in the so-called history plays – where one might expect the fates of individuals and societies to converge – we are left wondering: why did the representation of Prince Hal's accession as Henry V require the intensely vivid depiction of Falstaff? Or why, if Shakespeare meant to invoke a legend according to which Banquo was King James's ancestor, is Malcolm (and not Fleance) crowned at the conclusion of *Macbeth*? And what is the connection between, say, this broader history and Macduff's role as Macbeth's assassin?

One could go on and on with questions such as these, since no perspective in Shakespeare's work – neither the author's, nor the audience's, nor that of any individual character – is capable of presenting the events as a unified whole. In Shakespeare, subjective-individual and objective-worldly points of view never fully coincide. Indeed, exploring this non-coincidence has been, over the past century, the task of many critics whose work builds upon the philosophical tradition I am tracking here: critics such as Northrop Frye, Jan Kott, Stanley Cavell and others.[15]

To better see the implications of this, we should consider Shakespearean drama in the light of what we have come to regard as hallmark crises of the modern age. Recall, for instance, that by the time that Shakespeare wrote his plays, the view of our natural or social world as a finite, known cosmos had been thrown into irrevocable crisis – a crisis whose effects are still palpable today. For a start, the scientific revolution started by Copernicus (and continued in Shakespeare's own time by Galileo) did not simply furnish new knowledge about natural phenomena by replacing mythological views of the universe with 'truer' ones. Rather, with its ongoing 'discoveries' and explanatory power, the new science leaves us with no way to account for our place in the physical world whose laws are being laid bare to human scrutiny. Pressing questions result: are human beings just bodies in motion? Are our life-defining actions and most important practices mere effects of physical or biological laws?

At the same time, the so-called 'discovery' of the Americas, the mapping and exploration of the earth, increasingly complex economic practices, new occasions for social mobility, the disappearance of feudalism in Europe, the Reformation's expropriation of church wealth and its theological emphases on the individual subject, the rise of individual property and accumulated social wealth – all of these are part of Shakespeare's horizons. Our place in nature or society is no longer clear, even as our knowledge of the world 'out there' is increased exponentially.

Jean-Jacques Rousseau (1712–78) was one of the first to identify and explore the implications of these new horizons. In his widely influential writings he sought, for example, to define the inherent limitations of both modern science and theology when it comes to our self-knowledge, and thus to advocate what we now see as the 'humanities'. Rousseau emphasized the importance of those issues that could be solved neither by the new science nor by the old theologies of religious traditions. His approach was to underscore the importance of moral problems borne by individuals – those dramatic-ethical situations that cannot be resolved or explained by any appeal to a 'third-person' (objective) point of view, such as the dictates and laws of God, society or nature. Such predicaments or moral burdens go to the heart of our lives together, to the point of leaving us torn between the warmth of human passion ('nature', 'pity') and the coldness of rational knowledge. If society (or the voice of reason) tells us to obey quietly, while our passions revolt and urge us to act, then our objective, rational knowledge about a given situation cannot fully tell us how to handle – how to *live* – in that situation.

In the years after Rousseau wrote – and largely in response to his writings – German philosophers, especially, came to see tragic dramas as deepening the same issues and predicaments. It became possible – essential, even – to see both ancient and Shakespearean tragedies as perhaps our best resource for examining the ethical predicaments of modern individuals. Indeed, although such examinations might take the form of studying a work of ancient or Shakespearean drama, the impetus springs entirely from our modern world, from our need for self-understanding – rather than from some conservative desire to preserve inherited wisdom. In this way, the study of tragedy came to be seen as essential to humanistic inquiry *tout court*.

After all, while knowing a set of facts (as established by biology, social history or anthropology) might help us to understand something about the importance of burial rites in ancient Greece, and so in some sense 'explain' Antigone's actions in Sophocles's play – that knowledge would not be helpful to Antigone herself, or to anyone in her position. *She* is the one who has to act – and live or die accordingly. And while it is true that Antigone does act in accordance with an objective duty to bury her brother, that duty can only be accomplished if *she* acts and takes responsibility for these actions as *her own*. Tragic dramatists see human beings not as mere twigs floated here and there on a river of laws or forces (social-historical, biological, physical) beyond our control – but as actors in the world. If we are exposed to tragic downfalls, then it is because no matter what, we have to act. What tragedies reveal – and what humanistic inquiry into the 'tragic' explores – is the unavoidability of the first-personal, individual perspective. This is why tragedy is seen as essential to understanding what it is to be a modern individual – what it is to be someone who does not just passively accept one's fate but actively *leads* one's life.

Re-defining the tragic

Again, all this is worth bearing in mind not only because philosophers in Germany from the late eighteenth century onwards were greatly influenced by Rousseau's framing of these issues – but also because, although Rousseau's writings do not mention Shakespeare, German philosophy turned with gusto to Greek tragedy and to Shakespeare just when this split between the first-person and third-person views, this world-alienation, began to reach a fever pitch.

How, then, did looking at ancient and Shakespearean tragedy help these philosophers respond to the problems Rousseau raises?

Borrowing his terms from Immanuel Kant, the philosopher F. W. J. Schelling (1775–1854) explored the first-person/third-person split as an opposition between 'dogmatism' and 'criticism'. 'In dogmatism,' wrote

Schelling, 'my vocation is to annihilate all free causality in me; to let absolute causality act in me, but not to act myself . . . in short my destiny is the utmost unlimited passivity.'[16] In other words, dogmatism is the upshot of a scientific-rational world-view according to which all bodies are bodies in motion – such that the difference between living human bodies (individual subjects) and other material objects erodes, and all our actions and feelings appear to be nothing more than passive expressions of universal laws of motion.[17] By contrast 'in criticism,' wrote Schelling, 'my vocation is immutable selfhood, unconditional freedom, unlimited activity'.[18] Criticism puts everything in the subject, denying the objective – the way, for instance, that René Descartes' Second Meditation sought to demonstrate that we know our minds better than we know the material bodies that we touch or see (for example, a piece of wax); that what we know belongs not to anything in these bodies but to the activity of the thinking 'I'.

Like Rousseau before him, Schelling found both dogmatism and criticism to be unsatisfactory – because both, on their own, fail to account for how human beings act freely in the world. We are not free, Schelling thought, to simply deny the objective world – since that kind of freedom leaves us worldless, not free *in* the world. On the other hand, we cannot act freely if objective natural or social situations always require us to do such and such. So, freedom requires a perspective that is both subjective and objective – a perspective that, Schelling thought, could not be achieved theoretically but only practically, through action. And for a depiction of such action, the young Schelling – who was in his early twenties when he wrote these words – turned to tragedy.[19] 'One thing remains,' wrote Schelling:

> to know that there is an objective power which threatens our freedom with annihilation, and, with this firm and certain conviction in our heart, to fight *against* it exerting our whole freedom, and thus to go down . . . [The hero] must be *punished* for succumbing because he did not succumb *without a struggle*. That the malefactor who succumbed under the power of fate was punished, this tragic fact was the recognition of human freedom . . . Greek tragedy honored human freedom, letting its hero fight against the superior power of fate. It was a sublime thought, to suffer punishment willingly even for an inevitable crime, and so to prove one's freedom by the very loss of this freedom, and to go down with a declaration of free will.[20]

The tragic structure of subjective freedom, then, has two sides: first, the absolute assertion of the subject's own freedom in the face of fate, or whatever objectively comes her way – and, second, the way in which this assertion comes to light through her being made to suffer by some worldly power 'out there' (fate, nature, societal demands) for asserting her freedom in this way at all. In other words, the positive value of her freedom – the essence of her 'self' – is proved only by her defeat; her freedom, says Schelling, is proved 'precisely through the loss of this freedom'.[21] At the same time, because she is defeated – that is, because she struggles, rather than passing quietly into the night – her freedom is demonstrated by her having taken up the struggle at all.

Indeed – and this is the thrust of Schelling's argument – the 'struggle' or 'conflict' between subjective freedom and objective necessity (nature, fate, societal demands) is itself the fullest proof of the subject's unbounded freedom. The destructive power of objective necessities, after all, comes to light not in our inert reception of whatever befalls us. To succumb is not to passively acquiesce, since one who is passive cannot experience defeat after a struggle. If objective reality crushes whoever struggles against this reality, then it is her subjective freedom that is crushed and at the same time brought to light by this very defeat. Hence, Schelling concludes, the struggle itself is already 'fought' on the ground of human freedom. 'The essence of tragedy . . . the conflict of freedom and necessity [exists] only . . . where freedom is fought on its own ground.'[22]

Hegel's view of tragic situations, which evolved partly in response to Schelling, complicates Schelling's vision of 'objective necessity' by introducing what Hegel calls the 'absolute idea of ethical life' (*Sittlichkeit*). By 'ethical life', Hegel did not only mean the historical customs and practices of human societies – but also the ways that our ritual practices *both* distinguish our actions from objective facts of the matter (for example, to bury or cremate a dead body distinguishes the human deed of destruction from the biological processes of natural decay and death) *and* at the same time acknowledge an objective reality 'out there' (to bury someone is, after all, to acknowledge their natural death).

Now tragedy, in Hegel's view, shows ethical life to be rent with conflicts, latent and manifest – to be fragile and transformable, rather than permanent and stable. Tragedies do this, he thought, by depicting a word or deed that brings to light irreconcilable social demands – such as Antigone's duty to bury her brother and Creon's command that such burial not be given. The upshot of such a conflict is not only the destruction of the transgressor (Antigone, for instance), but the devastation of the social world in which these opposed powers might co-exist peacefully; in fact, it is the shattering of that (objective) peaceful world which occasions the (subjective) suffering. What makes an action 'tragic', therefore, is that it brings to light divisions and tears in the fabric of all our lives together. We may not all suffer the hero's fate, exactly, but none of us is off the hook. Tragic conflict and suffering are, therefore, different from mere misfortunes or isolated pieces of bad news. Tragic conflict and suffering expose a deep 'diremption' (Hegel's term) in the way we live together – to the point of showing a whole way of life to be impossible, self-cancelling – with only two possible outcomes on the horizon: either the suffering will give rise to some new understanding or transformation in the way we live together, or else it will show that this division cannot be healed.

It is the former possibility – namely, the need for reconciliation – that, for Hegel and others, makes the tragic 'dialectical'. The tragic is dialectical because a tragedy has, so to speak, two sides: on the one hand, it is through tragic suffering that a social world becomes painfully, subjectively aware of its own conflicts and divisions; on the other hand, a tragedy presents an 'objective' view of these divisions, and allows a reconciliation to come into view, if possible.

The tragic in Shakespeare

But are Shakespeare's dramas 'tragic' in this way? What if – as I have been intimating – Shakespearean drama withholds this dialectic perspective, in which the fates of objective social worlds and individual subjects coincide?

In his *Lectures on Fine Art*, Hegel himself seems to have sensed that Shakespeare, whom he saw as the exemplary modern tragedian, inaugurated something like a non-dialectical conception of tragedy. On the one hand, Hegel saw that modern tragedy – by which he meant Shakespearean drama above all – 'takes for its proper subject matter . . . the subjective inner life of the character who is not, as in classical tragedy, a purely individual embodiment of ethical powers'.[23] In other words, the interests, aims and actions of Shakespeare's characters are not fully absorbed or explained by those of the family, church, state and so on – which is why even minor characters in Shakespeare stand out to us as individuals who might be 'played' by actors in radically diverse ways, with different ticks, passions, motivations and so forth. But, on the other hand, Hegel also wanted to hold to the belief that 'in human action a basis of specific ends drawn from the concrete spheres of family, state, church etc. is never missing'. Our actions invariably throw us into the 'sphere of the real world and its particular concerns'.[24] Again, Hegel's thought is that tragedies show how our actions always implicate us in a broader social world, and by the same token how the fate of a social world itself unfolds through our actions. If there are no worldly consequences to our actions, then they do not appear as actions at all; if our worldly ties are not transformed by what particular human beings do, then no tragedy would be possible, and individual human agents would not come to light as such.

By these lights, we can see the conundrum that Shakespearean drama posed for Hegel's conception of the tragic as dialectical – namely, that the relationship between the actions of individual characters and objective 'powers' in Shakespeare's drama is far from clear.

Here is how Hegel attempted to resolve the conundrum: the 'aims' of Shakespeare's characters, he writes, 'are broadly and variously particularized and in such detail that what is truly substantial can often glimmer through them in only a very dim way'.[25] But even this seems inadequate. After all, it seems impossible to account for – say – Regan or Goneril's attachment to Edmund as (even dimly) expressing anything 'truly substantial', as revealing anything beyond the contingency of their passionate attachment to him, or their jealousy of one another. Think also of how Shakespeare's frequent and diverse explorations of the vicissitudes of sexual love show us attachments to which society is utterly blind and by which it cannot be explained. Desdemona's father openly declares, for instance, that he cannot see the legitimacy or meaning of his daughter's desire for Othello. And later, Desdemona's dying words will refute Othello's perception of himself as her murderer – challenging us to see her motivation as hers alone: 'Nobody; I myself. Farewell.' So, too, because Romeo's and Juliet's aims are not immediately those of their families or of Verona, their tragic end cannot be seen as the consequence of their prior actions. This is why their suicides still need explaining, even when the consequences for the family or the city are clear ('Go hence and have more talk of these sad things' (5.3.306)). What we perceive, therefore, is an uncanny split between the subjective tragedy of Romeo and Juliet (their joy and suffering) and the objective tragedy suffered by the families in Verona (the self-defeating enmity of Capulet and Montague).[26]

Not coincidentally, Shakespearean tragedy has often been understood to express a grievous conflict between the subjective desires or aims of individuals and the objective demands of social life. Here is a typical expression of this view, taken from Theodor Adorno's description of *Romeo and Juliet*: 'without the longing for a situation in which love would no longer be mutilated and condemned by patriarchal or any other powers, the presence of the two lost in one another would not have the sweetness – the wordless, imageless utopia – over which, to this day, the centuries have been powerless'.[27] Such an understanding does manage to solve at least part of the problem that Hegel encountered when he viewed Shakespearean tragedy with Sophoclean-coloured glasses. Rather than regard the tragedy as the result of some conflict *within* the social world that is brought to light by the lovers' actions, we come to see that what the lovers' actions have actually laid bare is a conflict *between* the social world and the concerns of individuals, a rift between worldly necessity and individual desires.

More than any other work by Shakespeare, it is *Hamlet* that has garnered the most critical attention in this regard – largely because many eighteenth-century readers saw the play as paradigmatic of this world-alienation. For example, in probably the single most influential interpretation of *Hamlet*, Goethe's Wilhelm Meister sees Hamlet's predicament both in terms of the Prince's disjointed time and as resulting from Hamlet's noble soul, which was 'unfit for the performance' of what is being asked.[28] For Goethe, then, the problem lay not only in Hamlet's external predicament but also in Hamlet himself – as if Hamlet were his own predicament. Extrapolating from Goethe's account, Hegel in fact tried to develop an account of modern 'Shakespearean' personae who 'are from the beginning in the midst of a wide field of more or less accidental circumstances and conditions within which it is possible to act in this way or in that'.[29] Hegel's intuition here is that the fragmentary, disjointed nature of modern society robs the protagonist of the 'ethical pathos' that animated the actions of Greek tragic heroes. The problem, then, is not only Hamlet's personality or character; rather, it is what Hamlet discovers over the course of his days and nights in the play – that it does not matter what he does. Whatever he may do, his words and deeds cannot reveal ethical stakes on the order of, say, Antigone and Creon. Indeed, nothing Hamlet does – not even his summary, albeit accidental, killing of Polonius – generates any meaningful response, let alone opposition, from anyone else in Denmark; at most, he is simply sent away by Claudius. And while perhaps he might have disobeyed Claudius and Gertrude – say, by demanding to return to Wittenberg – life at Elsinore entails dutiful obedience without actually being given anything to do.

Hamlet, in short, uncovers no absolute 'conflict' in the ethical life of Elsinore. There seem to be only accidents, contingencies and complicated external circumstances. If the Greek tragic hero is generated, in Hegel's and Schelling's accounts, through his or her necessarily ethical pathos, 'in modern tragedy it remains a matter of chance whether the individual's character is gripped by something intrinsically justified or whether he is led into crime or wrong'.[30] And if it is chance – sheer accident – that determines not only the protagonist's field of action but also the ethical stakes of those actions, then, as in *Hamlet*, 'character and an ethical end *may* coincide, but ... this coincidence is not the *essential* foundation and objective condition of the depth and beauty of a [modern] tragedy'.[31]

So, what then is the 'depth and beauty' of Shakespearean tragedy? If the conflict no longer lies in the ethical order of things, then perhaps – Hegel avers – it 'lies essentially in the character to which the individuals adhere in their passion, not because of any substantial justification but because they are what they are once and for all'.[32] Still, if the protagonist's conflicts are not bound up with anything objective, then their travails risk seeming like a tempest in a teapot – as if nothing more were at stake than 'the formal inevitability of [the character's] personality'.[33] On the one hand this might explain why Shakespeare's characters seem so real to us, so richly depicted. On the other hand, matters start to look an awful lot like a classic impasse of modern liberalism – individuals doing their own thing is either compatible with construction of a liveable society, or it is not.

Shakespeare offers, so says Hegel, 'the finest examples of firm and consistent characters who come to ruin simply because of this decisive adherence to themselves'.[34] Similarly Hegel's contemporary, the English critic William Hazlitt (1778–1830) – who, with his friend Samuel Coleridge, had been influenced by the German enthusiasm for Shakespeare – emphasized the importance of character-type in his *Characters of Shakespear's Plays* (1813). But it is really A. C. Bradley's 1904 lectures on Shakespeare that offer the most sustained and influential elaboration of this problem. In Shakespeare's tragedies, Bradley writes, 'action is essentially the expression of character'. Although Bradley claims that Hegel is the only writer on tragedy to compare with Aristotle, in a sense it is really Bradley who accomplishes the fullest reversal of Aristotle through his reading of Shakespeare. Whereas Aristotle maintained that character is a function of that character's actions and therefore of the plot, Bradley suggests that plot in Shakespearean tragedy is a function of character – 'character is destiny'.[35]

And yet, on precisely this point, Bradley finds something missing in the Hegelian-German reading of Shakespeare – a sense of lack that he repeatedly attributes to the failure of the philosophical reading to account for that which moves us in Shakespeare's plays. This attention to our affective response to the plays is perhaps the greatest virtue of Bradley's writings, however tendentious his suppositions in this regard may be. If Shakespeare's characters come to ruin – *pace* Hegel – because of a 'decisive adherence to themselves', because there is no indisputable governing set of social norms and principles to give their deeds meaning, then what Bradley wants to know – *contra* Hegel – is why, if this is all true, these plays are not 'depressing' like so many 'mis-called tragedies'. For Bradley, Hegel perceived roughly half of the picture – namely, the notion that Shakespeare's protagonists are 'free artists of themselves'. But what he failed to account for was how Shakespeare managed to conjure a compelling drama of these free artists that does not simply leave us with 'the reflection that all is vanity'.[36] How did Shakespeare manage to take characters whose fate derives from a decisive adherence to themselves and make them meaningful and moving to us?

More to the point, Bradley wonders, how did Shakespeare manage this without falling back upon moralistic caricatures, protagonists with whom we identify because they are basically 'good' people (the way Aristotle requires that tragic heroes be neither reprobates nor saints, but closer to the latter)? As Bradley notes, while all Shakespeare's tragic heroes are 'exceptional beings', they are not necessarily 'good' – in fact, they are often wilful criminals (Macbeth) or murderers (Hamlet, Othello) or worse. And yet, Shakespeare manages to instil in us more than a desire for their downfall; indeed, Bradley maintains that these protagonists elicit our 'sympathy' and, even, our 'admiration'.[37]

Such is Shakespeare's trick: he shows us protagonists with nothing to cling to but their own character, heroes who perform some of the most vicious things humans can do to one another – and, yet 'no one ever closes the book with the feeling that man is a poor mean creature'. 'He may be wretched and he may be awful,' writes Bradley, 'but he is not small. His lot may be heart-rending and mysterious, but it is not contemptible. The most confirmed of cynics ceases to be a cynic while he reads Shakespeare's plays.'[38]

Into the twenty-first century

You will perhaps have noticed the extent to which the study of Shakespeare in universities has, in recent decades, largely – though not entirely – abandoned the line of inquiry opened up by these explorations of the 'tragic'. The works of Hegel and Herder, for instance, are rarely assigned to students of Shakespeare. And Bradley's influence on students of Shakespeare in the early decades of the twentieth century has largely given way to a generation of scholars who – rather than look for a chance to consider the 'first-person' predicaments depicted by Shakespeare – look in the plays for the objective concerns of the early modern culture from which Shakespeare's work springs. Of course, one might still suspect that – inasmuch as Shakespeare presents the woe and weal of individual human beings in ways that cannot be fully explained by the fate of the society to which they belong (whether 'Denmark' or 'Venice,' or Elizabethan–Jacobean society) – a 'cultural materialist' approach to Shakespearean drama, if not to modern life *tout court*, cannot but fail to fully satisfy.

That said, insofar as scholarly approaches to Shakespeare provide a corrective to the naïve presentation of Shakespeare (or of literary works) as repositories of eternal truths, they also return us to Herder's riposte to the neo-classicists of his day. As I have been trying to show, the 'cult' of Shakespeare itself grew out of a deep sense of the historicity of Shakespeare's work, and of artistic practices generally – just as they sought to highlight in Shakespeare's works an occasion for us to become more historically self-aware. Even more strikingly, our two most powerful accounts of tragic drama – Aristotle's *Poetics* and Hegel's *Lectures on Fine Art* – both present tragic drama as the highest form of human artistry precisely because tragic dramas present a provisional vision of human beings as agents in history. As Aristotle makes clear, for instance, chronicles merely describe particular, actual pasts whereas tragedies present human beings in their potential as makers of History.

Shakespeare's plays also build upon particular, concrete past events, of course. They draw directly upon Plutarch and Holinshed's *Chronicles of England, Scotland and Ireland*, for a start, as well as all manner of (then) contemporary events. Many scholars are often keen to demonstrate this, in part because illuminating a historical or textual source can help us to better grasp how and with what implications Shakespeare turns that source into a drama. Others are keen to emphasize Shakespeare's dependence on actual historical events, to present the historical horizons of tragic drama or human artworks. For instance, Carl Schmitt (1888–1985), a political theorist and proponent of Nazi ideology, noted that James I was the son of a queen who took part in her husband's murder – James's mother, Mary Queen of Scots, married her husband's assassin only three months after the murder. Schmitt argues that the ambiguity surrounding Gertrude in *Hamlet* in fact alludes to this set of facts, and that this allusion is partly responsible for Hamlet's delay. Schmitt's larger purpose, in noting this, is not to 'historicize' *Hamlet*, although he shares with cultural-materialist readings of Shakespeare a resistance to approaching artworks only on their own terms, since this approach obscures – in the case of *Hamlet* – that which makes Shakespeare's drama more than mere artistic-literary-imaginative 'play'. Schmitt's purpose, rather, is to grasp what makes *Hamlet* 'tragic' in the fullest sense. 'An invented fate,' he writes, 'is no fate at all.' For, the 'core of tragic action, the source of genuine tragedy, is something so irrevocable that no mortal can invent it'.[39]

Georg Lukács, on the other hand, offers something like the exact reverse of Schmitt's claim about Shakespeare and tragic drama. For Lukács,

Shakespeare's poetic achievement lies in the construction of 'a powerful sequence of great scenes that depict and portray the tragic feelings of tragic figures' – scenes which are connected by the individual character, without the slightest regard for historical or mythical inevitability. For instance, Macbeth's castle in Inverness the morning after the murder, or the graveyard scene in *Hamlet*, or Lear's scenes on the heath shows such scene-setting to be what Lukács calls the 'form of an irretrievable moment' – the dramatic or poetic truth about history, rather than the historical truth of drama and poetry.[40]

The expression 'poetic truth about history' belongs to Agnes Heller, a student of Lukács. Heller suggests that Shakespeare's dramas reveal not simply what has happened, but rather that they are really more interested in how it happened and in that it has happened – the dramatic truth of history, rather than the historical truth of drama. Whereas, according to Heller, the historian or historiographer approximates 'what really happened' – namely, what no artist invents – Shakespeare offers history not as sheer fiction but as 'revelatory truth'.[41]

By using this phrase, Heller means to place Shakespeare's histories and tragedies alongside religious truth, but also to signal an important difference between them. What Shakespeare's histories and tragedies share with religious revelation is, so to speak, a certain self-referential or self-authorizing quality. 'Because the drama *is* the truth ... one is confronted with the question of what exactly that truth is, not with the question of whether this is the truth.'[42] But what makes Shakespeare's 'revelatory truth' different from religious revelation – and, by the same token, what makes Shakespeare our contemporary – is that in Shakespeare stories unfold, individuals act, 'without any kind of otherworldly interference or protection'.[43] Without gods or deities to participate in the action, Shakespeare leaves us the revelation of truth about human actions by leaving us no possible way to justify or excuse them – while nevertheless keeping us fascinated, keeping us challenged to make even our most astonishing actions intelligible. What to make of Othello's murder of Desdemona? Or Macbeth's visit to the witches? Of Edgar's self-abasement?

In short, Shakespeare reveals the truth of history in his plays not because he reveals the structural necessity of tragic happenings, causal relations of plot constructions, or transparent motives or facts. On the contrary, the interpretability of Shakespearean drama is connected to the way in which his plays show that history is full of secrets without trying to decode them, without aiming to show what those secrets might be. Which also means – to return to where we began, with Herder – that Shakespeare's poetic achievement is rooted in the way in which we ourselves are reflected in the dramas.

What Shakespeare's drama offers are not simply existential truths about human life. Rather, his plays stage for us our own finitude, our own historicity. The poetic truth of Shakespeare's drama has no other ground than its revelation of ourselves to ourselves.

Notes

1. Johann Gottfried Herder, 'Shakespeare', *Philosophers on Shakespeare*, ed. Paul A. Kottman (Stanford University Press, 2009), p. 37.
2. The best account of the philosophy of the tragic, its origins in Germany and its difference from a poetics of tragedy is Peter Szondi, *An Essay on the Tragic*, trans. Paul Fleming (Stanford University Press, 2002).
3. This was true at the level of theoretical exposition – as witnessed in the use of Horace's *Ars Poetica* in education; in the work of Roger Ascham, Thomas Lodge, John Harrington, George Puttenham and others – and at the level of practical exploration, in the rising interest in Seneca and ancient tragedy, both in pedagogical contexts and theatrical circles.
4. '. . . plot-structure [*mythos*] is the goal of tragedy'. *The Poetics of Aristotle*, trans. and ed. Stephen Halliwell (Chapel Hill: University of North Carolina Press, 1987), Chapter 6, p. 37.
5. For Aristotle, this refinement is, significantly, made manifest in the *katharsis* that tragic plot structures cannot fail to elicit: 'The plot [of a tragedy] should be so structured that, even without seeing it performed, the person who hears the events that occur experiences horror and pity at what comes about' (Aristotle, *Poetics* 1453b1–4, trans. Stephen Halliwell, in *Aristotle: 'Poetics'; Longinus: 'On the Sublime'; Demetrius: 'On Style'* (Cambridge, MA: Harvard University Press, 1995), p. 73).
6. Aristotle makes clear that the work of the tragic poet differs from that of the historian in precisely this way: 'The difference between [the historian and the poet] is this: that the one relates actual events, the other the kinds of things that might occur.' In this way, tragedy deals with the potentiality – and not just the actuality – of human actions and their consequences, and is therefore 'nobler' and more 'philosophical' than historical writing (Aristotle, *Poetics* 1451b4–7, p. 59).
7. *Ibid.*, 1452a3–4, 63.
8. Herder, 'Shakespeare', p. 24.
9. *Ibid.*
10. *Ibid.* The primary target of Herder's venom here is the French dramatist Corneille and French Classicism, as well German followers such as Johann Christoph Gottched (1700–66).
11. Herder, 'Shakespeare', pp. 23, 25.
12. *Ibid.*, p. 28. My emphasis.
13. This paragraph and the following one draw upon my remarks, in Paul A. Kottman, *Tragic Conditions in Shakespeare* (Baltimore, MD: Johns Hopkins University Press, 2009), pp. 11–12.
14. Herder, 'Shakespeare,' *Philosophers on Shakespeare*, p. 30.

15. See 'Further reading' at the end of the chapter.

16. F. W. J. Schelling, *The Unconditional in Human Knowledge: Four Early Essays 1794–1796*, trans. Fritz Marti (Lewisburg, PA: Bucknell University Press, 1980), p. 191.

17. 'Dogmatism,' writes Schelling, demands 'that the subject cease. . . to be something opposed' to the objective. *Ibid.*, pp. 191–2.

18. *Ibid.*, p. 192.

19. For what are, in part, historically accidental reasons – having to do with, for example, the massive impact of Johann Joachim Winckelmann's studies of Greek art in the eighteenth century – Greek drama was a primary focus for Schelling. For Shakespeare and the Elizabethans, by contrast, Roman dramatists like Seneca and Plautus constituted the primary 'ancient' model.

20. *Ibid.*, pp. 192–3. Emphases in original.

21. *Ibid.*

22. *Ibid.*, p. 253; cited in Szondi, *An Essay on the Tragic*, p. 9.

23. G. W. F. Hegel, 'Dramatic Poetry', *Philosophers on Shakespeare*, ed. Kottman, p. 73.

24. *Ibid.*

25. *Ibid.*

26. For my full reading of *Romeo and Juliet*, see Paul A. Kottman, 'Tragic Love as the Struggle for Freedom in *Romeo and Juliet*', *Shakespeare Quarterly* 63, 1 (2012): 1–38.

27. Theodor W. Adorno, *Aesthetic Theory*, trans. Robert Hullot-Kentor (Minneapolis: University of Minnesota Press, 1977), p. 247.

28. Johann Wolfgang von Goethe, *Wilhelm Meister* (New York: Collier, 1967), p. 236.

29. Hegel, 'Dramatic Poetry', p. 76.

30. *Ibid.*

31. *Ibid.*

32. *Ibid.*

33. *Ibid.*

34. *Ibid.*, p. 79

35. A. C. Bradley, *Shakespearean Tragedy: Hamlet, Othello, King Lear, Macbeth* (London: Macmillan, 1960), p. 13.

36. *Ibid.*, p. 23.

37. *Ibid.*

38. *Ibid.*

39. Carl Schmitt, 'The Source of the Tragic', *Philosophers on Shakespeare*, ed. Kottman, p. 151.

40. Georg Lukács, 'Shakespeare and Modern Drama', *Philosophers on Shakespeare*, ed. Kottman, p. 41.

41. Agnes Heller, 'Poetic Truth and Historical Truth', *Philosophers on Shakespeare*, ed. Kottman, p. 187.

42. *Ibid.*

43. *Ibid.*

Further reading

Auden, W. H., *The Dyer's Hand* (London: Vintage, 1988).

Bradley, A. C., *Shakespearean Tragedy* (New York: Penguin, 1991).

Cavell, Stanley, *Disowning Knowledge in Seven Plays of Shakespeare* (Cambridge University Press, 2003).

Frye, Northrop, *Fools of Time: Studies in Shakespearean Tragedy* (University of Toronto Press, 1991).

Hegel, G. W. F. 'Dramatic Poetry' from *Lectures on Fine Art*, *Philosophers on Shakespeare*, ed. Paul A. Kottman (Stanford University Press, 2009).

Heller, Agnes, *The Time is Out of Joint* (London, MD: Rowan and Littlefield, 2002).

Herder, J. G., 'Shakespeare', *Philosophers on Shakespeare*, ed. Kottman.

Kott, Jan, *Shakespeare Our Contemporary* (New York: W.W. Norton, 1964).

Kottman, Paul A., *Tragic Conditions in Shakespeare* (Baltimore, MD: Johns Hopkins University Press, 2009).

Szondi, Peter, *An Essay on the Tragic* (Stanford University Press, 2002).

CHAPTER 13

Shakespeare's tragedies in performance

Lucy Munro

In 1594, *Titus Andronicus*, probably Shakespeare's first experiment with tragedy, appeared on the stalls of London's booksellers. This moment has rightly been seen as a landmark in Shakespeare's career as a dramatist in print; however, the book itself foregrounds the play's identity as a piece designed for the stage. The title page advertises it as: 'The Most Lamentable Romaine Tragedie of Titus Andronicus: As it was Plaide by the Right Honourable the Earle of *Darbie*, Earl of *Pembrooke*, and Earl of *Sussex* their Seruants'. Theatre historians have puzzled over this attribution. Does it mean that members of all three companies combined to perform *Titus Andronicus*? That it was successively performed by these companies, during a period – the early 1590s – when the theatre industry and, therefore, the ownership of plays, were in a state of flux? For the purposes of this chapter, though, the title page's statement of theatrical ownership highlights an essential truism: Shakespeare's tragedies were written for the stage.

This would not appear to be a controversial claim. Yet while Shakespeare's tragedies have met with immense theatrical and, to a lesser extent, cinematic acclaim they have also been the focus of anxiety concerning their performance and even, at times, their very performability. Plays such as *Titus Andronicus* have disappeared from the stage for extended periods, the victims of changing moral and aesthetic standards; others, such as *King Lear*, *Timon of Athens*, *Macbeth*, *Romeo and Juliet* and *Coriolanus*, have been extensively rewritten. Few have gone as far as the early nineteenth-century critic Charles Lamb, who argued that stage representation could never capture what was great about Shakespeare's tragedies. Lamb's assertion that the role of King Lear 'is essentially impossible to be represented on a stage' is in keeping with his dislike for the physicality of performance: 'in acting, scenery, dress,' he writes, 'the most contemptible things, call upon us to judge of their naturalness'.[1] It is also the product of a distinctive nineteenth-century moment, in which some critics were beginning to treat Shakespeare's plays as matter for reading, not staging, and in which modes of reading appropriate to the novel were beginning to be applied to them.[2] Nonetheless, his views have been echoed by later scholars, such as A. C. Bradley, who argued in 1904 that '*King Lear* is too huge for the stage', or Harold Bloom, who wrote in 1998, 'Our directors and actors are defeated by this play, and I begin sadly to agree with Charles Lamb that we ought to keep rereading *King Lear* and avoid its staged travesties.'[3]

I dwell on Lamb not because I share his ambivalence about putting Shakespeare's tragedies on the stage, but because in expressing his doubts he highlights some factors crucial to their successful performance. In particular, when he writes 'I am not arguing that Hamlet should not be acted, but how much Hamlet is made another thing by being acted',[4] Lamb acknowledges the instability of the Shakespearean text in performance – in *any* performance, not only those productions that we would think of as adaptations, such as Shadwell's *The History of Timon of Athens, the Man-Hater* (1676), more recent plays such as Tom Stoppard's *Rosencrantz and Guildenstern are Dead* (1966), or Joe Calarco's *Shakespeare's R&J* (1998), and films such as Akira Kurosawa's *Ran* (1985), Baz Luhrmann's *William Shakespeare's Romeo + Juliet* (1996), Julie Taymor's *Titus* (1999) or Ralph Fiennes's *Coriolanus* (2011). The action of putting bodies on a stage, and putting words in the mouths of those bodies, inflects the play and changes its meaning, even before we consider changes in text, or the specific effects of scenery, costume or performance. Moreover, Lamb's anxieties draw our attention to aspects of tragic performance that are often simultaneously beneficial and potentially detrimental. While audiences in different ages have had differing expectations, some problems have been consistent: an actor's presentation of deep emotion might tip into self-parody, provoking amusement rather than wonder, pity or horror; practical problems can undermine tragedy's pretensions to solemnity and grandeur; stage violence might be either unconvincing or all-too-believable; the costumes, props or scenery used in a specific production might enthral or alienate spectators.

Taking Lamb's observation about *Hamlet* as its starting point, this chapter explores four issues central to the performance of Shakespearean tragedy on stage and screen. The first section focuses on text. The existence of more than one early text of many of Shakespeare's tragedies suggests that they have always been subject to revision, and the history of performance demonstrates the many ways in which these plays have been brought into line with prevailing tastes and concerns. If the first section is concerned to a large extent with what audience members hear, the second, which focuses on spectacle, is concerned with what they see. It considers changes in the ways in which Shakespeare's tragedies have been staged, looking in detail at choices regarding sets, scenery, costumes and props. The third section returns to the issue of bodies on stage, comparing casting practices and actors' strategies in different periods. In particular, it looks at the soliloquy, a convention crucial to tragedy and one that poses specific challenges for performers. Finally, the last section pulls together some aspects of the first three sections, focusing on another characteristic intrinsic to tragedy and its effect on spectators: violence.

Text

Lamb castigates Nahum Tate's 1681 adaptation of *King Lear* and Colley Cibber's version of *Richard III*, first performed in 1700, which were still current on the stage in the early nineteenth century, as 'ribald trash' , and he dwells on Tate's *Lear* because it emblematizes, for him, the debased tastes of theatregoers. In Tate's version of what we might now call a 'Hollywood ending', Lear survives, Edgar is betrothed to Cordelia, and the Fool is omitted entirely. Lamb castigates David Garrick – who actually did much to maintain *King Lear*'s place within the eighteenth-century theatrical repertory, and restored much of Shakespeare's dialogue in his acting version – for clinging to Tate's ending. 'Tate,' he writes, 'has put his hook in the nostrils of this Leviathan, for Garrick and his followers, the showmen of the scene, to draw the mighty beast about more easily.'[5] For Lamb, the Shakespearean text is a great whale, a beast that can be tamed for the stage only with massive, and perhaps misguided, exertion.

Adaptation tells us something about the changing tastes of audiences over the last four hundred years, and what they have expected to find in a tragedy. Despite Lamb's distaste for it, the longevity of Tate's version demonstrates the affection that can adhere to particular adaptations, since both the Cordelia/Edgar romance and the happy ending appear to have been highly popular. In an article that first appeared in November 1771, *The Theatrical Review* claimed that

> the happy change in the catastrophe, if not more natural, is abundantly more pleasing ... What mind is so pleased with melancholy Ideas, or the struggles of injured virtue in distress, as not to receive much heart-felt satisfaction, in the last Scene, where *Edgar* and *Cordelia*, surmounting all difficulties, are made happy in each others love, as a reward for their loyalty and virtue[?][6]

From this perspective, Shakespeare's original ending violates poetic and moral justice, and it is therefore right that it should be amended, even if the new version seems more contrived. When Edmund Kean finally restored the original ending in 1823 it was not universally welcomed, and Tate's version was still being performed in London as late as 1857.[7] A reviewer in *The Morning Post* commented favourably on Kean's performance in the final act, saying that with the exception of his delivery of the repeated word 'never', which 'was exactly like a pettish girl who is quarrelling with her first lover', 'it was throughout one of his most transcendent efforts'. As Cordelia, Sarah West was 'beautiful, and deeply affecting'.[8] However, a legend that dates back at least as far as 1853 has it that 'Kean ... was scarcely strong enough to carry [West]. This tempted the risibility of the house, and pit, boxes, and gallery joined in a laugh which lasted until the curtain fell.'[9] Tragic tone is difficult to maintain in the face of practical mishap, and tragedy in performance is always vulnerable to a sudden descent into comedy.

If Restoration adaptations such as Tate's are examples of his era's disinclination to treat Shakespeare's plays as monumental or impervious to dramatic fashion, they are also extreme examples of the general instability of Shakespearean tragedy in performance. As Michael Warren describes elsewhere in this volume, many of Shakespeare's tragedies survive in two or more different early texts. Variations between these texts – which vary in scale from the addition or excision of individual words and speeches to the inclusion of a new scenes – mean that any director or theatre company wishing to stage one of these plays must decide which text their production is to use. Many directors will simply choose a modern edition and accede to their chosen editor's textual choices; many, however, think through their textual options in great detail.

Hamlet survives in three different texts – two versions in small-format quartos, published in 1603 and 1605, plus a third version in the large-format folio edition of Shakespeare's works published in 1623 – and directors' choices for this play are therefore especially loaded. Adrian Noble's decision to use an uncut version of Philip Edwards's New Cambridge Edition – itself a combination of the Folio and second quarto texts – in his 1992 production for the Royal Shakespeare Company (RSC), starring Kenneth Branagh, was mentioned in a number of reviews, and was viewed either as an interpretative decision in itself or a refusal to make such decisions. Frank Rich commented rather archly in *The New York Times* that '*Hamlet* is rarely produced without trims, and one wonders if the full version used here reflects not so much artistic purity as the lack of focus in Mr Branagh's characterization.'[10] Similar criticisms might be levelled at Branagh's 1996 film, strongly indebted in this respect to Noble's production, in which the director's devotion to a full, conflated text leads him to retain topical allusions such as the discussion of the 'little eyases' in Act 2, Scene 2, an allusion to the all-boy theatre companies of the early seventeenth century which sits uneasily in the film's nineteenth-century setting.

Some productions of *Hamlet* have opted instead for the first published text: the so-called 'bad' quarto. The earliest was directed by William Poel at St George's Hall, London, in 1881, and was the first of his experiments with staging Shakespeare in Elizabethan costume with minimal set and scenery.[11] The first quarto is gradually developing its own performance tradition, complete with relatively faithful renderings – such as Robert David MacDonald's 1981 production at Glasgow's Citizens' Theatre, Ralph Cohen's production for the Shenandoah Shakespeare Express (1995) and Red Shift's *Hamlet: First Cut* (1999), directed by Jonathan Holloway – and more radical adaptations, such as Two Gents' *Kupenga Kwa Hamlet*, directed by Arne Pohlmeier (2010), a township-style adaptation performed by only two actors in a mixture of English and Shona, and *Hamlet, House of Horror* (2009), directed by Chris Barton, a 75-minute vaudeville-style musical version.

Mainstream productions of *Hamlet* have also been influenced by the first quarto. Many have used its earlier placing of the 'To be or not to be' soliloquy, while Matthew Warchus's 1997 RSC production incorporated the scene between Gertrude and Horatio in which Gertrude pledges to assist Hamlet in his revenge, which does not appear in the second quarto or Folio texts. Warchus also excised Fortinbras and the war with Norway, and the play was established as a domestic tragedy in an opening sequence which, as Michael Billington describes, 'begins with an image of a besuited Jennings gravely emptying the ashes from his father's urn against background film of his boyhood self romping with his dad in the snow, then cuts to a gaudy wedding party, all balloons and fireworks, in which the mature Hamlet is a looker-on taking Polaroids of the canoodling Claudius'.[12] The incorporated material from the first quarto was therefore part of a strategic focus on the family and on the power of the past to shape the present.

If the tradition of Shakespearean adaptation is long, so is that of performing his tragedies in languages other than English. German and Dutch adaptations of *Titus Andronicus*, *Romeo and Juliet* and *Hamlet* dating from the seventeenth century survive, of which the best-known is *Der bestrafte Brudermord*, a version of *Hamlet*, which was produced in English by Poel in 1924 under the title *Fratricide Punished*. By 1900, the tragedies had been performed in local adaptations in countries including Canada, France, Germany, India, Poland, Russia and the USA, and at the 'Globe-to-Globe' festival held at Shakespeare's Globe, London, in 2012,

Shakespearean tragedies were performed in languages including Brazilian Portuguese, Belarussian, Cantonese, German, Japanese, Lithuanian, Palestinian Arabic, Polish, Turkish and 'Hip Hop'.

Like performances in English, these productions – and, correspondingly, their scripts – have long been affected by prevailing conventions and tastes. We might look, for example, to Jean François Ducis's translation/adaptation of *Othello*, performed at the Théâtre de la République in 1792. Ducis adapted Shakespeare's play to the aesthetic and social requirements of his own culture: Othello is 'jaune et cuivré' – a coppery yellow – rather than black, the relationship between Hédelmone (Desdemona) and her father is emphasized, and the part of Pézare (Iago) is radically reduced.[13] Ducis commented of the latter, 'Je suis bien persuadé que si les Anglais peuvent observer tranquillement les manœuvres d'un pareil monstre sur la scène, les Français ne pourraient jamais un moment y souffrir sa présence' ('I am convinced that if the English can calmly watch the manoeuvres of such a monster on the stage, the French could never for a moment stand his presence there').[14] However, breaking with neo-classical convention, Joseph Talma's Othello killed Magdelaine-Marie Desgarcins's Hédelmone on-stage, and even though she was killed with a dagger rather than a pillow this caused a sensation. In the words of an English observer, '[t]ears, groans, and menaces resounded from all parts of the theatre, and what was still more demonstrative, and more alarming, several of the prettiest women in Paris fainted in the most conspicuous boxes, and were publicly carried out of the house. Ducis was alarmed for his tragedy, for his fame, and for his life.'[15] Shakespeare's tragedy challenged local conventions, even as it was assimilated into them, and the self-conscious transgression involved with the adaptation of *Othello* can be seen in an engraving published with Ducis's text in 1813, representing Othello and Hédelmone in Act 5, Scene 4 (Figure 2).

Ducis referred to his adaptation as 'le sans-culotte Othello',[16] linking it with the French Revolution and its principles, and changes to texts have also reflected local social and political concerns elsewhere. For instance, Monadhil Daood's version of *Romeo and Juliet*, performed at Iraq's National Theatre and in the UK as part of the 2012 World Shakespeare Festival, evoked his country's sectarian divide by making Romeo a Shiite Muslim and Juliet a Sunni, signalling the families' allegiances through the costume of their patriarchs: Capulet was 'denoted as a Sunni by his red-and-white checkered keffiyeh', while Montague wore 'a black-and-white scarf more commonly worn by Shiites' (Figure 3).[17] Daood also refashioned the ending so that Romeo and Juliet did not commit suicide but were killed by

Figure 2. Works of J. F. Ducis (1913), after p. 242: Othello standing, Hédelmone asleep.

Figure 3. Monadhil Daood's *Romeo and Juliet in Baghdad*, Swan Theatre, 2012.

Paris, Juliet's rejected suitor, who 'enters the church wearing a belt of explosives and blows himself up, killing Romeo and Juliet'.[18] The narrative was thus reconfigured, and suicide took on a new set of associations, ones with an all-too-current relevance. 'Now,' commented Ahmed Salah Moneka, who played Romeo, 'it is an Iraqi story.'[19]

Spectacle

Ducis's and Daood's productions of Shakespearean tragedies are examples of not just changes to the text, but also the potential for visual elements to create theatrical meaning. Ducis's *Othello* was performed with perspective scenery indicating the location of each act: the Venetian senate chamber for Act 1, Othello's palace for Acts 2–4, and Hédelmone's bedchamber for Act 5. In Daood's production, place was suggested in part by costume. Such tactics are common on the contemporary stage and screen, in which Shakespeare's tragedies can be seen in a wide range of settings and costumes: Elizabethan and Jacobean; those suiting the period in which a play is set (e.g. Renaissance Italy for *Romeo and Juliet*; medieval England for *Richard III*, and ancient Rome for *Antony and Cleopatra* or *Julius Caesar*); alternative time periods or locations; eclectic; or modern. However, each of these choices has at times aroused controversy. Tragedy is often viewed as the most timeless or abstract of dramatic genres, and there is a history of critics being unnerved by its physicality on stage, or being hostile to the imaginative demands made by particular settings.

If we focus momentarily on productions of *Macbeth*, we can see the ways in which staging and the demands that it makes on spectators have shifted over four hundred years. *Macbeth* was first performed by the King's Men at the Globe playhouse around 1606. Like all of the playhouses in which Shakespeare's tragedies were first performed, the Globe was a round amphitheatre, open to the elements, with a thrust stage extending into the 'pit' in which a large proportion of the audience stood. It was a non-naturalistic playing space in which elaborate scenery was rarely used and the majority of props – tables, beds, thrones, tombs, and so on – were portable. Even the 'great horse with his leages' (probably representing the wooden horse of Troy) and the hell-mouth, mentioned in the accounts of the theatrical impresario Philip Henslowe, could have been easily and quickly installed and removed.[20] The Globe's bare stage was therefore capable of representing a wide variety of imagined locations in quick succession. Act 1 of *Macbeth*, for instance, is located first on the battlefield, then in various rooms within the Macbeths' castle; Act 4 takes place in the witches' lair, the Macduffs' home and the English court. Costume generally appears to have been modern dress – meaning that Shakespeare's protagonists appeared in breeches, hose and doublet, or bodice and kirtle, whatever the play's setting – although details such as Roman togas appeared in some tragedies, resulting in a historically eclectic *mélange*.[21] Visual display is restricted to costume – a major part of playing companies' financial outlay – and specific moments of violent or supernatural spectacle, such as the appearance of Macbeth with bloodstained hands after the murder of Duncan, the sequence in Act 4, Scene 1, in which the witches present three apparitions and a display of eight future kings of Scotland to Macbeth, and the moment in the final scene when Macduff appears with Macbeth's head in his hands. According to the stage directions in the surviving text, published in the 1623 Folio, the apparitions were to be accompanied by thunder, a sound effect produced by rolling a cannonball down a wooden trough or metal sheet, or with drums. The effect of these conventions is thus to throw attention on to the performance of the actors – in particular those playing Macbeth and Lady Macbeth, who are given the majority of the soliloquies and set-piece scenes.

The first large-scale change in the performance of *Macbeth* came after the Restoration, in the 1660s, when the impresarios William Davenant and

Thomas Killigrew built new playhouses along French lines, with proscenium arches, stages with a much smaller thrust, perspective scenery and a clearer division between actor and audience. For Shakespeare's tragedies, this meant a new emphasis on stage spectacle and song. In Davenant's version of *Macbeth*, first performed around 1666, the first scene opens with the '*Thunder and lightning*' also specified in the 1623 text, but at its conclusion the witches '*Ex[it] flying*'. Later directions specify scenery for 'a heath' and 'Birnam Wood', while in Act 3, Scene 1, the scene opens to show '*a Banquet prepar'd*'. Additional songs are added for the witches, and in Act 3 Hecate is lifted to the heavens on a '*Machine*'. [22] The effect is captured by Samuel Pepys, who saw *Macbeth* eight times between 1664 and 1669, and wrote in his diary on 7 January 1667 that it 'appears a most excellent play in all respects, but especially in divertissement, though it be a deep tragedy; which is a strange perfection in a tragedy, it being most proper here, and suitable'.[23] Although some critics have argued, with Bernice Kliman, that 'Davenant's operatic enhancements, intentionally or not, scattered rather than intensified the effect of supernatural power over Macbeth', Pepys clearly found the effect of the mixture of visual and aural elements disconcertingly potent.[24]

By the nineteenth century, Davenant's innovations had been rejected in favour of a return to a more 'authentic' text. However, performance styles were even more distant from the conventions of Shakespeare's day. Productions of *Macbeth* in Scottish dress in Edinburgh in 1757 and in London in 1773 signalled a movement towards period settings and, later, pictorial realism.[25] Whereas Garrick in 1744 costumed Macbeth as 'a prosperous, red-coated Georgian general', to adopt Michael Dobson's description,[26] John Philip Kemble in the 1790s wore chain mail with plaid over it, and a bonnet with a single feather, Charles Kean in 1853 wore a 'Saxon' tunic and cross-garters, and Henry Irving in 1888 had a winged, copper helmet, accompanied by Ellen Terry's Lady Macbeth in a serpentine green gown and long, red plaits (Figure 4).[27] The three witches swelled into a chorus, a development viewed with cynicism by some observers; *The Daily News* remarked of a production at Drury Lane in 1864, '[t]he wild poetic grandeur of the drama is certainly diminished by the introduction of a hundred or more pretty singing witches, but trading managers are bound to be practical'.[28]

Historically authentic costume was matched by the sets. Elizabeth Inchbald was struck by '[t]he huge rocks, the enormous caverns, and blasted heaths of Scotland, in the scenery; – the highland warrior's dress, of centuries past, worn by the soldiers and their generals; – the

Figure 4. *Macbeth*, Act 2. Sir Henry Irving as Macbeth, Ellen Terry as Lady Macbeth;
Lyceum Theatre, January 26, 1889/J. Jellicoe; H. Railton.

splendid robes and banquet at the royal court held at Fores; – the awful, yet inspiring music, which accompanies words assimilated to each sound' of Kemble's *Macbeth*.[29] Irving's production at the Lyceum was still more spectacular, featuring some twenty-one changes of scene, and laboriously realistic sets designed by Hawes Craven. As Richard Foulkes describes, '[a]n entire month was spent searching the British Museum and South Kensington Museum to guarantee Celtic or Anglo-Saxon eleventh-century authenticity in every scenic detail, from such practical implements as swords and helmets to household utensils such as salt-cellars and Anglo-Saxon wine pots'.[30] Research was accompanied by the use of up-to-date technology, a reviewer in *The Standard* commenting that the witches were 'aided greatly by the management of the lights which play upon the lonesome and gloomy cavern' and that 'the figures of the future Kings of Banquo's line are seen as through a thick mist, steam being utilised'.[31]

Irving and his followers took pictorial realism as far as it could go before the invention of cinema, and it is perhaps unsurprising that the twentieth century saw a backlash against such techniques, and a swing back to non-illusionist staging. Experiments in this line had been produced in Germany during the nineteenth century by Ludwig Tieck and Adolphe Appia, who 'at one swoop cleared the clutter of proscenium arch, painted scenery and stage machinery'.[32] In Britain, Poel, who staged *Macbeth* at the Fulham Grand Theatre in 1909, advocated a return to the staging conventions of the early modern theatre, with bare stage, minimal scenery and thrust stages. Performed on a 'platform stage',[33] Poel's *Macbeth* employed Elizabethan costume – a strategy viewed as wilful and arid archaism by many at that time – but by the time of his 1931 production of *Coriolanus* he had rejected period dress in favour of historically eclectic costume of a kind that would become widespread for staging Shakespeare's tragedies in the later twentieth century.

As performance styles began to proliferate, moves were also made to present Shakespeare in modern dress. The tragedies were central to this development. In 1925 the Birmingham Repertory Theatre mounted a modern-dress production of *Hamlet* – widely dubbed '*Hamlet* in plus-fours' – directed by H. J. Ayliff and designed by Paul Shelving, and the same team's *Macbeth* (1928) was set during the First World War.[34] Richard Jennings described the disorientating effect of the opening sequence:

> We see, first . . . a shattered hut and a windmill – apparently on the Western front. Is it a war play?

> The witches appear, and behave in the usual manner with the usual cackles cut up by the usual thunderstorm. Enter some smart officers in khaki with tabs.
>
> Yes: A war play. But what on earth is the matter? The officers speak. 'What bloody man is that?' Modern language – bad language – has made this a sufficiently familiar phrase. But 'of the revolt the newest state'? What dug-out would deal in inversions of that type? These officers are rehearsing for an amateur performance of *Macbeth*, somewhere behind the lines.[35]

Barry Jackson, founder of the Birmingham Repertory Theatre, wrote in a programme note that the aim was to 'give to the tale of "old, unhappy, far-off things" the vividness and actuality of present-day happenings'.[36] As Claire Cochrane notes, '[i]t seems curious now that the generation which had endured the carnage of the First World War should have been unconscious of the implications of Shakespeare's text married to the sights and sounds of modern battle'.[37] It was, however, a step too far for audiences: Jackson and Ayliff's *Hamlet* was safely distanced to a far-off Ruritanian kingdom, despite its modern dress, whereas a wartime *Macbeth*, in a Scottish setting, was apparently too close to home, and its violence became raw and jarring.

In recent years, alternative settings for *Macbeth* and the other tragedies have proliferated in ways which would have been incomprehensible to reviewers of Ayliff's production. Screen versions of *Macbeth*, for instance, include Kurosawa's *Throne of Blood* (1957), set in medieval Japan, Vishal Bhardwaj's *Maqbool* (2004), set in the criminal underworld of Mumbai, and Billy Morrissette's *Scotland, PA* (2001), in which the 'kingdom' is a fast-food restaurant in 1970s, suburban Pennsylvania. In these films, and similar stage productions, set and costume mediate the text for spectators and function as an interpretative aid, foregrounding some aspects of the tragedy's narrative while obscuring others. For instance, both *Throne of Blood* and *Maqbool* invoke male-dominated cultures – of the samurai and the criminal gang respectively – which have significant effects on their presentation of Macbeth and Lady Macbeth. Similarly, casting Duncan as warlord, gang-leader or restaurateur affects spectators' interpretations of the 'king' and Macbeth's act of regicide.

Performance

Audiences have traditionally held strong views about what they consider appropriate in the performance of Shakespeare's tragedies. Reviewers of Ayliff's *Macbeth* were not made uneasy merely by the setting but by the actors' performance style and delivery, which stubbornly refused – in the view of many critics – to reach after tragic grandeur. Although Scott Sunderland as Macduff was praised as 'unaffectedly poetic' in his expression of grief for his wife and children, Eric Maturin's delivery of Macbeth's lines was widely thought to be overly modern; Cochrane comments, '[m]ost notoriously "blasted" in "blasted heath" became an expletive', and Maturin turned 'turned "thanks" into "thengks"'.[38] Other critics have also found details of performance distracting; Lamb, for instance, thought that dwelling on moments of virtuoso skill, such as Sarah Siddons dismissing the guests in the banquet scene in *Macbeth*, granted 'non-essentials' an importance they did not merit.[39] Yet the performance of an individual actor and the sense of a group of actors working together as an ensemble are at the heart of many spectators' enjoyment of Shakespearean tragedy.

As early as 1610, Henry Jackson praised the performance of an unknown boy actor as Desdemona, referring to him throughout as female: 'although she always acted the matter very well, in her death [she] moved us still more greatly; when lying in bed she implored the pity of those watching with her countenance alone'.[40] The transcendent moment, for this spectator, comes when the actor's performance goes beyond text and gesture, and exists solely in facial expression; this technique was to become highly significant in cinematic interpretations of the tragedies, as in Asta Nielsen's performance as Hamlet in Svend Gade's 1921 silent film. On the Restoration, Desdemona was one of the first roles to be played by an actress, and a prologue survives, written by the former actor Thomas Jordan – who had himself played female roles in the 1630s – which teases spectators with the novel casting, and foregrounds some of the problems that the actresses faced from the first:

> I Come, unknown to any of the rest
> To tell you news; I saw the Lady drest;
> The Woman playes to day; mistake me not,
> No Man in Gown, or Page in Petty-Coat;
> A Woman to my knowledge, yet I cann't
> (If I should dye) make *Affidavit* on't.
> Do you not twitter Gentlemen? I know
> You will be censuring; do't fairly though;
> 'Tis possible a vertuous woman may
> Abhor all sorts of looseness, and yet play;
> Play on the Stage, where all eyes are upon her; –
> Shall we count that a crime *France* calls an honour?
> In other Kingdoms Husbands safely trust'em,
> The difference lies only in the custom[.][41]

The prologue's tone seems out of keeping with the tragedy that follows, and it also suggests that actresses were often assumed to be unchaste, or treated as sex objects. Audience reactions, however, also demonstrated their power to move their spectators; Pepys noted in his diary that at a performance on 11 October 1660, at the Cockpit, 'a very pretty lady that sat by me, called out, to see Desdemona smothered'.[42]

Conventions associated with tragedy, such as the extended soliloquy, have always made specific demands on actors. There are a variety of ways in which soliloquies might be performed, including self-address, address to the entire audience, or address to a specific spectator.[43] Lamb assumes that the soliloquy is addressed to the audience, wondering how in *Hamlet* '[t]hese profound sorrows, these light-and-noise-abhorring ruminations, which the tongue scarce dares utter to deaf walls and chambers' could be represented 'by a gesticulating actor, who comes and mouths them out before an audience, making four hundred people his confidants at once'.[44] The bravura performance of soliloquies at this time is also suggested by references to audiences applauding them; in 1803, for instance, *The Morning Post* noted of the American actor Thomas Cooper's performance at Drury Lane, '[t]he soliloquy, at the end of the second act, was managed in a masterly manner, and was received with unbounded applause'.[45] However, performance conventions were not consistent: playing Hamlet some fifty years earlier Garrick 'never addressed himself to the audience ... but, with arms occasionally folded and thoughtful brow, appeared ... to be uttering his thoughts aloud to himself, without regard either to the manner or the spectators'.[46]

Recent productions of *Hamlet* have approached the soliloquy in a number of different ways. In a period-dress production directed by Giles Block and designed by Jenny Tiramani at Shakespeare's Globe in 2000, Mark Rylance exploited his experience of playing at the reconstructed Globe theatre, and the often startlingly direct connection that it can offer between actor and spectator, one reviewer complimenting the way in which 'he can launch into a soliloquy with his back turned to the audience or with his hands full of ridiculous props'.[47] A year later, Stephen Pimlott's modern-dress RSC production, designed by Alison Chitty, created a more direct rapport. The spare, almost empty, white set was thrust forward, with a walkway into the stalls from which Sam West's Hamlet delivered parts of his soliloquies; Susannah Clapp comments,

> The rotten state is a vast and echoing space in which characters are isolated, struggling to contact each other over huge distances. At the same time, the

audience is much closer to the actors. Soliloquies, addressed to them directly, are arguments rather than lyrical musings. For 'To be or not to be', West marches furiously up to the edge of the stage and puts his question as a matter of urgency. When he talks of guilty creatures sitting at a play, he rakes his eyes over the stalls.[48]

In both of these productions, the delivery of the soliloquies was in keeping with both the actor's presentation of role and their broader stage persona. Rylance's Hamlet was a self-consciously mercurial and iconoclastic Renaissance prince, West's a more thoughtful intellectual, in a production that was widely acclaimed for putting the politics back into the play.

When Shakespeare's tragedies have been translated into different languages or media, the soliloquies have often come under pressure. A 1903 production of *Hamlet* in Tokyo, set in contemporary Japan, cut the soliloquies or recast them as dialogue. As Yasunari Takahashi suggests in his account of the production, this was not because soliloquies are unknown in Japanese theatre – in *kabuki* theatre they are accompanied by music and 'half-sung', having a function similar to that of an aria in opera – but because director Otojiro Kawakami rejected the artificiality of *kabuki* and, having done so, could find no way of integrating the soliloquy into his vision of a Japanese Shakespearean theatre.[49] The place of the soliloquy on screen has also been ambiguous. Although direct address has been used in some television adaptations of *Hamlet*, film directors are generally uneasy with it, and the soliloquies of screen Hamlets have generally been delivered in self-address or, in some cases, voice-over, meaning that they become a more straightforward expression of a character's mental processes. In the films of both Laurence Olivier (1948) and Michael Almereyda (2000) 'To be or not to be' is delivered partly in voice-over and partly aloud, yet the same technique creates different effects. Where the cliff-top setting of Olivier's scene suggest loneliness and alienation, the video-store location used by Almereyda, in which Ethan Hawkes's Hamlet delivers his speech walking down the aisle of the 'Action' section, both ironizes Hamlet's musings on suicide and suggests, in the fact that he speaks his thoughts aloud, a more genuine madness than productions generally allow.

Across the years, reviewers and other commentators have drawn attention to the expression, movement or tone of an actor, and its capacity to bring a character to life. An elegy on Richard Burbage, who originated the roles of Hamlet, Macbeth, Othello, King Lear and others, describes how the actor

> leap[ed] into a Graue
> Suiting y[e] person (w[ch] he us'd to haue)

of a mad Louer wth so true an Eye
That there I would haue sworne hee meant to dye[50]

This piece of business was still being employed by actors in the early
twentieth century, when John Barrymore was attacked for refusing to follow
it.[51] The fidgety energy of Sarah Bernhardt's Hamlet (Figure 5) was epito-
mized for one reviewer by her mockery of Polonius in Act 2, Scene 2, when
on the line 'Buzz, buzz' 'she runs after an imaginary fly, pretends to catch it,
and then plays a schoolboy "sell" on the Chamberlain, by opening her hand
and showing him it empty'.[52]

Trailed at length in the British newspapers, Bernhardt's Hamlet was
also an example of the ways in which star performances have been used to
'sell' Shakespeare's tragedies in performance. In the 1950s the Stratford
Memorial Theatre actively pursued a policy of star casting, and John
Gielgud, Ralph Richardson, Peggy Ashcroft, Michael Redgrave, Vivien
Leigh, Laurence Olivier, Edith Evans, Paul Robeson and Charles
Laughton all appeared in leading roles in Shakespeare's tragedies. More
recently, the casting of David Tennant – then starring in the lead role in
the BBC series *Doctor Who* – as Hamlet for the RSC in 2008 and the
comedian Lenny Henry as Othello for Northern Broadsides in 2009 made
headlines in the UK, while the New York Shakespeare Festival's penchant
for celebrity casting was mocked in Charlie Varon's 1994 satire *Rush
Limbaugh in Night School*, in which the 'shock-jock' ends up playing
Othello opposite Garrison Keillor as Iago.

Casting also affects the performance of Shakespeare's tragedies in other
ways. There is a sustained tradition of women playing Hamlet and King
Lear, and recent years have seen performances of tragedies such as *Antony
and Cleopatra* and *Richard III* by both male and female single-sex casts –
pioneered by Poel in an all-male production of *Hamlet* in 1900 – and
reverse-gender productions, such as Lee Breuer's production of *King Lear*
for Mabou Mines at the Triplex Theatre, New York, in 1990.[53] While some
have pursued authenticity, others have instead used such casting to inter-
rogate the gender dynamic of the tragedies, and the very nature of
Shakespeare's tragic heroes. The tragedies have also been performed with
reduced casts, and even – taking culture's fascination with the tragic hero a
step further – as one-actor shows, as in Robert Lepage's *Elsinore*, first
performed in French in 1995 and in English in 1996, Susanna Hamnett's
Nearly Lear (2011), or Alan Cummings's *Macbeth* (2012), set in a mental
hospital, in which a disturbed patient repeatedly plays *Macbeth* to himself.
Elsewhere, productions have employed colour-blind casting or thematic

MME. SARAH BERNHARDT AS "HAMLET."

COPYRIGHT.

Lafayette LTD.

LONDON, DUBLIN, GLASGOW, MANCHESTER & BELFAST.

Figure 5. Sarah Bernhardt (1844–1923) as Hamlet in the 1899 production at the Adelphi Theatre.

casting, as in the many productions of *Romeo and Juliet* in which the protagonists are played by actors from different racial backgrounds.

Casting has been an especially pressing problem for *Othello*. Richard Burbage played the role in black make-up, a tradition that persisted until the 1980s on stage and screen; it is still periodically employed in productions of Verdi's *Otello*. However, black actors were cast as early as the 1820s, when Ira Aldridge played Othello in provincial English theatres and, later, the West End, and since Laurence Fishburne's performance in Oliver Parker's film in 1995 they have dominated the role on screen. It is difficult, though, to present this as a simple progress narrative, and a number of actors and commentators have been uneasy about the effects of casting a black actor as Othello. In an influential essay written in the late 1990s, the British actor Hugh Quarshie describes it as 'a role written for a white actor in black make-up and for a predominantly white audience', and comments, '[o]f all the parts in the canon, perhaps Othello is the one which should most definitely not be played by a black actor'. 'If a black actor plays a role written for a white actor', he asks, 'does he not risk making racial stereotypes seem legitimate and even true[?]'[54] A decade earlier, in 1989, Quarshie co-directed a modern-dress production of *Othello* with Sue Dunderdale at the Greenwich Theatre, London, in which both Othello and Iago were played by black actors, Clarke Peters and Paul Barber; the play has also seen a 'photo-negative' production, directed by Jude Kelly at the Shakespeare Theatre, Washington, DC, in 1997, in which Othello was played by the white British actor Patrick Stewart and Iago by the African American actor Ron Canada. More recently, Vishal Bhardwaj relocated the narrative to rural India in his 2006 film *Omkara*, and transformed the racial difference between Othello and Iago into an issue of caste. If none of these productions has been fully successful in negotiating the play's racial politics, each suggests the complexity of the problem.

Violence

Violence is at the dark heart of Shakespearean tragedy, and actors' and directors' responses to it tell us as much about their own age as they tell us about their understanding of Shakespeare. Poel's *Macbeth* broke new ground in retaining the scene in which Lady Macduff's children are slaughtered on Macbeth's orders. Contending that 'Shakespeare's tragedies were written to be acted neither as grand opera nor as grand tragedy but as domestic tragedy', Poel argues that the major impact of the changes is to create 'a new interpretation of the character of Lady Macbeth, and the abandonment of the conventional stage-business of to-day'.[55] Elsewhere he makes it clear that the function of the changes was to set up a comparison between Lady Macbeth and Lady Macduff, writing that '[t]he appearance of Lady Macduff on the stage affords opportunity for the reflection that Duncan's murder would never have taken place had she been Macbeth's wife'.[56] However, as Carol Chillington Rutter notes, the scene has been used in recent British productions to mark 'a growing sense of pain and incomprehension at human atrocity on a global scale ... to focus culture's stunned revulsion to casual violence, to terrorism and to the slaughter of innocents, locating what the Victorians couldn't bear to look at in the violated space of domesticity'.[57]

Violence's capacity to challenge both aesthetic and societal conventions has exercised consistent pressure on the performance of Shakespeare's tragedies. As noted above, directors and audiences have occasionally found Shakespeare's violence unconvincing, but they have also considered it too real or disturbing to be performed. Poel himself omitted the blinding of Gloucester in *King Lear*, a practice adopted by many Victorian producers, while the rape and mutilation of Lavinia in *Titus Andronicus* has forced directors including Peter Brook, Julie Taymor and Yukio Ninagawa into textual cuts and/or stylization.[58] Taymor, who has directed *Titus* for stage and screen, comments, '[t]here is a danger in a literal and graphic portrayal of an image such as Lavinia's dismemberment. It is easily too grotesque and horrific, and can upstage the larger picture of events'.[59] However, this perspective is challenged by Pascale Aebischer, who argues that '[i]n the obscene figure of the dismembered and violated Lavinia, Shakespeare displays the unspeakable and unrepresentable in a manner that leaves the viewer or reader hardly any way of responding adequately without replicating and potentially even reinforcing the obscenity of her representation'.[60] In this reading, the obscenity of the violence against Lavinia is precisely the point; even now, Shakespeare's tragedies push at the limits of what is performable.

Two recent productions of *Macbeth* have thematized violence in rather different ways. The Folger Shakespeare Theatre's 2008 co-production with Two River Theater Company, directed by Aaron Posner and the stage-magician Teller, opened with a faux pre-show educational message about stage violence, one rudely interrupted when the speaker was herself unexpectedly stabbed. This set the tone for the production that followed, which was alert to both the play's violence and its moments of humour. Teller contributed a series of set-piece illusions, some expected – such as the appearance of the dagger in Act 2, Scene 1 – some less so. Particularly striking was the moment in Lady Macbeth's sleep-walking scene when, as Paul Harris describes, '[s]econds after she utters "out damned spot", splotches of bright red blood appear on the white nightgown of actress Kate Eastwood Norris, until the character is nearly drenched in the incriminating fluid' (Figure 6).[61] The effect was not dependent solely on these illusions; sound and other aspects of stage action were also important factors: fight director Dale Anthony Girard contributed 'harsh, earthy and convincing stage violence', while '[t]he percussive score by Kenny Wollesen – all bells and screeching wheels – feels less like accompaniment than audible needles to the nerves'.[62] Teller described the play as 'Shakespeare's supernatural horror story', and the production – strongly influenced by contemporary horror film – both supported his view that 'violence on a stage is a blast because you know it's not real . . . It's like the scary drop on a roller coaster – all the thrill, none of the hurt' and suggested that stage violence can be at once self-consciously artificial and viscerally effective.[63]

Teller's attention to the impact of stage violence was shared by a rather different production of *Macbeth* at Shakespeare's Globe in 2010, directed by Lucy Bailey. Bailey had directed a notoriously bloody production of *Titus Andronicus* at the Globe in 2006, in which summer heat, violent spectacle and the stifling effect of a black canvas velarium or roof contributed to a record number of spectators being evacuated during performances.[64] *Macbeth* pushed things even further. In an interview, Bailey asked, 'How do you do a play about night, and dark, and hell, in a sunlit open space?'[65] Although her question is not one that Shakespeare or his actors would have recognised, her solution was striking. She refashioned the Globe into a Dantean vision of Hell: spectators in the yard stood beneath black sheeting, with only their heads protruding, and were periodically confronted by 'writhing, blood-smeared bodies which suddenly sho[t] through slits in the cloth right next to them'.[66] The witches rose from slits in the stage surface which appeared to render it somehow porous, and the stage was surrounded by a semi-transparent curtain, giving the action 'an hallucinatory quality'.[67] Bagpipes wailed, bells tolled, and the ghost of Banquo, 'dripping blood, worm[ed] out of a vast platter of cooked meats'.[68] For many reviewers, this was good, gruesome fun in the same vein as the Folger *Macbeth*; Sam Marlowe, for instance, describes it as 'at once oozing with dark, pornographic Jacobean superstition and as crowd-pleasing and horribly titillating as an afternoon at the London Dungeon'.[69] Marlowe's allusion to a tourist attraction not far from Shakespeare's Globe neatly conveys his impression that the violence of Bailey's production was merely

Figure 6. Kate Eastwood Norris as Lady Macbeth in a 2008 production of *Macbeth*, directed by Teller and Aaron Posner.

theatrical display. However, some aspects of the production suggest a more serious purpose. The Thane of Cawdor, whose death takes place offstage in the 1623 text, was brought onstage, 'chained to a pillar, deprived of his tongue and, it seems, agonisingly garrotted', before his tongue was thrown at the groundlings.[70] Stage violence was not, therefore, merely entertaining spectacle, but an attempt to explore the darkest aspects of warfare and politics, in a deeply pessimistic reading of the play.

As this chapter has described, textual adaptation, stage spectacle and actors' performance styles and strategies all contribute to the impact of Shakespeare's tragedies on the stage and screen. However, these basic elements of theatrical and cinematic interpretation can still be controversial, nearly two hundred years after Lamb expressed his concerns about how tragedy should or could be performed. Bailey's production of *Macbeth* was generally well received, but one critic, Michael Billington, worried that its visual excess was a sign that British theatre is 'gradually retreating to a Victorian theatre of spectacle'.[71] Others expressed similar fears about a reversion to Victorian standards in Doran's 2008 *Hamlet*, in which the final words of the play were not Fortinbras's 'Go bid the soldiers shoot', but Horatio's 'Good night sweet prince, / And flights of angels sing thee to thy rest', arguing that this textual cut threw too much attention on Tennant's Hamlet. Stanley Wells, for instance, commented that it was a return to the romanticism of Irving and his contemporary, Herbert Beerbohm Tree.[72] Visual spectacle, textual emendation and the power of the star actor are all associated here with outmoded 'Victorian' models of performance. Yet if these strategies are potential liabilities they are also – as we have seen – at the heart of the performance of Shakespearean tragedy and its power to move and disturb successive generations of spectators.

Notes

1. 'On the Tragedies of Shakespeare, Considered with Reference to their Fitness for Stage Representation', *The Works of Charles Lamb*, 2 vols. (London: C. and J. Oliver, 1818), vol. II, pp. 1–36; 26, 34.
2. For background see Gail Marshall, ed., *Nineteenth-Century Shakespeare* (Cambridge University Press, 2012).
3. A. C. Bradley, *Shakespearean Tragedy: Lectures on Hamlet, Othello, King Lear, Macbeth* (London: Macmillan, 1904), p. 247; Harold Bloom, *Shakespeare and the Invention of the Human* (New York: Riverhead Books, 1998), p. 476.
4. Lamb, 'On the Tragedies of Shakespeare', p. 10.
5. *Ibid.*, pp. 20, 26.

6. *The Theatrical Review, or, New Companion to the Play-house*, 2 vols. (London, 1772), pp. 211, 212.

7. See 'Drury Lane Theatre', *The Standard*, 24 September 1857, p. 4.

8. 'Theatre: Drury Lane', *The Morning Post*, 11 February 1823, p. 3.

9. Wiltshire Stanton Austin and John Ralph, *The Lives of the Poets-Laureate* (London: Richard Bentley, 1853), p. 205; see also Jeffrey Kahan, 'Introduction: Shakespeare's *King Lear*', *King Lear: New Critical Essays*, ed. Kahan (New York: Routledge, 2008), pp. 1–103, 26.

10. 'Branagh's Hamlet as a Young Conservative', *The New York Times*, 24 December 1992, Section C, p. 9.

11. See J. S. Styan, *The Shakespeare Revolution* (Cambridge University Press, 1977), pp. 47–63; Marion O'Connor, *William Poel and the Elizabethan Stage Society* (Cambridge: Chadwyck Healy, 1987), pp. 18–21.

12. Michael Billington, 'The Cracker: Get Shorter', *The Guardian*, 10 May 1997, p. 10. Productions using the first quarto's placing of 'To be...' include Declan Donnellan's for Cheek by Jowl (1990), Tim Pigott-Smith's at the Regent's Park Open Air Theatre (1994), Greg Doran's for the RSC (2008) and Ian Rickson's at the Young Vic (2011).

13. *Oeuvres de J.F. Ducis*, 2 vols. (Paris: Nepveu, 1813), vol. II, p. 162.

14. *Ibid.*, p. 161.

15. 'Talma', *Blackwood's Magazine* 18 (September 1825): 297–302; 299. On Ducis's *Othello* see also John Golder, *Shakespeare for the Age of Reason: The Earliest Stage Adaptations of Jean-François Ducis 1769–1792* (Oxford: Voltaire Foundation, 1992); Julie Hankey, *Shakespeare in Production: Othello*, second edition (Cambridge University Press, 2005), pp. 51–3.

16. Hankey, *Shakespeare in Production: Othello*, p. 51.

17. Tim Arango, ' "Romeo and Juliet" Recast as Sectarian Tragedy that Unfolds in Modern Times', *International Herald Tribune*, 30 April 2012, news section, p. 2.

18. 'Shakespeare Tragedy set Amid Iraq Strife', *Agence France-Presse*, 24 April 2012. www. afp.com/en/node/65294.

19. *Ibid.*

20. R. A. Foakes, ed., *Henslowe's Diary* (Cambridge University Press, 2002), pp. 319–20.

21. The fullest recent account of early modern stage costume is Robert I. Lublin's *Costuming the Shakespearean Stage: Visual Codes of Representation in Early Modern Theatre and Culture* (Farnham: Ashgate, 2011).

22. *Macbeth, a Tragædy. With all the Alterations, Amendments, Additions, and New Songs. As it's now Acted at the Dukes Theatre* (London, 1674), pp. 1, 25, 49, 38, 44.

23. Quoted in John Munro, ed., *The Shakspere Allusion Book*, 2 vols. (London: Chatto and Windus, 1909), vol. II, pp. 92–3.

24. Bernice Kliman, *Shakespeare in Performance: Macbeth*, second edition (Manchester University Press, 2004), p. 18.

25. See John Wilders, ed., *Macbeth* (Cambridge University Press, 2004), p. 16.

26. Michael Dobson, *The Making of the National Poet: Shakespeare, Adaptation and Authorship* (Oxford: Clarendon Press, 1992), p. 93. See also Stephen Orgel,

'The Authentic Shakespeare', *Representations* 21 (1988): 1–25; Kliman, *Shakespeare in Performance*, p. 27.

27. On these productions see Dennis Bartholomeusz, *Macbeth and the Players* (Cambridge University Press, 1969). For a recent approach to costume and discussion of the costumes of various Lady Macbeths, see Barbara Hodgdon, 'Shopping in the Archives: Material Memories', *Shakespeare, Memory and Performance*, ed. Peter Holland (Cambridge University Press, 2006), pp. 135–67; 151–4.

28. 'Drama: Drury-Lane', *The Daily News*, 4 November 1864, p. 2. On choruses of witches see Kliman, *Shakespeare in Performance*, pp. 46–8.

29. *Macbeth . . . As performed at the Theatres Royal, Covent Garden and Drury Lane. Printed under the Authority of the Managers from the Prompt Book. With Remarks by Mrs Inchbald* (London: Longman, Hurst, Rees and Orme, 1808), p. 4.

30. Richard Foulkes, *Henry Irving: A Re-evaluation of the Pre-eminent Victorian Actor-Manager* (Aldershot: Ashgate, 2008), p. 151.

31. '"Macbeth" at the Lyceum', *The Standard*, 31 December 1888, p. 2.

32. Sybil Rosenfeld, *A Short History of Scene Design in Great Britain* (Oxford: Blackwell, 1973), p. 146.

33. O'Connor, *William Poel*, 90, quoting a playbill advertising the Elizabethan Stage Season at Fulham, 22–26 June 1909.

34. For a concise comparison of these productions see Dennis Kennedy, *Looking at Shakespeare: A Visual History of Twentieth-Century Performance*, second edition (Cambridge University Press, 2001), pp. 109–13.

35. Richard Jennings, ' "Macbeth" in Modern Dress. At the Court Theatre', *The Spectator*, 1 February 1928, p. 188.

36. Quoted in 'Court Theatre: "Macbeth" in Modern Dress', *The Times*, 7 February 1928, p. 12.

37. Claire Cochrane, *Shakespeare and the Birmingham Repertory Theatre, 1913–1929* (London: Society for Theatre Research, 1993), p. 144.

38. Jennings, ' "Macbeth" in Modern Dress', p. 188; Cochrane, *Shakespeare and the Birmingham Repertory Theatre*, p. 138.

39. Lamb, 'On the Tragedies of Shakespeare', p. 36.

40. Andrew Gurr, *The Shakespearean Stage*, third edition (Cambridge University Press, 1992), p. 226 (translation of Latin original).

41. *A Royal Arbor of Loyal Poesie* (London, 1663), pp. 21–2.

42. Munro, *Shakspere Allusion Book*, vol. II, p. 89.

43. On the variety of options available see Mary Maher, *Modern Hamlets and their Soliloquies* (Iowa City: University of Iowa Press, 2003), pp. xiv–xv.

44. Lamb, 'On the Tragedies of Shakespeare', p. 10.

45. *The Morning Post*, 8 March 1803, p. 3.

46. Julian Charles Young, *A Memoir of Charles Mayne Young, Tragedian*, 2 vols. (London: Macmillan, 1871), vol. I, pp. 41–2.

47. 'Fresh and Daring, Rylance's Prince Creates a Rapport That Nears Genius', *The Independent*, 10 June 2000, p. 7.

48. Susannah Clapp, 'There's Nothing Rotten in this State', *The Observer*, 6 May 2001, Review, p. 12.
49. Yasunari Takahashi, '*Hamlet* and the Anxiety of Modern Japan', *Shakespeare Survey* 48 (1995): 99–112; 104–5.
50. Munro, *Shakspere Allusion Book*, vol. 1, p. 272.
51. See, for instance, James Agate, *Brief Chronicles: A Survey of the Plays of Shakespeare and the Elizabethans in Actual Performance* (London: Jonathan Cape, 1943), pp. 248–9.
52. 'Madame Bernhardt as Hamlet', *The Era*, 17 June 1899, p. 13.
53. On such productions see Tony Howard, *Women as Hamlet: Performance and Interpretation in Theatre, Film and Fiction* (Cambridge University Press, 2007) and the essays in James C. Bulman, ed., *Shakespeare Re-Dressed: Cross-Gender Casting in Contemporary Performance* (Cranbury, NJ: Associated University Presses, 2008).
54. Hugh Quarshie, *Second Thoughts About Othello*, International Shakespeare Association Occasional Paper 7 (Chipping Camden: Clouds Hill Printers, 1999), p. 5. For further discussion see Virginia Mason Vaughan, *Performing Blackness on English Stages, 1500–1800* (Cambridge University Press, 2005), pp. 104–5; Ayanna Thompson, *Passing Strange: Shakespeare, Race and Contemporary America* (New York: Oxford University Press, 2011), pp. 97–117.
55. Quoted in Carol Chillington Rutter, *Shakespeare and Child's Play: Performing Lost Boys on Stage and Screen* (London: Routledge, 2007), p. 231.
56. Willam Poel, *Shakespeare in the Theatre* (London and Toronto: Sidgwick and Jackson, 1913), p. 61.
57. Rutter, *Shakespeare and Child's Play*, pp. 193–4.
58. On the theatrical and cinematic treatment of these moments see Pascale Aebischer, *Shakespeare's Violated Bodies: Stage and Screen Performances* (Cambridge University Press, 2004), pp. 24–63; Alexander Leggatt, *Shakespeare's Tragedies: Violation and Identity* (Cambridge University Press, 2005), pp. 8–28.
59. Eileen Blumenthal and Julie Taymor, *Julie Taymor: Playing with Fire* (New York: Abrams, 1999), p. 226.
60. Aebischer, *Shakespeare's Violated Bodies*, p. 30.
61. Paul Harris, 'Macbeth', *Variety*, 10–16 March 2008.
62. Missy Frederick, 'Folger's (and Teller's) Magical *Macbeth*', *DCist*, 4 March 2008 http://dcist.com/2008/03/04/folgers_and_tel.php; Peter Marks, 'At the Folger, a Wickedly Good "Macbeth"', *The Washington Post*, 4 March 2008, C01.
63. Geof Koss, 'Folger Production Gives *Macbeth* a Bold Makeover', *Roll Call*, 17 March 2008 www.rollcall.com/issues/53_109/-22608-1.html.
64. 'Globe Warns Over "Gruesome" Play', *BBC News*, 2 June 2006, http://news.bbc.co.uk/1/hi/entertainment/5042516.stm.
65. Nick Curtis, 'Lucy Bailey is Putting the Sex into Shakespeare', *The Evening Standard*, 21 April 2010 www.standard.co.uk/goingout/theatre/lucy-bailey-is-putting-the-sex-into-shakespeare-6461405.

66. Charles Spenser, 'Blood and Gore, but No Humanity', *The Daily Telegraph*, 3 May 2010, p. 23.
67. Michael Billington, 'Violence, Blood and Savage Spectacle in Scotland's Hell on Earth', *The Guardian*, 1 May 2010, p. 44.
68. Kate Bassett, 'Wait a Moment. Is That the Crack of Doom I See?', *The Independent on Sunday*, 9 May 2010, p. 58.
69. Sam Marlowe, Review of *Macbeth*, *Time Out*, 6 May 2010, p. 101.
70. Benedict Nightingale, 'He is Restless, Desperate and Scary – It's Strong Stuff', *The Times*, 1 May 2010, p. 21.
71. Billington, 'Violence'.
72. See Andrew James Hartley, 'Time Lord of Infinite Space: Celebrity Casting, Romanticism, and British Identity in the RSC's "*Doctor Who Hamlet*"', *Borrowers and Lenders* 4.2 (2009): 1–16; 8.

Further reading

Aebischer, Pascale, *Shakespeare's Violated Bodies: Stage and Screen Performances* (Cambridge University Press, 2004).
Dobson, Michael, ed., *Performing Shakespeare's Tragedies Today: The Actor's Perspective* (Cambridge University Press, 2006).
Gurr, Andrew, *The Shakespearean Stage*, third edition (Cambridge University Press, 1992).
Kennedy, Dennis, *Looking at Shakespeare: A Visual History of Twentieth-Century Performance*, second edition (Cambridge University Press, 2001).
Leggatt, Alexander, *Shakespeare's Tragedies: Violation and Identity* (Cambridge University Press, 2005).
Marshall, Gail, ed., *Nineteenth-Century Shakespeare* (Cambridge University Press, 2012).
Oya, Reiko, *Representing Shakespearean Tragedy: Garrick, the Kembles, and Kean* (Cambridge University Press, 2007).
Ritchie, Fiona and Peter Sabor, eds., *Shakespeare in the Eighteenth Century* (Cambridge University Press, 2012).
Stern, Tiffany, *Making Shakespeare: From Stage to Page* (London: Routledge, 2004).
Styan, J. S., *The Shakespeare Revolution* (Cambridge University Press, 1977).

Select bibliography

Adelman, Janet, *Suffocating Mothers: Fantasies of Maternal Origin in Shakespeare's Plays, 'Hamlet' to 'The Tempest'* (New York and London: Routledge, 1992).
  The Common Liar: An Essay on 'Antony and Cleopatra' (New Haven: Yale University Press, 1973).
Aebischer, Pascale, *Shakespeare's Violated Bodies: Stage and Screen Performances* (Cambridge University Press, 2004).
Allen, Michael J. B. and Kenneth Muir, eds., *Shakespeare's Plays in Quarto: A Facsimile Edition of Copies Primarily from the Henry E. Huntington Library* (Berkeley and Los Angeles: University of California Press, 1981).
Altman, J. B., *The Improbability of Othello: Rhetorical Anthropology and Shakespearean Selfhood* (Chicago and London: University of Chicago Press, 2010).
Anderson, Linda Marie, *A Kind of Wild Justice: Revenge in Shakespeare's Comedies* (Newark: University of Delaware Press, 1987).
Andrews, Michael Cameron, *'Hamlet*: Revenge and the Critical Mirror', *English Literary Renaissance* 8 (1978): 9–23.
Auden, W.H., *The Dyer's Hand* (London: Vintage, 1988).
Axton, Marie, *The Queen's Two Bodies: Drama and the Elizabethan Succession* (London: Royal Historical Society, 1977).
Ayres, Philip J., 'Degrees of Heresy: Justified Revenge and Elizabethan Narratives', *Studies in Philology* 69 (1972): 461–74.
Baldwin, T. W., *William Shakespere's Small Latine and Lesse Greeke*, 2 vols. (Urbana: University of Illinois Press, 1944).
Bartels, Emily, *Speaking of the Moor: From Alcazar to Othello* (Philadelphia: University of Pennsylvania Press, 2008).
Barton, Anne, *Shakespeare and the Idea of the Play* (New York: Greenwood, 1977).
Bate, Jonathan, ed., *The Romantics on Shakespeare* (London and New York: Penguin Books, 1992).
Bayley, John, *The Characters of Love* (London: Constable, 1960).
Belsey, Catherine, *Shakespeare and the Loss of Eden: The Construction of Family Values in Early Modern Culture* (London: Macmillan, 1999; New Brunswick, NJ: Rutgers University Press, 2000).
  The Subject of Tragedy: Identity and Difference in Renaissance Drama (London and New York: Routledge, 1985).

'Tragedy, Justice and the Subject', *1642: Literature and Power in the Seventeenth Century*, ed. Francis Barker (Colchester: University of Essex, 1981), pp. 166–86.

Bennett, Susan, *Performing Nostalgia: Shifting Shakespeare and the Contemporary Past* (London and New York: Routledge, 1996).

Bentley, Gerald Eades, *The Profession of Dramatist in Shakespeare's Time* (Princeton University Press, 1971).

Berger, Harry, Jr, 'Text against Performance: the Gloucester Family Romance', *Shakespeare's Rough Magic: Essays in Honor of C. L. Barber*, ed. Peter Erickson and Coppélia Kahn (Newark, NJ: University of Delaware Press, 1985).

Bevington, David, *Murder Most Foul: Hamlet through the Ages* (Oxford University Press, 2011).

'Mutius: an Obstacle Removed in *Titus Andronicus*', *George Peele*, ed. David Bevington, (London: Ashgate, 2011), pp. 449–62.

Tudor Drama and Politics (Cambridge, MA: Harvard University Press, 1968).

Blayney, Peter W. M., *The First Folio of Shakespeare* (Washington, DC: The Folger Shakespeare Library, 1991).

Booth, Stephen, *'King Lear', 'Macbeth', Indefinition, and Tragedy* (New Haven: Yale University Press, 1983).

Bowers, Fredson, *Elizabethan Revenge Tragedy, 1587–1642* (Princeton University Press, 1940).

Bradbrook, Muriel, *Themes and Conventions in Elizabethan Tragedy* (Cambridge University Press, 1960).

Braden, Gordon, *Renaissance Tragedy and the Senecan Tradition: Anger's Privilege* (New Haven and London: Yale University Press, 1985).

Bradley, A. C., *Oxford Lectures on Poetry* (London: Macmillan, 1909, rpt 1962).

Shakespearean Tragedy: Lectures on 'Hamlet', 'Othello', 'King Lear', and 'Macbeth' (London: Macmillan, 1904; 2nd edn, 1905).

Brodwin, Leonora, *Elizabethan Love Tragedy, 1587–1625* (London and New York University Presses, 1971).

Broude, Ronald, 'Revenge and Revenge Tragedy in Renaissance England', *Renaissance Quarterly* 28 (1975): 38–58.

Brower, Reuben, *Hero and Saint: Shakespeare and the Graeco-Roman Heroic Tradition* (Oxford: Clarendon Press, 1971).

Burckhardt, Sigurd, 'How Not to Murder Caesar', *Shakespearean Meanings* (Princeton University Press, 1968), p. 9.

Bushnell, Rebecca W., *Tragedies of Tyrants: Political Thought and Theater in the English Renaissance* (Ithaca, NY: Cornell University Press, 1985)

Callaghan, Dympna, *Women and Gender in Renaissance Tragedy* (Atlantic Highlands, NJ: Harvester Wheatsheaf, 1989).

Campbell, Lily B., *Shakespeare's Tragic Heroes: Slaves of Passion* (Cambridge University Press, 1930).

'Theories of Revenge in Renaissance England', *Modern Philology* 28 (1931): 281–96.

Cavell, Stanley, *Disowning Knowledge in Six Plays of Shakespeare* (Cambridge University Press, 1987).

Chambers, E. K., *William Shakespeare: A Study of Facts and Problems*, 2 vols. (Oxford: Clarendon Press, 1930).

Charnes, Linda, *Notorious Identity: Materializing the Subject in Shakespeare's Plays* (Cambridge, MA: Harvard University Press, 1993).

Clemen, Wolfgang, *Shakespeare's Dramatic Art* (London: Methuen, 1972).

Coghill, Nevill, *Shakespeare's Professional Skills* (Cambridge University Press, 1964).

Cole, Susan, *The Absent One: Mourning Ritual, Tragedy, and the Performance of Ambivalence* (University Park: Pennsylvania State University Press, 1985).

Collinson, Patrick, *The Religion of Protestants: The Church in English Society, 1559–1625* (Oxford University Press, 1982).

Cooper, Helen, *The English Romance in Time: Transforming Motifs from Geoffrey of Monmouth to the Death of Shakespeare* (Oxford University Press, 2004).

Cox, John D., *Shakespeare and the Dramaturgy of Power* (Princeton University Press, 1989).

Crockett, Bryan, *The Play of Paradox: Stage and Sermon in Renaissance England* (Philadelphia: University of Pennsylvania Press, 1996).

Cunliffe, John William, *The Influence of Seneca on Elizabethan Tragedy: An Essay* (London: Macmillan, 1893).

Dabhoiwala, Faramerz, *The Origins of Sex: A History of the First Sexual Revolution* (London: Allen Lane, 2011).

Davies, Horton, *Worship and Theology in England from Cranmer to Hooker 1534–1603*, 5 vols. (Princeton University Press, 1970).

Davis, Lloyd, 'Embodied Masculinity in Shakespeare's *Julius Caesar*', *Entertext* 2, 1 (2003): 161–82.

De Grazia, Margreta, *'Hamlet' without Hamlet* (Cambridge University Press, 2007).

Shakespeare Verbatim: The Reproduction of Authenticity and the 1790 Apparatus (Oxford: Clarendon Press, 1991).

Dickey, Franklin M., *Not Wisely But Too Well: Shakespeare's Love Tragedies* (San Marino, CA: Huntington Library, 1957).

Diehl, Huston, *Staging Reform, Reforming the Stage: Protestantism and Popular Theater in Early Modern Drama* (Ithaca, NY: Cornell University Press, 1997).

Dillon, Janette, 'Is There a Performance in this Text?', *Shakespeare Quarterly* 45 (1994): 74–86.

Dobson, Michael, *The Making of the National Poet: Shakespeare, Adaptation and Authorship, 1660–1769* (Oxford: Clarendon Press, 1992).

Performing Shakespeare's Tragedies Today: The Actor's Perspective (Cambridge University Press, 2006).

Dollimore, Jonathan, *Radical Tragedy: Religion, Ideology and Power in the Drama of Shakespeare and his Contemporaries* (Brighton: Harvester Press, 1984).

Doran, Madeleine, 'History and Tragedy', *Endeavors of Art: A Study of Form in Elizabethan Drama* (Madison: University of Wisconsin Press, 1954).

Drakakis, John, ed., *Shakespearean Tragedy* (London: Longman, 1992).

Duffy, Eamon, *The Stripping of the Altars: Traditional Religion in England c. 1400–1580* (New Haven, CT: Yale University Press, 1992).

Dutton, Richard, Alison Findlay and Richard L. Wilson, eds., *Lancastrian Shakespeare: Region, Religion and Patronage* (Manchester University Press, 2004).

Elias, Norbert, *The Civilizing Process*, trans. Edmund Jephcott, 2 vols. (Oxford: Blackwell, 1982).

Ellis-Fermor, Una, 'The Equilibrium of Tragedy', *The Frontiers of Drama* (London: Methuen, 1948).

Elton, William R., *King Lear and the Gods* (San Marino, CA: Huntington Library, 1966).

Erne, Lukas, ed., *The First Quarto of 'Romeo and Juliet'* (Cambridge University Press, 2007).

Esler, Anthony, *The Aspiring Mind of the Elizabethan Younger Generation* (Durham, NC: University of North Carolina Press, 1966).

Falco, Raphael, *Charismatic Authority in Early Modern English Tragedy* (Baltimore, MD: Johns Hopkins University Press, 2000).

Fernie, Ewan, *Shame in Shakespeare* (London and New York: Routledge, 2002).

Fineman, Joel, *Shakespeare's Perjured Eye: The Invention of Poetic Subjectivity in the Sonnets* (Berkeley: University of California Press, 1986).

Fitz, Linda T., 'Egyptian Queens and Male Reviewers: Sexist Attitudes in *Antony and Cleopatra* Criticism', *Shakespeare Quarterly* 28 (1977): 217–316.

Foakes, R. A., *'Hamlet' Versus 'Lear': Cultural Politics and Shakespeare's Art* (Cambridge University Press, 1993).

Fowler, Alistair, *Kinds of Literature: An Introduction to the Theory of Genres and Modes* (Oxford: Clarendon Press, 1982).

Frye, Northrop, *Anatomy of Criticism* (London: Penguin, 1957).
  Fools of Time: Studies in Shakespearean Tragedy (University of Toronto Press, 1991).

Frye, Roland Mushat, *Shakespeare: The Art of the Dramatist* (London: Allen and Unwin, 1982).

Gardiner, Helen, *Shakespeare and Religion* (London: Faber, 1971).

Garner, Shirley Nelson and Madelon Sprengnether, eds., *Shakespearean Tragedy and Gender* (Bloomington: Indiana University Press, 1996).

Giddens, Eugene, '"Honorable Men": Militancy and Masculinity in *Julius Caesar*', *Renaissance Forum* 5, 2 (2001): 1–16.

Gillies, John, *Shakespeare and the Geography of Difference* (Cambridge University Press, 1994).

Girard, René, *Violence and the Sacred*, trans. Patrick Gregory (Baltimore, MD: Johns Hopkins University Press, 1977).

Goldberg, Jonathan, *James I and the Politics of Literature: Jonson, Shakespeare, Donne and Their Contemporaries* (Baltimore, MD: Johns Hopkins University Press, 1983).

Grady, Hugh, *The Modernist Shakespeare* (Oxford: Clarendon Press, 1991).

Graham, Kenneth J. E., *The Performance of Conviction: Plainness and Rhetoric in the Early English Renaissance* (Ithaca, NY: Cornell University Press, 1994).

Green, Douglas E., 'Interpreting "Her Martyr'd Signs": Gender and Tragedy in *Titus Andronicus*', *Shakespeare Quarterly* 40 (1989): 317–26.

Greenblatt, Stephen, *Hamlet in Purgatory* (Princeton University Press, 2002).

Renaissance Self-Fashioning from More to Shakespeare (University of Chicago Press, 1980).

'Shakespeare and the Ethics of Authority', *Shakespeare and Early Modern Political Thought*, ed. David Armitage, Conal Condren and Andrew Fitzmaurice (Cambridge University Press, 2009), pp. 64–79.

Shakespearean Negotiations: The Circulation of Social Energy in Renaissance England (Berkeley: University of California Press, 1988).

Greg, W. W., *The Editorial Problem in Shakespeare*, 3rd edn (Oxford: Clarendon Press, 1954).

The Shakespeare First Folio: Its Bibliographical and Textual History (Oxford: Clarendon Press, 1955).

Griswold, Wendy, *Renaissance Revivals: City Comedy and Revenge Tragedy in the London Theatre, 1576–1980* (Chicago and London: University of Chicago Press, 1986).

Gurr, Andrew, *The Shakespearean Stage*, 3rd edn (Cambridge University Press, 1992).

Hall, Kim F., *Things of Darkness: Economies of Race and Gender in Early Modern England* (Ithaca, NY: Cornell University Press, 1995).

Hallett, Charles and Elaine S. Hallett, *The Revenger's Madness: A Study of Revenge Tragedy Motifs* (Lincoln: University of Nebraska Press, 1980).

Halliwell, Stephen. *Aristotle's Poetics* (London: Duckworth, 1986).

Hammond, Paul, *The Strangeness of Tragedy* (Oxford University Press, 2009).

Hanna, Sara, 'Shakespeare's Greek World: the Temptations of the Sea', *Playing the Globe: Genre and Geography in Renaissance Drama*, ed. John Gillies and Virginia Mason Vaughan (Madison: Fairleigh Dickinson University Press, 1998), pp. 107–28.

Harbage, Alfred, *Twentieth-Century Views of Shakespeare's Tragedies* (Englewood Cliffs, NJ: Prentice-Hall, 1964).

Hegel, Georg Wilhelm Friedrich, *Aesthetics: Lectures on Fine Art*, ed. and trans. T. M. Knox, 2 vols. (Oxford University Press, 1975).

Hegel on Tragedy, ed. Anne and Henry Paolucci (New York: Harper and Row, 1975).

Heller, Agnes, *The Time is out of Joint: Shakespeare as Philosopher of History* (Lanham, MD: Rowan and Littlefield, 2002).

Henn, T. R., *The Harvest of Tragedy* (London: Methuen, 1956).

Herman, Peter, 'Tragedy and the Crisis of Authority in Shakespeare's *Romeo and Juliet*', *Intertext* 1–2 (2008): 89–109.

Hibbard, G. R., '*King Lear*: a Retrospect', *Shakespeare Survey* 33 (1980): 1–12.

Hillman, David, 'Visceral Knowledge: Shakespeare, Skepticism, and the Interior of the Early Modern Body', *The Body in Parts: Fantasies of Corporeality in Early Modern England*, ed. David Hillman and Carla Mazzio (New York and London: Routledge, 1997), pp. 81–105.

Hinman, Charlton, *The Printing and Proof-Reading of the First Folio of Shakespeare*, 2 vols. (Oxford: Clarendon Press, 1963).

Hinman, Charlton, ed., *The Norton Facsimile: The First Folio of Shakespeare*, 2nd edn, intro. by Peter W. M. Blayney (New York: W. W. Norton, 1996).

Hodgdon, Barbara, 'Doing the Egyptian', *The Shakespeare Trade: Performances and Appropriations* (Philadelphia: University of Pennsylvania Press, 1998), pp. 81–94.

Homan, Sidney, *Shakespeare's Theater of Presence* (Lewisburg: University of Kentucky Press, 1986).

Honigmann, E. A. J., *The Stability of Shakespeare's Text* (London: Edward Arnold, 1965).

Hopkins, Lisa, *The Cultural Uses of the Caesars on the Renaissance Stage* (Aldershot and Burlington, VT: Ashgate, 2008).

Howard, Jean E., *Shakespeare's Art of Orchestration* (Urbana: University of Illinois Press, 1984).

Hunter, G. K., *Dramatic Identities and Cultural Tradition: Studies in Shakespeare and his Contemporaries* (Liverpool University Press, 1978).

'The Heroism of Hamlet', *Hamlet*, ed. J. R. Brown and Bernard Harris (Stratford-upon-Avon Studies, 5; London: Arnold, 1963).

Hunter, Robert Grams, *Shakespeare and the Comedy of Forgiveness* (New York: Columbia University Press, 1965).

Hutson, Lorna, *The Invention of Suspicion: Law And Mimesis in Shakespeare and Renaissance Drama* (Oxford University Press, 2007).

Ioppolo, Grace, *Revising Shakespeare* (Cambridge, MA: Harvard University Press, 1991).

Jackson, Ken, ' "One Wish" or the Possibility of the Impossible: Derrida, the Gift and God in *Timon of Athens*', *Shakespeare Quarterly* 52, 1 (2001): 34–66.

Jacoby, Susan, *Wild Justice: The Evolution of Revenge* (New York: Harper & Row, 1983).

Jones, Emrys, *The Origins of Shakespeare* (Oxford University Press, 1977).

Hamlet and Oedipus, rev. edn (New York: Doubleday, 1949, 1954).

Scenic Form in Shakespeare (Oxford: Clarendon Press, 1971).

Jones, John, *On Aristotle and Greek Tragedy* (Stanford University Press, 1962).

Jowett, John, 'After Oxford: Recent Developments in Textual Studies', *The Shakespearean International Yearbook*, ed. W. R. Elton and John M. Mucciolo (Aldershot: Ashgate, 1999), pp. 65–86.

Kahn, Coppélia, ' "Magic of Bounty": *Timon of Athens*, Jacobean Patronage, and Maternal Power', *Shakespeare Quarterly* 38, 1 (1987): 34–57.

Kastan, David Scott, ' "His Semblable Is His Mirror": Hamlet and the Imitation of Revenge', *Shakespeare Studies* 19 (1987): 111–24.

' "Proud Majesty Made a Subject": Representing Authority on the Early Modern Stage', *Shakespeare After Theory* (London: Routledge, 1999).

Shakespeare and the Shapes of Time (Hanover, NH: University Press of New England, 1982).

Kaufman, Peter, *Prayer, Despair and Drama* (Urbana and Chicago: University of Illinois Press, 1996).

Kennedy, Dennis, *Looking at Shakespeare: A Visual History of Twentieth-Century Performance*, 2nd edn (Cambridge University Press, 2001).

Kerrigan, John, *Revenge Tragedy: Aeschylus to Armageddon* (New York: Oxford University Press, 1996).

Keyishian, Harry, *The Shapes of Revenge: Victimization, Vengeance, and Vindictiveness in Shakespeare* (Atlantic Highlands, NJ: Humanities Press, 1995).

King, John N., *Tudor Royal Iconography* (Princeton University Press, 1989).

Kirsch, Arthur C., *The Passions of Shakespeare's Tragic Heroes* (Charlottesville: University Press of Virginia, 1990).

Knapp, Jeff, *Shakespeare's Tribe: Church, Nation and Theater in Shakespeare's England* (Chicago and London: University of Chicago Press, 2002).

Kottman, Paul A., 'Defying the Stars: Tragic Love and the Struggle for Freedom in *Romeo and Juliet*', *Shakespeare Quarterly* 63 (2012): 1–38.

Tragic Conditions in Shakespeare: Disinheriting the Globe (Baltimore, MD: Johns Hopkins University Press, 2009).

Kottman, Paul A., ed., *Philosophers on Shakespeare* (Stanford University Press, 2009).

Kyd, Thomas, *The Spanish Tragedy*, ed. Philip Edwards (London: Methuen, 1959).

Lamb, Margaret, *Antony and Cleopatra on the English Stage* (London: Associated University Presses, 1980).

Leech, Clifford, *Tragedy* (London: Methuen, 1969).

Leggatt, Alexander, *Shakespeare's Political Drama: The History Plays and the Roman Plays* (London: Routledge, 1988).

Shakespeare's Tragedies: Violation and Identity (Cambridge University Press, 2005).

Lever, J. W., *The Tragedy of State* (London: Methuen, 1971).

Levin, Harry, *The Overreacher* (Cambridge, MA: Harvard University Press, 1952).

Limon, Jerzy, 'Revenge Tragedy, or, a Decayed Form – a Review Essay', *Southern Humanities Review* 16 (1982): 257–67.

Loomba, Ania, 'Shakespeare and Cultural Difference', *Alternative Shakespeares* 2, ed. Terence Hawkes (London: Routledge, 1996).

Lucas, F. L., *Tragedy in Relation to Aristotle's Poetics* (London: Hogarth Press, 1927).

Lyne, Raphael, *Shakespeare, Rhetoric and Cognition* (Cambridge University Press 2011).

Mack, Maynard, 'The World of *Hamlet*', *Yale Review*, new series, 41 (1951–2): 515.

Maguire, Laurie E., *Shakespearean Suspect Texts* (Cambridge University Press, 1996).

Mahood, M. M., *Shakespeare's Wordplay* (London: Methuen, 1957).

Marsden, Jean I., *The Re-imagined Text: Shakespeare, Adaptation, and Eighteenth-Century Literary Theory* (Lexington: University Press of Kentucky, 1995).

Marshall, Cynthia, 'Man of Steel Done Got the Blues: Melancholic Subversion of Presence in *Antony and Cleopatra*', *Shakespeare Quarterly* 44 (1993): 385–408.

Marshall, Gail, ed., *Nineteenth-Century Shakespeare* (Cambridge University Press, 2012).

Mason, H. A., *Shakespeare's Tragedies of Love* (London: Chatto and Windus, 1970).

Maus, Katharine Eisaman, *Inwardness and Theater in the English Renaissance* (Chicago and London: University of Chicago Press, 1995).

McAlindon, T., 'Cultural Materialism and the Ethics of Reading: or, the Radicalizing of Jacobean Tragedy', *The Modern Language Review* 90 (1995): 830–46.

Shakespeare's Tragic Cosmos (Cambridge University Press, 1991).

'Tragedy, *King Lear*, and the Politics of the Heart', *Shakespeare Survey* 44 (1992): 85–90.

McDonald, Russ, *Shakespeare and the Arts of Language* (Oxford University Press, 2001).

McEachern, Claire, *The Poetics of English Nationhood, 1590–1612* (Cambridge University Press, 1996).

McEachern, Claire and Debora Shuger, eds., *Religion and Culture in Renaissance England* (Cambridge University Press, 1997).

McElroy, Bernard, *Shakespeare's Mature Tragedies* (Princeton University Press, 1973).

Mehl, Dieter, *Shakespeare's Tragedies: An Introduction* (Cambridge University Press, 1986).

Mercer, Peter, *Hamlet and the Acting of Revenge* (University of Iowa Press, 1987).

Miles, Gary B., 'How Roman are Shakespeare's "Romans"?', *Shakespeare Quarterly* 41, 3 (1989): 257–83.

Miola, Robert S., *Shakespeare and Classical Comedy: The Influence of Plautus and Terence* (Oxford University Press, 1994).

Shakespeare and Classical Tragedy: The Influence of Seneca (Oxford: Clarendon Press, 1992).

Shakespeare's Rome (Cambridge University Press, 1983).

Montrose, Louis, *The Purpose of Playing: Shakespeare and the Cultural Politics of the Elizabethan Theatre* (University of Chicago Press, 1996).

Mortimer, Nigel, *John Lydgate's Fall of Princes: Narrative Tragedy in its Literary and Political Contexts* (Oxford University Press, 2005).

Moschovakis, Nicholas R., 'Irreligious Piety and Christian History: Persecution and Pagan Anachronism in *Titus Adronicus*', *Shakespeare Quarterly* 53, 4 (2002): 460–86.

Muir, Kenneth, *Shakespeare's Tragic Sequence* (London: Methuen, 1972).

Munro, Lucy, 'Tragic Forms', *The Cambridge Companion to Renaissance Tragedy*, ed. Emma Smith, and Garrett A. Sullivan, Jr (Cambridge University Press, 2010), pp. 86–101.

Nevo, Ruth, *Tragic Form in Shakespeare* (Princeton University Press, 1972).

Newman, Karen, 'Cultural Capital's Gold Standard: Shakespeare and the Critical Apostrophe in Renaissance Studies', *Discontinuities: New Essays in Renaissance Literature and Criticism*, ed. Viviana Comensoli and Paul Stevens (University of Toronto Press, 1998), pp. 96–113.

Nietzsche, Friedrich, '*The Birth of Tragedy*' and '*The Genealogy of Morals*', trans. Francis Golffing (New York: Doubleday, 1956).

O'Connell, Michael, *The Idolatrous Eye: Iconoclasm and Theater in Early Modern England* (Oxford University Press, 2000).

Orgel, Stephen, 'The Authentic Shakespeare', *Representations* 21 (1988): 1–25.

'Nobody's Perfect: or, Why Did the English Stage Take Boys for Women?', *South Atlantic Quarterly* 88 (1989): 7–29.

Orgel, Stephen and Sean Keilen, eds., *Shakespeare and the Editorial Tradition* (New York: Garland, 1999).

Ozment, Steven, *The Age of Reform 1250–1550* (New Haven, CT: Yale University Press, 1980).

  When Fathers Ruled: Family Life in Reformation Europe (Cambridge, MA: Harvard University Press, 1983).

Oya, Reiko, *Representing Shakespearean Tragedy: Garrick, the Kembles, and Kean* (Cambridge University Press, 2007).

Palfrey, Simon and Tiffany Stern, *Shakespeare in Parts* (Oxford University Press, 2007).

Parker, Kenneth, *William Shakespeare: Antony and Cleopatra* (Tavistock: Northcote House, 2000).

Parker, Patricia and Geoffrey Hartman, eds., *Shakespeare and the Question of Theory* (London: Methuen, 1985).

Paster, Gail Kern, *Humoring the Body: Emotions and the Shakespearean Stage* (Chicago and London: University of Chicago Press, 2004).

  The Idea of the City in the Age of Shakespeare (Athens: University of Georgia Press, 1985).

Patterson, Annabel, *Shakespeare and the Popular Voice* (Oxford University Press, 1989).

Paulin, Roger, *The Critical Reception of Shakespeare in Germany 1682–1914: Native Literatures and Foreign Genius* (New York: George Olms Verlag, 2003).

Prosser, Eleanor, *Hamlet and Revenge*, 2nd edn (Stanford University Press, 1971).

Puttenham, George, *The Arte of English Poesie (1589)*, ed. G. D. Willcock and A. Walker (Cambridge University Press, 1936).

Rabkin, Norman, *Shakespeare and the Common Understanding* (New York: Free Press, 1967).

Rackin, Phyllis, 'Shakespeare's Boy Cleopatra, the Decorum of Nature, and the Golden World of Poetry', *PMLA* 87 (1972): 201–12.

Rebhorn, Wayne A., 'The Crisis of the Aristocracy in *Julius Caesar*', *Renaissance Quarterly* 43, 1 (1990): 75–111.

Reiss, Timothy, *Mirages of the Self: Patterns of Personhood in Ancient and Early Modern Europe* (Stanford University Press, 2003).

Richards, I. A., *Principles of Literary Criticism* (London: Routledge, 1926).

Ritchie, Fiona and Peter Sabor, eds., *Shakespeare in the Eighteenth Century* (Cambridge University Press, 2012).

Rose, Mark, *Shakespearean Design* (Cambridge, MA: Belknap Press of Harvard University Press, 1972).

Rosenmeyer, Thomas G., *Senecan Drama and Stoic Cosmology* (Berkeley, Los Angeles, and London: University of California Press, 1989).

Rossiter, A. P., *Angel with Horns: Fifteen Lectures on Shakespeare* (London: Hutchinson, 1961).

Rozett, Martha Tucker, *The Doctrine of Election and the Emergence of Elizabethan Tragedy* (Princeton University Press, 1984).

Rutter, Carol Chillington, *Enter the Body: Women and Representation on Shakespeare's Stage* (London: Routledge, 2001).

Sanders, Eve Rachel, 'The Body of the Actor in *Coriolanus*', *Shakespeare Quarterly* 57, 4 (2006): 387–412

Schoenfeldt, Michael C., *Bodies and Selves in Early Modern England: Physiology and Inwardness in Spenser, Shakespeare, Herbert, and Milton* (Cambridge University Press, 1999).

Schwartz, Murray and Coppélia Kahn, eds., *Representing Shakespeare: New Psychoanalytic Essays* (Baltimore, MD: Johns Hopkins University Press, 1980).

Scott, Amy, '"Romans, Countrymen and Lovers": Performing Politics, Sovereign Amity, and Masculinity in *Julius Caesar*', *Renaissance Papers* (2003): 99–117.

Seneca, *Four Tragedies and 'Octavia'*, trans. E. F. Watling (London: Penguin, 1966).

Sharrock, Alison, *Reading Roman Comedy: Poetics and Playfulness in Plautus and Terence* (Cambridge University Press, 2005).

Shuger, Debora, *Habits of Thought in the English Renaissance: Religion, Politics, and the Dominant Culture* (Berkeley: University of California Press, 1990).

Sibly, John, 'The Duty of Revenge in Tudor and Stuart Drama', *Review of English Literature* 8 (1967): 46–54.

Sidney, Sir Philip, *An Apology for Poetry* (1595), ed. Geoffrey Shepherd (London: Nelson, 1965).

Siegel, Paul N., '"Hamlet, Revenge": The Uses and Abuses of Historical Criticism', *Shakespeare Survey* 45 (1993): 15–26.

Siemon, James R., *Shakespearean Iconoclasm* (Berkeley: University of California Press, 1985).

Simpson, Percy, 'The Theme of Revenge in Elizabethan Tragedy', *Proceedings of the British Academy* 21 (London: Humphrey Milford, 1935).

Singh, Jyotsna, 'Renaissance Antitheatricality, Antifeminism, and Shakespeare's *Antony and Cleopatra*', *Renaissance Drama* 20 (1989): 99–121.

Smith, Bruce, *Homosexual Desire in Shakespeare's England: A Cultural Poetics* (Chicago and London: University of Chicago Press, 1991).

  Shakespeare and Masculinity (Oxford University Press, 2000).

Smith, Emma, *Shakespeare's Tragedies* (Oxford: Blackwell, 2004).

Spencer, T. J. B., '"Greeks" and "Merrygreeks": a Background to *Timon of Athens* and *Troilus and Cressida*', *Essays on Shakespeare and Elizabethan Drama in Honor of Hardin Craig*, ed. Richard Hosley (Columbia: University of Missouri Press, 1962), pp. 223–33.

  'Shakespeare and the Elizabethan Romans', *Shakespeare Survey* 10 (1957): 27–38.

Spurgeon, Caroline, *Shakespeare's Imagery and What it Tells Us* (1935; rpt Boston: Beacon Hill Press, 1958).

Stavanage, Liberty, '"I fear she cannot love at all": Unnatural Female Sexuality in the Revenge Tragedy', *Genre: An International Journal of Literature and the Arts* 28 (2008): 125–43.

Stern, Tiffany, *Making Shakespeare: From Stage to Page* (London: Routledge, 2004).

Styan, J. S., *The Shakespeare Revolution* (Cambridge University Press, 1977).

Szondi, Peter, *An Essay on the Tragic* (Stanford University Press, 2002).

Szonyi, György E. and Rowland Wymer, eds., *The Iconography of Power: Ideas and Images of Rulership on the English Renaissance Stage* (Szeged: JATE Press, 2000).

Tassi, Marguerite A., *Women and Revenge in Shakespeare: Gender, Genre, and Ethics* (Cranbury, NJ: Associated University Presses, 2011).

Taylor, Gary and Michael Warren, eds., *The Division of the Kingdoms* (Oxford: Clarendon Press, 1983).

Thompson, Marvin and Ruth Thompson, eds., *Shakespeare and the Sense of Performance* (Newark: University of Delaware Press, 1990).

Urkowitz, Steven, *Shakespeare's Revision of 'King Lear'* (Princeton University Press, 1980).

Vickers, Brian, *Appropriating Shakespeare: Contemporary Critical Quarrels* (New Haven and London: Yale University Press, 1993).

Shakespeare, Co-Author (Oxford University Press, 2002).

Shakespeare: The Critical Heritage, 6 vols. (London: Routledge, 1974).

Waith, Eugene M., *Ideas of Greatness: Heroic Drama in England* (London: Hutchinson, 1971).

Walker, Greg, *Writing under Tyranny: English Literature and the Henrician Reformation* (Oxford University Press, 2005).

Watson, Robert N., *Shakespeare and the Hazards of Ambition* (Cambridge, MA: Harvard University Press, 1984).

'Shakespeare's New Words', *Shakespeare Survey* 65 (2012): 358–77.

Wayne, Valerie, ed., *The Matter of Difference: Materialist Feminist Criticism of Shakespeare* (Ithaca, NY, and London: Cornell University Press, 1991).

Wiemann, Robert, 'Representation and Performance: the Uses of Authority in Shakespeare's Theater', *Materialist Shakespeare: A History*, ed. Ivo Kamps (London: Verso, 1995), pp. 198–217.

Wells, Robin Headlam, *Shakespeare, Politics and the State* (Basingstoke: Macmillan, 1986).

Wells, Stanley, *Re-Editing Shakespeare for the Modern Reader* (Oxford: Clarendon Press, 1984).

Wells, Stanley, ed., *The Cambridge Companion to Shakespeare Studies* (Cambridge University Press, 1986).

Werstine, Paul, 'A Century of "Bad" Shakespeare Quartos', *Shakespeare Quarterly* 50 (1999): 310–33.

'Narratives about Printed Shakespeare Texts: "Foul Papers" and "Bad" Quartos', *Shakespeare Quarterly* 41 (1990): 67–86.

Wheeler, Richard P., *Shakespeare's Development and the Problem Comedies: Turn and Counter-Turn* (Berkeley: University of California Press, 1981).

Whigham, Frank and Wayne A. Rebhorn, eds., *The Art of English Poesy by George Puttenham* (Ithaca, NY: Cornell University Press, 2007).

White, Paul, *Theatre and Reformation* (Cambridge University Press, 1993).

Williams, Raymond, *Modern Tragedy* (London: Chatto and Windus, 1966).

Willis, Debora, '"The gnawing vulture": Revenge, Trauma Theory, and *Titus Andronicus*', *Shakespeare Quarterly* 53, 1 (2002): 21–52.

Woodbridge, Linda, *English Revenge Drama: Money, Resistance, Equality* (Cambridge University Press, 2010).

Wright, George T., *Shakespeare's Metrical Art* (Berkeley and Los Angeles: University of California Press, 1988).

Index

CAMBRIDGE COMPANIONS TO...

Authors

Edward Albee edited by STEPHEN J. BOTTOMS
Margaret Atwood edited by CORAL ANN HOWELLS
W. H. Auden edited by STAN SMITH
Jane Austen edited by EDWARD COPELAND and JULIET McMASTER (second edition)
Beckett edited by JOHN PILLING
Bede edited by SCOTT DEGREGORIO
Aphra Behn edited by DEREK HUGHES and JANET TODD
Walter Benjamin edited by DAVID S. FERRIS
William Blake edited by MORRIS EAVES
Brecht edited by PETER THOMSON and GLENDYR SACKS (second edition)
The Brontës edited by HEATHER GLEN
Bunyan edited by ANNE DUNAN-PAGE
Frances Burney edited by PETER SABOR
Byron edited by DRUMMOND BONE
Albert Camus edited by EDWARD J. HUGHES
Willa Cather edited by MARILEE LINDEMANN
Cervantes edited by ANTHONY J. CASCARDI
Chaucer edited by PIERO BOITANI and JILL MANN (second edition)
Chekhov edited by VERA GOTTLIEB and PAUL ALLAIN
Kate Chopin edited by JANET BEER
Caryl Churchill edited by ELAINE ASTON and ELIN DIAMOND
Coleridge edited by LUCY NEWLYN
Wilkie Collins edited by JENNY BOURNE TAYLOR
Joseph Conrad edited by J. H. STAPE
H. D. edited by NEPHIE J. CHRISTODOULIDES and POLINA MACKAY
Dante edited by RACHEL JACOFF (second edition)
Daniel Defoe edited by JOHN RICHETTI
Don DeLillo edited by JOHN N. DUVALL
Charles Dickens edited by JOHN O. JORDAN
Emily Dickinson edited by WENDY MARTIN
John Donne edited by ACHSAH GUIBBORY
Dostoevskii edited by W. J. LEATHERBARROW
Theodore Dreiser edited by LEONARD CASSUTO and CLAIRE VIRGINIA EBY
John Dryden edited by STEVEN N. ZWICKER
W. E. B. Du Bois edited by SHAMOON ZAMIR
George Eliot edited by GEORGE LEVINE
T. S. Eliot edited by A. DAVID MOODY
Ralph Ellison edited by ROSS POSNOCK
Ralph Waldo Emerson edited by JOEL PORTE and SAUNDRA MORRIS

Walt Whitman edited by EZRA GREENSPAN
Oscar Wilde edited by PETER RABY
Tennessee Williams edited by MATTHEW C. ROUDANÉ
August Wilson edited by CHRISTOPHER BIGSBY
Mary Wollstonecraft edited by CLAUDIA L. JOHNSON
Virginia Woolf edited by SUSAN SELLERS (second edition)
Wordsworth edited by STEPHEN GILL
W. B. Yeats edited by MARJORIE HOWES and JOHN KELLY
Zola edited by BRIAN NELSON

Topics

The Actress edited by MAGGIE B. GALE and JOHN STOKES
The African American Novel edited by MARYEMMA GRAHAM
The African American Slave Narrative edited by AUDREY A. FISCH
Theatre History by DAVID WILES and CHRISTINE DYMKOWSKI
African American Theatre by HARVEY YOUNG
Allegory edited by RITA COPELAND and PETER STRUCK
American Crime Fiction edited by CATHERINE ROSS NICKERSON
American Modernism edited by WALTER KALAIDJIAN
American Poetry Since 1945 edited by JENNIFER ASHTON
American Realism and Naturalism edited by DONALD PIZER
American Travel Writing edited by ALFRED BENDIXEN and JUDITH HAMERA
American Women Playwrights edited by BRENDA MURPHY
Ancient Rhetoric edited by ERIK GUNDERSON
Arthurian Legend edited by ELIZABETH ARCHIBALD and AD PUTTER
Australian Literature edited by ELIZABETH WEBBY
British Literature of the French Revolution edited by PAMELA CLEMIT
British Romanticism edited by STUART CURRAN (second edition)
British Romantic Poetry edited by JAMES CHANDLER and MAUREEN N. McLANE
British Theatre, 1730–1830, edited by JANE MOODY and DANIEL O'QUINN
Canadian Literature edited by EVA-MARIE KRÖLLER
Children's Literature edited by M. O. GRENBY and ANDREA IMMEL
The Classic Russian Novel edited by MALCOLM V. JONES and
    ROBIN FEUER MILLER
Contemporary Irish Poetry edited by MATTHEW CAMPBELL
Creative Writing edited by DAVID MORLEY and PHILIP NEILSEN
Crime Fiction edited by MARTIN PRIESTMAN
Early Modern Women's Writing edited by LAURA LUNGER KNOPPERS
The Eighteenth-Century Novel edited by JOHN RICHETTI
Eighteenth-Century Poetry edited by JOHN SITTER
English Literature, 1500–1600 edited by ARTHUR F. KINNEY
English Literature, 1650–1740 edited by STEVEN N. ZWICKER
English Literature, 1740–1830 edited by THOMAS KEYMER and JON MEE
English Literature, 1830–1914 edited by JOANNE SHATTOCK